JFK and de Gaulle

JFK and de Gaulle

How America and France Failed in Vietnam, 1961-1963

Sean J. McLaughlin

UNIVERSITY PRESS OF KENTUCKY

Scholarly publisher for the Commonwealth,
serving Bellarmine University, Berea College, Centre College of Kentucky, Eastern Kentucky University, The Filson Historical Society, Georgetown College, Kentucky Historical Society, Kentucky State University, Morehead State University, Murray State University, Northern Kentucky University, Transylvania University, University of Kentucky, University of Louisville, and Western Kentucky University.

Editorial and Sales Offices: The University Press of Kentucky
663 South Limestone Street, Lexington, Kentucky 40508–4008
www.kentuckypress.com

Library of Congress Cataloging-in-Publication Data

Names: McLaughlin, Sean J., 1978– author.
Title: JFK and de Gaulle : how America and France failed in Vietnam, 1961–1963 / Sean J. McLaughlin.
Description: Lexington : University Press of Kentucky, [2019] | Series: Studies in conflict, diplomacy, and peace | Includes bibliographical references and index.
Identifiers: LCCN 2019014999| ISBN 9780813177748 (hardcover : alk. paper) | ISBN 9780813177762 (pdf) | ISBN 9780813177779 (epub)
Subjects: LCSH: Kennedy, John F. (John Fitzgerald), 1917–1963. | Gaulle, Charles de, 1890–1970. | Vietnam War, 1961–1975—United States. | United States—Foreign relations—France. | France—Foreign relations—United States. | United States—Foreign relations—1953–1961. | United States--Foreign relations—1961–1963.
Classification: LCC DS558 .M425 2019 | DDC 959.704/32—dc23

This book is printed on acid-free paper meeting the requirements of the American National Standard for Permanence in Paper for Printed Library Materials.

Manufactured in the United States of America

Member of the Association of University Presses

To Selina, Olivia, and the hope of a more peaceful American future.

Contents

Introduction

At the end of January 1963, France's long-tenured ambassador to the United States, Hervé Alphand, reported back to Paris on a top secret American exercise at Camp David that laid bare many of the stark differences between the two NATO allies. As Alphand noted to French foreign minister Maurice Couve de Murville, his old colleague from the Free French days of World War II, the Kennedy administration had decided the previous October (either before, during, or after the Cuban Missile Crisis—he does not specify) to include representatives from Britain, France, and West Germany in a three-day series of politico-military simulations of potential conflict scenarios in divided Berlin. During the Cuban Missile Crisis, French president Charles de Gaulle had barely concealed his frustration from former Secretary of State Dean Acheson when he discovered that the Kennedy administration had no intention of coordinating strategy with the NATO allies it could have plunged into nuclear war. This may have convinced the White House to pull back the veil and show Washington's closest allies how its planning culture operated.[1] Never before had foreigners been invited into this world of role-playing simulations, an elaborate process based on advanced math and probability calculations, that involved the most powerful men in the Kennedy administration and even on occasion the president himself as participants.[2]

A French team took part in a series of simulations from November 23 to 25, 1962, that were organized by the Rand Corporation and the Pentagon. Specialists and scientists had been working on the simulations for years. There were three different sorts of exercises, strategic, limited conflict, and politico-military, and the Ambassadors Group participants were divided according to the Kriegsspiel method into red, blue, and control teams. The American hosts created a comfortable environment to promote deep concentration, while the players were equipped with advanced technology, such as teleprinters, to facilitate rapid communication between teams. As the game began, players were expected to be, as Alphand described, "pragmatic and analytical without any preconceived notions."[3] Each participant would be afforded an opportunity to speak his mind on his own component of the game along with general matters that could extend beyond his specific area of professional expertise. He wrote, "In doing so, the subject is exhausted by systematic research on every possible situation," and with repetition State Department and Pentagon functionaries came to acquire "theoretical understanding and practice that was almost unimaginable." Alphand was deeply impressed by the sheer planning and intellectual energy that went into this undertaking, but he could not withhold comment on what he saw as its glaring shortcomings.

As hypermodern and technologically advanced as it appeared on the surface, the Kennedy administration's style of contingency planning was to the French mind "tedious and useless." These exercises stressed summaries of military matters including logistics, tactics, and the use of arms, all of which would be vital in the event of war. Yet Alphand curiously noted that there was no consideration of the cost or resources required for each decision. Also absent was any serious reflection on the "emotional, sentimental, or even historical" factors that would affect the allies on which the United States depended for the defense of Western Europe. "When Americans set out to imagine formulas for the use of multilateral NATO force," Alphand wrote, "Germany, France, and Italy are pawns on a chessboard as though the memories of the past had been totally forgotten." This was an exercise that Americans saw as a cool and rational approach to the exigencies of the Cold War, whereas to the French it came across as utterly dehumanizing. Intuition was minimized, hindering creativity, yet the Americans believed that they could employ these methods to foresee every possible outcome. At the end of this rigorous and thoroughly prepared exercise, the French participants were taken aback by the "extraordinary confidence [their American hosts held] in their methods and judgement."[4] How then would France's American friends fare, Alphand must have been left to wonder, when this rich, mighty colossus committed itself to an overseas crisis that did not play out according to the expectations of the war game planners at Camp David?

In its broadest conception, this work is a study of bilateral Franco-American relations during the Kennedy presidency. Its first aim is to explain how John F. Kennedy came to view France as a world power from his college days at Harvard through to the end of his pre-presidential political career. The second is to explore why France and the United States fundamentally disagreed over Western strategy for Vietnam. These are vital concerns, given that Kennedy's commitments to Vietnam came during a crucial turning point when both direct military intervention and disengagement were still equally viable options. I believe that there is a clear connection between these two threads and seek to build a case that de Gaulle's government made a yeoman's effort to convince Kennedy that American military intervention in South Vietnam would backfire horribly, but Kennedy chose not to heed the advice because he did not take France seriously as a member of the Atlantic alliance.

After almost six long years of trying in vain to convince the Kennedy and Johnson administrations that military intervention in Vietnam would end in failure, de Gaulle delivered a captivating speech in the Cambodian capital Phnom Penh on September 1, 1966, that brought his assessment of the Vietnam conflict to a global audience. This was, nevertheless, an almost futile gesture after the Johnson administration had decided to send in American combat troops. Though frequently derided in American circles for the "vagueness" of his earlier suggestions on Southeast Asia, de Gaulle touched on four major themes that he and his lieutenants had been diligently hammering away at in private since his first face-to-face meeting with Kennedy in May 1961. His program included recognition of the principle of Vietnamese self-determination, the withdrawal of American troops from South Vietnam, acceptance of controlled neutrality for Southeast Asia, and the necessity of dealing with mainland China directly. De Gaulle's Phnom Penh speech very succinctly recapitulated not only the nearly unanimous French critique of America's involvement in Vietnam, but also a point of view that resonated with a growing number of Americans who felt the original decision to go to war had been a mistake and that the conflict was unwinnable.

De Gaulle confounded and infuriated a succession of American presidents, from Franklin Roosevelt to Lyndon Johnson. He straddled the line between the socialist and capitalist worlds and had shaken off his hard-line imperialist past by the time Kennedy took office. He yearned to overthrow the Yalta system status quo that created a bipolar, US-Soviet-dominated world order and pursued his aims through traditional forms of European diplomacy that harkened back to a pre-revolutionary era. He came off at times as an authoritarian nationalist and at others as the champion of poor and weak countries, making him one of the most difficult world leaders to read. Americans tended to view President de Gaulle with a mix of the respect due for a genuine war hero and an ill-defined discomfort over how France's growing assertiveness would impact American interests. In official Washington of the Kennedy era, long-standing American anti-Gaullism translated into a strong tendency to equate French opposition to American designs as the insignificant bluster of a second-rate ally.

The Kennedy administration's reaction to the Gaullist critique of America's growing military and political engagement with South Vietnam from 1961 to Kennedy's assassination in November 1963 was bitter silence and inaction. Kennedy's decision to sideline de Gaulle's correct assessment of America's disastrous intervention in Vietnam was largely the result of his own long-standing Francophobic prejudices. The motives behind de Gaulle's Vietnam critique—chiefly, to keep American attention focused on Europe, to explore the possibility of bringing the Cold War to an early conclusion, and to prevent American encroachment in a former colony where France still retained considerable influence—were fairly straightforward. Proceeding from the conviction that de Gaulle operated with good intentions on this particular subject, the more vexing question is why the Kennedy administration reacted so negatively to his views on Vietnam.[5]

Had each president not initially approached the other with high hopes as their official relationship began, there would be little story to tell. In the beginning, Kennedy, like many Americans, viewed his French counterpart as one of the great heroes of World War II, while de Gaulle placed great stock in the abilities of the young, charismatic, Harvard-educated American leader to resolve many of the outstanding Franco-American roadblocks left over from the Eisenhower presidency. Both men sought a cooperative working relationship, but were completely unable to establish one due to a variety of factors ranging from temperament, generational and cultural differences, and the unavoidable power imbalance between their two countries. Consequently, Franco-American divergence over Vietnam during the Kennedy years unfolded within the broader context of a failing bilateral relationship.

Soon after extricating France from its own long and bloody counterinsurgency campaign in Algeria, de Gaulle became the most vocal opponent of escalation of the war in Vietnam within the Western camp. The international landscape was changing dramatically by this point, particularly in Europe, where an impressive economic recovery had taken hold and the larger powers had mostly shed the colonial millstones round their necks. The Cuban Missile Crisis had encouraged both superpowers to reexamine the amount of risk they were willing to take in Cold War standoffs, ushering in a new period of relative calm. This breathing space gave European powers more room to pursue their own interests than at any point since the end of World War II.[6] These were the conditions that birthed a very trenchant French critique of American politico-military intervention in Vietnam.

In de Gaulle's view, there was little that any foreign power could do to suppress the revolutionary fervor of Vietnamese nationalists, who had so recently humiliated the best of the French army at Dien Bien Phu. Regardless, any attempt to do so would prove a costly distraction from more pressing Western security concerns in Europe. Left to their own devices, he predicted that the Vietnamese would choose an independent, nonthreatening course in international affairs somewhat akin to Marshal Tito's socialist but nonaligned regime in Yugoslavia. The alternative for Washington to this imperfect but tolerable arrangement was launching a war that would consume untold resources and drag on to the point of exhaustion. By the time President Richard Nixon arrived in the White House in 1969 there were over a half million American military personnel in South Vietnam and the prospects for victory looked no better than they had when America's war there had begun four years earlier. As the military stalemate finally gave way to a flimsy peace deal in 1973 and then Saigon's collapse two years later, de Gaulle's dire forecast was proven sadly accurate. Never before had the United States spilled so much blood and treasure on a failed enterprise.

While de Gaulle's complex relationship with the "Anglo-Saxon" powers has been subject to numerous high-quality studies by renowned scholars in both French and English, the Kennedy administration's reaction to his Vietnam critique has been given little attention despite a deluge of new works that have done much to provide a badly needed international context to the history of the war.[7] After a period of close study during the 1970s and early 1980s in the aftermath of American withdrawal, the origins of the Vietnam War came under intense scrutiny once again following the 1995 publication of former Secretary of Defense Robert S. McNamara's Vietnam memoir, *In Retrospect: The Tragedy and Lessons of Vietnam*.[8] The leading historians in this new wave of scholarship were nearly unanimous in their assessment that Kennedy and then Johnson had committed a grave error in leading their country down the path to war in Vietnam, that the conflict could and should have been avoided, that presidential decision-making on Vietnam was faulty to the extreme, and that both presidents pursued the hopeless task of forcing South

Vietnamese leaders to conform to American modes of thought because of their complete failure to understand the intricacies of Vietnamese culture.[9]

While these works were the product of prodigious, and frequently international, multi-lingual archival research, they all show a tendency to overlook the Kennedy administration's crucial rejection of the Gaullist critique of its Vietnam policy, instead focusing on general factors behind the Kennedy administration's interest in Vietnam, bureaucratic politics, mistaken assumptions, the transition from Kennedy to Johnson, and ultimately the fateful decision to go to war after the Tonkin Gulf Incident in the summer of 1964.

One very welcome recent historiographical trend has been a movement toward placing greater emphasis on the role of Vietnamese actors that have traditionally been ignored or marginalized in US-centric accounts of the war. Almost thirty years ago noted historian George C. Herring identified the relative absence of individual Vietnamese players as one of the main weaknesses of existing scholarship.[10] As Hanoi opened records of the former Saigon regime to foreign researchers in the mid-1990s, younger historians finally gained the means to respond to his lament.[11] Around the same time, the opening of archives in former communist bloc countries in Eastern and Central Europe similarly created backdoor insight into Hanoi's role via interested third-party countries that have unfairly been viewed as stooges of Moscow.[12]

This move toward inclusiveness of Vietnamese and communist bloc actors was not, however, coupled with a parallel impetus to reevaluate France's role in American Vietnam policy during the Kennedy years.[13] France was a signatory to the Geneva Accords with residual responsibilities to its former colony, while de Gaulle was a major international player with a vested interest in a diplomatic solution in Vietnam.[14] French officials who served in Vietnam, journalists who worked there, and a legion of talented historians—too few of whom have seen their work translated into English—have covered the war from different angles.[15] Nevertheless, there is no detailed study in French of how American perceptions of France shaped the Kennedy administration's rejection of de Gaulle's critique of American policy in Vietnam.

The French repeatedly emerge as the cultural "other" against which Kennedy administration officials contrasted their goals and prospects for success in Southeast Asia, but this work also aims to illuminate an underexplored facet of the American experience in Vietnam: a tragic and missed opportunity for a French-supported peace deal in the summer of 1963. Despite long odds for success, French diplomats had very quietly laid the groundwork for dialogue between Hanoi and Saigon, while players at the highest levels in both Vietnamese governments had expressed interest in at least exploring the possibility of a negotiated settlement. The French program did not guarantee that the South would stay out of communist hands in the long term, but it would, however, have greatly improved the prospects for the establishment of a more moderate, Cold War neutral regime. Perhaps more importantly to American interests, it also would have created enough breathing room to allow the United States to disengage from a long-running and intractable problem with its international prestige intact before irreversible commitments had been made.

Just as this process was about to begin in earnest, the Kennedy administration literally killed any hopes for a French-brokered peace deal by authorizing a coup against the South Vietnamese government, leaving Lyndon Johnson in a virtual trap where military escalation appeared to be the only path forward. This colossal miscalculation was partially the result of a soft, but persistent anti-French influence on the Kennedy White House's decision-making process. The administration viewed France with a curious blend of historically rooted gendered stereotypes, contrasts between the contemporary geopolitical weakness of postwar France and American strength, contempt for France's record as a colonial power, and the "GI Generation's" overconfidence in American military power in an era when the French army had recently suffered numerous defeats across the globe. The United States ultimately ended up paying a terrible price for the Kennedy administration's distrust of France's motives in Vietnam.

The Kennedy administration was ideologically predisposed against a legitimate dialogue of equals with France and dismissed out of hand most Gaullist positions, including his noninterventionist approach toward Vietnam. Anti-French sentiment had unwittingly been absorbed into the administration's foreign policy ideology and colored all dealings between Kennedy and de Gaulle. The main actors in the Kennedy administration were born between 1908 and 1925 and served as witnesses from afar to one of the most turbulent periods in French and European history. As adolescents, college students, and veterans they formed a thoroughly negative portrait of France from the 1920s to 1950s that later shaped their official contacts with de Gaulle's government. These men were born into an era in which most American elites were inculcated with a belief in Anglo-Saxon supremacy. They grew up during the 1920s and 1930s as France was vilified in the United States for its post-Versailles intransigence on a raft of postwar issues, from war debt repayment to its supposedly vindictive line on Weimar Germany. As young men, they witnessed the French collapse in June 1940 as confirmation of most Americans' preconceived notions of French decadence. In government service in the late 1940s and early 1950s, they witnessed obstinance from weak and divided Fourth Republic governments that were alternatively pacifistic or aggressive, seemingly whichever caused Washington the greatest difficulty at any given moment. Meanwhile, every government from the outbreak of hostilities in Algeria in 1954 to de Gaulle's return to power four years later appeared tone-deaf to Washington's pleas for a negotiated peace.

By the time they reached the White House, Kennedy's men had formed an overwhelmingly negative picture of France that created a reflexive ideological firewall they applied to any major policy proposal that came from de Gaulle. Robert Dean's *Imperial Brotherhood: Gender and the Making of Cold War Foreign Policy* provides a fascinating explanatory framework in arguing that the strikingly homogenous group of American decision-making elites of the era was socially conditioned by all-male boarding schools to expect deference from those who were less powerful and to view independence or nonconformity as a threat.[16] The inability or unwillingness of de Gaulle's France to accept a compliant, subordinate role in the Western alliance like all the other former great powers of Europe unsurprisingly confounded and angered many Kennedy- and Johnson-era elites. Not knowing how to force de Gaulle into obedience, ignoring the French president appeared to be the best means of reigning in his mischief-making capacity.

This work breaks with other studies of the origins of the Vietnam War by focusing on late summer 1963 as a crucial missed opportunity for American disengagement from a hopeless conflict rather than the events of the "Long 1964" that have occupied the attention of many other scholars. In July and August of 1963 the Kennedy administration had a relatively broad range of options, running from direct American military intervention, to increased military aid, to forced regime change in South Vietnam, to limited or total withdrawal of American personnel and resources. Each path came with its own set of consequences, but if Kennedy had been willing to consider the latter option, de Gaulle was both willing and able to help facilitate a face-saving American exit. Kennedy certainly would have faced considerable flak from hawkish elements at home had he moved in this direction, but American public opinion was growing increasingly sour toward the conflict and likely could have been reconciled to cutting loose an unresponsive and heavy-handed client. Once the Kennedy administration made the ill-fated late summer decision to authorize a coup against the Diem regime, which had ruled the country since independence, Saigon was essentially reduced to a protectorate of Washington and the possibility of American disengagement had all but evaporated.

Various disunited individual and institutional voices within the American government concurred with de Gaulle that a diplomatic solution for an independent, neutralized, and united Vietnam would have adequately achieved American aims in Southeast Asia at a marginal cost. The tentative efforts of men such as Chester Bowles, John Kenneth Galbraith, James Gavin, Mike Mansfield, and George Ball to dissuade Kennedy from escalating the American military role in Vietnam were unlikely to succeed because they appeared to align with Washington's chief antagonist within the Western camp. The Kennedy administration's gendered perceptions of France as an effete, decaying old world power fed its mistaken view that it could successfully manage a counterinsurgency in Vietnam even though Paris had already failed in the same endeavor. Kennedy's men, overconfident in the supposed effects of the vigor and drive that they brought to the conflict, summarily rejected de Gaulle's realist position in part because of the national banner he carried.

A series of questions arise from this conclusion: could *any* foreign leader have deterred the Kennedy team from its folly in Vietnam? Why were the lessons of the disastrous French war so easily dismissed? Why were diplomatic efforts rejected? Would de Gaulle's words of caution have carried more weight in Washington had the messenger more closely conformed to elite American ideals of masculinity and lacked the burden of a long, difficult relationship with the United States?

One must engage in a deeper study of the breakdown in Franco-American relations in the early 1960s in order to find a plausible explanation as to why de Gaulle could not become a trusted outside opinion for the Kennedy White House.[17] There was a long germination period for Kennedy's suspicions of France, while his fellow New Frontiersmen independently brought their own similar reservations to the White House. In due course, it will emerge that the Kennedy administration's gendered, stereotype-laden perceptions of France and de Gaulle were a direct cause of its failure to consider a course of action in Vietnam that was far better tailored to American national security interests.

In seeking to explain the administration's rejection of de Gaulle's Vietnam position, the childhood images of France internalized by Kennedy and the prevalent views of France in American culture must be explored. The long-term approach in this work historicizes Kennedy and helps contextualize his administration's rigid approach to de Gaulle in the early 1960s. Elite American perceptions of France during the turbulent first four decades of the twentieth century help demonstrate the sorts of prejudices the Kennedy men unwittingly absorbed during their formative years. As this work shifts to the Kennedy presidency, relevant official documents from the John F. Kennedy Presidential Library in Boston, the National Archives in College Park, Maryland, and *Foreign Relations of the United States* help illustrate how his anti-French prejudices translated into policy.

Kennedy's counterproductive use of military pressure alone in Vietnam is all the more disappointing in retrospect given the wise leadership he showed in other areas. Kennedy staked his claim as a serious presidential candidate by publishing a book, *Profiles in Courage,* which lauded past American politicians who made unpopular decisions for the good of the nation. After the savage race riots at the University of Mississippi in September 1962 following the enrollment of veteran James Meredith, the institution's first African American student, Kennedy shed his caution on civil rights and began to prepare the groundwork for noble-minded antidiscriminatory legislation that would cleave his party in two later in the decade. In the foreign policy realm, he rejected the notion of monolithic communism when it came to Yugoslavia, understanding relatively early in his political career that its independent socialist course posed no threat to the United States. Later, as president, he may well have saved the world from nuclear annihilation by resisting pressure from his military advisers to attack Cuba in October 1962, giving the Soviet Union time to consider his terms for a negotiated settlement to the Cuban Missile Crisis. Here and elsewhere, Kennedy demonstrated a talent for patience, nuance, and creative problem-solving, but it was one that completely deserted him when it came to Vietnam.

There is an almost impossibly high burden of proof when it comes to most reasoned arguments pertaining to John F. Kennedy as a result of the tragic circumstances surrounding his assassination. Despite the meticulous research efforts of Vincent Bugliosi that largely confirmed the findings of the Warren Commission, nearly two-thirds of Americans still cling to the belief that there was a wider conspiracy behind the Kennedy assassination.[18] When it comes to his foreign policy, Kennedy has a fanatical army of defenders who insist that had he lived to serve a second term he would have wrapped up

American involvement in Vietnam by 1965, citing the existence of pre-Diem coup plans based on an overly optimistic view of the war effort as evidence that Kennedy would have implemented a pullout. They typically and conveniently dismiss the vitally important question of how Kennedy would have been able to stick to this program under the real-world developments Lyndon Johnson faced in 1964 and early 1965, when the Saigon government was on the verge of collapse.[19] Accepting this argument means believing that a man who had done nothing but escalate the American presence in Vietnam and who had shown no inclination to back out even during the worst of the Buddhist Crisis of 1963 would have abruptly reversed course by washing his hands of this mess right after his reelection campaign. This line of thinking assumes that Kennedy was just as cynical about the world as Richard Nixon, the author of a 1972 Vietnam peace deal he knew was doomed to failure, and would have been willing to abandon a long-standing ally just as soon as he was free from facing American voters again. This is a terrible misreading of Kennedy's character, but one that fits with a general trend of plucking at one single thread from the file rather than examining the story as a whole.

I proceed with an understanding that large numbers of readers simply cannot be convinced that their core assumptions about John F. Kennedy are wrong and that there will be considerable resistance to the conclusions presented here. I concede that there is no published, publically available document at present in which any member of the administration openly discloses that Francophobia and anti-Gaullism motivated Kennedy's Vietnam decisions. One of the most frustrating aspects for historians researching Kennedy is that by the time he reached middle age his handwriting had become mostly indecipherable. There are bits and fragments that hint at President Kennedy's real views of France and de Gaulle in his notes and doodles, but none are legible enough to confidently present as confirmation of his prejudices. Still, the circumstantial case for my argument is quite strong.

Earlier Kennedy diaries from his pre-presidential years definitively illustrate that he subscribed to popular negative American stereotypes of France. These views are more subtly reflected in several speeches from the House of Representatives and the Senate in the 1950s. After assuming the presidency, Kennedy understandably became more guarded about expressing his real impressions of de Gaulle's France, but most official American correspondence on Vietnam contained a very strong thread of irritation at French assessments of the situation in Southeast Asia, a nearly automatic willingness to place sinister motives on French actions, and a generally accepted premise that de Gaulle's mode of thought was simply incomprehensible to rational-thinking Americans. The anti-France tone of Kennedy's subordinates was a reflection of suspicions the president himself had repeatedly expressed throughout his political career.

Three years of embassy telegrams, White House memos, and minutes of related meetings have been carefully examined for language that sheds light on the administration's core assumptions about and prejudices concerning France. This approach reveals "emotives," described by Frank Costigliola as "performative statements that translate into language—and in the process clarify, reinforce, and communicate—emotions that often were previously inchoate."[20] Costigliola continues, "Discerning the role of emotions in shaping the judgement of policy-makers at particular instances can yield a more nearly complete understanding of foreign relations history."[21] These emotives reveal themselves on numerous occasions, as Kennedy and his subordinates used feminizing language or resorted to irrelevant cultural stereotypes that reflected a deep-seated antipathy toward France. Through much internal administration correspondence on de Gaulle and France there is a recurring, unspoken assumption—subtly reflected in word choices and turns of phrase—that France was flawed, inferior, and hardly worth taking seriously.

The existence of two contrasting worldviews translated into very little solicited, meaningful dialogue on Vietnam between Paris and Washington during the period in question and well beyond the Kennedy era. Neither side had made any significant departure from positions dating back to the Geneva Accords of 1954, nor was any reappraisal seriously considered by either party.[22] Kennedy could not accept the French assessment of the weakness of the West's position in Vietnam, and de Gaulle was unable to persuade him. Unsurprisingly, the Vietnam dossier soon became subsumed in a wider breakdown in Franco-American relations that had been brewing since de Gaulle returned to the Élysée in 1958.

In the early 1960s, France and the United States were locked into contradictory positions on the gravity of the Cold War, the stakes for the West in Southeast Asia, and American hegemony within the Western alliance. To Kennedy's White House, even a small local triumph for Vietnamese communists would cause great damage to American prestige and diminish its credibility as an ally. Ironically though, none of America's allies shared Washington's willingness to use large-scale military force in Vietnam, much less viewed it as an essential test of America's Cold War fortitude. For Kennedy, the thought of negotiations with Ho Chi Minh held connotations of weakness and signaled a failure to learn "the lessons of Munich," an unthinkable abrogation of America's global duty from a president who idolized Winston Churchill. De Gaulle, viewing the Cold War as an artificial construction, preferred a pro-Western regime in Vietnam but knew that a second attempt to use outside military force would not produce one. This broad philosophical divergence between de Gaulle and Kennedy on Vietnam was further complicated by an unspoken American practice of nonconsultation with European allies during decision-making on strategic matters.[23]

Personal factors compounded the structural and ideological causes of Franco-American divergence on Vietnam. Kennedy firmly rejected France's position on Vietnam from the moment de Gaulle first articulated it to him in Paris in the spring of 1961. In many respects, Kennedy's stance marked the continuation of a long-standing postwar American pattern of deliberately opposing French designs when it came to major foreign policy issues of joint concern. De Gaulle naturally resented being treated by Washington as the leader of a junior ally that was too weak or irresponsible to shape its own destiny. His frustration over the wrong-headed American position on Vietnam reached a boiling point when lumped in with old grievances over American moral support for Algerian rebels fighting against French rule, Kennedy's rejection of his proposal for a top-tier NATO decision-making *directoire* composed of Britain, France, and the United States, and American unwillingness to help assist in the building of an independent French nuclear "*force de frappe*" (strike force).[24] Regardless of whether he felt he could shape American policy or not, de Gaulle became emboldened by a series of major slights from Kennedy and by his American counterpart's complete disregard for his discrete counsel on Vietnam. On August 28, 1963, just as the Kennedy administration was debating how it would respond to growing civil unrest in South Vietnam, de Gaulle released an unusually direct public statement calling for the withdrawal of all foreign powers from Vietnam and neutralization for the divided country.

The timing of de Gaulle's August 1963 statement on the need for a negotiated, nonmilitary settlement in South Vietnam caused considerable alarm and discomfort for Kennedy. Late summer 1963 was a high-stress period for the administration, and Vietnam was its principal headache. Kennedy, agonizing over whether to green-light a coup against South Vietnam's President Ngo Dinh Diem in the hopes of bringing in a more popular, less repressive regime, had convinced himself that his administration was too heavily invested to simply withdraw. Kennedy contained his anger over de Gaulle's words in a televised interview with legendary CBS journalist Walter Cronkite the following week, but he still made it clear that he felt France had little right to interfere with American efforts in Southeast Asia unless it dramatically ratcheted up its economic and military assistance there.

The point was moot to de Gaulle, who had no interest in prosecuting Diem's war or siding with his regime over Ho Chi Minh's. Kennedy had personalized de Gaulle's critique of American management of the counterinsurgency campaign in Vietnam and was unable to step back and consider the real question of whether the war was worth fighting. This indirect exchange between two presidents clearly indicated that after a little over two years of uneasy coexistence both governments had found themselves completely unable to communicate with, understand, or sympathize with one another. De Gaulle's statement was much discussed over the following weeks, but Kennedy's men gritted their teeth and chose to tune de Gaulle out completely rather than issue a tart reply.

It was at this point that all of the unspoken American prejudices against the French emerged in embassy cables, conversation memos, telegrams, and the like. The French were trying to interfere in South Vietnam despite having offered little to nothing by way of military or economic aid over the previous decade; they went to the press because they lacked the "guts" to take their position to the Americans face to face[25]; they were pushing on Vietnam the same sort of neutralization plan that was failing in Laos; and worst of all, they were intriguing with Diem's brother, Ngo Dinh Nhu, and the North Vietnamese to do an end run around Washington and reach a neutralization deal with Soviet support. However, there was no veracity to any of these wild claims.

McGeorge Bundy, Kennedy's special assistant for national security affairs, summed up the administration's frustration with de Gaulle best when he wrote a draft memo to Kennedy that stated, "We find only our own personal irritation as an argument against [the] well-established conclusion that we do best when we ignore Nosey Charlie."[26] Kennedy was felled by an assassin's bullet a little over two and a half months later, leaving his public breach with de Gaulle over Vietnam in the waning days of the summer of 1963 as the final salvo of a pitched Franco-American battle over the shape of NATO, Western Cold War policy, and Vietnam that had been raging since 1961.

1

Cultural Imaging of the French "Other"

Belief in the existence of "national character" dates back to at least the writings of Greek traveler-historian Herodotus. Enlightenment writers such as Vico, Montesquieu, Hume, Voltaire, Herder, and Diderot began to apply pseudo-scientific ideas to their examinations of national character in the seventeenth and eighteenth centuries, but their subject increasingly became a matter of public debate along with the rise of Social Darwinism in the nineteenth century.[1] William L. Chew, who has studied "imagology" in a general historical and Franco-American context, argues that national stereotypes, while malleable over time, are in large part rooted in "historical circumstances."[2] While Americans have traditionally clung to a general antipathy toward Europeans that is rooted in notions of American exceptionalism, France has often been singled out as one of the most offensive nations on the continent for a variety of reasons. At various points over time, Americans were cautious of conniving French diplomats, alarmed at France's sexual and racial permissiveness, and dismissive of France's supposedly weak republican system of government.

When Franco-American relations are healthy, American observers typically invoke the revolutionary services of the Marquis de Lafayette, after whom countless American towns and counties are named, and the Statue of Liberty, a late nineteenth-century French gift to celebrate the heady early days of the bilateral alliance; when they are strained, one is reminded that brief Franco-American partnerships in war almost always give way to bitterness in peace, be it after the American Revolution or following both world wars. Those familiar with the short-lived and widely mocked rebranding of French fries as "freedom fries" as a backlash against France's opposition to the 2003 war in Iraq know just how instinctively anti-French views surface in the United States at the merest hint of trouble.

However, it was not until the late nineteenth century that the core perceptions of each nation's respective elites would firmly take hold in a fashion that had implications for mid-twentieth-century foreign relations. Set against a backdrop of Social Darwinism, intense nationalism, Anglo-Saxonism, and conceptions of a racial hierarchy, the parent generation of the future men of the Kennedy administration began to ascribe hard, negative attributes to France and the French that they would pass down to their offspring. By casting the French as overly emotional, excessively proud, vain, cruel, conservative, backward, and effeminate, these elites were better able to rationalize their own perceived racial superiority and legacy as inheritors of sound British traditions. This chapter explains the evolution of American views of France to illustrate the perceptions and stereotypes that were common currency during Kennedy's formative years. The candid notations in Kennedy's 1937 diary from his summer trip to Europe, during which he spent several weeks in France, clearly show that he had absorbed many of the popular Francophobic themes in circulation during the interwar years.

American Anglo-Saxonism

Writing during a period of high Franco-American tension during the mid-1920s, historian John Gazley argues that "hatred for France" dating back to the early reign of Napoleon III was a large contributing factor behind American sympathy for Prussia during the Franco-Prussian War of 1870–71.[3] Just as they had in 1789, Americans greeted news of the 1848 revolution in France and the establishment of a new republican government in imitation of their own with almost universal enthusiasm.[4] This goodwill turned to distrust with Louis Napoleon's 1851 coup, which convinced many Americans that "the French people were unfit for republican institutions. They were fickle, unstable, impractical . . . for they had little political education and were enamored of a unified, centralized government."[5] Subsequent commentary across the American press in the early 1850s lambasting the faults of French national and political character clearly demonstrated that the temporary surge of pro-French sentiment was solely based on the mistaken belief that France was about to import an unadulterated version of the American political model.

Anti-French sentiment ran high, even in liberal eastern quarters, through the 1860s thanks to Napoleon III's flirtation with the Confederacy and his interference in Mexican politics.[6] Cable telegraphy technology allowed American newspapers to receive prompt reporting from their European correspondents during the Franco-Prussian War of 1870, which was probably followed more closely than any other foreign event during the late nineteenth century. American public opinion was strongly pro-German and anti-French, fueled by American perceptions that Germany was undemocratic yet forward-looking and that German immigrants were of the highest quality in terms of their education, disposition toward the United States, and propensity for democracy.[7]

Later, Anglo-Saxonists on both sides of the Atlantic dismissed the rapid postwar expansion of the French empire into Southeast Asia and North, West, and Central Africa as the meaningless conquest of large but economically marginal territories that Britain had passed over. While Anglo-Saxonists of the nineteenth century viewed the French, owners of a colonial empire second in size only to Britain's, as their primary competitor, they did not view them as a serious threat to the English-speaking peoples. A variety of factors ranging from military defeats dating back to the Napoleonic era, a growing industrial gap with Britain and Germany, second-rate colonies, and demographic stagnation stoked Anglo-Saxonist perceptions of French inferiority. To many, it appeared that France had not only ceded its position as the dominant power in continental Europe to Otto von Bismarck's Germany, but was also gradually sliding down the path toward Spanish irrelevance.[8]

There was by century's end little American interest in France on a "psychological and intellectual plane" beyond small Francophile groups.[9] The absence of French immigration to the United States meant that there was no domestic ethnic lobby to promote sentimental ties with Paris.[10] The one unambiguously pro-French segment of American society during this period were wealthy white women who looked to Parisian fashion designers to help them project a cosmopolitan image, and middle-class women with upward pretensions who sought to copy them by wearing knock-off designs.[11] This constituency had virtually no political power.

In *Ideology and U.S. Foreign Policy,* Michael Hunt presents a persuasive case that American ideology has been shaped in large part by perceptions of a racial hierarchy.[12] By the mid- to late nineteenth century, American race thinking increasingly revolved around notions of Anglo-Saxonism, a belief that Americans and Britons shared positive racial characteristics that explained the success of the American republic and the British empire.[13] A great deal of the jingoistic imperialism that drove the United States to war with Spain in 1898 was rooted in the belief that Washington had a responsibility to share the white man's burden with its transatlantic cousins in London.

Anglo-Saxonism proved equally popular across class lines on both sides of the Atlantic mainly because it was simple, abstract, and based on the premise of an innate superiority of the British and American peoples.[14] While there was significant opposition in American quarters to using Anglo-Saxonism as a justification for following Britain's lead in civilizing the "lesser races" of the world in places such as Cuba and the Philippines, it did resonate with a younger generation of American elites who led the imperial drive of the 1890s.[15] Anglo-Saxonism had a firm believer in the White House in Theodore Roosevelt, though his was a more open-minded sort and he counted French ambassador Jean Jules Jusserand as a close friend and confidant. As a concept, it gained further traction in the United States as white Anglo-Saxon Protestants, especially those in elite circles on the Eastern seaboard, reacted against the arrival of millions of Catholics, Eastern Orthodox Christians, and Jews from Eastern and Southern Europe.[16]

Stuart Anderson and Hunt both demonstrate that Americans conceived of Anglo-Saxons as industrious, intelligent, driven by moral purpose, and possessing an innate talent for government. The combination of these qualities supposedly contributed to the respective successes of English-speaking civilizations. Germans were admired as racial cousins, but they could not be considered equals because "they had lost their love of liberty" and accepted autocratic rule.[17] The Latin peoples of Europe, of which the French were considered the most formidable, were ever lower down the race hierarchy because "they lacked vigor; they were sentimental, undisciplined and superstitious; and consequently they were of small account in international affairs."[18] This crude, romanticized Anglo-Saxonist view of the world, coupled with the arrival of just over 5 million politically organized Germans in the nineteenth century, helped create an instinctive sympathy for Germany and corresponding distrust for France in American opinion through the interwar years.[19] As we shall see later, Kennedy's residual Anglo-Saxonist worldview manifested itself in his natural empathy with the Cold War plight of West Germans and a corresponding disdain for France.

If not couched in overtly racial terms, the French adopted strong and enduring negative stereotypes of Americans over the course of the nineteenth century. Even Alexis de Tocqueville, the oft-quoted nineteenth-century French aristocrat who penned the classic examination of American institutions and characteristics, *Democracy in America,* had mixed views of the United States. Tocqueville lamented in great detail how the institution of slavery had debased southern whites and threatened to tear the union apart.[20] Despite their many positive characteristics, Tocqueville saw Americans as obsessed with money, reduced "to preferring equality in slavery to inequality with freedom," lacking in "true independence of mind," and unable to separate an interpretation of Christianity "which seems to vegetate in the soul rather than to live" from notions of liberty.[21]

By the founding of the Third Republic in the wake of the Franco-Prussian War, the United States was no longer held up as the beacon of liberty it had been seen as during Tocqueville's lifetime.[22] The United States was much observed in France during the early industrial era, and its political aura began to wane as it rapidly shed the idealized agrarian, patriarchal, and colonial features that had endeared it to the French in the early nineteenth century. Americans themselves were increasingly perceived to be driven by the lure of a quick dollar and a ceaseless hunger for technological innovations that undermined time-tested traditions. Most of the contact between the two peoples took place in France, where American businessmen and expatriates frequently came across as obnoxious and pampered. The French formed ideas about Americans based on these interactions, which predictably framed French opinion about the United States as a whole.[23] It made it all the more difficult for the French to contend with the exponential growth of American military and industrial power when the individual Americans they encountered in France typically came off as crass and uncivilized.

Both countries had roughly the same population and economic base in 1870, but France remained relatively stagnant compared to the explosive growth in both areas in the United States. The shock of the American declaration of war on Spain in 1898 was seen from France as a challenge from an aggressive, powerful New World rival that might well end up dominating the world if the British threw their lot in with their Anglo-Saxon cousins. Jealousy and contempt for upstart America naturally ensued in this crucial era, during which French policy-makers of the post-1914 period, de Gaulle included, established their formative views of the United States.[24]

Predictably, pre–Great War stereotypes proved equally enduring in France as in the United States. Irwin Wall writes, "America was regarded as uncultured, a society of overgrown children imbued with naïve optimism, a country of pragmatists devoid of theoretical understanding."[25] French opinion from the conservative right to the socialist left disdained American society's extreme emphasis on individual happiness at the expense of the collective good, while most of the French deplored America's Calvinistic pursuit of trade and profits in addition to its decentralized, laissez-faire state.[26]

The racial assumptions that drove Anglo-Saxonism as a belief system nurtured an informal Anglo-American partnership that developed at the turn of the twentieth century.[27] This growing spirit of Anglo-American cooperation transformed into an increasingly close relationship as the Republican administrations of the 1920s placed new emphasis on collaboration between private businesses as a means of addressing major international economic concerns.[28] Put into practice, key bankers and businessmen in the United States and Britain increasingly looked to coordinate their efforts on financial matters, the radio and cable industries, and oil diplomacy. This partnership survived the Great Depression and deepened in the run-up to America's entry into World War II as the theme of "cooperative competition" gave way to a new Anglo-American partnership that was marked by an unprecedented peaceful transfer of international dominance.[29]

Robert J. Young describes the boost in pro-French feeling in the United States during the latter stages of World War I as a "national mood swing" rather than a long-term reevaluation of national stereotypes. Well before 1919 was out, Anglo-American opinion had already adopted the German line that the Treaty of Versailles was excessively harsh, while the American press had begun to turn on France before peace negotiations had even wrapped up.[30] The general mood in the United States had shifted and a supposedly vindictive France was increasingly viewed as more of an obstacle to normalization than defeated Germany.[31] Recognizing postwar French weakness, successive French governments put great stock in maintaining the wartime entente with the United States, banking on American support for a linkage between reparations and war debt repayment, privileged access to American markets and resources, and postwar assistance. The reality they were confronted with after the Versailles peace talks, however, was one of constant peppering from American officials over how and when Paris would commit to a repayment scheme with specific schedules and interest rates for the $3 billion war debt it had accumulated.[32]

Events in the 1920s served to further sweep away the vestiges of wartime solidarity and buttress traditional negative American stereotypes of France.[33]

Through the decade of Kennedy's formative childhood years, French foreign policy was continually attacked by large swaths of the American press that had little to no sympathy for the political, economic, and security difficulties Paris was facing. As evidenced by Kennedy's writings in the 1930s, there is every reason to speculate that at some point during this period popular negative cultural imaging of France permeated its way into the young boy's consciousness.

The laundry list of American complaints against France was long, running from issues of national policy, such as its unwillingness to pay its war debts, militarism in the Ruhr, a "Napoleon Complex," and vengefulness against Germany. There were other sweeping assumptions of a cultural nature, such as indolence, while many returning American soldiers brought lurid tales of French sexual permissiveness and racial tolerance that would have been considered shocking by Jim Crow standards.[34] President Woodrow Wilson's inability to deliver for France the security pact he had promised and bitterness over the inability to find a mutually acceptable compromise over the complicated war debts-reparations issue were at the heart of the postwar breakdown in Franco-American relations.

In Kennedy's early years, the two major New England newspapers, the *Boston Daily Globe* and the *Hartford Courant,* were broadly sympathetic to France during the Ruhr Crisis of 1923–24, when a French-led force occupied Germany's industrial heartland in response to the Weimar regime's refusal to pay reparations. *The Globe* lamented Washington's role in the crisis in failing to honor Wilson's promise of a peacetime American security guarantee to France. The paper was sympathetic toward attempts of French industrial magnate Eugene Schneider to create a mutually beneficial steel cartel with German concerns and bring peace to the Ruhr.[35] The *Courant* cheered on the French bid to make the intractable Germans back down and honor the treaty at gunpoint.[36] Even moderately critical reporting on French actions in the Ruhr was often tempered by an acknowledgment that laconic President Calvin Coolidge was not working constructively to bring the crisis to an end.[37] This relatively favorable coverage of France came when Kennedy was only six years old, however, too early to have any real impact on his worldview. By the time Kennedy could have been expected to begin following the news in his early adolescent years, the focus of the American press shifted to a far more emotive issue, that of European repayment of war debts to American creditors.

The Republican administrations of Warren G. Harding (1921–23), Coolidge (1923–29), and Herbert Hoover (1929–33) put their faith in the unregulated free market as the best corrective, and thus conducted their business with Europe largely through unofficial and private economic channels. In and out of government, France was viewed as an obstacle to Washington's designs because of its resistance to American disarmament initiatives and its frequent attempts to evade repayment on its crippling war debts. For Americans, repayment was an emotional issue rooted in the sanctity of honoring business contracts. The "Uncle Shylock" barbs from French voices arguing that debts accrued while fighting a common cause would have been wiped off the books by a true friend only salted the wound. In sum, the contentious nature of bilateral affairs served to fuel and perpetuate crude cultural stereotypes on both sides of the Atlantic during Kennedy's formative years.[38]

Anglo-Saxonism waned as a loose ideology in the early years of the twentieth century, but it created in the United States an enduring sense of partnership with Britain and helped entrench popular condescension for France that has lasted to the present. Frank Costigliola argues convincingly in *France and the United States: The Cold Alliance, 1940–1990* that American perceptions of the French as a lesser people endured well into the Cold War years largely on the same grounds cited by turn-of-the-century Anglo-Saxonists.[39] Negative stereotypes of France did not emerge from nowhere when Kennedy assumed the White House; they had traceable roots in the events of the interwar period and earlier.

John F. Kennedy's Earliest Views of France

John F. Kennedy was born on May 29, 1917, in the leafy West Boston suburb of Brookline, Massachusetts, to Joseph Patrick Kennedy, a rising star in the local banking industry, and Rose Fitzgerald Kennedy, daughter of an establishment family from the north end of the city.[40] He was the second of nine Kennedy children, four of whom were boys—Joseph Patrick Jr., John Fitzgerald, Robert "Bobby" Francis, and Edward "Teddy" Moore—who enjoyed tremendous success in public life, or would have had war not intervened.

The Kennedy boys had politics in their blood. Their maternal grandfather, John Francis "Honey Fitz" Fitzgerald, was a former US congressman and Boston mayor, while their paternal grandfather, Patrick Joseph Kennedy, was a state senator, congressman, and powerful ward boss in East Boston. Joseph Kennedy, father to the future president, was extremely well-connected in the Boston business community and probably could have secured an elected office of his own, but he chose to remain in the private sector. This proved to be a shrewd decision. Joseph Kennedy became a millionaire thanks to clever wartime dealings with Columbia Trust, the Massachusetts Electric Company, and Bethlehem Steel, followed by a series of timely investments in the early American film, real estate, and liquor import industries. Joseph Kennedy was one of the rare investors to actually profit from the Great Depression, liquidating many of his riskier stocks before the 1929 Wall Street Crash and funneling the proceeds into real estate once property values bottomed out. By the mid-1930s he had transformed himself from a wealthy Bostonian to one of the richest men in America. He astutely offered financial backing to Franklin Delano Roosevelt's 1932 presidential campaign and followed with a 1936 book, *I'm for Roosevelt,* that helped persuade fellow business magnates to cast their vote for the New Deal.[41] This political investment paid off handsomely, as Roosevelt rewarded Joe Sr. in December 1937 by appointing him ambassador to the Court of St. James, the greatest prize in diplomatic postings. At this point Joe Sr. began working to use his vast fortune and personal connections with influential power brokers to set his sons up for political success at the national level.

The Kennedy children spent leisurely summers swimming and playing sports at the family's second home in the affluent village of Hyannis Port on Cape Cod, but were bundled off to elite boarding schools every September. John studied at the Canterbury School and then Choate, both in Connecticut, receiving poor marks in all subjects except the two that really interested him: English and history. Being popular, relatively athletic, and the son of a rich, politically connected businessman, his grades did not present an obstacle to further study, and John entered Harvard, his father's alma mater, in the autumn of 1936. John's work ethic improved little upon his entry into an elite Ivy League school, and it appeared that his elder brother Joe, already an upperclassman at Harvard, was a far more suitable vessel for Joe Sr.'s political ambitions. However, with war clouds looming in Europe and Asia as he began his second year at Harvard, John's interest in continental affairs and international politics began to grow and he started to take his studies more seriously. His father's appointment as ambassador to Britain in December created a unique opportunity to gain firsthand insight into international relations, further stoking his curiosity.

The Irish Catholic Kennedy clan of Boston made a surprisingly easy transition to the aristocratic society of late 1930s England, reveling in their liberation from American provincialism. Joe Kennedy lacked the instinctive Anglophobia of most Boston Irish, taking pride in his opulent suite at Windsor Castle and boasting of his connections with British nobility.[42] He had long been trying to shake the "Irish" label that had dogged him through all of his business and political dealings at home. It was in Britain that he was finally accepted as an American.[43]

Joe Sr.'s business acumen did not exactly prepare him for the formalities of his new posting, and his tour ended badly after only two and a half years. He did, however, make a tremendous first impression in London by breaking many of the staid diplomatic conventions that had become clearly anachronistic by the early twentieth century.[44] Kennedy Senior soon ingratiated himself with the like-minded isolationist elites in the right-wing Cliveden Set, and later went against his wife's wishes by supporting the marriage of his daughter Kathleen, a darling of London social circles, to Billy Cavendish, the Anglican Marquess of Hartington.[45]

Joe Kennedy had lobbied President Roosevelt hard for his ambassadorship, which he viewed as confirmation of his social superiority over established Boston Brahmins and as a springboard to create future opportunities for his children. Kennedy was, however, a wholly inappropriate candidate for the job at this critical juncture in world history due to his defeatist instincts and a lack of foreign policy knowledge that was a source of constant embarrassment for the professional diplomats in the State Department. His British hosts took an even dimmer view, vowing never to forgive him for his pessimistic assessments of London's ability to withstand German aggression and his flight to the countryside after the Blitz began. He was forced to give up his position and return home in 1940, formally resigning after Roosevelt secured his unprecedented third presidential election.[46]

Life had nevertheless been good for the Kennedys in Britain, at least before war broke out and Joe fell from grace. Young John in particular became an ardent Anglophile and built lifelong friendships with the aristocratic acquaintances of his sister Kathleen, such as future ambassador to the United States David Ormsby-Gore, who enjoyed privileged access to the White House during the Cuban Missile Crisis.[47] British elitism, as it turned out, dovetailed nicely with the sense of social superiority Joe Kennedy had been trying to instill in his children.

Joe used his position in London to get John a summer job working at the American embassy there in 1938, opening up a new vantage point on the world for the young Harvard undergraduate.[48] This was, Barbara Leaming argues, also a time when the arch anti-appeaser, Winston Churchill, would play a "monumental influence" in turning Kennedy away from his father's worldview of narrow isolationism and willingness to cohabitate with aggressive dictatorships. A frail, bookish Kennedy first became acquainted with Churchill's ideas in detail at age fifteen, reading his account of the First World War, *The World Crisis,* while he was laid up in a Boston hospital. Leaming credits *The World Crisis* with introducing Kennedy to ideas like "duty and honor before self-interest," arguing that his "encounter with the work was the start of his lifelong fascination with how wars begin—and how to prevent them."[49]

In 1940, Kennedy's senior thesis at Harvard on Britain's unpreparedness for war with Germany became the basis of his first book, *Why England Slept.*[50] The work's title, *While England Slept: A Survey of World Affairs,* paid homage to Churchill's survey of international relations from 1932 to 1938, though its central argument reflected much of his father's laissez-faire worldview.[51] Joe Kennedy's influence over *Why England Slept* was pervasive. Joe had selected the topic for his son's thesis—which John eventually completed with the aid of a personal secretary and five stenographers—and the final product "echoed the ambassador's sympathetic attitude toward Neville Chamberlain," author of the infamous Munich Agreement with Hitler. Thomas C. Reeves implies further intervention from Kennedy Senior, noting that the two faculty readers at Harvard agreed to award John magna cum laude standing for his work despite "poor writing and faulty analysis."[52] Joe then arranged for John to send a copy of the thesis to Arthur Krock, a *New York Times* reporter to whom Joe had been feeding information in exchange for friendly reporting, for assistance in transforming the hastily written effort into a full-length book. Joseph Kennedy arranged for heavy editing from his personal speechwriter and Krock, a promotional campaign from family friend Henry Luce at *Time-Life* magazines, and favorable reviews in Kennedy family-friendly newspapers. These steps, coupled with a fortuitous summer 1940 publication date just months in advance of the Luftwaffe's blitz against Britain, turned an otherwise unremarkable student project into a best-seller.[53]

The disheartening experience of appeasement did not dampen John Kennedy's Anglophilia, and he rather apologetically explained the politics of 1930s Britain as "a case of a democratic form of government, with a capitalistic economy, trying to compete with the new totalitarian system, based on an economy of rigid state control."[54] His book was meant to serve as a cautionary tale to the

United States, which shared similar values, institutions, and economic principles, and was generally sympathetic to Britain. Kennedy took solace in the knowledge that even when Britain suffered through the inept leadership of Prime Minister Stanley Baldwin and the flawed assumptions of Neville Chamberlain, there were more courageous men like Anthony Eden and Winston Churchill to replace them.[55] Garry Wills writes that the book illustrated just how much "[Kennedy] admired [British] adventurer aristocrats, who could save the people by guiding them, sometimes without their knowledge."[56]

As revealing as *Why England Slept* is in regard to Kennedy's views of Britain, there is very little corresponding work from his Harvard years that sheds light on his perceptions of France. It is, however, abundantly clear from Kennedy's fifteen-page travel diary from his three-week summer tour of France with lifelong friend LeMoyne "Lem" Billings as a twenty-year-old in 1937 that Kennedy had absorbed the crude French stereotypes common of his generation long before ever setting foot in the country.

The terrifying rise of fascism in Europe between the world wars led many talented psychologists into a deeper examination of social identity, prejudice, in-group/out-group dynamics, and a host of other related subjects. Academics working in these fields typically distinguish prejudice from bigotry, a harsher and more active manifestation of the dislike of a particular out-group, and at the furthest extreme group hate, the foundation for violent political organizations. Kennedy's views of France occasionally showed signs of prejudice, though this ebbed and flowed at different times, and never strayed remotely close to the latter two categories. It would be informative here to briefly outline some of the theoretical explanations as to why, how, and when prejudices take root.

Gordon Allport, a pioneering American psychologist whose work from the 1950s has largely stood up to a half-century of academic scrutiny, argued that children mimic the prejudices they encounter and that these prejudices grow stronger with the passage of time.[57] Later, British-based scholar Henri Tajfel, a Polish Jew and French army prisoner of war, advanced social identity theory from the late 1960s into the 1980s as a means of explaining how individuals identify with groups in order to accentuate their own positive characteristics and put up boundaries with other groups.[58] Tajfel's former student Michael Billig argues that there is nothing particularly nefarious about the existence of prejudice, itself a "cognitive short cut" that helps individuals "make sense of, and thereby bring coherence to, their understanding of the world." It would be impossible for our brains to process large quantities of complex information without a degree of categorization and simplification, but the danger is that this unwitting action distorts our views of the various people with whom we have relationships.[59]

Understanding the psychology of prejudice helps provide an explanation as to how and why a politician would respond to certain challenges. In the case of John F. Kennedy, a prevailing anti-French sentiment circulated in American society during his formative years that would have been impossible to avoid and, consequently, is highly likely to have shaped his views of the country. Stanley Allen Renshon, a professor of psychology of social and political behavior at The City University of New York who has written extensively on presidential leadership, argues that "the child acquires basic beliefs about the nature of the world at an early age . . . [and] this process of basic belief acquisition has crucial implications for the political socialisation process."[60] Essentially, what we learn about the world at an early age is both enduring and hugely influential on our views through adulthood. As an elected official after the war, Kennedy was understandably wise enough not to put his prejudices to paper, making his 1937 travel diary an invaluable source for discerning his unfiltered views on France and the French.

In the early twentieth century, growing numbers of middle- and upper-class Americans like Kennedy traveled to Europe, an experience that unintentionally helped them shape their own national identity. Christopher Endy writes, "Voyaging to Europe compelled travelers to reflect on what it meant to be an American . . . it was a process of testing a worldview or sense of national self by encountering a European 'other.'"[61] He argues that European travel reinforced the traditional stereotypes about the differences that separated Americans from their European cousins, though many travelers relished exploring a more traditional, aesthetically conscious society that contrasted the modern, evolving, and industrial America they left behind.[62] For most Americans, travel to France around the turn of the century "strengthened U.S. sympathy for [the country] in part because of France's ability to satisfy Americans' expectations of a romantic Old World."[63] In Kennedy's case in the late 1930s, the experience of visiting France firsthand led him to the quite opposite conclusion that the country was backward in every sense and naively ill-prepared for trouble ahead with Hitler's Germany.

On July 1, 1937, Kennedy embarked on his first major trip to Europe, a six-week tour that began in France and took him through Mussolini's Italy and Hitler's Germany. One of the recurring themes running throughout his diary entries was his perception of French complacency in the face of major upheaval in neighboring Germany. Spiritually, economically, and politically, he felt that the French were simply unready to defend the hard-fought gains of the Great War.[64] Kennedy did encounter plenty of individual acts of kindness from the French, but he tended to note them dismissively in passing, saving his most colorful language for observations of the numerous flaws in the French national character.

Kennedy's travel journal began with his arrival by sea at the bustling English Channel seaport Le Havre and follows a leisurely journey southward to Monte Carlo. His first entry on July 9 marked his impressions of the Rheims Cathedral, a World War I fort, and the Roman-built red chalk caves of the Champagne region. As Kennedy put pen to paper, he contrasted the general air of political disorder in France with the progressive, unifying reform program of President Roosevelt back home in the United States. French prime minister Léon Blum, a polarizing Jewish socialist, had resigned in June after months of agonizing over whether his government should intervene on behalf of the motley collection of Republican Common Front allies fighting against German- and Italian-backed fascists in the Spanish Civil War. The French Popular Front survived Blum's fall, but it was a shaky coalition characterized by considerable infighting among its Socialist, Radical, and Communist members until it collapsed entirely over the Munich Agreement in 1938.

Though he felt that he was "treated very well" by the locals, his conversation with the kindly manager of the restaurant in which he had lunch (and, to his delight, was offered a free bottle of champagne) led him to this conclusion:

> The general impression seems to be that while they would like Roosevelt, his type of government would not succeed in a country like France which seems to lack the ability of seeing a problem as a whole—They don't like [Prime Minister Léon] Blum as he takes away their money and gives it to someone else. That to a Frenchman is tres 'mauvais.' The general impression also seems to be that there will *not* be a war in the near future and that France is much too well prepared for Germany. The permanence of the alliance of Germany and Italy is also questionable.[65]

Kennedy's remark that the French "lack the ability to see problems as a whole" is a broad assessment of a serious national character defect, assigning a fundamental lack of logical thinking to an entire people as a whole. Though he does not explicitly compare the French to Americans (or the British) in this passage, the comment would not have been worth making if this was a common fault he encountered with his fellow Americans. Kennedy made these sweeping observations based on one conversation with a bourgeois restaurateur only two days after setting foot in the country, signaling that many of his strongest views of France had been formed well before his trip began.

In noting that Blum "takes away their money," Kennedy was echoing a common American jab at the French, who were frequently derided in the American press for the ease at which they were perceived to have been taken in by the destructive policies of the Radical, Socialist, and Communist parties. The issue of low French taxation was a sore point in the United States in the 1920s, where a wide segment of American opinion held that France had been deliberate in keeping its tax rates low as a means of crying poor and avoiding repayment of its war debts. Kennedy's final comment on the French belief that there would be no war with Germany in the near future because France was "much too well prepared" further hints that he bought into popular interwar American perceptions that the French were both militaristic and excessively proud of their martial prowess.

The following day, July 10, Kennedy moved on from quiet, provincial Rheims to the City of Light, but what he found there was highly disagreeable. Kennedy's journal entries from Paris demonstrate that he took a cynical view of French claims to civilization, and the landmarks that have so delighted generations of American travelers left him feeling empty. On an individual level, Kennedy made hyperbolic complaints that urban-dwelling French had the hygiene habits of peasants, were backward in every sense of the word, and could hardly contain their greed. For example, shortly after he reached the city, Kennedy recorded this encounter: "Arrived at 1:00. Found a new place to stay for 40 Francs. Have now acquired the habit of leaving the car around the block to keep the price from going up. Had the lights fixed and got another screwing—These French will try to rob at every turn."[66]

The French had earned a reputation for price gouging the horde of bargain-seeking American tourists who flocked to Paris in the 1920s, and Kennedy took it at face value. His 40 Franc room cost the 2015 equivalent of $22, which is slightly less than one would pay for a spot in a better youth hostel in Boston.

The following day Kennedy made the following observations of French hygiene: "Went to church then after lunch went out to Fontainebleau. Very interesting but not given to what you would expect as all seems very artificial. Rather crowded and the distinguishing mark of the Frenchman is his cabbage breath and the fact that there are no bath-tubs."[67]

He went on to mention that café fare did not agree with him and he was "having difficulty with the eggs as it necessary to ask for them about six minutes as the stove is a bit off."[68] His impression of Fontainebleau seems to indicate that he viewed the trappings of French civilization to be more of the garish, tourist-drawing sort rather than authentic manifestations of the high culture the French projected abroad. Additionally, he seemed to take a schoolboy's pleasure in observing the irony that the French, who viewed themselves and their culture in such high esteem, frequently lacked even the most basic of amenities, such as a bathtub or properly working stove, and were oblivious to their own body odor.

The following week Kennedy traveled south to Orléans, where his inspection of the rural hinterland provided further fuel for his perception of French backwardness. While Kennedy found Orléans itself to be "amazing," he immediately noted that "France is really quite a primitive nation."[69] He elaborates in these comments on the French countryside: "Very impressed by the little farms we have been driving thru. America does not realize how fortunate they are. These people are satisfied with very little and they have very little so it is really a very conservative country, at least outside of Paris."[70]

Kennedy seems more surprised than impressed by rural French poverty and the seemingly inferior state of French agriculture to that of the United States, though an honest comparison with the share-cropping belt in the old Confederacy would have been more favorable to the Loire valley. Kennedy felt French peasants might have been living a seemingly idyllic life in the country's bucolic regions, but they were simply too ignorant to realize how poorly off they were in comparison to farmers in other advanced Western countries. The juxtaposition of French claims of high civilization when a large swath of the country was made up of peasants who lived in primitive conditions seemed to confirm to Kennedy that France was not as special as it perceived itself to be.

Kennedy then moved further south to Saint-Jean-de-Luz, a small community on the frontier with war-torn Spain. News of the various atrocities committed during the civil war raging to the south were on his mind as

Kennedy took in his first bull fight, a sport typically associated with Spain that, now as then, is only popular in a handful of towns in southern France. Nevertheless, he used the spectacle to again make sweeping generalizations about the French that served as further evidence of a defect in their national character: "In the afternoon went to a bull-fight. Very interesting but very cruel, especially when the bull gored the horse. Believe all the atrocity stories now, as these southerners, such as the French and Spanish, are happiest at scenes of cruelty. They thought funniest sight was when horse ran out of the ring with his guts trailing. Managed to try some spears later for 20¢ each."[71]

While Kennedy claims that he found the practice of bullfighting disgusting, he was still curious enough to try his hand with a spear. It is also notable that he lumps the French and Spanish, "these southerners," together as though they belonged to the same civilization, which was quite typical of late nineteenth-century Anglo-Saxonists who saw both peoples as members of a common "Latin" race.

Other entries show that Kennedy was unimpressed by French women, who were both excessively conservative and insufficiently attractive for the young playboy's tastes, but these impressions were most likely the result of frustration from his lack of sexual conquests during the French leg of the trip.[72] It is fair to speculate that his unfavorable impression of French women provided additional fodder for his negative views of the country as a whole, given that France has typically been ascribed womanly traits by Americans. Just after he said goodbye to the country on August 1 when he crossed over into Italy, Kennedy offered one final parting shot for posterity that now seems quite embarrassing. He wrote, "went to the beach. . . . Saw our first good-looking foreign girls. . . . The Italian streets are much more full and lively than those of [the] French and the whole race seeming more attractive. Fascism seems to treat them well."[73]

Earlier in the trip Kennedy had expressed his disapproval of France's leftist Popular Front government, but he held no similar qualms about Mussolini's fascist regime, such was his relief at finally leaving the country behind. At the tail end of his voyage, Kennedy traveled up the German Rhine on his way back to England, noting that it was "very beautiful as there are many castles all along the way. All the towns are very attractive, showing that the Nordic races certainly seem superior to the Latins. The Germans really are too good—it makes people gang against them for protection."[74] These words indicate that Kennedy had adopted a crude and articulated racial hierarchy by age twenty. He held Britons out as the most exemplary people of Europe, followed by Germans—who did unnerve him with their militaristic overconfidence—then came Italians, and bringing up the rear were the French.

Kennedy's European travel journal provides the best evidence that he had absorbed popular American prejudices of France by his early adult years. His European trip took place during a particularly turbulent period of world history, but also at a time when Kennedy was maturing into an identity of his own.[75] Hamilton argues that when Kennedy returned to Harvard in the autumn of 1937 he had adopted a "deeper emotional coolness [that] accorded with Anglo-Saxon society . . . [and] increasingly . . . saw England as the political anchor of Europe, the guarantor of peace between arrogant Germans, complacent French, noisy Latins, and Communist Russians."[76] He found confirmation of these national stereotypes in his travels and ultimately brought them into the White House, where they shaped his dealings with European countries. Kennedy's perceptions of France formed at this juncture remained largely intact through his political career, though they revealed themselves more subtly when he spoke out against European colonialism—its French form in particular—as a young senator in Washington after the war.

2

Building the Perfect Candidate

By the end of World War II, John F. Kennedy had emerged as a well-connected Harvard graduate, the author of a popular book, a decorated navy veteran of the Pacific war, and a reporter with the Hearst chain assigned to cover the peace conferences in the summer of 1945. He was clearly a rising star in the making, and his political career officially began the following year when he was elected as congressman for Massachusetts's 11th Congressional District, a position he held until being elected to the Senate in 1952. In Washington he soon gained a reputation for sharp anticolonial rhetoric at a time when France was fighting a losing battle to retain control of Vietnam and local nationalist movements were organizing themselves to fight against European rule elsewhere. Throughout his prepresidential political career from 1946 to 1960, Kennedy's most biting commentary was consistently reserved for the French, be it for their policy in Vietnam or later Algeria.[1] While Britain had successfully negotiated its peaceful disengagement from India and was taking the fight to Malayan rebels, Kennedy openly worried that ham-fisted French colonial rule would drive the most rebellious of the Fourth Republic's subjects into communist arms, undermining America's Cold War campaign to woo Third World nationalists away from the Soviet bloc.

Discussion of the French colonial legacy in Indochina or the strengths and weaknesses of the Fourth Republic is tangential to American foreign policy in Southeast Asia during the Kennedy administration, but an exploration of the manner in which Kennedy viewed French colonial rule in the 1950s helps establish a link between his negative prewar perceptions of France and his unwillingness to collaborate with de Gaulle on peace in Vietnam in the early 1960s.[2]

Kennedy's negative views of French colonial policy in turn shaped his outlook of French leaders as advice givers and later predisposed him against de Gaulle's counsel when it came to this particular corner of its former empire. Kennedy's 1945 postwar diary of his second extended trip to Europe reveals that while his views of France had become more politically mature since his first visit to the country in the late 1930s, he still retained many of the underlying assumptions that fueled his earlier negative assessment of French national character. This diary confirms that Kennedy saw France as an annoying distraction from more pressing issues facing Washington. Within, Kennedy reserved some backhanded compliments for de Gaulle, but generally clung to the view that France was a decadent exporter of luxury goods and a bumbling, overly ambitious colonial ruler that contributed nothing of value to the development of its empire.

In a series of public addresses through the 1950s, Kennedy repeatedly charged France with standing in the way of the establishment of a "free and independent" Vietnam that would be able to resist communist advances. He also firmly rejected suggestions that the United States could reach a modus operandi with Ho Chi Minh that would see the establishment of a unified, but nonaligned, socialist Vietnam along the lines of Tito's Yugoslavia.[3] Kennedy met with Tito on several occasions both before and after becoming president, finding the Yugoslav leader to be a generally agreeable man with whom the United States could do business despite his socialist reorganization of Yugoslavian society. The great tragedy of Kennedy's Vietnam policy was that he was unwilling to make the same bargain with Ho, who unlike Tito had not broken off relations with the Soviet Union. After France suffered its humiliating penultimate defeat at the hands of the Viet Minh at Dien Bien Phu and withdrew from the country in 1954, Kennedy turned his sights to rebelling Algeria, which he sympathetically viewed as another badly mismanaged corner of the French empire in danger of falling under the sway of radicals who made easy prey for Moscow.

Kennedy's postwar diaries span from late June to early August 1945, during which time he ventured from San Francisco to Berlin via London, Dublin, and Paris as a Hearst correspondent charged with making sense of the negotiations that wrapped up the war from a veteran's perspective. Hugh Sidey, the friendly Kennedy biographer and *Time* magazine journalist who edited the diary in the mid-1990s, calls it "the only known personal record of the future President at this stage of his development."[4] His diary, spanning sixty-two mostly type-written pages, reveals a more thoughtful Kennedy than the young man who had visited Europe almost a decade earlier. Surveying firsthand the massive wartime destruction across the heart of Western Europe, Kennedy was naturally fixated on postwar elections, establishing political stability, and the mean task ahead for those responsible for bringing about economic recovery. He was deeply concerned for the future and recognized that the short-term outlook for the continental powers was grim.

Reviewing the state of affairs across the major European powers, Kennedy lamentably noted the rise of Labour Party rule in Britain and the electoral defeat of his idol, Winston Churchill, but remained confident that socialist experimentation would not snuff out the best British traditions of individual liberty. As dire as the situation was in Berlin, Kennedy was pleased at how orderly ordinary Germans were in the Western occupation zone.[5] He viewed German bureaucrats and workers as highly skilled and efficient, characteristics that augured well for their future integration into the Western alliance. When it came to France, however, Kennedy did not recognize the importance of de Gaulle's leadership to this extremely fractious and geopolitically invaluable American ally. Sidey argues that Kennedy had reached the conclusion that France was "a difficult woman" (in Sidey's words) and the United States was better off "leav[ing] de Gaulle and his France alone and pass on to other more important things . . . sentiments [that] seemed to echo right down to Kennedy's White House."[6]

Anglophilism and Francophobia are frequently two sides of the same coin, and this remained the case for Kennedy after the war. In his June 29, 1945, diary entry for a high society soirée in Eastbourne at the estate of the duke of Devonshire, then undersecretary of state for colonies, he made unfavorable comparisons between British and French policy in India and the Levant respectively. Kennedy had a mixed assessment of the duke, referring to him as "a statesman of mediocre ability but outstanding integrity," though he nodded approvingly at the duke's comments implying that Britain had little choice but to disengage from India.[7]

Whereas the British were seemingly bracing themselves for the loss of what had long been the jewel of their empire, Kennedy noted critically that the French were vainly fighting tooth and nail to retain their position in the Eastern Mediterranean. Kennedy wrote, "In the Levant, France had been consistently warned. It was France's traditional policy of domination of this part of the middle East [*sic*] which was carried out at a time when French prestige and power was too weak to successfully carry it through."[8] The comment is left to dangle without further elaboration, but it is notable how Kennedy's implied approval of British realism in India contrasted to his perception of hopelessly wrongheaded selfishness that motivated France in Lebanon and Syria during the later stages of World War II.

By 1945, Britain simply lacked the money and resources to hold roughly 300 million colonial subjects in South Asia against their will, so it reluctantly chose to withdraw from an increasingly untenable position in the face of growing civil unrest. This in no way indicated any general policy of turning over other colonies to national liberation movements just yet, as London proved itself quite willing and able to meet Malayan rebels (1948 to 1960) and Mau Maus in Kenya (1952 to 1960) with force when colonial subjects tried to push the independence agenda faster than Britain was willing to tolerate. The wartime split between rival Vichy and Free French governments spelled the end of French rule in Lebanon and Syria, both post–World War I mandates where French control had never run deep and the economic gain for Paris was marginal at best, and the French did withdraw the last of their forces relatively bloodlessly from the Levant in early 1946. Comparing the two decolonizations, Kennedy would have had little reason to conclude that one policy was conducted any better than the other unless he was predisposed to believe that the British were innately capable of pulling off a limited colonial withdrawal better than the French.

Later entries from France show that Kennedy projected a late wartime Anglo-Saxon dissatisfaction with an increasingly assertive de Gaulle, who had transitioned from leader of the Free French to chairman of the Provisional Government of the French Republic, onto the French people as a whole.[9] On July 28, 1945, he wrote, "People are disappointed with DeGaulle [*sic*]. He has not pleased any group (which may be a sign of fair government) and has made himself extremely unpopular with most."[10] This backhanded compliment did at least acknowledge that de Gaulle had more backbone than France's revolving door of interwar leaders. Kennedy also implied that a conservative de Gaulle was at least the lesser of two evils when he wrote, "Any movement against DeGaulle [*sic*] will take the form of a swing to the Left—the victory of the socialists in Britain may accentuate this swing."[11]

Kennedy did show some sympathy for the plight of French civilians and recognized that American actions in France could be seen as heavy-handed. He wrote: "Food is hard to get for people in the city because of lack of transportation. . . . United States unpopularity is strengthened by the fact that we control most of the rolling stock (railroad, cars, trucks, etc.) and use it to feed and supply our own forces. The French have nothing."

Still, subsequent notes indicate that he chose to perceive France as a decadent exporter of luxury goods, a view that came with a corresponding set of unspoken assumptions regarding the feminine nature of the French as a people.[12] France certainly was internationally known for a wide range of luxury goods, contrasting it with more industrialized Britain and Germany, but it was also heavily engaged in many supposedly masculine economic pursuits, such as agriculture, auto making, and banking, that did not fit into Kennedy's preconceived gender-laden notions.

In a very brief entry on monetary matters, such as exchange rates, tariffs, and their implications for importers/exporters, Kennedy noted, "Perfume and luxury goods are no longer of first class quality. Perfumes are not the musk base of former days. The musk supply, which comes from the East, has been turned off."[13] When addressing the challenges facing French exporters, he wrote that brandy and wine merchants would take the biggest hit because of the franc's artificial postwar exchange rate. No mention was made of the French automotive industry or mining concerns, elements of which had been as modern or professionally run as those found anywhere else in the world before the war. A later entry lamented "the laxity of Paris" compared to "perfect" army discipline through Germany, further underlining his view of France as a country lacking the masculine, Anglo-Saxon characteristics of vigor, determination, and efficiency.

Unsurprisingly, Kennedy demonstrated a keen interest in foreign affairs from the moment he won election as the representative for Massachusetts's 11th Congressional District in 1946. As a junior congressman gearing up for a Senate run in 1952, Kennedy delivered his first major foreign policy address on February 6, 1951, speaking broadly on European affairs. He had spent five weeks in Europe during the winter of 1950–51 surveying the military preparedness of NATO allies Britain, France, and Italy as well as anti-Soviet, pro-Western states outside the NATO umbrella, such as West Germany, Yugoslavia, and Spain.

Kennedy devoted nearly as much air time to addressing the issue of each respective nation's "will to resist" Soviet aggression as he did more quantifiable issues related to armaments, manpower, and training. In shaping the "Issues in the Defense of the West" address this way, Kennedy left himself considerable room for subjective deliberations that subtly reflected his core perceptions of various European peoples. His conclusions generally conformed to his preexisting beliefs regarding each nation's national character: the British were war-weary and cautious, but sensible and willing to fight if pushed; the Germans were competent, efficient, redeemable despite past transgressions, and would be a welcome addition to the Western alliance; the French, however, were still as weak, timid, and riven by factionalism as they had been before the war.

Kennedy's language in this radio address revealed the masculine characteristics he hoped to find in reliable allies: determination, willingness to sacrifice, and efficiency.[14] Kennedy found that one of America's greatest difficulties was convincing Europeans to fully commit to their own self-defense, "to make sacrifices, to face deprivation, even to starve in defense of freedom." He continued, "These are the things without which armies destined for victory cannot be built, and we must find them within ourselves and our allies and those who might become our allies."[15] Of the traditional European powers most capable of making a significant contribution to the collective security of the West, Kennedy found France to be the most lacking. He confessed that "France gives me a sense of division and confusion, of hesitation and doubt," an outlook that would carry on through his presidency.[16]

As a supporter of West German rearmament, Kennedy saw France paralyzed in a hypocritical contradiction. He noted that "she looks longingly to German manpower for assistance and relief from her burden [as the backbone of the Western European defensive alliance], but at the same time she is unwilling to pay the price that Germany demands for rearming."[17] After conversations with Jules Moch, the minister of war, and former premier Georges Bidault, Kennedy concluded that the French were unwilling to allow West Germany independent control over a "national army," but felt Bonn had little reason to run the risk of becoming embroiled in wider conflicts with the communist bloc if not offered the carrot of increased autonomy from Allied occupiers.[18]

Kennedy's sympathies clearly fell with what he perceived to be entirely reasonable demands from the West Germans, implying that the reticence of Fourth Republic governments to endorse German rearmament threatened to undermine Western European defenses. Furthermore, his remarks showed little acknowledgment of just how emotive this issue was for countries that had recently been subjected to a four-year Nazi occupation. On the implications of German rearmament, Kennedy noted approvingly that the West German brass "had a more realistic and less fearsome appreciation of Russian military power . . . [because] they had met the Russian armies in the field and felt they knew them and their weaknesses." By arguing that the "realistic" Western Germans were "distrustful of France's military strength [with] . . . the rout in 1940 . . . still vivid in their minds," he agreed with their dismissive assessment of the French army rather than recognizing it as the largest non-communist force on the continent and an essential component to Western European defense.[19] More importantly, Kennedy's words reflected the Rooseveltian view of the fall of France as a "supine capitulation" that undercut France's great power status. There was in these comments so much instinctive praise for Germany and such casual willingness to dismiss French concerns that, if read in isolation, one might be left to wonder which had been America's ally and which its enemy during the war.

Kennedy did approve of the more robust Cold War stance of the Gaullist opposition in France, though it was politically isolated through much of the Fourth Republic period thanks to the concerted efforts of centrist and socialist parties determined to block it and the Communist Party from power. He was pleased to note that Gaullists rejected the fears of successive *Troisième Force* coalition governments that German rearmament might provoke a preemptive attack from the Soviet Union. He reported that General Pierre Billotte, a military aide to de Gaulle, promised that if Gaullists took power they would reverse the "weak" war effort of the current government by almost quadrupling the number of divisions in the French army from twenty to seventy-five and concede greater independence to West Germany in exchange for rearmament. By contrast, Kennedy argued that France's coalition governments were not only undermanning the army, but had also done nothing to prepare the economy for war.[20] As a result, French governments demonstrated a distinct lack of determination, or "will to resist" in Kennedy's words, that exposed them as weak, passive, cowardly, and effete when faced with the Soviet menace.

Kennedy took even greater satisfaction with the Gaullist camp for its divergence with the government on how best to deal with the Soviet-controlled *Parti Communiste Français* (PCF). French coalition governments came together with relative ease during the Fourth Republic in order to keep the PCF on the political sidelines, but Kennedy remained highly concerned with this passive approach toward a 5 million-strong potential Fifth Column that could sabotage war efforts against the Eastern Bloc. Kennedy blamed the French government's economic mismanagement, citing low wages, inflation, and insufficient price controls, for the continued appeal of the PCF, charging that a "prevalent criticism of France's government is that it is unable to get through to working people whereas the Communists succeed in doing so."[21] Billotte's pledge that he and de Gaulle would take "stern measures to destroy the party were they to come to power" was music to Kennedy's ears when compared to the waffling ineffectiveness of the government's laissez-faire approach.[22] As appealing as the Gaullist military platform and firm stance against communism was to Kennedy, the United States still had to deal with what it considered soft Troisième Force governments until the Algerian crisis brought de Gaulle back to power in 1958. This undoubtedly helped stoke his perceptions of France as an unreliable sick man of Europe that lacked the sort of vigor and determination Americans should expect from their closest allies.

The Senator and Colonial Vietnam

Vietnam was an unknown backwater of the French empire to most Americans when World War II broke out, but within twenty years the country had taken on a strong emotional association in the American psyche, thanks to the Japanese attack on Pearl Harbor, the "loss" of China to Mao's communists, and the bloody stalemate in Korea. American interest in Vietnam grew even before Pearl Harbor as a handful of astute observers commented on its geographic suitability as a jumping-off point for a Japanese push into resource-rich and weakly defended Malaya and Indonesia, then colonies of Britain and the Netherlands, respectively, and as a southern cordon for occupied China.[23]

Even after the war, Americans associated Southeast Asia with resources, strategic air bases, and vital communications hubs, especially after China was taken over by a hostile communist party in 1949. In particularly vivid language in a September 1954 address on communist advances in Indochina, Francis Cardinal Spellman, the highly influential conservative archbishop of New York, told an American Legion audience, "Time is running out for us also, because, given the present pace of the Communist advance, it cannot be long before its encircling pincers will be turning upon ourselves. The danger of another Pearl Harbor embracing the whole American people is definitely possible and possibly imminent."[24] Determined to never be taken by surprise again, the United States signed a series of defense groupings into effect, most notably the Southeast Asia Treaty Organization (SEATO), as part of an effort to cobble together an effective anticommunist force that could fill Britain's former role as the regional hegemon.

President Roosevelt's pre–Pearl Harbor war planning was thrown into disarray by France's shocking collapse in the spring of 1940, which eliminated his preferred, more limited option of containing Hitler by providing military assistance to his enemies. The collaborationist Vichy regime surrendered Vietnam to the Japanese military by the summer of 1941, handing it possession of strategic airbases and naval facilities at a time when Roosevelt was trying to deter further Japanese expansionism by imposing an embargo on scrap iron and oil. This craven act infuriated Roosevelt and, consequently, engendered his sympathy toward Vietnamese nationalists who were trying to free themselves from the French and Japanese yoke. Roosevelt frequently brought up the subject of Indochina at various junctures during the war, proposing a UN trusteeship that was designed to serve as part reward for the Vietnamese and part punishment for France's cowardly performance on the battlefield.[25] Soviet leader Joseph Stalin had no objection to this arrangement during meetings with Roosevelt at the Tehran and Cairo conferences in late 1943, viewing Indochina as one component of a broader anticolonial consensus that had been developing between Washington and Moscow.[26] Whether or not abruptly dismantling the French empire in this fashion would have been practical at war's end became a moot point when Roosevelt died in office on April 12, 1945.

Harry Truman, by contrast, had very little interest in Southeast Asia when he assumed the presidency and, unaware of the extent of Roosevelt's colonial dealings with Stalin, preferred to postpone any major decisions on the region until after the war.[27] Truman ultimately yielded to Churchill's pressure to allow the European powers to retain their colonies, placating France in a bid to turn it into a strong partner for Britain in postwar Europe. Despite private sympathy for Vietnamese nationalists, Truman recognized French sovereignty as the war with Japan drew to a close. He did so out of the belief that American geopolitical interests demanded stability—and potential access to the same military facilities used by the Japanese—in Southeast Asia. Abrupt changes there would have negative reverberations for American designs for postwar Europe, which was Truman's overriding priority.[28]

Truman was caught in a bind in the years that followed. Seeking to tie a fragile postwar France to the Western alliance and fearful that a Viet Minh triumph would give ammunition to McCarthyites, who would blame his administration for "losing" Vietnam just as it had supposedly lost China, he felt that he had no alternative but to provide material support for the French counterinsurgency effort aimed at perpetuating an anachronistic system of European colonial rule.[29] As Richard Immerman writes, the outbreak of war in Korea in June 1950 "reinforced perceptions of America's stake in Indochina . . . by confirming that the Communists, unchecked, were capable of military expansion [while the Chinese intervention] magnified the threat of the Sino-Soviet alliance."[30] So important was Vietnam in the domino theory as the gateway to the rubber, tin, and rice of nearby Malaya and Thailand that Truman's successor, Dwight Eisenhower, continued to prop up the doomed French effort until 1954, when Paris finally agreed to withdraw its forces and grant independence after suffering a humiliating defeat to the Viet Minh at Dien Bien Phu.

American frustration with developments in Vietnam deepened as the United States found itself caught in a position where it had to work through the French, who did little to appeal to the loyalty of their colonial subjects and were losing ground in the field despite massive amounts of American military aid, but could not push them too hard for fear of alienating France from NATO. Premier Joseph Laniel's government had promised that France would continue the war to victory in 1953 in order to secure American financing for the Navarre Plan, a disastrously executed bid to draw the Viet Minh out into open combat at Dien Bien Phu, but Fourth Republic governments measured their duration in months rather than years.[31] Laniel was ousted in June 1954 after France's defeat at Dien Bien Phu in favor of Pierre Mendès France, who had been committed to a negotiated withdrawal long before growing public opposition in France forced the conflict to a close. Mendès France rapidly concluded a peace settlement, the Geneva Accords, that granted Vietnam its independence, but this rapid about-face left many Americans feeling used and betrayed.

Whereas most in France were ready to put the war behind them by 1954 and withdraw with a small measure of national dignity intact, the Geneva Accords were bitterly rejected in Washington. Both President Eisenhower and opposition senator John F. Kennedy shared a belief that the West should not negotiate from a position of military weakness, arguing that a negotiated partition would lead to civil war, heighten the prestige of Ho Chi Minh, and provide the Soviets with an opportunity to engineer a Czechoslovakian-style power grab that installed pliant Vietnamese communists.[32] In actuality, the Soviet Union and China, both cautious of being drawn into a peripheral conflict with the United States after the recently concluded bloodletting in Korea, pressured the Viet Minh into taking a lesser settlement from France than its battlefield advantages merited, but the Eisenhower administration was unable to move beyond its strategic conception of a monolithic communist bloc making a push for Southeast Asian resources.[33]

If there was one blessing to France's exit from the Eisenhower administration's perspective, it was that it created an opportunity for the United States to take on a direct managerial approach in Vietnam free of the interfering French bureaucracy. In *Replacing France: The Origins of American Intervention in Vietnam,* Kathryn C. Statler demonstrates that after Geneva the Eisenhower administration accelerated its program to "systematically replace . . . French control in South Vietnam with American influence."[34] Statler's work is based on the premise that France and the United States had proven themselves fundamentally incapable of agreeing on a program to halt the communist advance in Vietnam from the earliest stages of the Indochina War. This roadblock fed a view in Washington that "replacing France in Indochina was one way for the United States to score against both communism and colonialism."[35] What it should have done was prompt questions about whether the conflict itself was winnable given the geopolitical shift in East Asia. Americans had demanded a voice in shaping French Vietnam policy that corresponded with its growing aid flow to Paris before the Geneva Accords. Once the French granted independence, the Eisenhower administration simply transferred these resources directly to anticommunist Vietnamese. Eisenhower saw France as "an unreliable and weak ally . . . [and] perceived the French as dupes of communist political warfare that raised false hopes for a relaxation of tensions and sowed dissension in the Western alliance."[36]

As Statler argues, Eisenhower "reject[ed] the lessons that the French experience in Indochina had to offer [and] saw French eagerness to negotiate an end to the First Indochina War as a betrayal of the Western alliance."[37] As a result, he set out on a path Kennedy built on: have the United States replace "the French political, military, economic, and cultural presence in Vietnam with an American one and then escalat[e] the conflict despite repeated warnings by French leaders that escalation would not lead to victory."[38] Rather than allow the conflict to wind down with national elections in 1956 as prescribed in the Geneva peace settlement, Eisenhower instead reoriented American efforts into building up a client state in the noncommunist South that would be strong enough to resist pressure from the communist North.[39] By the late 1950s, the United States had billions of dollars invested in its South Vietnamese "nation-building operation" and "the American presence eventually pervaded every aspect of South Vietnamese life."[40]

Despite viciously attacking much of the president's foreign policy record from his perch in the Senate, Kennedy did agree with the direction of Eisenhower's Vietnam policy.[41] Even if Kennedy was more hesitant to commit American troops than Eisenhower, as many historians have conceded, he did retain his predecessor's full commitment to holding the line against communist advance in the region and similarly rejected the notion that France could still play a constructive role in the country's future.

Fredrik Logevall is rightly skeptical of the "incipient withdrawal thesis," which posits that Kennedy had decided to disengage from the conflict by the time of his assassination and would not have Americanized the war in early 1965 as Lyndon Johnson did. In addition to the dearth of evidence to support the thesis, Logevall cites "a pronounced fear of a premature negotiated settlement [and] . . . a strong determination to remove Ngo Dinh Nhu from effective policy-making power, if necessary by removing President Diem himself" as further indication that Kennedy had in fact decided strongly against American disengagement in the fall of 1963. Logevall adds, "The administration's fear that Nhu and Diem might opt for a deal with the enemy, perhaps with French help, made the administration all the more determined to oust them."[42]

Long before these fatal decisions were made, however, Kennedy had already fixated on Vietnam as one the most pressing trouble spots in America's Cold War campaign. In 1952 Kennedy won an upset victory over moderate three-term Republican senator Henry Cabot Lodge Jr., quickly thereafter earning himself a reputation as a rising star in the Democratic Party with a keen interest in foreign policy issues. It was during this time that his interest in Indochina deepened and his perception of French misrule there grew more concrete.

Kennedy's Senate files contain seventy-one pages of hand-written and typed notes he took on Philippe Devillers's *Histoire du Viêt-Nam de 1940 à 1952,* which he presumably read in preparation for his Mutual Security Act amendment speech to the Senate on June 30, 1953. Devillers was the Indochina correspondent for *Le Monde,* a French equivalent to the *New York Times,* in the late 1940s who later became a preeminent French historian of the era and an expert on the final decade of French rule in Indochina. Specialists still consider his *Histoire du Viêt-Nam* a classic in the field of Asian Studies.[43] Nevertheless, Kennedy laughed off many of Devillers's arguments, especially his position that the West needed to negotiate with Ho Chi Minh.

In *Histoire du Viêt-Nam,* Devillers locates the rightward shift of French domestic politics in 1946, culminating in the ascendance of the *Mouvement Républicain Populaire* (MRP), as the postwar turning point in Franco-Vietnamese relations. The MRP controlled foreign and colonial policies in 1940s Troisième Force coalition governments and made the fateful decision to abandon concessions toward real autonomy in the colony that had been promised by leftist Jean Sainteny, the author of a 1946 deal with Ho that would have given Vietnam considerable autonomy in exchange for staying in the Union Française, and General Jacques-Philippe Leclerc, who was equally amenable to negotiating with Ho as the top French military commander in Indochina in 1946, just as Mao's communists were marching ever closer to victory in neighboring China. As events in Vietnam became subsumed in larger Cold War developments in Asia, the MRP turned a limited war of reconquest into a full-scale civil war in a blundered attempt to retain power through a puppet government under Bao Dai. Arguing from a realist approach that reflected a shifting balance of power in the region, Devillers concludes that French authorities should have stuck with the Sainteny-Leclerc program and negotiated autonomy with Ho in good faith.

Kennedy's private, unguarded notes on the book reveal much of his thinking on France, de Gaulle, and Indochina because they were not meant for public consumption. Within, he condemned France's colonial record, slammed any suggestion of Titoism or neutralism for an independent Vietnam, and personally blamed de Gaulle for failing to make serious concessions as head of the provisional French government in 1945. Very early on Kennedy makes clear that his sympathies lay with the Vietnamese rebels rather than French officials desperately seeking to salve badly wounded national pride. Kennedy took great interest in passages where Devillers illustrated poor decision-making—or, as Kennedy liked to call it, a "lack of realism"—from the French or implied selfish motives behind their colonial rule and desire to return to Vietnam in 1945.[44]

On his first page Kennedy made a handwritten note of approval on the following quote from André Malraux, a postwar Gaullist minister and long-standing opponent to French colonial policy in Indochina, a "courageous Annamite could not help but be a revolutionary."[45] Kennedy expressed similar approval for the tone of a message from Bao Dai, the half-interested playboy who spent most of his time as Vietnam's titular emperor living in the French Riviera, to de Gaulle on August 20, 1945, urging the French to show more empathy for the Vietnamese.[46]

Kennedy believed that de Gaulle, who as head of the provisional government in 1945 made the ill-fated decision to send an expeditionary force to retake Vietnam, was acting out of national pride rather than the best interests of his people or France's colonial subjects. Kennedy was correct on this point, one that de Gaulle himself likely would have conceded in retrospect. He noted that de Gaulle's creation of a semiautonomous Indochinese Federation on March 24, 1945, "came 15 years too late. . . . What de Gaulle really wanted was for France to join as one of the great powers in the fight against Japan. Knowing how the wind blew in Washington, he thought this was the best way to get back into Indo China."[47] Kennedy believed de Gaulle had narrow, self-serving motives in Vietnam in the immediate postwar period, which was a fair position, but one that if held too rigidly ran the danger of preventing him from later acknowledging that de Gaulle was both willing and able to atone for this original sin.

Kennedy employed negative gendered stereotypes of the French deeper into his notes on *Histoire du Viêt-Nam.* In reference to France's precarious position in Vietnam in February 1945, he wrote, "south of the 16th parallel France is mistress but there's still plenty of trouble in the North."[48] Kennedy's decision to tag France as a "mistress" rather than a "master" was not an accident; this label acknowledges a position of power, but carries with it connotations of feminine deviousness, intrigue, and domination for the purposes of pleasure. Kennedy later accused France of one of the gravest purported female character flaws: irrationality. Commenting on the failure of negotiations toward autonomy for a united Vietnam in 1946, Kennedy writes, "France shows her lack of realism—refuses [Vietnamese demands for the establishment of a neutral provisional Cochin Chinese government in advance of a future referendum on the territory's future]—Viets leave in tears—conference ends in disaccord."[49]

Kennedy contrasted this "lack of realism" from the French with his own "Objective Analysis." It was his view that "Paris should have, in the spring of 1947, talked to Indo China the way London had just talked to India. . . . *If*—France had made a 'Declaration of Policy'—like England—new parties in Indo China would have negotiated with her without being suspected by the Viet Minh of 'collaborating with the colonialists.'"[50]

While this comparison fails to acknowledge even a modicum of local nuance—Britain had little choice but to withdraw from India or face a costly insurrection that would stretch its battered finances to the limit, whereas the form of Vietnam's future affiliation with France was still very much in play through the early 1950s—it conforms to Kennedy's well-established Anglophilia and corresponding Francophobia. When coupled with earlier observations, Kennedy's appraisal here underlines a worldview in which "realism" was the preserve of vigorous, masculine Anglo-Saxons and beyond the grasp of the feminine French.

These notes also contain the earliest written germination of Kennedy's political blueprint for a united noncommunist Vietnam. Little would change from the ideas sketched out roughly here and those he sought to implement as president almost a decade later. Kennedy felt that the French had gotten it all wrong, zeroing in on three main faults: unwillingness to grant full independence, attempts to partition the country, and a willingness to deal with Ho Chi Minh as a legitimate standard-bearer for Vietnamese nationalism. Kennedy highlighted how Devillers apportioned blame on the French for radicalizing the conflict, concurring with his assessment that war could have been avoided had they conceded a fair, negotiated settlement before the CCP's triumph in China in 1949. He accused the government of Paul Ramadier, a socialist, of the dual fault of "hypnotiz[ing itself] with Ho's communistic convictions" and failing to recognize that "only nationalism, independence and unity could rally the Viets [*sic*]."[51]

Kennedy disagreed vehemently, however, with Devillers's suggestion that communists be admitted to the negotiating table on the grounds that their camp contained the most capable, respected statesmen in nationalist circles. He felt that an immediate and full French withdrawal with a transfer of sovereignty "to a representative Vietnam group [excluding communists] . . . wouldn't have brought civil war, but would have stabilized the regime."[52] Devillers saw the major problem for the West, one that Kennedy did not recognize, as the complete absence of any acceptable noncommunist candidate who enjoyed anything resembling Ho's level of prestige or popular support. Unlike in Taiwan and South Korea, where deeply flawed but reliably noncommunist strongman like Chiang Kai-shek and Syngman Rhee held power respectively, there simply was no Vietnamese counterpart through which the United States could project its aspirations. Nevertheless, Kennedy fallaciously believed that with this move "the French administrative and military apparatus could have been withdrawn on a friendly basis [and] The Union française would then have been truly formed" with the willing participation of a united Vietnam.[53] Kennedy did not ask himself how communists forces, battle-hardened after a decade of guerrilla warfare, would have reconciled themselves to this arrangement that left them totally marginalized.

At the heart of Kennedy's plans for Vietnam was a conviction that there was a strong, liberal, progressive, noncommunist element within the country that yearned for the sort of freedom that could be cultivated through the right amount of support from the West. Kennedy agreed wholeheartedly with Devillers's assessment that France had failed miserably in Vietnam, radicalizing a solvable problem and bolstering a communist camp that was unamicable to Western interests in the process.[54] By escalating the conflict and failing to recognize real Vietnamese independence, France was, in Kennedy's mind, squeezing the nascent liberal, democratic element of Vietnamese society further to the political margins. He argued that "France has solemnly recognized Viet independence . . . [and] should now follow up her words with actions—in letting the people freely choose their own destiny," a move that he seemed to believe would usher in a new era of peace and stability.[55] The unfortunate reality was that a truly free and fair vote shortly after World War II ended would have brought communists, not liberal nationalists, to power in Vietnam just as it likely would have in either Italy or France. Kennedy conflated what the United States wanted to happen in Vietnam with what was far more likely to take place if events were allowed to run their course naturally.

This wishful thinking flew in the face of Devillers's position that the communists were well-organized, highly committed, and had a superior caliber of political leadership while enjoying the support of the youth, intelligentsia, and most ordinary Vietnamese. Foreshadowing de Gaulle's own assessment years later, Devillers rejected the notion that a communist regime in Vietnam would be automatically pro-Soviet or closed to the West, arguing that peace could only be secured if outside powers dealt directly with the most dynamic political bloc in the country rather than attempting to prop up a weaker internal rival. To this, Kennedy noted rather flippantly, "This is lovely—I dare you to say in your speech that we should give Indo-China to the communists because they are the ones with the most integrity!"[56]

Here we have an early indication that Kennedy had no intention whatsoever of permitting negotiations with Ho Chi Minh designed at securing a Cold War neutral Vietnam. De Gaulle was probably the only man in the world who could have talked Kennedy into seeing the merits of this approach by explaining his experience dealing with Ho over the years. De Gaulle too was at first hostile to Ho, but then gradually abandoned his enmity for a grudging respect that later grew into acceptance of the legitimacy of many of his positions. Unfortunately, de Gaulle did not open up to Kennedy on how and why this evolution in this thinking unfolded, nor was Kennedy receptive enough as a listener to have appreciated it.

Kennedy's Mutual Security Act amendment speech in the Senate contained an elaboration on many of the key themes from his notes on Devillers's work, picking apart the French colonial record in Vietnam, rejecting claims that Ho Chi Minh might go down the road of Marshall Tito, and pinning the blame on de Gaulle for failing to go deep enough in concessions in 1945 during his brief stint as president of the provisional French government.[57] Kennedy began this speech by stating unequivocally that the French must withdraw politically, culturally, and eventually militarily if there was to be any hope of defeating the communists. There was cruel irony at play in 1961 when, with the French and American roles in Vietnam reversed, de Gaulle advanced a remarkably similar argument to Kennedy, to no effect.

In his speech Kennedy argued that "regardless of our united effort, it is a truism that the war can never be successful unless the people of Vietnam are won over from their sullen neutrality and open hostility to it and fully support its successful conclusion. This can never be done unless they are assured beyond doubt that complete independence will be theirs at the conclusion of the war."[58] As colonial rulers, he continued, the French had historically treated the region as little more than a rich plantation zone ripe for economic exploitation. French control was paramount and the Vietnamese had no say in how they were ruled or who enjoyed the spoils from their resources.[59] These points could hardly be denied, though they were not unique characteristics of French colonial rule.

After summarizing wartime developments during the Japanese occupation culminating in Ho's declaration of independence on September 2, 1945, Kennedy explained his unwillingness to accept gestures from the communist camp that were clearly designed to curry favor with the United States. He stated:

> Many people have since argued that Ho Chi Minh was at that time ripe for Titoism if the French had been willing to grant him sufficient political concessions. It is difficult to be wholly convinced of this, although it is true that in November 1945 he did dissolve the Indochinese Communist party and took similar conciliatory steps to

> gain the support of a majority of the people. But his long previous attachment to Communist causes argues against this theory, and the seizure of control by the Communists in China at a later date would have placed him in a most difficult position if he had attempted to break his ties with Moscow.[60]

Although this line of thinking—that all communists operated nefariously in all instances—was common currency in postwar America, it revealed that Kennedy was either unaware of the profound distrust Vietnamese nationalists like Ho held for China, which had controlled Vietnam as a vassal state for more than half of the previous two millennia, or felt that it was no longer relevant in a Cold War world. In any event, Kennedy implied that the Japanese occupation should have been a bookend to French rule in Indochina, singling out de Gaulle for botching the transition to Vietnamese independence in March 1945.

Kennedy derided de Gaulle's deliberately vague proposals for an Indochinese Federation, where a French governor general and French ministers held real power over a local assembly that had little role aside from rubber-stamping decisions made in Paris.[61] While de Gaulle did leave office in January 1946 without having secured any formal deal on Vietnam, the accord Ho signed with the French two months later differed little from the program de Gaulle had proposed a year earlier. This process had plenty of similarities to the British settlement with Ireland after World War I, in which both parties made painful concessions to loosen their union, but Kennedy did not acknowledge it as a step toward independence. Kennedy decried the lack of military, diplomatic, and economic concessions from the French in 1946, overtly criticizing de Gaulle for failing to reach an equitable solution when he had the means and political capital at his disposal.[62] After a nationalist Vietnamese rebellion broke out in late 1946, the French finally began to offer more ground on autonomy while still holding on to as much control as possible. He noted, "The concessions which the French have made to the successive governments have been considerable, and if extended to Ho Chi Minh in 1945 and 1946 might have changed the entire history of that area."[63]

Kennedy went on argue that subsequent "French offers of limited independence to the people of Vietnam have always been too little and too late."[64] The consequences of this were dire; with little prospect of real independence, noncommunist Vietnamese lacked a real cause to fight for, while French lives and American money were being wasted.[65] Through the early 1950s, Kennedy noted that France had given Vietnam some of the trappings of independence without adding any substance to them. For example, France still controlled Vietnam's foreign and defense policy, higher education was conducted in French, and French citizens controlled nearly every facet of the economy, enjoyed extraterritoriality, and could be exempted from local taxes.[66] There was no popular assembly to represent Vietnamese interests, and all major policy decisions were made in Paris.[67] In continuing to prop up the French war effort in Indochina, Kennedy argued, the United States was not only delaying the implementation of real reforms that would bring peace, but also doing great damage to its own reputation across Asia.[68]

As lamentable as an American breach with France may have been, Kennedy argued that the consequences of the status quo were far worse in the long run for both the Vietnamese people and America's Cold War campaign. Kennedy saw France as an obstacle in Vietnam, not a partner, after having made mistakes that he could neither forgive nor forget. In Kennedy's eyes, de Gaulle bore considerable personal responsibility here as well, even though he was out of power eleven months before the First Indochina War began.

Kennedy refined and then reiterated this message before the Senate two years later on April 6, 1954, as French forces at the jungle fortress of Dien Bien Phu were locked in the fierce fight with the Viet Minh that would become the decisive engagement of the war. His Indochina speech was delivered at roughly the halfway point of the three-month battle, as French prospects for victory were growing increasingly remote. The French defeat there effectively ended the war and ushered in a complete French military withdrawal, rendering Kennedy's exhortations against continued American support for the French effort moot. Nevertheless, the speech reinforces the argument that Kennedy saw France as an impediment toward the establishment of pro-Western regimes in Southeast Asia, making it a malevolent force that needed to be excised from the region before the damage it had done became permanent.

Though taking care "not to disparage [French] valor," Kennedy clearly stated that France was simply not up to the task of "achiev[ing] the necessary victory over the forces of communism, and thus preserv[ing] the security and freedom of all of southeast Asia."[69] Coming from a diehard Cold Warrior such as Kennedy, these carefully chosen words represented a barely concealed condescension toward a broken great power that lacked the psychological "will to resist" or the resources necessary to shape world events rather than simply respond passively to them. Kennedy lamented that every time the French came calling for more money and weapons to prosecute the war in Indochina, the United States always conceded, time and time again choosing to believe rosy prognostications that victory was just around the corner. The end to this charade, he believed, had to come sooner rather than later.[70]

Kennedy repeated an argument that he had been making publicly for over three years: France had failed to win over enough of the Vietnamese public to triumph in the war and as such had no hope of military victory even with a limitless American commitment to prop up its war effort.[71] He went on to add that the French had reneged on all of the promises they made to grant real independence in Indochina in order to secure pledges of aid from Washington. Vietnam still lacked a popular assembly, was subject to arbitrary decisions made in Paris, and its economy remained almost entirely under the control of French interests. To Kennedy, "all of this flies in the face of repeated assurances to the American people by our own officials that complete independence has been or will be granted."[72]

Without a popular assembly, Vietnamese negotiators had a difficult time reflecting the will of the people, thus enabling the French to continue postponing a real political settlement.[73] Here Kennedy made perfectly clear that he believed France, aided and abetted by short-sighted patrons in Washington, was compromising the Western cause in the Cold War. He did demonstrate an understanding of the difficulty of fighting on Indochinese terrain and the shortcomings of using modern Western weaponry against an enemy that was highly mobile, blended in with the population, and enjoyed widespread public support. Still, Kennedy did not accept France's inability to reassert its control over Indochina as a cautionary tale for the United States, while his later actions from the White House demonstrate that he believed his administration could succeed where successive governments of the Fourth Republic had failed. Seven years later de Gaulle—as wary of American meddling in Vietnam as Senator Kennedy had been of France's—found a surprising degree of resistance when he repeated these very same sound, logical arguments from the Indochina speech back to Kennedy and his administration.

Kennedy's interest in Vietnam did not wane with the 1954 Geneva Accords that brought independence from France and partitioned the country into communist and noncommunist halves with provisions for full elections within two years. In a foreign policy speech at Temple Emmanuel in New

York City on November 17, 1957, Kennedy identified Indochina as no less of a concern than other more prominent divided Cold War nations, such as Germany and Korea. While he held little doubt that the United States could match the Soviet Union scientifically and militarily, he argued that the Third World would become the new central front of the Cold War.[74] Countries like Vietnam were not, in Kennedy's mind, backwaters that could be comfortably ignored, but were rather the battleground of the future. Kennedy's future rival, Soviet premier Nikita Khrushchev, was thinking along the same strategic, geopolitical lines when he pledged Soviet support for "wars of national liberation" in a January 6, 1961, speech from Moscow that was subjected to heavy analysis by the Kennedy White House.[75]

Ugly Americans No Longer

Fellow supporters of a strong American Third World policy in the late 1950s found their call to arms in Eugene Burdick and William Lederer's *The Ugly American,* a fictionalized account of the failure of American Third World aid efforts and France's disastrous counterinsurgency campaign in Vietnam.[76] This best-selling novel, which was given an uninspired Hollywood turn in 1963, was deliberately controversial; it contained an alarmist message that the United States was losing the war for hearts and minds in the newly independent countries of the Third World to the Soviet Union. Burdick and Lederer, both navy veterans of World War II, located a scapegoat that provoked considerable debate in official Washington: overseas American bureaucrats who were soft careerists in search of easy living rather than dedicated, capable Cold Warriors. This charge found a receptive audience with an American public that had been conditioned by years of vile attacks on civil servants from the witch hunting Senator Joseph McCarthy. Robert Dean argues that *The Ugly American* became one of Kennedy's favorite books "as an ideological buttress to his political exhortations . . . congruent with his calls for a tougher, smarter policy of confrontation with the communists in postcolonial regions." The aspiring presidential candidate was so moved by this piece of fiction that he sent a copy to every member of the Senate.[77]

Dean devotes a large part of chapter 7 of *Imperial Brotherhood* analyzing how *The Ugly American* related to the "masculine imperial narrative" that shaped the Kennedy administration's foreign policy, but the novel also contains a significant feminizing portrayal of French colonial officials that he does not explore. Although the story takes place mostly in the fictional Southeast Asian country of Sarkhan, Burdick and Lederer devoted three chapters to the French guerrilla war in Vietnam. Their stereotypes of the French conformed entirely to those Kennedy already held and almost certainly reinforced Kennedy's previously held assumptions about French national character, the flaws of French counterinsurgency strategy, and the illegitimacy of the French colonial project in Vietnam.

The general tone of these *Ugly American* chapters on colonial Vietnam is that individual French soldiers—a motley lot, including some former Nazi collaborators—were tough as nails, well-trained, well-armed, and commanded by generally competent, tactically sound officers. Hard-headed French generals, however, were convinced they knew everything about warfare from their extensive readings of military classics from Clausewitz and others, assuming that they had nothing to learn from more contemporary communist tacticians.

Burdick and Lederer use two officers, Major Monet of the French army and Major "Tex" Wolchek, as a vehicle for comparing and contrasting French and American approaches to guerrilla warfare. The sophisticated Major Monet, a St. Cyr graduate from a proud military family, is arrogant, haughty, and bookish in comparison to salt-of-the-earth Texan Major Wolchek, the son of poor Lithuanian immigrants who was innately capable of solving complex problems with simple logic rather than extensive study. As their part of the story unfolds, Burdick and Lederer allege that the French were not open to new ideas about guerrilla warfare and foolishly chose to keep on trying failed old tactics over and over again until their inevitable defeat. This was very much a cautionary message to American leaders who later engaged the same foe on the same terrain, but it was also explicitly framed as one related to a French national character flaw: stubbornness.

As the Cold War approached a stalemate in nuclear and conventional forces around the time *The Ugly American* was published, Kennedy turned his attention to the Special Forces and counterinsurgency efforts coupled with Third World modernization programs promoting progressive government, liberal capitalism, and professionalism from the military in a bid to win hearts and minds. Kennedy truly took *The Ugly American*'s message to heart; he felt that Americans had to borrow communist tactics, read Mao and Che Guevara's works on guerrilla warfare, and generally approach the Third World with a greater sense of urgency.[78] Much of the language Burdick and Lederer use to describe the French effort in Vietnam echoes Kennedy's assumptions about the ineffectiveness of the early French approach to anticolonial nationalism and, by contrast, highlights how a robust new generation of American leaders could fare better.

In a long passage from chapter 11, Major Wolchek describes the problem behind the French counterinsurgency efforts with Ambassador Harrison MacWhite and Major Monet over a bottle in Hanoi as a pitched battle is being fought outside the city. A flustered, downcast Monet admits, "I feel I'm living in a nightmare, but I don't know what the plan or the key to it is," prompting Wolchek to begin a simplistic lecture on why everything the French army had done in Indochina was wrong. Wolchek compares the battle to "trying to fight a mountain of syrup blindfolded" and compliments Monet's ability to lead his men in combat, but provokes the Frenchman's ire by castigating him for following "the rules of the classic western warfare" when he should have been reading up on communist guerrilla warfare strategies. Monet "wearily" dismisses Wolchek's suggestion that he read Chairman Mao's military writings because "everything that can be written on war was already written long before him. Clausewitz and Jomini went over the whole thing. It's impossible to write anything new on war." MacWhite lends his support to Wolchek based on his impression of Mao as a political leader who is "a shrewd student of men" and the author of a "kind of fight [that] . . . may have become the model by which all Asian Communists fight." Monet still refuses to concede the point, however, as Wolchek is forced to accept "that Monet did not want to be forced to learn a new kind of warfare."[79] Using simple metaphors and inelegant prose, Burdick and Lederer provide a very succinct theory as to why the obstinate, classically minded French were indeed "yesterday's men" when it came to the Third World.

The Ugly American does not simply argue that the French failed in Vietnam for a lack of creativity on the battlefield, but perhaps unintentionally subsumed this component of the defeat into a broader portrait of American perceptions of French shortcomings. The stereotypes contained in the chapters that deal directly with the French fully conform with those held by Anglo-Saxonists over a half-century earlier and are echoed in Kennedy's own writings as a young man. There is no doubt that Burdick and Lederer had France's humiliating collapse in 1940 in mind as they wrote. They saw France as a nation that took to the battlefield with the "smell of defeat" already in the air before a shot had been fired.[80] When Major Wolchek, a decorated American war hero injured in Korea, discusses dropping into Dien Bien Phu for a closer look at the fighting, Major Monet is forced to make the humiliating admission that he had never parachuted into enemy fire because "there has never been an opportunity."[81]

When the fighting began, the French simply lacked the masculine toughness of their American counterparts. When Majors Wolchek and Monet were both injured during the defense of Hanoi, Monet left his command to have the bones in his left elbow set after being shot with a burp gun. By contrast, "Tex was hit by hand-grenade fragments in the buttocks; with a sigh he told the French corpsman not to bother taking a probe to him. Tex now had the iron of three wars in his body and in some dim way he knew he had expected to all along."[82] When the tide turned against them, the French would give way to self-pity and indulge in past glories rather than use adversity as a pretext for self-examination. With Hanoi about to fall, Monet lamented, "imagine a nation which produced Napoleon, Foch, and Lyautey being beaten by so primitive an enemy."[83]

The Ugly American perpetuated other myths about the French counterinsurgency campaign in Vietnam that encouraged Americans to summarily dismiss the notion they had anything to learn about the Third World from Paris. The French, so confident of their civilizational superiority, supposedly never attempted to make use of local resources in the struggle against communism. Instead, they employed "mercenaries"—in Vietnam, these were North Africans, mostly Algerians, many of whom were battle-hardened veterans of World War II—rather than use local manpower even if this meant alienating the Vietnamese. Burdick and Lederer assume that the French chose to deploy "foreign" troops to Vietnam because they felt the passive, undisciplined Vietnamese were unfit as a people for soldiering alongside French troops despite clear evidence that Vietnamese communists were capable of fighting with ferocity and ragged determination.[84] At no point do they acknowledge that there was some sound strategic thinking behind French reluctance to arm large numbers of Vietnamese of dubious loyalty and give the Viet Minh a perfect opportunity to infiltrate the French army. British commanders during the American Revolution held a similar reluctance to rely on local forces and met with a similar fate.

Burdick and Lederer tried to fit Vietnam into the American revolutionary tradition by arguing that the French sparked even more Vietnamese resentment through their bureaucratic, mercantilist economic policies that led to monopolies and excessive red tape that retarded Vietnamese economic growth and perpetuated backwardness.[85] If Burdick and Lederer did concede that the French had one skill, it was the feminine ability to seduce gullible American senators into offering their support for continued American aid for the French campaign by plying them with fine food and wine.[86] *The Ugly American* was more than a work of simple fiction, however; it was a window into underlying cultural assumptions that reflected and confirmed Kennedy's views on France's role in Southeast Asia. These themes were subtly referenced in speeches from the future president during the 1950s and ultimately reinforced his decision to reject de Gaulle's neutralization program for Vietnam.

3

Masculinity and Modernization in Democratic Party Politics during the 1950s

The men of the Kennedy administration were products of a dominant postwar political framework that demanded a certain ideal of robust manhood in response to international and domestic circumstances.[1] K. A. Cuordileone charts the development of "a political culture that put a premium on hard masculine toughness and rendered anything less than that soft and feminine and, as such, a real or potential threat to the security of the nation."[2] This rediscovered emphasis on toughness had its roots in the upheaval of World War II and the rise of totalitarian ideologies, both of which had taken place on the Democrats' watch, factors which led postwar liberal Democrats to revamp the entire way they viewed the world.

During the same period from the late 1940s to the mid-1950s, while de Gaulle was on the political sidelines or in retirement, France was led by a series of seemingly weak, unstable Fourth Republic coalition governments. This did not, however, prevent France from mounting a successful opposition to American-supported initiatives, such as the European Defense Community (EDC), negotiating peace with communists in Vietnam against Washington's wishes, and generally resisting American "coca-colonization" of Europe.[3] According to Costigliola, Americans generally "referred to the French in ways that suggested a flighty, not-so-capable female: emotional, hypersensitive, frivolous, impractical, unrestrained, too concerned with food, drink, fashion, art, and love. Meanwhile Americans usually cast themselves in a 'masculine' mode—rational, calm, pragmatic, and efficient."[4] These perceptions of French decadence and irrationality were coupled with fears that acts of resistance from Fourth Republic governments were undermining Washington's efforts to win the Cold War.

Many Democrats shared Arthur Schlesinger's view that liberals in the United States and Britain had shied away from conflict for far too long, and that they had been complacent and cowardly in appeasing Hitler.[5] Clinging to old views that man was inherently rational and failing to reconcile oneself with humankind's capacity for depravity were mistakes that could not be repeated in a Cold War age of anxiety. The liberal prescription Schlesinger advocated in his 1949 tome *The Vital Center* was designed to "masculinize the liberal reform tradition and the radical democrats who rightly stood to inherit it."[6] Young Democrats coming of age in the 1950s, he argued, should start to take their cues more from Teddy Roosevelt than his distant cousin Franklin.

Liberal democrats were motivated to reevaluate their own ideological approach to international relations as a result of the "lessons of Munich," where an overmatched Neville Chamberlain backed down in the face of German pressure in 1938. Relentless attacks from conservative quarters in the 1950s created an added impetus for a shift toward overt "toughness." They found themselves on the defensive through the early postwar period, attacked for their privilege and "softness" by McCarthyites and right-wing conservatives. The Right typically attacked liberal intellectuals as "overly emotional and feminine . . . eggheads" and "bleeding hearts" that were jealous of the more experienced, rational, and masculine men of the Republican Party.[7] Democrats subsequently attempted to deflect charges of softness by embracing the Republican position that the early Cold War dictated more "outward physical manliness" in response to a new totalitarian challenge posed by the Soviet Union. During these years, the Republican Party, which had scuppered American membership in the League of Nations after World War I and had a strong isolationist wing in opposition before and immediately after World War II, successfully created a narrative that it had a better command of foreign policy issues than Democrats. While McCarthyism petered out after the mendacious senator's official censure in 1954, his assault had strong lingering effects on Democrats into the 1960s. Just as Kennedy was beginning to make his mark in American politics, leading liberal Democrats began to adopt an exaggerated "tough" approach as a defense mechanism.[8]

The Democratic Party split between two rival foreign policy camps in the early 1950s over the issue of whether Washington should adopt a more aggressive policy with the communist bloc.[9] The "realists" were led by Truman-era

Secretary of State Dean Acheson, while a group of "idealists" rallied around twice-failed Democratic presidential nominee and Illinois governor Adlai Stevenson.[10] Acheson, with the support of Paul Nitze, a former head of the State Department policy planning staff who in 1950 authored the hard-line strategy in NSC-68, argued that the Cold War was an enduring feature of the international landscape and that negotiations with the Soviet Union were futile and dangerous due to the autocratic and secretive nature of the Soviet state. This faction, backed by former President Truman, future President Lyndon Johnson, and Speaker of the House of Representatives Sam Rayburn, believed that the United States could best maintain its position by building up its military power and strengthening NATO.

Stevenson's primary ally was Chester Bowles, who was later chosen as Kennedy's first undersecretary of state and then almost immediately marginalized for his opposition to the Bay of Pigs invasion and deepening American military intervention in South Vietnam.[11] The Stevenson-Bowles faction countered that American foreign policy aims were best served by delivering economic aid to underdeveloped countries, expanding international trade, and maintaining good relations with neutrals in the United Nations. Supporters, including Senators Hubert H. Humphrey and J. William Fulbright, Roosevelt-Truman-era diplomat William Averell Harriman, and economist John Kenneth Galbraith, tended to be optimists when it came to prospects for a *modus vivendi* with the Soviet Union, but they did not deny that Washington had the right to use military force to counter aggression from the communist bloc.[12] The factional struggle was settled by American voters, who rejected Stevenson soundly in favor of Dwight Eisenhower in both the 1952 and 1956 presidential elections, creating an opportunity for Acheson to steer the Democratic foreign policy platform back in an uncompromisingly hawkish direction in advance of Kennedy's selection as the party's presidential nominee in 1960.

In the early 1950s the Democratic leadership was even more supportive of Eisenhower's foreign policy, which they viewed largely as a continuation of Truman's, than most rank-and-file Republicans. Still, some Democrats did begin to oppose Eisenhower early in his first term, but they were for the most part divided and ineffective, which created the appearance that party leadership supported a cooperative bipartisan approach to foreign affairs. It was not until after Eisenhower's reelection in 1956 that Democrats began to rally around an alternative foreign policy program that would help return one of their own to the White House in 1960.[13]

Acheson saw the Soviet Union's successful launch of the Sputnik spacecraft in October 1957 as a means of reuniting Democrats around the issue of a military buildup, which became easier to sell to the party after the humiliation of the failed American Project Vanguard satellite launches in December 1957 and February 1958. If the United States was losing the space race, there was reason for voters to believe it was also falling behind elsewhere. Acheson successfully drew major media attention to the so-called missile gap between the United States and the Soviet Union, which he knew was a future threat rather than a present danger, as a means of scoring political points against the popular Eisenhower administration. It was at this point that the Democrats began to turn the tables on Republicans, accusing them of being soft on communism, promising to reverse Republican cuts to military spending, pushing NATO allies to bolster their military capacities, encouraging neutrals to join the Western camp, and working on new limited war strategies to replace Eisenhower's massive retaliation nuclear doctrine.

By the late 1950s Acheson had effectively outmaneuvered party liberals who saw rapprochement with Moscow's post-Stalin leadership as a more productive long-term strategy, shifting the Democratic Cold War foreign policy program back to its NSC-68 incarnation.[14] J. K. Galbraith, the witty Canadian-born economist, writes in his memoirs that he and other vocal liberal Democrats in the Democratic Advisory Committee in the late 1950s were uncomfortable with how Acheson and Nitze placed greater importance on positioning the party to retake the White House than on holding a rational internal debate on Cold War policy. Their objections to the party's knee-jerk condemnations of every Eisenhower administration foreign policy action as "soft on communism" were, however, mostly futile. He writes, "Many, in fact, recognized the need for accommodation with the Soviets, but it was going too far to say this out loud. That the Soviets, either directly or through their Chinese puppets (as the latter were automatically regarded), were moving to dominate the former colonial world was not contested."[15] Galbraith argued that this climate within the party, one that emphasized conformity over debate, contributed to fateful decisions on Vietnam under later Democrat presidents.[16]

The defeat of party liberals suited Kennedy, who sided with Acheson and was positioning himself as a hard-line anticommunist candidate for the presidential nomination.[17] Their alignment, however, was solely issue-based. Acheson had never got on well with Kennedy, whom he dismissed as a spoiled, vapid youth who had bought his way into Congress with the proceeds of his appeasing father's various shady business dealings. When it came to alliance policy, they had disagreed sharply over France; Acheson encouraged greater sympathy for an ally undergoing a painful decolonization process, in contrast to Kennedy's demand that it grant Algerian independence immediately.

Acheson threw his weight behind the Kennedy-Johnson ticket in 1960 because it held the best hope of defeating the Republicans, but by early 1963 he had become thoroughly disillusioned with the "Best and the Brightest" of the administration.[18] Acheson had in fact initially backed Senator Stuart Symington of Missouri for the Democratic presidential nomination in an attempt to block Kennedy, but Kennedy still retained "more admiration for the cool toughness and unflinching pragmatism of . . . Acheson than he did for his more liberal advisors, men like Bowles and Galbraith, whom he considered idealistic but slightly mushy."[19] Whatever regrets he may have had later, Acheson played a major role in shifting the national foreign policy debate in a manner that set Kennedy up to take the White House.

By the late 1950s, a sense of "cultural malaise and national softness" began to deepen with the Soviet launch of Sputnik in 1957. As a result, many of the major themes that dominated the crisis in American masculinity emerged in the 1960 presidential election. Liberals rallied behind John Kennedy because they wanted to see a "liberal superman" president as counter to the supposedly soft, conformist bureaucrats of the Eisenhower administration. As K. A. Cuordileone argues, liberals sought a leader who was "capable of restoring muscularity to what were once political liabilities: intellectuality, wealth, style, and Ivy League pedigree, and not least of all a liberal Democratic politics."[20] Backing down from the communist challenge in Vietnam, as de Gaulle later seemed to advocate with his proposals for a negotiated neutralization of the South, flew in the face of the central tenets of the new Democratic "cult of toughness" that Kennedy rode to the White House. The Kennedy administration simply could not fathom taking the advice of a foreign leader it perceived as advocating the same stance as the vacillating Frenchmen who signed off on the disastrous Munich Pact two decades earlier.

As Democrats were taking on an exaggerated masculine posture in advance of the 1960 presidential election, many Americans looked at political developments in France with growing disdain. By Stalin's death in 1953, Cold War dividing lines had solidified in Europe and the PCF had been effectively marginalized by centrist coalitions, factors that contributed to a growing sense in France that Paris no longer had to choose between East and West and could opt for a more neutral course.[21] France, like Britain, turned its attention to reestablishing itself as a great power, whereas the principal American aims in Europe were to contain the Soviet Union and tie West Germany to the Atlantic alliance.[22] These goals were not necessarily in opposition to one another, but they did contain the potential for conflict. Successive postwar French governments were primarily concerned with rapidly modernizing a country that had long lagged behind its more dynamic European rivals, Germany especially. In theory, rapprochement with the East would create the tantalizing possibility of allowing the French government to redirect resources from the military to its recovery effort, meaning that France was willing to at least consider deescalating the Cold War if circumstances warranted. This economics-first focus was primarily a natural response to the very real prospect of falling from the ranks of the great powers after the humiliation of 1940 and the collapse of the Third Republic.[23] By contrast, Costigliola argues that Americans, viewing France as inferior and feminine from their position of relative strength and security, simply could not accept that the French had "legitimate national interests and perspectives significantly different from those of the United States."[24] This fundamental contradiction over postwar priorities helped exacerbate long-standing cultural stereotypes that fed Franco-American tensions.

The EDC affair demonstrated that there had been considerable and effective French efforts to curb American hegemony long before de Gaulle returned to power in 1958. By negotiating a French withdrawal from Vietnam in July 1954 in the face of American efforts to keep France fighting, Mendès France had openly placed French interests above relations with the United States, a first for a Fourth Republic prime minister and a harbinger of the most assertive Gaullist tone to come. Thereafter, "neutralist-tinged nationalism" characterized French dealings with the United States.[25]

The French National Assembly's refusal to ratify the EDC treaty the following month led many Americans to conclude that Washington should rely more on West Germany as its principal continental European partner. Compliance trumped wartime solidarity. *Time* accused Mendès France of indecisiveness and failure to give direction to the assembly, while crediting "ailing old Edouard Herriot, honorary President of the Assembly, who for years has appealed more to French emotions than to French intelligence," with tipping the balance against the treaty after an overly dramatic anti-EDC speech.[26]

It also noted that the "impulse [in Washington] was to say: 'The French be damned,'" but lamented that "France still would have to be taken into account" solely by virtue of its geographical importance to NATO logistics in Western Europe. In any event, "the West could never again accept France at quite the same valuation, which was a sad fact but one that the French nation had created for itself."[27]

Of the major dailies, the *Washington Post,* argued that "all of the weaknesses of the French political system became more evident during the long and wearisome debate over ratification of the European Defense Community treaty." Despite living in a "state of paralysis under the threat of weapons of absolute destruction . . . [French] people are preoccupied with other things, with high prices, with the effort to get a little pleasure out of the few days at the end of summer when the sun has at last appeared after an unprecedented spell of cold, gloomy weather."[28] The usually liberal, pro-European *Hartford Courant* overdramatically accused "a psychotic France" of "cut[ting] the ground out from under the moderate, internationalist, western-minded, and thoroughly civilized Chancellor Adenauer—its best friend in Germany." The French vote seemed to confirm irrational France's status as "a declining civilization" that looked to past alliances with the Anglo-Saxon powers during the world wars that were completely inappropriate given the political realities of the 1950s.[29] The *Wall Street Journal* noted that Mendès France led a country that "long ceased to be a great military power" and was now sending dangerously mixed messages to young Germans who hoped to integrate their country into the West.[30] Only the sober *New York Times* argued that "it would be stupid and politically immoral to turn on France now or to regard her as anything but the valued friend and ally that she has always been," but it quietly noted that "just about everybody in the free world outside France thinks the French are wrong."[31]

The Anglo-French-Israeli invasion of the Suez Canal in October 1956, an action that ushered in the transition from British to American hegemony in the Middle East, exacerbated tensions in the Franco-American relationship even further. At issue for Washington was less the fact that Britain and France were acting like unreformed nineteenth-century imperial powers—the Eisenhower administration had no qualms about removing democratically elected, unfriendly governments in Iran in 1953 and Guatemala in 1954—but that they had done so without first consulting their superpower patron. The president was alarmed by President Gamal Abdel Nasser's hasty decision to nationalize the canal as punishment for the withdrawal of an offer of Anglo-American financing for the Aswan High Dam project, but not to the same extent as its counterparts in Paris and London, who feared that he would choke Europe off from its oil supply in the Persian Gulf. The Eisenhower administration was even more furious given that the invasion coincided with the brutal Soviet repression of an anticommunist uprising in Hungary and drew world attention away from what should have been a huge propaganda win for the West.

France, seeking to punish Nasser for his moral and material support for Algerian rebels fighting for independence, had won British and Israeli support for a joint military scheme, which was executed flawlessly. The French government was furious when Washington denied France its first clear military victory since World War I, viewing Eisenhower's call for an immediate cease-fire as a betrayal in the face of a common Western enemy.[32] The whole affair had completely opposite effects in Paris and London; the Suez humiliation forced Britain to retreat even further into its so-called special relationship with the United States, but it marked a definite break between France and its erstwhile Anglo-Saxon allies. The biggest long-term consequence of the Suez Crisis was an even more decisive French turn toward a policy of independence, closer ties with European partners rather than Washington, and even greater assertiveness on colonial and Third World issues.[33]

Americans were generally unwilling to forgive this series of policy disputes, from the EDC to the Suez Crisis, as part of France's awkward transition into a postcolonial global role. This fit with a trend that Costigliola identified in which the United States has generally had great difficulty acknowledging, much less debating, differing points of view within the Western alliance since taking on the self-proclaimed role of "leader of the free world." European opposition to American designs was frequently described in feminizing language that reflected a shifting power dynamic with the United States; it could be argued that this phenomenon was essentially a Cold War update of traditional American stereotypes of the Old World.[34]

Costigliola shows, for example, that George F. Kennan's "long telegram" of February 1946 painted the Soviet Union as a rapist seeking to take advantage of weak, feminine European nations. At the outset of the Cold War, Americans understood themselves to be the masculine hero who would ride in to the rescue, leading them to view the Western alliance more in terms of a marriage headed by a clear-thinking patriarchal leader than a partnership of equals. Costigliola writes:

> U.S. officials often responded to an ally's resistance to American policy with emotive language that depoliticized and trivialized the difference of opinion. Such emotion-laden language read political disagreements as evidence that the ally was unreasonable or incapable. . . . With varying and probably unknowable degrees of intentionality, U.S. officials used language that depicted difficult allies as beings that were in some way diminished from the norm of a healthy heterosexual male: sick patients, hysterical women, naive children, emasculated men. Such images of the needy activated altruistic language and so helped transform American control into American caring.[35]

In relation to France specifically, Costigliola finds a "pattern in which U.S. officials represented France's resistance to American policy as evidence that Fourth Republic France suffered from mental sickness, from an insufficiency of masculinity, and from a moral corruption in its politics and society."[36] Further, "from 1940 to 1958, Americans often represented France or the French government as one or more of a series of stock characters who were wayward but ultimately unthreatening and who were usually maligned women: the whimsical airhead, the flirt, the hysteric, the seductress, the female who was willful and wrongheaded, and the woman who was out of place in the public sphere."[37]

Subsequently, the perfectly reasonable misgivings that led the French government to sink the EDC as an unacceptable infringement on national sovereignty were overlooked by "outraged U.S. officials who trivialized French concerns by representing them as evidence of irrationality."[38] Two years later, when France expressed its displeasure at Washington's condemnation of the Franco-British conduct during the Suez Crisis, "U.S. officials again represented French resentment as evidence of a client's psychological problem . . . because it fit their conception of the Western alliance: an association of nations with differences in mental stability as well as military power."[39] American usage of this sort of gender-coded language to describe France dropped off sharply when de Gaulle reclaimed the French presidency in 1958, but the pop psychology approach to his agenda persisted into the 1960s.[40]

The New Frontiersmen

After defeating Vice President Richard Nixon by a razor-thin margin in November 1960, Kennedy set about filling his cabinet with fellow "New Frontiersman" who would reinvigorate American foreign policy after eight years of drift under Eisenhower's old, weak, decadent, and effeminate "organization men."[41] As Robert Dean writes, each of Kennedy's New Frontiersmen "had performed brilliantly as a scholar and athlete at an Ivy League university . . . had been decorated for bravery during service as a junior officer in the Second World War, and . . . had gone on to serve the nation through a brilliant 'establishment' career in government, academia, law, or banking."[42] Dean continues, "Central to the self-definition of Kennedy's stoic warrior-intellectual foreign policy administrators was a commitment to struggle, engagement, and relentless competition with America's imperial rivals, the Communist 'bloc.'"[43] There was a striking degree of conformity to what Dean calls Kennedy's "elite ideology of masculinity" among the New Frontiersman, and this translated into an unquestioning agreement on accepted Cold War wisdom.[44] In practice, Kennedy administration debates on Vietnam typically focused on what form American intervention should take rather than the broader question of whether Washington's national security needs really demanded the establishment of a stable, pro-Western client regime in Saigon.

Some of the dysfunction in the Franco-American relationship in the early 1960s was the byproduct of the generational gap between the elderly de Gaulle (born in 1890) and the relatively youthful Kennedy administration, made up mostly of men who were twenty to thirty years de Gaulle's junior. De Gaulle was an unabashed product of nineteenth-century Europe, his worldview shaped by the pre-Soviet era of intense Darwinian national rivalries. As a general, rebel leader, and president, his experience spanned a period of incredible turmoil that saw the collapse of empires, revolution, and the rise of totalitarian ideologies of the right and left, giving him a broader perspective on world affairs. Truman-era figures of Gilded Age vintage such as Dean Acheson and George Marshall had their own earlier disagreements with de Gaulle, but they usually had a better general understanding of his motives. The members of the Kennedy administration, however, had not known a precommunist era and defined their mission thoroughly by America's global ideological struggle against the Soviet Union. They came of age during the 1930s, when their country was preoccupied by the domestic troubles of the Great Depression and had largely detached itself from international affairs. They were young men while the United States was locked in mortal struggle with Nazi Germany and imperial Japan, and then resumed or started their civilian lives as their country emerged from the crucible of war only to find itself bogged down in a strange, new conflict with the Soviet Union. During their formative years they had seen aggressive totalitarian states on the march, leading them to the conclusion that the United States could never forget "the lessons of Munich," especially after the "loss" of China to Mao's communists in 1949. Whereas de Gaulle was able to imagine a world beyond the Cold War because he had lived through the era that came before it, the brilliant men in the Kennedy administration were totally absorbed by the immediate, short-term implications of Washington's geopolitical rivalry with the Soviet Union.

The generational gap between de Gaulle and the Kennedy administration did more than offer differing frames of historical reference; it also produced a wholly different tone and methodology for the diplomacy they conducted. The Kennedy men had the confident aggressiveness of a younger generation of leaders and saw no limit to their problem-solving abilities. In his inaugural address, Kennedy served notice that his would be an active administration, indicating particular interest in supporting newly independent regimes in the emerging Third World. He and his New Frontiersmen would not shirk from the enormous responsibility of protecting the "free world" they had placed on their own shoulders.[45] This was not simply empty rhetoric, and the approach had serious implications for Franco-American relations. Kennedy signaled an impatience with traditional European diplomacy—was the backwardness of Southeast Asia not the fault of selfish French colonialists, and did this backwardness not encourage locals to flirt with communism?—and "yesterday's men" who practiced it. De Gaulle was seen as the worst offender, the sort of leader who simply could not understand how the administration's urgent modernization plans for Vietnam fit into its broader Cold War strategy.

The Kennedy administration's actions, if not always its words, strongly indicated that it did not view France as a world power, at least not one on par with Britain, nor did it believe Paris had any credibility in Southeast Asia. One might be tempted to speculate that some of President Franklin Roosevelt's legendary Francophobia had filtered down to Kennedy as a young Democrat, but after launching his political career Kennedy's opposition to

French policy was at least publicly contained to the impersonal level of grand strategy as opposed to the crude, schoolboy barbs Roosevelt lobbed at de Gaulle during the war. In his 1954 Indochina speech to the Senate, Kennedy had emphasized his standard Cold War line that the struggle against communism was a necessary one, while success would be predicated upon winning hearts and minds in the Third World. As colonizers, he charged the French with never having lived up to their promises of autonomy, with economic exploitation, and with failing to train a political class to run the country after independence—the unspoken implication being that this was a major obstacle in the sort of hearts and minds campaign necessary for victory over the communist camp.[46]

Kennedy later applied the same themes with increasing frequency to France's efforts to retain control over Algeria, which he saw as a byproduct of "a residue of defensive nationalism" after the Anglo-French debacle at Suez in 1956.[47] For well over a half-decade before becoming president, Kennedy continually spoke of his frustration with France's decision to cling to an anachronistic colonial policy in the face of such violent opposition from its subjects. That Paris resisted what he saw as an obvious reality—Europeans had to give up their empires—left France totally discredited when it came to Third World issues. These views were so deeply ingrained in Kennedy's mind by 1961 that it was unlikely that any amount of framing from de Gaulle or any other French leader could have convinced him that France, despite past mistakes, still had regional expertise that deserved to be taken into account. The New Frontiersmen concurred.

Dean Rusk, Kennedy's obdurate secretary of state, was born in Cherokee County, Georgia, in 1909, lifting himself from humble rural Southern origins through a mix of hard work and rough charm.[48] He spent two years working for a lawyer in Atlanta to finance his undergraduate education at a small, well-regarded liberal arts school, Davidson College, in North Carolina, later earning a master's degree from St. John's College at Oxford as a Rhodes Scholar. Rusk was working as an associate professor of government and the dean of faculty at another small liberal arts school, Mills College, in Oakland, California, when he was called up for active duty as a junior staff officer in the US Army in 1940. The industrious Rusk rose to the rank of colonel, eventually becoming the deputy chief of staff in the China-Burma-India theater, where he was awarded the Legion of Merit with Oak Leaf Cluster. Rusk's military and academic background opened the door for postwar government work, and he served in a variety of relatively high-level roles during the Truman years.[49] He rode out the Eisenhower presidency as head of the Rockefeller Foundation, though his appointment as Kennedy's secretary of state at age fifty-two took most observers by surprise. For some, the tag of being a "compromise candidate" was meant to be derisive.

While he was more patient than other New Frontiersmen, Rusk emerges from Warren Cohen's biography as indifferent to public opinion and unwilling to challenge authority even when he held deep reservations, such as he did during the Bay of Pigs invasion. Rusk was, however, a well-intentioned, loyal, and hard-working bureaucrat, "the consummate Wilsonian . . . responding to Lenin with the precepts of American liberalism."[50] Rusk nevertheless remained a firmly anti-intellectual New Frontiersman despite his Oxford background. He would later disparage academic theories and research projects, preferring to apply himself in an administrator's role. As a result, Rusk was generally ill-disposed to cerebral leaders like de Gaulle and found it much easier to get on with the rough-hewn vice president, Lyndon Johnson, than other New Frontiersmen. Although Rusk was widely viewed as an expert on Asia and foreign affairs, he accepted stock positions on Vietnam and followed the Democratic pack by taking generic anticommunist, global interventionist positions.[51]

Rusk was a classic compromise pick as secretary of state, one who never staked out bold positions or pushed back against his colleagues.[52] Unsurprisingly, he would emerge as one of the administration's strongest advocates of expanding the American intervention in South Vietnam and showed little regret for his actions even decades after he had left office. Rusk believed that primacy in foreign policy formation should be granted to the president and that there should be a clear military hierarchy in the bureaucracy, a position that excused him from taking the initiative to chart an alternate course in Vietnam.[53] Rusk was the sort of ultra-loyalist who viewed those who withdrew their initial support for the president's Vietnam policy—men like Senator Mike Mansfield and Undersecretary of State George Ball, who have been viewed much more kindly by history—as "Benedict Arnolds."[54]

Rusk professed a general dislike for "the inevitable entanglement of summit diplomacy with domestic politics" in head of state meetings with friend and foe alike. When it came to France, he posed what was to him a rhetorical question: "Is the President of the United States to be caught up personally in the difficult task of satisfying General de Gaulle's appetite for grandeur?"[55]

On policy formation, Rusk would later invoke Winston Churchill to rationalize his predisposition for holding firm as his State Department faced "the endless, laborious, challenging human job of getting on with the day's work to create a decent world order."[56] Logevall finds irony in Kennedy's selection of a chief diplomat who "had little faith in the power of diplomacy to settle international disputes, at least where communists were involved," noting that there was little record of any contingency planning for diplomatic efforts in Vietnam in Rusk's State Department from 1961 to 1965.[57] Little surprise then that he compared meetings with de Gaulle, which were usually accompanied by a critique of American policy, to "crawling up a mountainside on your knees, opening a little portal at the top, and waiting for the oracle to speak."[58]

McGeorge Bundy, Kennedy's proud, intelligent, and athletic national security advisor, was a Republican and late convert to the Kennedy team, which he joined only in 1960 out of dissatisfaction with his party's nomination of Richard Nixon for the presidency.[59] Like Kennedy, Bundy had been born into a respected establishment family in Boston in 1919, later making his way to army intelligence in 1941 via Yale and Harvard. After the war he briefly served as an assistant to and ghostwriter for Roosevelt and Truman's former secretary of war, Henry L. Stimson, then worked for a spell as a political analyst at the influential Council on Foreign Relations. He returned to Harvard as a visiting lecturer in 1949, quickly working his way up to dean of the faculty of arts and sciences in 1953, a position he held until joining the Kennedy cabinet.

While Bundy was considered by many to hold the most impressive mind of the Best and Brightest, he, like Rusk, disdained political theory and philosophy.[60] As a Harvard dean he had quietly purged "politically suspect untenured employees and graduate students who refused to name names" despite his public declarations against McCarthyism and loyalty purges.[61] Still, Bundy was a man of stature in American academia who had taken all the hard positions Kennedy expected of his New Frontiersmen. Schlesinger described Bundy as a man of "unlimited self-confidence . . . trenchant and uninhibited," characteristics that shine through in his writings on the Cold War during the 1940s and 1950s.[62]

Ideologically, Bundy was more cautious in his internationalism than Rusk, but backed taking a strong stance against perceived aggressors as part of getting the lessons of World War II right. Bundy fell in line with the pack when it came to his views on foreign policy and, like Kennedy, he was a crisis manager who expected that "the good statesman would be a pragmatic anti-Communist" capable of thinking clearly under extreme pressure.[63]

De Gaulle was irksome to Bundy, who took pleasure at a banquet during the spring 1961 Paris summit in embarrassing the general for his slow, deliberate attempt at conversation with a display of "easy and fluent" French.[64] He later expressed mischievous delight at the annoyance it would cause France when the Peace Corps was deployed to post-independence Algeria.[65] Hawkish on Vietnam, Bundy left the Johnson administration, where his elite Boston pedigree held less sway, in 1966 out of frustration with its conduct of the war, particularly the decision not to expand retaliatory bombings on North Vietnam.

Secretary of Defense Robert McNamara, the most immediately recognizable New Frontiersman thanks to his slicked back hair and rimless glasses, shared Bundy's Harvard background and Republican affiliation, but was unique in the sense that he came to the administration from the private sector rather than academia.[66] He was born into a comfortably middle-class family in San Francisco in 1916, gaining a bachelor's degree from the University of California, Berkeley, at age twenty-one and an MBA from Harvard by twenty-three. McNamara remained at Harvard as an assistant professor of business administration until 1943, when he joined the Army Air Force at the rank of captain. Like Rusk and Bundy, however, McNamara's war service came in a strictly administrative capacity rather than a combat role.[67]

McNamara left the service in 1946 to join the Ford Motor Company with ten fellow "Whiz Kids" who had introduced statistical control to the Air Force, rising up the corporate ladder until he became in 1960 the first president in company history to come from outside the Ford family. By all accounts he was quite satisfied at having reached the top of the American automotive industry in Detroit, but he found it impossible to resist Kennedy's appeal to his sense of national duty and joined the administration in early 1961. As one of the most dynamic business executives in the country, McNamara was expected to use his strong managerial expertise to organize and rationalize the Department of Defense along corporate lines.

Time magazine's profile of McNamara in December 1960 emphasized his stern Presbyterian work ethic, modesty bordering on cheapness, distaste for typical executive glad-handing, and willingness to sacrifice a lucrative career in the private sector for public service.[68] McNamara was a different sort from the other New Frontiersmen in both background and temperament. Whereas Rusk and Bundy were inclined to believe that the war in Vietnam was not progressing as expected by the later 1960s because it was not being prosecuted aggressively enough, McNamara became haunted by nagging doubts that his government had committed a grave error by extending itself so deeply in the country. McNamara harbored his reservations privately, though, resigning from the Johnson administration in 1968 and later attempting to publicly analyze his role in the conflict as a cautionary tale for future generations.[69] From his distant vantage point in the Department of Defense, McNamara had approached the conflict as a business executive, operating on the assumption that the competition could be bested with a superior product and exemplary management. McNamara did not personalize the war to the extent that Kennedy, Rusk, Bundy, and others did, which meant that he did not share their emotional response to de Gaulle's opposition to America's Vietnam policy.

Of the junior men in the president's foreign policy coterie, Walt Whitman Rostow brought the most decidedly academic profile to the White House.[70] Rostow was born in New York to Russian-Jewish socialists in 1916, excelling academically at Yale and as a Rhodes Scholar at Oxford before joining the Office of Strategic Services as a major in 1942. He spent most of the later 1940s in Europe working on various economic recovery programs and lecturing on American history at Oxford and Cambridge. In the 1950s he worked as an economic history professor at MIT, where his prodigious writings on economic modernization drew Senator Kennedy's attention. Rostow joined the Kennedy campaign in 1958—he was credited with developing the catchy Kennedy campaign slogan "Let's get the country moving again"—and developed an easy rapport with the future president.

The prism of economics locked Rostow into his own unique fallacies about Vietnam. In 1960 he had authored *The Stages of Economic Growth: A Non-Communist Manifesto,* a hugely influential liberal democratic blueprint for Third World modernization.[71] Rostow, a prolific economic historian, argued in *The Stages of Economic Growth* that the United States should accelerate the modernization of countries like Vietnam by stimulating key economic sectors and shielding vulnerable regimes from communist incursion by any means necessary. Combined, this would give Third World economies time to grow, winning public support for a noncommunist approach to development. Supremely confident in his modernization theory and obsessed by statistical data that seemed to support it, Rostow was a consistent, unwavering supporter of escalating the war at every turn through both the Kennedy and Johnson administrations.

Bundy, who held many reservations about Rostow, nevertheless agreed to take him on as a deputy special assistant to the president for national security affairs as penance for failing to provide Kennedy with active support during the 1960 presidential campaign.[72] When the administration began drawing up a counterinsurgency plan for Vietnam in 1961, the bookish Rostow proposed committing thousands of American combat troops to the country and a bombing campaign against the North, a program that was far too aggressive for Kennedy's taste. Kennedy quickly distanced himself from Rostow, who was given a sideways promotion to chair of the State Department's Policy Planning Council. His ideas had little influence over Kennedy, Rusk, Bundy, or McNamara and were mostly ignored from late 1961 onward.[73]

In the early 1970s, Undersecretary of State George Ball, along with Senator Mike Mansfield, emerged from *The Pentagon Papers* as one of the few courageous opponents of escalation during the tragic march to war.[74] Ball, born in Des Moines, Iowa, in 1909 and raised in Illinois, was a Midwestern outsider who never really accepted the inherent elitism of the "Best and the Brightest."[75] He studied literature and classics at Northwestern University rather than pursue an Ivy League education and put on anti-intellectual airs. Ball was dispatched to France to assist with American Marshall Plan reconstruction efforts in the late 1940s and formed a deep friendship with the French architect of the European Economic Community (EEC), Jean Monnet, who shared his passion for a new, increasingly integrated Western European political entity firmly anchored in the Atlantic community. Later, de Gaulle's opposition to surrendering French sovereignty to supranational institutions and his independent streak put him at odds with everything Ball believed was in the best interests of both the United States and Western Europe. As a staunch Europeanist with little background or interest in Southeast Asia, Ball was by far the most pessimistic voice in the administration about the prospects for success in Vietnam after the decision had been made for military escalation.

Fearing that an intensification of the air campaign against the North would leave Washington unable to choose its exit strategy, he was one of few officials who favored a political solution and "covert probing of a deal with the Viet Cong elements."[76] Ball never accepted the Kennedy-Rusk-Bundy position that an American defeat in Southeast Asia would do untold damage to America's standing in Western Europe, holding that an unwarranted commitment in Vietnam would raise more questions about the American leadership of NATO than it answered. This was exactly the same message de Gaulle and his foreign policy team tried to share with the Kennedy administration.[77] In the end, however, the problem with Ball's advice on Vietnam was that it was neither sharp nor consistent, it failed to answer practical questions about how to deescalate, and it was presented with the lack of confidence one would expect of one of the lone inner circle voices challenging the president's wisdom.[78]

A parallel to Ball's Eurocentrism was his dim view of the Third World, skepticism toward development theories, and a general ambivalence to Southeast Asia that distinguished him from other members of the administration. Ball was an anti-Rostowian, yet another position he unconsciously shared with de Gaulle. He agreed in principle with aid to help newly independent countries resist communism, but opposed the seemingly limitless "nation-building" assistance associated with popular developmental economics of the Kennedy era and far-flung military commitments incommensurate with Washington's resources.[79]

Ball did little to conceal his views early after taking office and never really fit with the tone or style of New Frontier administration, but he was nevertheless tolerated as the voice of "domesticated dissent."[80] He was elevated to the position of undersecretary of state for political affairs in the wake of the late 1961 ouster of Chester Bowles, whose punishment for leaking his opposition to the Bay of Pigs invasion served as a cautionary tale for other subordinates willing to challenge the president's authority. Ball was privately worried about Kennedy's foreign policy, specifically signals that he would make Southeast Asia a test case for resisting communism. He thought Vietnam was a trap and had long admired former French prime minister Pierre Mendès France for finding a way out of an unwinnable conflict.

Ball voiced his opposition to American escalation in Vietnam directly with Kennedy only once, on November 7, 1961. He described the recommendation of the recently released Taylor-Rostow Report to expand the military aid program to the Diem regime and introduce 6,000 to 8,000 American combat troops under the guise of flood relief work as an "enormous mistake" that would ultimately lead to the repetition of the French calamity a decade earlier. Ball went on to predict that if Kennedy approved the plan the United States would have 300,000 troops bogged down in "hostile country" within five years (a number that ended up being 200,000 men too few), to which Kennedy replied, "George, I always thought you were one of the brightest guys in town, but you're crazier than hell, this isn't going to happen."[81] Ball was shocked by the president's tart response and quickly surmised that internal administration debate centered on how to deny victory to the communists rather than whether the logic of American military intervention was sound, an approach that severely limited policy options. Hemmed in by the more influential McNamara and Rusk, he chose silence over sustained opposition that would have certainly led to his early dismissal.[82]

Modernization Theory

Kennedy arrived in the White House in January 1961 possessing, like the rest of the New Frontiersmen, a long record of interest in Vietnam. He had been a strong supporter of Ngo Dinh Diem in the Senate as a member of the American Friends of Vietnam, an influential lobby group, and first gained national attention as a foreign policy expert in the early 1950s for his speeches on Southeast Asia. Kennedy saw the Third World as the key battleground of the future and was determined to launch a new iron-willed foreign policy that was no longer bound by the economic constraints that stayed Eisenhower's hand.[83] In Diem, Kennedy saw exactly the sort of anticommunist nationalist leader he and fellow Third Worlders in the administration could heartily support.[84] His views of the Vietnamese as a whole, however, were shaped by paternalistic liberal views of Asian backwardness and a political missionary's obligation to provide uplift to the downtrodden masses.[85]

Kennedy's willingness to commit to South Vietnam was fueled both by his faith in contemporary modernization theories and overconfidence in his administration's managerial abilities.[86] While the administration viewed victory in the Vietnam conflict as crucial to setting a precedent for the defeat of other communist national liberation movements, it still felt it was "a small and relatively manageable part of a worldwide contest."[87] In the early 1950s Kennedy concluded that South Vietnam's liberal, democratic nationalist elites were trapped between French colonialists and communist rebels, just waiting for an opportunity to break free. He assumed that these nationalists would be eager to work with anticolonial American advisers who would help them steer South Vietnam in a pro-Western direction.[88] In retrospect, it would soon become apparent that both of these assumptions were fatally flawed.

Kennedy's men felt excessively confident that their approach to Vietnam would succeed where France had failed because it was grounded in rational, logical, American social science and was motivated by an altruistic modernization program rather than colonial greed. World War II, the Korean War, and the nuclear arms race fueled the rapid development of a "national security structure" that bound together many disparate public and private institutions into a larger framework. Under this new structure, intellectuals from foreign policy institutes and elite universities were able to play an ever larger role in shaping the political and cultural assumptions that drove American foreign policy. The conclusion they reached by the late 1950s was that American leadership of the free world required a technocratic approach to national security that married the needs of foreign, economic, and domestic policies. Orrin Schwab writes, "The state needed to be multifaceted and multidimensional, organizing the Free World's response to communism militarily, economically, politically, and psychologically; it needed to work intensively within countries, within regions, and within the United States itself."[89] Kennedy's men embraced these new ideas and set about applying them once they reached the White House.

Kennedy-era policy-makers looked to modernization theory as a promising new means of containing revolutionary communist expansion. Through the 1950s a small army of social scientists—most notably Rostow, Lucian Pye, Daniel Lerner, Gabriel Almond, and James Coleman—had been studying how economics, political systems, and social values had shaped development across the globe, leading to the creation of the new, influential academic field of modernization by the early 1960s. As Michael E. Latham argues, modernization theory was built on the beliefs that: "(1) 'traditional' and 'modern' societies are separated by a sharp dichotomy; (2) economic, political and social changes are integrated and interdependent; (3) development tends to proceed toward the modern state along a common, linear path; and (4) the process of developing societies can be dramatically accelerated through contact with developed ones."[90]

At its core, modernization theory was essentially a combination of established American views on the backwardness of non-Europeans and the white man's burden dressed in the academic language of social scientists.[91] The modernization theorists' core assumption was that the industrial capitalist democracies of the West, most of all the United States, set the benchmark for developing countries, which could and should be encouraged to adopt their path. This message appealed to the Kennedy administration's sense of global mission and was seamlessly integrated into the New Frontiersmen's foreign policy program.

Modernization ideology was based on a belief in the altruism, benevolence, and determination of the American people that was rooted in the exceptional historical circumstances that had shaped them. Believing its own foreign policy to be rooted in sound, pragmatic American social science, the Kennedy administration rejected the model of Gaullist foreign policy formation, which they viewed as little more than a byproduct of French intuition and emotion. The administration was convinced that it was promoting a universal, science-based path to development that would enable it to solve the myriad problems facing Third World nations and thwart Soviet attempts to swing them over to the communist camp. Rival foreign visions of how to manage Western relations in the Third World could be dismissed as the products of selfishness. Implicit in American modernization ideology as it was applied to Southeast Asia was a complete and total rejection of the counterproductive French colonial model; as such, it provided further justification for the administration's determination to box de Gaulle out of policy-making decisions on Vietnam.

The administration bought into the myth that the Viet Cong could be defeated if the United States used American technology and management strategies to alleviate economic backwardness, then introduced new liberal democratic institutions that would help integrate South Vietnam with the West. It assumed that American methodology and values were universally applicable, though the administration made little effort to familiarize itself with local history and culture or even consult the Vietnamese on what sort of future they wanted for their country.[92] Soviet premier Nikita Khrushchev's January 1961 speech declaring Soviet support for anticolonial movements and wars of national liberation, coupled with communist advances in Cuba, Congo, and South Vietnam, exacerbated the Kennedy administration's concerns over the fragility of the developing world and intensified its commitment to making this new strategy of containment work.

Through 1961 an informal hard-line anticommunist coalition consisting of Kennedy, liberal internationalists in the State Department, right-wing members of the senior officer corps, and modernization theorists working in the social sciences threw its support behind the doctrine of counterinsurgency. Orrin Schwab describes counterinsurgency doctrine as "a theory of war that departed from the military's traditional concept but captured the support of civilian foreign policy experts throughout the executive branch."[93] It was assumed both in the White House and the Pentagon that the Soviet Union was orchestrating an aggressive campaign against the West and pro-Western regimes across the globe. Key policy-makers saw communist pressure in both Vietnam and Berlin as related elements of this struggle and committed themselves to holding the line on both fronts.[94] In the former, it was imperative to show the Vietnamese the tangible economic benefits of Westernization before their country was lost to the communists. Success here could be applied elsewhere.[95]

In his first year in office, Kennedy reshuffled the bureaucracy, installing hawks in positions of influence and sidelining doves and neutralists, in preparation for an expansion of the American program in Vietnam to support Diem. On Thanksgiving, Averell Harriman, a highly regarded wartime ambassador to Moscow and Truman's secretary of commerce, was promoted in the State Department to assistant secretary for Far Eastern affairs, while Michael Forrestal, Harriman's protégé and the son of Truman's secretary of defense, James Forrestal, took over the Indochina desk at the National Security Council. Harriman had been a strong supporter of George Kennan's push for a more robust containment strategy toward the Soviet Union and had later played a leading role in implementing the Marshall Plan. These two men had increasing influence with Kennedy, who began to feel more confident with his policy direction in Vietnam by the end of the year. Their dovish rivals never wielded much clout; Galbraith came across as a pacifist, Bowles had committed career suicide after the Bay of Pigs, while Abram Chayes had relatively little influence over policy formation in his role as legal adviser for the Department of State.

Disengagement or neutralization would have broken with seven years of American policy and been viewed as a repudiation of the Diem regime, an unacceptable reversal for Kennedy in 1961.[96] By the end of his first year in office he had boosted American aid to South Vietnam from $42 million to $220 million, agreed to General Maxwell Taylor's proposal for "more assertive use of armed forces," dispatched 400 Green Berets to lead the Montagnards guarding North Vietnamese infiltration routes, dispatched hundreds of additional training officers to the ARVN (3,205 by the end of 1961, and 9,000 by the end of 1962), authorized CIA commando raids on the North, and permitted the delivery of weapons to anticommunist militias.[97] This marked a very substantial expansion of American military intervention in

Vietnam, one that served as a necessary precursor to establishing a security environment that would allow for the full implementation of the administration's modernization program.

The corollary to playing such an ambitious role in the modernization process of Third World countries was, as Andrew Preston notes, an increased likelihood that the United States would be drawn into long bush wars to prop up willing client regimes. Rostow and Kennedy understood this risk, but it did not deter them; they felt the United States had an undeniable responsibility to protect the weakest nations targeted by communist "scavengers of the modernization process."[98] For their part, Western European leaders were naturally concerned that Kennedy's new rigorous focus on the Third World was a distraction from the central front of the Cold War, Berlin, and that more robust American intervention in developing countries threatened to draw NATO into a global conflict with the communist bloc over peripheral concerns.

The combination of modernization theory and the threat of American military intervention to suppress communist insurgencies would, Kennedy and Rostow assumed, demonstrate American resolve and check Soviet advances in the Middle East, Africa, and Asia. The chief obstacle American modernization theory encountered in South Vietnam, however, was one of security: the insurgency proved so widespread that Americans could not effectively institute the new programs designed to improve the local standard of living and deliver South Vietnam to the Western camp. Rostowians did not abandon modernization theory in the face of the Viet Cong's challenge; rather, they shifted their focus to more conventional military thinking in order to defeat it on the battlefield as a necessary precursor to the establishment of their cherished economic programs.[99] From this compromise emerged a framework for the subsequent reports, plans, and programs that would draw the Kennedy administration deeper and deeper into Vietnam over the next two years, to de Gaulle's great chagrin.

Modernization theory and counterinsurgency doctrine did not emerge from sinister motives despite the havoc American intervention ultimately wreaked across Southeast Asia, though they were embraced so unquestioningly by the men of the Kennedy administration because many Democrats had felt that they needed to exaggerate their toughness to counter McCarthyite charges of softness in the 1950s.[100] In practice, there was so little regard for local sensibilities in modernization planning that it is hardly surprising that the administration's highly ambitious program for Vietnam failed.

Despite their ostensibly good intentions, Kennedy and the New Frontiersmen let their confidence in idealistic and untested economic and nation-building theories lock them into a rigid mode of thought on Vietnam. The industrialization efforts, resettlement programs, and helicopter raids they developed for use against the Viet Cong held very little appeal for the average Vietnamese peasant. Collectively, these actions propped up the deeply unpopular Diem regime and assisted his security forces as they extended new forms of landlord rule in the countryside, alienating the United States from the poor farmers who made up the bulk of South Vietnam's population.[101] Kennedy's program simply could not succeed in Vietnam, however, without a Vietnamese proxy who completely shared his vision; rather than reevaluate his core assumptions, he devoted his presidency to a vain search for a local leader who simply did not exist.

4

Toward the First Encounter

Franco-American relations during the first four months of the Kennedy presidency were characterized by the White House's cautious, guarded assessment of de Gaulle in advance of a major Franco-American summit meeting between the two presidents in Paris starting at the end of May.[1] Though the attention of both men was diverted by major crises during this period—in April, Kennedy oversaw the debacle that was the Bay of Pigs invasion of Cuba, while de Gaulle successfully faced down a coup attempt from generals in Algeria angered by his willingness to grant independence to the rebelling colony—there was some measure of optimism that their first meeting would go a long way toward resolving many of the issues that had troubled their governments' bilateral relationship during the latter years of the Eisenhower administration. This was not to be the case.

As the months unfolded in advance of the summit, Kennedy's early genuine enthusiasm for greater Franco-American dialogue was quickly tempered by de Gaulle's total disagreement with the American president's plan to reconstitute the chaotic UN peacekeeping operation in post-independence Congo. Nevertheless, American policy-makers close to Kennedy continued to emphasize during this period that there were plenty of potential areas for Franco-American agreement (such as the EEC, Africa, Latin America, Berlin, and the omnibus category of "East-West affairs") that outweighed areas of divergence (such as UN legitimacy, the French nuclear weapons program, and "NATO" broadly conceived).

While the youthful Kennedy was eager to break from the past by employing a modern Cold War-influenced approach with the emerging Third World, de Gaulle's conceptions of how international diplomacy should be conducted harkened back to the long era of European international supremacy when French norms were widely accepted.[2] Born in the northern city of Lille near the Belgian frontier in 1890, just two decades after the Franco-Prussian War, de Gaulle retained a distinctly "long nineteenth century" view of French security interests throughout his political life and was most wary of neighboring Germany rather than Russia or the Soviet Union. His conception of France's traditional role in the world made him enormously sensitive to any gesture that would exclude Paris from the ranks of the great powers, thus explaining how his obsession with status led to a tremendous degree of friction with both Roosevelt and Churchill during the war years. While Churchill often sparred with de Gaulle, there was a grudging respect between the two men and Churchill always understood that British interests would be served in restoring France as a counterbalance to Germany at war's end. Roosevelt, by contrast, initially refused to acknowledge de Gaulle as the French leader in liberated North Africa in late 1942, poisoning relations by backing his rival, General Henri Giraud.

Almost completely unknown outside his own country before 1940, de Gaulle's prickly relations with the Allies during this period of extreme French vulnerability largely and permanently shaped the way Americans subsequently viewed him. The reality was, however, that de Gaulle had gained valuable political experience during the war and the early years of the Fourth Republic, eventually becoming much more confident of his and France's position by 1958. Stanley Hoffman describes him at this point as "not only older, but also more relaxed, avuncular, and serene—rounder both physically and in manner." This confidence, Hoffman argues, came from the satisfaction of knowing that his unheeded warnings on the need to mechanize the French army in the 1930s and grant strong presidential powers in the mid-1940s were both proven correct in hindsight.[3] De Gaulle's confidence often seemed more like arrogance to many, but it was rooted in a long series of victories over some of the best French military and political minds of his generation.

Temperamentally, Kennedy was a pragmatist who focused on Cold War crisis management without dwelling heavily on long-term trends. This sharply distinguished the president and other New Frontiersmen from de Gaulle, who rarely allowed immediate problems to disturb his meditation on the outlook for the international system decades into the future.[4] These contrasting approaches to diplomacy, however, emerged from differing national mythologies rooted in France's *mission civilisatrice* and America's Manifest Destiny and exceptionalism as much as the makeup of individual policymakers. Phil Melling and Jon Roper write, "France, with its experience of a fractured revolutionary past, had a more tolerant attitude towards diverse ideologies and different cultures, seeking at least to investigate colonial societies before attempting to assimilate them. The United States, with a self-confidence endorsed in its ideologically monolithic 'liberal tradition' did not travel in search of utopia."[5] Under different circumstances, these two approaches to international relations could have complimented each other nicely for a more nuanced Western approach to the Cold War. In practice, however, they served to underline the cultural and philosophical differences that had long separated Paris and Washington.

While Eisenhower Republicans were the ostensible foil for the New Frontiersmen, the de Gaulle-era French political elite similarly failed to live up to the New Frontiersmen's masculine ideal and did not command American respect. De Gaulle was a resolute and courageous wartime leader, but he had quarreled endlessly with his Anglo-American counterparts and had seemingly shown a lack of pragmatism by negotiating with Moscow when it suited his interests. Foreign Minister Maurice Couve de Murville had served the collaborationist Vichy government as an administrator until 1943, shortly after Americans troops landed in North Africa. Ambassador to the United States Hervé Alphand had spent the war as an economics attaché in Washington and later became economic director for the Free French in London instead of serving in the military. Both were of service age during the war, but neither saw glory on the battlefield. De Gaulle confidant and minister of cultural affairs André Malraux's heavily decorated service in the French Resistance was somewhat tainted by earlier adventurism in Spain on behalf of a left-wing Republican government many Americans found more offensive than the ultra-conservative Franco regime that replaced it. Kennedy's idealized list of heroic soldier-statesmen who dedicated their lives to American notions of freedom ran from Thomas Jefferson to Winston Churchill via John Quincy Adams and Theodore Roosevelt.[6] None of the men in de Gaulle's inner circle, carrying ambiguous pasts that reflected the turmoil France had undergone during the first half of the twentieth century, came remotely close to fitting this mold in the eyes of the New Frontiersmen.

The immediate questions for the Kennedy administration regarding de Gaulle revolved around determining what he really wanted from Washington and then deciding whether it was worth conceding his demands.[7] De Gaulle had for the previous two years been waging a sustained campaign to convince the Eisenhower administration of the merits of his *directoire* plan, which the

Americans attempted to bury in low-level committee discussions (to de Gaulle's great annoyance) rather than dismiss it outright. De Gaulle's conception of the *directoire* was relatively straightforward. NATO had swelled to fifteen members with West Germany's entry in 1955 and there was a large disparity in wealth, military resources, and global footprint between them. The *directoire* would in effect serve as an inner council comprising the Western alliance's three most powerful members, the United States, Britain, and France. Washington's role in the proposed grouping was automatic due to its wealth, nuclear umbrella, and military power, but de Gaulle felt that the latter two warranted inclusion thanks to centuries of experience in the Third World, extensive economic and political ties in their former colonies, their ability to project force abroad, and the reality that both would end up shouldering much of the burden if war returned to the continent. Once assembled, the *directoire* would ideally discuss issues of global import, reach a consensus, and then address NATO as a whole. This would have functioned to a degree in a role analogous to the UN Security Council vis-à-vis the General Assembly.

De Gaulle dispatched Jacques Chaban-Delmas, president of the National Assembly, to Washington in early 1961 in a bid to resurrect the *directoire* plan with the new administration and impress upon Kennedy the importance of shared decision-making within the Western alliance. The results, however, were no different than they had been under the old regime. De Gaulle continued pushing for a top tier of NATO composed of the United States, Britain, and France until 1962, when it became clear that Kennedy had no intention of even considering the proposal. There was so little American interest that discussions never even advanced to the point of outlining how such a *directoire* might function, though it appeared by 1961 that de Gaulle was hoping for little more than a consultative body. While such a rearrangement would undoubtedly have brought a wave of protest from excluded Western alliance members, such as West Germany, Italy, and the Netherlands, there was in Gaullist eyes a good deal of logic to having NATO's big three, all permanent members of the UN Security Council and nuclear powers, collaborate more closely. De Gaulle, a proud man who hated to ask for anything, awkwardly broached the proposal again with Kennedy after it appeared that Eisenhower had agreed in principle to an unofficial consultative *directoire* just before leaving office. Kennedy was less receptive, however, and chose to ignore the most pressing French concern with NATO in the early 1960s.[8]

Kennedy, like Eisenhower, was offended by charges that Washington's imperial management of NATO was threatening to undermine its relationship with Western Europe when de Gaulle's program appeared to be a blatant scheme to assert French dominion over Germany and win a veto over American foreign policy. American leaders generally appreciated the stabilizing influence de Gaulle restored to France, but they resented his initiatives to undercut American management of NATO or, when they failed, to distance Paris from Washington.[9] As Kennedy arrived in the White House, the United States and France were moving in two different directions: Washington was principled, domineering, and prepared to "bear all burdens" in defense of the free world, while Paris was shedding its empire, redefining its place in the world, and adopting a narrower national focus. Kennedy's "Grand Design" and de Gaulle's "Grand Vision" set the stage for a clash between Paris and Washington over the nature of the Atlantic alliance, Europe, and beyond.[10]

Still, there is an interpretation in the best recent literature on de Gaulle's political philosophy that his policy of *grandeur* was more a show for domestic audiences and that his aims were actually quite limited. It should be noted that the historians in this school are almost exclusively French, Andrew Moravcsik of Princeton being the most notable American exception. The first wave of major Anglo-American studies of de Gaulle during the late 1960s and early 1970s generally took de Gaulle's various pronouncements at face value and ridiculed his pretensions.[11] Philip G. Cerny argues that Gaullism was not a revolutionary approach to international affairs; it was meant to modify the existing balance rather than overthrow it. He claims that "for de Gaulle, *grandeur* was a qualitative, not a quantitative, concept, and that, as a consequence, the Franco-American conflict of the sixties appears in a rather different light. French goals were essentially symbolic and did little to alter the substantive power relationship between France and the United States."[12] De Gaulle's *grandeur* emerged as a "limitationist ideology" mostly concerned with "internal moral unity and worthiness."[13] Had this been understood in Washington at the time, the Kennedy administration almost certainly would have felt less defensive in discussions with French officials on its Vietnam policy.

Maurice Vaïsse portrays de Gaulle as a resolute pragmatist who dedicated himself above all to transforming the bipolar (East-West) Cold War order into a multipolar system in which an independent Europe would sit astride the two superpowers. It was de Gaulle's aim to see this new European grouping build strong ties with the emerging Third World, a move that dictated French withdrawal from Algeria and sub-Saharan Africa. Accordingly, his stance toward the United States, Britain, and NATO should be understood within the context of his efforts to build an independent and French-dominated Europe.[14] Frédéric Bozo adds, "In contrast to his predecessors, de Gaulle's objective was not to place France on a par with Great Britain as second fiddle to the United States, but actually to make its allies recognize its status as a world power—a goal he judged incompatible with integration within NATO."[15]

De Gaulle's concerns with American leadership were abundant and profound. He feared that Americans would not come to Western Europe's defense if doing so would provoke a Soviet nuclear missile strike on the United States, that the rigidity of the bloc system threatened to drag allies such as France into war with the Warsaw Pact over issues that were of no concern to it (such as Taiwan), and that the superpowers had a shared interest in keeping tensions artificially high as a means of maintaining full control over the countries in their respective spheres of influence. To break up this highly volatile arrangement, de Gaulle envisioned a post–Cold War world in which the newly independent states of the Third World and "old Europe" counterbalanced the superpowers. His foreign policy had "two complementary faces": one was revisionist and outward-looking, that of the champion of smaller states, while the other was inward-looking, seeing foreign policy as a means of entrenching a strong state in the national interest when historically France had been prone to divisiveness.[16]

It is crucial to note that these conclusions, in general terms, were not relegated to hindsight as the work of historians who had spent years digging through archives and various other sources. The Kennedy administration's own frequently consulted in-house France expert, Nicholas Wahl of Harvard, shared a similar assessment with Secretary of State Rusk as early as the summer of 1961 that will be discussed in greater detail in chapter 5. The fundamental problem with Franco-American relations in the early 1960s was not that de Gaulle was concealing his motives—this most certainly was not the case with the *directoire* proposal—but that addressing them would have forced the Kennedy administration to launch an unpleasant self-critique of American foreign policy.

The New Frontiersmen brought to the White House very specific ideas about America's role as "leader of the free world," which they saw as a deep moral obligation. These beliefs shaped their conviction that Washington had a duty to defend Diem's South Vietnam against communist aggression, and, by extension, colored their views of de Gaulle's contrarian and outwardly laissez-faire position. Kennedy's "GI Generation" advisors were nearly unanimous in their view that they had a duty to resist communist expansion everywhere across the globe and that negotiation with the enemy was fraught with danger.[17] In the New Frontiersmen's most hopeful World War II analogy, coming from Vice President Johnson in May 1961, Diem was the "Winston Churchill of Southeast Asia" and Vietnam was no less important than pre-Munich Conference Czechoslovakia.[18] As Washington's commitment to the Saigon government grew progressively deeper, the administration became increasingly annoyed with suggestions that it entertain a compromise settlement to wind down the conflict.

Anne Sa'adah argues that the views de Gaulle expressed on Vietnam at the 1961 summit were separate from other NATO issues and were shaped more by ideological differences rather than any concrete action taken by the Kennedy administration. She defines the disagreement as part of what de Gaulle saw as "an American *idée simple*—unity of interest in the Free World" and the "Gaullist *idée fixe*—national independence."[19] De Gaulle believed that he had identified a pattern of diplomatic behavior rooted in notions of American exceptionalism that both restricted French independence and thwarted his foreign policy aims. Sa'adah argues that de Gaulle was probably unaware that Kennedy had already authorized an expansion of the American aid program in Vietnam beyond the limits set out in the Geneva Accords when they met in Paris. He was mainly concerned that "American intervention . . . reflected an inability to recognize neutrality as a respectable political posture in the international arena, and represented a misapplication of force. It was, in other words, part of a familiar pattern of American behavior."[20]

While acknowledging that "the vagueness of de Gaulle's plan might have been imaginatively utilized by an administration genuinely interested in negotiations [and] it would certainly have been utilized by a president determined to withdraw from South Vietnam," Logevall argues that the Kennedy administration's campaign to sabotage all foreign peace initiatives is more significant than its rejection of the de Gaulle program.[21] Counterintuitively, the more difficult the situation in South Vietnam became, the more unwilling the administration grew to negotiating an end to the conflict. He attributes this to the administration's desire to fully manage the conflict and its aversion to allowing either French or Vietnamese actors to steal credit for solving it.

This position raises the question over whether Francophobia had anything to do with the administration's dismissal of de Gaulle's plan or if it was simply determined to apply force in Vietnam regardless of other alternatives.

The New Frontiersmen took offense not to a French position that they knew to be wrong, but to the fact that Paris had the temerity to vocalize its opposition to American designs. The administration's emotional response to de Gaulle's first public call for peace in Vietnam at the end of August 1963 illustrates that the New Frontiersmen rejected the notion that the French, the craven appeasers and capitulators of World War II, had any moral authority to influence American policy in Vietnam. It is extremely difficult to envision a similar reaction from the White House had London been equally forthright with its reservations over the conduct of the war, and it is impossible to explain the rejection of de Gaulle's push for peace without examining it against the broader context of American disdain for France.[22]

Vietnam was, however, far removed from the focal point of the Cold War in early 1961, when plans for a reorganization and expansion of the American effort there had only just been outlined. Kennedy had not committed American combat troops to Vietnam; concerns that would later occupy de Gaulle, such as American usurpation of French influence in a former colony, the dangers of unnecessarily drawing the Soviets and Chinese into the conflict, and binding emerging Third World states to an independent European grouping that stood astride the superpowers, were nebulous and long-term. De Gaulle may even have attached little material importance to the future political orientation of Vietnam. Left-leaning biographer Jean Lacouture writes, "Lieutenant, then Captain, then Major de Gaulle, saw the problems of his work and life only in 'European' terms and in the perspective of the industrial universe of which he was a part. No Frenchman was less concerned with what is now called the 'third world' than this Parisian native of Lille."[23]

Perceptions of Kennedy at the top of the French diplomatic corps in the spring of 1961 were characterized by pessimism. Hervé Alphand, the French ambassador in Washington, shared his pre-summit impressions of Kennedy in a communiqué to Foreign Minister Couve de Murville on May 11, 1961. Citing American setbacks in Cuba, Laos, Congo, and South Vietnam, he wrote that "it appeared that the administration lost control of its foreign policy, at the same time that they lacked experience and judgment before the manoeuvres of an adversary infinitely more perspicacious and better armed."[24] While Kennedy was able to maintain his calm, self-confidence, and problem-solving abilities through adversity, he did display some alarming character traits in crisis situations, most notably impulsiveness, indecisiveness, and a general lack of reflection on the potential consequences of his actions.[25] Alphand concluded on a somewhat fatalistic note that one at least hoped that Kennedy had learned some valuable lessons from this first round of setbacks that could be applied to future decision-making.

De Gaulle even expressed a profound glumness about Kennedy's upcoming round of international summitry with Khrushchev to German chancellor Konrad Adenauer in conversations in Germany nine days later.[26] During this exchange between two elderly European statesmen separated from Kennedy by age, temperament, and worldview, de Gaulle was quick to assume the worst-case scenario while Adenauer sought to gently reassure his colleague. Adenauer said that he was favorably disposed to the young American president, expressing his view that he appeared "intelligent, energetic, understanding quickly and knowing how to listen, if lacking in experience."[27] De Gaulle responded by opining that the Kennedy-Khrushchev meeting in Vienna immediately after the Paris summit was premature and that Khrushchev would talk of peaceful coexistence to lull Kennedy into a false sense of security before launching a "major operation" in Western Europe. De Gaulle was concerned that Kennedy would not be prepared for the coming crisis and that Europeans were unclear as to how far he would go to defend them.[28] Adenauer responded that he was not worried about the Vienna meeting, which would be "a useful test allowing us to judge Mr. Kennedy on the job."[29]

When de Gaulle fretted that "Mr. Kennedy had never been the man of Europe . . . and more particularly the problem of Berlin does not belong to the issues that interest him greatly," Adenauer tried to assuage his worries by arguing that Kennedy was surrounded by able men such as Johnson, Acheson, and Henry Kissinger—a curious point given that Johnson had little role in the administration's foreign policy formation, while the latter two were mistakenly assumed to be active members of Kennedy's inner circle—who knew Europe well and would make sure he was adequately prepared for Vienna.[30] Adenauer's hopeful tone that NATO would become more responsive to European concerns did not sway de Gaulle, who remained convinced that Americans saw themselves as solely responsible for the defense of the free world and would reserve an exclusive decision-making prerogative.[31]

Pre-summit reports on de Gaulle solicited by the White House emphasized character traits that set him up as old-fashioned, stodgy, encumbered by protocol and appearances, highlighting the generational and cultural gap between the septuagenarian general and his youthful American counterpart. There was no acknowledgment that he had mellowed considerably with age and was no longer facing the same wartime stresses that shaped his dealings with Churchill and Roosevelt. Still, de Gaulle had gone a long way toward reestablishing his credentials as a great statesman in Kennedy's eyes by taking bold steps designed to bring peace and independence to Algeria. Kennedy approached the summit with de Gaulle with equal measures of curiosity and caution, unsure of what sort of outcome to expect. While Vietnam was on the agenda in Paris, it was not a policy sphere where Kennedy, still contemptuous of the French colonial record in Indochina, sought French input. At this juncture de Gaulle had fully formed ideas on the proper course of action in Vietnam, but the opposition to American military intervention he articulated in his first conversation with Kennedy was nowhere near as vigorous as he would later portray it to be.

The tone of Kennedy's first letter to de Gaulle on February 2, 1961, roughly a week and a half after his inauguration, stands out as that of a confident rookie seeking and expecting the approval of an older, more experienced colleague. Whether or not de Gaulle appreciated Kennedy's humble deference at the outset, it was not in his nature to cultivate their relationship on this level if it meant endorsing policies he could not support. From our vantage point today, however, it strains the imagination that an allied leader would communicate with an American president with such complete disregard for the reaction his or her words would produce. De Gaulle's rejection, even though he was clearly in the right, served to alienate Kennedy rather than draw him into a conversation between equals that may well have produced a more desirable outcome for both parties.

Kennedy's memo on the Congo Crisis stands out from future correspondence in that it was clearly penned by the president himself without going through the filter of his advisers.[32] He wrote in a tone that hinted at self-satisfaction with his intellectual capacity for solving major international problems as well as an eagerness for validation from a respected peer. No doubt Kennedy felt that his approach to the Congo was characterized by the sort of thoughtful consideration that de Gaulle practiced in the Élysée. This personal, flattering approach to de Gaulle was not to last the week, however. Stung by de Gaulle's sudden, total rejection of a plan he had crafted with great care and attention immediately after assuming the presidency, Kennedy turned over responsibility for future correspondence with de Gaulle to his aides, most of whom carried anti-French or anti-de Gaulle prejudices. The emotional element of his first letter was replaced with an official tone and detached correctness in subsequent correspondence, giving reason to believe that the Kennedy-de Gaulle relationship nearly broke on first contact.

Although the Kennedy White House saw little imminent threat of communist penetration in Africa and was generally content to let Britain and France take the lead on Western policy on the continent, the Congo was an exception because of its size, large population, and lucrative natural resources. Almost immediately after winning its independence from Belgium in June 1960, the Congo descended into a chaotic mash of anti-European violence, an army mutiny, and political disintegration—with the CIA, the Belgians and the Soviets all muddying the waters by providing support for rival factions.[33] The UN dispatched peacekeepers the following month, but failed to agree on a clear mandate for the country, leaving the UN force powerless to stop the secession of the mineral-rich Katanga province and the murder of Soviet-backed Prime Minister Patrice Lumumba by Belgian-supported rebels. The worst of the crisis took place while Kennedy was on the campaign trail in 1960, but renewed international efforts to salvage the UN mission and find a workable political settlement were to begin in earnest around the time of his inauguration. The Congo Crisis served as an early foreign policy test for Kennedy, though the stakes there were relatively low because Africa was still at this point a tertiary Cold War theater. Kennedy hoped to author a plan that would end the crisis, reestablish UN credibility, and provide him with an early opportunity to secure Franco-American cooperation. De Gaulle slapped down key proposals Kennedy offered to resolve the crisis, thwarting each and every one of these aims.

In the early February letter to de Gaulle, Kennedy emphasized the importance he placed on the Congo and expressed his hopes for a "continuing exchange of views" on the troubled country. Kennedy fretted over the failure of the UN mission and Soviet/United Arab Republic support for dissidents, speculating that a communist takeover in the Congo could have a domino effect for the rest of Africa.[34] Though admitting that the UN had failed miserably to date, Kennedy expressed his desire to continue working under its aegis and asked for de Gaulle's support for a new blue helmet mandate to neutralize the Congolese Army and rebel elements, get soldiers out of politics, retrain politicized soldiers, and "prevent all outside assistance from coming into the Congo."[35] He went on to outline an ambitious program that called for the formation of a coalition government, constitutional reforms, federalism, and a ban on secession followed by the release of all political prisoners. UN advisors would play a "much greater administrative role" to prevent Lumumba from seizing levers of power (news of his January 17 execution had not yet been made public at the time Kennedy was writing) and the West would provide technical help to the beleaguered country.[36]

Kennedy acknowledged that de Gaulle had previously expressed his opposition to the UN role in the Congo, but hoped he would change his mind or at least not oppose American attempts to buttress the UN effort. He closed with a personal appeal for greater Franco-American cooperation by using nostalgic language that evoked the two nations' fruitful partnership during the American Revolution, emphasizing shared "ideals and objectives." Kennedy went beyond the required niceties by expressing his "deep appreciation of the great role [de Gaulle was] playing in the world," and referred to him as "a Captain in this climactic struggle for two decades."

Kennedy expressed hopes "that it [would] be possible in 1961 for France and the United States to stand side by side, in terms of the closest comradeship, in the defense of the West" and sheepishly asked permission to start a running dialogue "on matters which are broader in nature and of fundamental, if less immediate concern to us both."[37] Kennedy's reference to de Gaulle, universally known as "le général," by the lower rank of captain is odd, but was perhaps an innocent byproduct of his naval background. Kennedy may have been subconsciously implying that France carried significant responsibilities but was clearly not at the head of the chain of command, or this could merely have been a turn of phrase. Nevertheless, Kennedy's overall tone in his first official correspondence with de Gaulle was positive; it illustrated a desire for greater cooperation with a man he had grown to respect as a voice of authority within the Western camp. This departure from Kennedy's earlier reservations about de Gaulle was a reflection of the considerable amount of political capital the French president had accumulated by bringing strong leadership to a weak, long-divided country and the bold action he was taking to bring the Algerian War to a close.

De Gaulle's response was correct in tone, expressing an appreciation for Kennedy's effort, pleasure with this exchange of ideas, and a willingness to put himself at the American president's disposal. This did not stop him from dissecting Kennedy's plan, most of which he found to be unworkable or inadvisable, with the sort of care an engaged teacher would have for a brighter pupil. De Gaulle expressed his support for an exchange of ideas on major international questions facing the West, promising to "respond with the most complete straightforwardness" in that regard.[38] After politely outlining his preferred course of action, de Gaulle professed his surprise that Kennedy preferred a UN-centered approach when the international body had failed to reestablish order or lay the foundation for a political solution. De Gaulle gently chided Kennedy here, explaining that he had no faith in a reinforced UN peacekeeping force knowing full well that it would inevitably contain a strong contingent from Soviet allies like the United Arab Republic, Indonesia, Ghana, Guinea, and others that could not be expected to act impartially.[39] He stated that his preference was tripartite consultation between Paris, London, and Washington because "the actual composition of the UN excludes, in reality, the organization's capability of acting in a coherent, effective, and politically unbiased manner."[40]

De Gaulle thought it better that Paris, London, and Washington exclude the UN, which he viewed as a Trojan horse for the Soviet bloc, and concentrate their diplomatic efforts on pressuring the Congolese and Belgians into fully complying with the independence treaty they had already signed.[41] He claimed that "in general, a coordinated policy of the US, Great Britain, and France on the issues facing the world would be the best guarantee, and even the only guarantee, that these issues do not degenerate into angry and dangerous events." De Gaulle did approve of elements of Kennedy's Congo plan, especially his pledge to offer support to moderate President Joseph Kasavubu's government that would enable it to successfully resist intrigue from the Soviet bloc-supported faction.[42] He agreed that a broad-based Congolese government was needed, as was military reorganization and depoliticization, and a guarantee of the indivisibility of national territory. Nevertheless, he felt these were initiatives that had to come from within the Congo, from the national government, with support from the West. He argued that the West should present this united view to President Kasavubu and let him accept it willingly rather than impose terms. De Gaulle expected that he would come around and that France would use its local resources discretely to help achieve this end.[43]

In broad terms, de Gaulle felt that Kennedy's plan was overly ambitious and that the administrative role he envisioned likely contravened the UN charter by interfering so greatly in sovereign affairs of state, observations that foreshadowed future opposition to Kennedy's policy in Vietnam. De Gaulle warned that if Kennedy did proceed in this direction he would set a precedent for future UN operations that went well beyond the organization's capabilities and would jeopardize the very survival of a world body Kennedy valued so much by transforming it into a vehicle for pursuing Western aims in Africa.[44] He concluded by expressing hope that Kennedy's government would not present a motion for a new UN mandate for the Congo because France would not be able to offer its support.[45]

This exchange on the Congo may have been brief, but it appeared to impact the White House in a manner that would have implications on later Franco-American discussions about Vietnam. De Gaulle most likely came away moderately perturbed by Kennedy's inclination to directly engage such a messy, remote problem, by his disregard for national sovereignty, and by his willingness for strong-arm solutions when an *approche douce* was more likely to yield the desired result. Kennedy most likely came away suspicious that de Gaulle was a knee-jerk contrarian; his aides certainly had already come to the conclusion that de Gaulle's France was a roadblock that must be carefully avoided as much as possible. Dean Rusk, Kennedy's secretary of state, concluded in a February 9, 1961, memo to Kennedy that "General de Gaulle's letter to you . . . is almost wholly negative, not only in response to your request for his views on our proposed course of action on the Congo problem, but also with respect to our reliance on the United Nations from the beginning of the Congo crisis."[46] Rusk did acknowledge that de Gaulle had carefully worded his statement "presumably to give France sufficient flexibility to abstain in the Security Council instead of flatly opposing our efforts," which was a small victory for the White House.

Rusk recommended that "no purpose would be served in encouraging further correspondence with [de Gaulle] on the Congo at this time" and that American interests would be better served by focusing instead on securing a French abstention for a future UN vote to extend the mandate there.[47] McGeorge Bundy concurred with Rusk that "the President should not continue his dialogue with de Gaulle at this time."[48] Bundy even went further, suggesting that Kennedy cut the ambassador to France, Lieutenant General James Gavin, out of the loop on the administration's thinking on the Congo so as to ensure a definite end to the exchange.

The French did not seem to put much stock in Franco-American differences over the UN role in the Congo, nor were they aware that de Gaulle's position was seen as grounds for breaking off dialogue by Kennedy's key advisors. Alphand met with Woodruff Wallner, an American codirector of UN Affairs at the State Department, in early February, acknowledging the Kennedy administration's fears that the UN was at grave risk of losing all credibility in the Third World if it could not stabilize the Congo. His response was a statement of the obvious: Kennedy's plan would be extremely difficult to implement in a country with little infrastructure, grinding poverty, and a sprawling expanse over an area the size of Western Europe.[49]

The Rusk-Bundy response comes across as somewhat drastic considering that Kennedy had initiated the dialogue, amounting to only one exceedingly polite letter each, by writing de Gaulle to seek his feedback on a proposed Congo plan. De Gaulle had responded to Kennedy by offering a thorough, perceptive review of his ideas, just as he had been requested. While the Kennedy White House thanked de Gaulle for his frankness, they clearly did not appreciate the sentiment when it meant suggesting alterations to predetermined American policy. This early episode augured ill for de Gaulle's future attempts to sway the administration's Vietnam policy in a similar direction. Still, the president was at least more willing to continue working with the French than his subordinates. In an early February meeting with Alphand, Kennedy sang the praises of the new ambassador to France, James Gavin, describing him as a personal friend who had been his advisor on all defense-related questions during the campaign, and expressed hopes that Alphand would be a frequent visitor to the White House.[50] Later that month, Rusk, by contrast, abruptly cut the length of his second meeting with Alphand in half.[51]

As the bilateral discussion of the Congo came to an abrupt halt, new dialogue began on other Third World regions that fell under the French sphere of influence, principally Laos and Algeria, where de Gaulle's ideas were more favorably received in the White House. Small, land-locked Laos had been granted full independence from France with the Geneva Accords in 1954, but its weak, neutrality-inclined government found itself under pressure from a low-level communist insurgency directed from North Vietnam.[52] The Pathet Lao under the leadership of the "Red Prince" Souphanouvong, a longstanding ally of Ho Chi Minh, however, did not threaten the government to the same degree as its comrades across the border in South Vietnam. Laotian communists were also at least willing to enter into discussions with centrist parties on neutrality agreements and the formation of a coalition government in the early 1960s. While the Americans had far fewer local resources in Laos than in South Vietnam, the communist challenge there was considerably weaker. The Kennedy administration recognized the unique set of circumstances in Laos and opted for a diplomatic approach, cautiously supportive of de Gaulle's program: "a ceasefire . . . the convening of the International Control Commission and an international conference . . . for negotiated Laotian Cold War neutrality."[53]

At the same point the *Front de Libération Nationale*'s (FLN) nationalist revolt against French rule in Algeria was winding down as a costly military victory for Paris that ended in political defeat.[54] To win on the battlefield, the French army was forced to resort to a series of brutal tactics ranging from torture, to mass civilian relocations, to the use of concentration camps, bringing international condemnation and pushing France itself to the brink of civil war. De Gaulle, facing growing domestic opposition to a war prosecuted mostly by conscripted troops, was forced to reconcile his countrymen with the political reality that independence was inevitable. He had been slow to publicly accept the principle of Algerian self-determination, but committed to it fully in the wake of a brief insurrection from radical *pieds noirs* settlers and rightist army officers during the *Semaine des barricades* at the end of January 1960.[55] Though his actions were not designed to curry foreign favor, de Gaulle had built up considerable political capital with Kennedy during the final act of the Algerian War of Independence by taking the difficult steps necessary to secure a resolution to the long-running conflict.[56] As brutal as the Algerian anticolonial struggle had become, the Kennedy administration was satisfied that de Gaulle had effectively blocked communist elements from hijacking the newly independent regimes across the formerly French stretch of North Africa. This left the White House comfortable enough to concede the continent as a Franco-British sphere of interest so American resources could be allocated in more sensitive regions.

A curious debate related to Laos, Algeria, and broader Franco-American cooperation in postcolonial regions began in the White House in late March 1961 and continued through the lead-up to the Paris summit. In internal discussions through the spring, Kennedy and many of his key aides conceded the logic of tripartism, de Gaulle's frequently invoked solution for international crises from Congo to Laos, and stressed the importance of greater coordination of Franco-British-American policy in Third World hot spots. Nevertheless, they still chose to deny de Gaulle the satisfaction of formally accepting his *directoire* plan despite all of the more obvious points in its favor.

Tripartism emerged as a subject of discussion in the White House as the American-trained and -supplied Royal Lao Army wilted in the face of a Pathet Lao-North Vietnamese advance that left most of northern Laos in communist hands by mid-March 1961. Recognizing that emergency American material support to the government alone would have done little to turn the tide without motivated, experienced troops capable of taking the fight to the communists, the Kennedy administration had little alternative but to turn its sights to salvaging anything it could with a diplomatic solution.[57] Kennedy's inability to influence the situation in Laos on his own in turn created an opportunity for de Gaulle, who had responsibilities to the country (given that France was a signatory to the Geneva Accords), the will to intervene, a considerable degree of influence with the Laotian government, and a line of communication to the Pathet Lao's sponsors in Hanoi. Kennedy and his aides were thoroughly unimpressed with the job France had done training the Laotian army after independence, but the administration found little to object to in de Gaulle's overtures for a coordinated Franco-British-American response.

De Gaulle wrote Kennedy at the end of March to propose an international discussion modeled on the Geneva Conference to secure recognition of Laotian neutrality and national unity, a Control Commission (such as the one comprised of Canada, India, and Poland that was called for in the Geneva Accords) to stop arms shipments and monitor a cease-fire between the government and the communists, and the formation of a broad-based government under neutralist Prince Souvanna Phouma, Souphanouvong's brother and rival.[58] De Gaulle remained consistent with his opposition to operating through the UN in the Congo, making clear that he was not disposed toward using SEATO as cover for direct Western intervention in Laos. He argued that the two presidents and Britain's Prime Minister Harold Macmillan should agree to stand shoulder to shoulder on Laos before launching a whole-hearted tripartite diplomatic effort with Moscow rather than escalating the crisis with a Western military intervention.[59]

This call for unity, coupled with de Gaulle's strong condemnation of Moscow's role in precipitating the crisis, shielded his neutralization and pacification plan from charges of "softness" in American quarters. Conference diplomacy bore fruit later that spring, leading to the creation of a shaky coalition government with Pathet Lao participation. By mid-decade, the government fell as Laos was subsumed by the intensifying conflict in Vietnam, but the Gaullist approach had at the very least bought time when the Americans lacked the means to secure a better alternative.[60]

The constructive role de Gaulle played during the Laotian Crisis prompted the Kennedy administration to discuss the merits of his *directoire* plan as they understood it, which was not particularly well. Walt Rostow wrote Kennedy in late March to suggest that the United States and France "ought to talk long before crises are hot" when it came to areas presently or formerly in the French sphere of influence.[61] Rostow had just met with Michel Habib-Deloncle, a Gaullist member of the National Assembly who was lobbying him on de Gaulle's behalf for the *directoire.* Rostow reported that Habib-Deloncle cautioned him on the dangers of Western disunity in the Third World, chiefly "running very grave risks of repeating the situation in Laos in other parts of the underdeveloped areas . . . [if] there was no serious effort made to concert British, French, and American policy." He suggested that establishing the principle of consultation would make problems regarding NATO and nuclear weapons "vastly easier to solve."

Rostow added his own thoughts for the president's behalf, conceding that "where there are French interests—notably in Africa—we ought to talk with them as serious dignified partners. . . . They know a lot—including a lot painfully learned about guerrilla warfare."[62] Nevertheless, Rostow advised Kennedy that the administration "need not accept de Gaulle's tripartitism in theory or carry it out with Gallic logic," despite his acceptance of the merits of greater coordination with the French in Third World trouble spots. He concluded by recommending that tripartite discussion be buried "in the functional sub-committees of the NATO Council," an offer that undoubtedly would not have satisfied de Gaulle's bid for greater consultation with Washington.[63]

Rostow returned to the theme of tripartism in an early May memo to Bundy that seemed to indicate that Kennedy was on the verge of making a major concession to de Gaulle just weeks in advance of their bilateral summit. Rostow called for increased coordination between the United States, Britain, and France in Africa and Southeast Asia because communists were exploiting their divisions and "may draw us close to a test of military strength."[64] The president considered the risk of war grave enough to warrant a closing of the ranks, arguing that "high level tripartite discussions of a Western strategy in Africa and Asia are urgent." Rostow added, "in this matter he finds himself close to the views of General de Gaulle."[65] Kennedy told

Rostow that he wanted to let Britain and France take the lead in Africa, which was in the midst of revolutionary upheaval, because he felt confident that they could neutralize any potential military-political threat emerging from the continent and might be able to eventually reincorporate it as "a constructive part of the Western system."[66]

The president's plan to defer to Britain and France in Africa was motivated largely by American overextension elsewhere and his unwillingness to take on new responsibilities "where [Washington's] allies, much strengthened by their remarkable growth in the 1950's can deal with the situation."[67] Kennedy envisioned a tripartite Africa policy where all parties agreed to "a common strategy and how the day to day tactics and tasks of execution may best be allocated and managed . . . where positions of potential political stability and strength exist." From these bases, "[Britain, France, and the United States] should work with all the wisdom and resources we can muster to create islands of responsibility," preventing communists from hijacking revolutionary movements and keeping the decolonization process as bloodless as possible.[68]

At the same time that perceived communist advances in the Third World spurred the Kennedy administration to reexamine tripartitism, de Gaulle's stock in Washington was at an all-time high. Rostow reported that "with respect to North Africa, the President has been impressed by General de Gaulle's vision of the kind of regional development which would be possible after the Algerian settlement is achieved." Kennedy had such a positive view of de Gaulle's efforts at achieving a "constructive regional solution in the long run . . . [that] could conceivably contribute to the pacification of the North African area" that "[he] would be interested to hear De Gaulle's [*sic*] views on the appropriate broad strategy which we should all pursue in Africa; and believes that these matters should promptly be explored on a communal basis by the Western nations most concerned."[69] While de Gaulle conceived of the *directoire* as a clearing house for all pressing foreign policy matters of joint concern, the Kennedy administration took a much narrower view. Its newfound respect for de Gaulle's counsel was confined solely to African affairs rather than alliance policy as a whole.

The Kennedy administration viewed Southeast Asia, where Soviet-backed communists posed a greater, more immediate threat and proximity to Mao's China allowed for much easier resupply, as an entirely different ball game with much higher stakes. While the Kennedy administration was willing at this point to let the British and French play a minor supporting role in the region, they would not allow them to take the lead as they had in Africa. Kennedy ranked defending Vietnam as a top foreign policy priority, and on March 1, 1961, he approved a counterinsurgency plan to ramp up American antiguerrilla training programs, increase the number of Ranger companies at the expense of regular infantry units, improve border patrols, infiltrate the Viet Cong, and establish "safe areas" where the loyalties of Vietnamese peasants could be bought with schools, doctors, land reform, and farm supplies.[70] The White House hoped that these efforts would see South Vietnam through an eighteen- to twenty-four-month danger period of increased communist pressure. Kennedy's general views on consultation with America's allies are illuminated by his stipulation that his counterinsurgency plan was to commence immediately, regardless of whether the Saigon government had given its approval.[71]

In April, Kennedy's attention was temporarily diverted from Vietnam by the disastrous Bay of Pigs invasion of Fidel Castro's Cuba by American-trained anticommunist exiles, but by the end of the month he had refocused American efforts in Southeast Asia.[72] On April 20 he formed a presidential task force charged with developing "a program of action to prevent Communist domination of South Viet-Nam."[73] This task force, headed by Roswell L. Gilpatric, the deputy secretary of defense, was charged with building on the counterinsurgency plan Kennedy had approved the previous month by focusing greater attention on the socioeconomic factors that he perceived to be feeding the Viet Cong insurgency.

Gilpatric's review of American political, economic, and military policy in Vietnam was aimed at, among other things, increasing coordination between the White House, Department of Defense, State Department, CIA, and USIA (US Information Agency, the government's public diplomacy organ). The task force report he produced within a week met with general philosophical agreement by all parties involved in its formation, but there were major concerns regarding the vagueness of its timetables and cost estimates, how to secure Diem's acquiescence and cooperation from neighboring countries, and bureaucratic questions over whether the State Department, the military, or the ambassador in Saigon should coordinate the plan.[74] For the time being, the various organs involved in the project agreed to leave these matters for further clarification after a vice presidential visit to South Vietnam, content that there was no opposition to the broader contours of the report.

Gilpatric's program called for a major intensification of American efforts in Vietnam and clearly signaled that Washington would be taking the initiative for "saving" the country from communism. The report "includ[ed] a range of mutually supporting actions of a political, military, economic, psychological and covert character which can be refined periodically on the basis of further recommendations from the Ambassador in the field."[75] American concerns over South Vietnam's fate were so serious that an unspoken assumption that input from the South Vietnamese was neither necessary nor desirable ran throughout Gilpatric's writing.[76] While Gilpatric accepted that the United States would have to work with Diem, who had hitherto resisted or delayed most American suggestions, he viewed him more as an obstacle than a partner in the democratization and economic development of the country. It was his assessment that securing Diem's cooperation would "require very astute dealing between U.S. Government personnel and the Vietnamese . . . [and a] combination of positive inducements plus . . . discreet pressure."[77] He understood this was a tall order, but Kennedy had declared Vietnam a "critical area" that demanded nothing less than an all-out effort from all relevant arms of the American government.

Gilpatric's report made brief reference to multilateral support for the American program in Vietnam, but it was the British, and to a lesser degree Australians, Malayans and Filipinos, not the French, whose assistance he hoped to enlist. In February, Lord Samuel Hood, minister-counsellor at the British embassy in Washington, shared his pessimism at the general direction in which South Vietnam was heading to the State Department, but he did express British willingness to cooperate with the Americans by sharing the counterinsurgency expertise they had gained during the Malayan Emergency during the 1950s. After its diplomatic defeat during the Suez Crisis in 1956, Britain's window for independent maneuver had narrowed considerably and London was generally disinclined to press its opposition to American policy. The prospect of British cooperation was viewed favorably in the State Department, which was hoping to enlist Franco-British support in normalizing South Vietnamese-Cambodian relations so as to secure at least one of Diem's borders.[78]

The Gilpatric report acknowledged the British offer to provide counterinsurgency training and financial support to the South Vietnamese and concluded that "the political benefits to be obtained within the western alliance by sharing responsibility for this difficult problem" were worth the "administrative problems" caused by "the use of third country personnel."[79] No mention was made of enlisting France to a similar end, most likely because of the perceived ineffectiveness of its counterinsurgency campaign in Indochina in the early 1950s and the French inability to give the Vietnamese a cause worth fighting for, deficiencies that looked considerably worse when contrasted with British success in Malaya.[80] Gilpatric did not acknowledge any of the successful tactics the French had employed in Algeria following their defeat in Vietnam.[81] It was also easier for American decision-makers to accept a British role when London shared Washington's view of the best way forward (albeit one that was more pessimistic about the prospects for success) and would not pose awkward philosophical questions about what Americans were doing in the country.

Kennedy already had a much clearer sense at this early juncture of what he wanted to accomplish in Vietnam and more confidence in his ability to succeed there than in other former European colonies. He was committed to taking great measures in support of Diem, who, despite his weaknesses, was seen to be manning the front line in a global struggle in which the "non-Communist base in the Indian Peninsula and the control of the Indian Ocean and the Western Pacific was ultimately at stake."[82] The conviction and urgency the Kennedy administration brought to its pursuit of the interrelated goals in Vietnam of beating the guerrillas, overcoming the social, political, and economic problems that fueled the insurgency, and containing China left no room for serious multilateral consultation with tentative European allies. This did not, however, indicate that Kennedy had arrived at the conclusion that France was entirely without use in Southeast Asia just yet.

Rostow reiterated in a mid-May memo that Kennedy viewed American policy in Laos as a complete shambles and that Western interests there could only be defended by the development of a common tripartite policy in advance of the difficult conference diplomacy to come. Kennedy recognized America's "weak position on the ground" and accepted the need to apply French "bargaining resources" to keep the country out of communist hands.[83] As Rostow put it, "We are all together now in the effort to negotiate a neutral Laos . . . and the United States is quite prepared to see France and Britain assume increased long-run responsibilities in Laos."[84] In his desperation, it appeared as though Kennedy might have been willing to give tripartism a conditional test run in Vietnam's neighbor.

Just days before Kennedy was to fly off to Paris to meet de Gaulle, Vice President Lyndon Johnson submitted his assessment of the situation in

Vietnam after a two-week whistle-stop tour of Southeast Asia and the Indian subcontinent. While Johnson's report now reads as a surprisingly balanced, nuanced account from the man who later made the fateful decision to opt for a full-out American military intervention, he did preemptively reject the sort of neutralization program for Vietnam that de Gaulle should have been expected to present to Kennedy in Paris. Johnson admitted that there was "a serious danger in Viet Nam . . . of the progressive disintegration of the government's hold on the nation," but cautioned that "the picture we receive at home has been colored by journalistic sensationalism."[85]

Nevertheless, the general thrust of Johnson's evaluation was prescient.[86] Johnson noted that "danger flags [were] flying," evidenced by the rapid increase of the Viet Minh from three or four thousand fighters to twelve thousand despite reports that government forces were inflicting heavy casualties, "the increasing tendency of the palace bureaucracy to isolate itself and President Diem from the people," and an intelligentsia that was becoming increasingly alienated from the government and at risk of drifting over to the communist camp. Nevertheless, Johnson "emphasized that this point of no return has not yet been reached."

Johnson did not underestimate the difficulty Washington faced in South Vietnam, cautioning that increased American aid was no guarantee of success if not accompanied by greater accountability and responsiveness from the Diem regime. He felt that the lack of viable rival leadership candidates to Diem—who, faults and all, was resolutely committed to defeating the Viet Minh—within the noncommunist camp meant that "in present circumstances there is no visible solution to the instability in Viet Nam on the basis of neutralization." Recognizing Diem's weaknesses, the vice president recommended implementing a three-year plan (this would coincide with Kennedy's first term in office) where increased military and economic aid was to be allocated on American terms, with the expectation that specific, measurable benchmarks would be met from the village level on up to the presidential palace.

Johnson hoped that, with close American guidance and supervision, "in time, the Saigon government may become less dependent on aid and lay a valid claim to represent the entire Vietnamese people, north and south." Still, he strongly advised making clear to Diem that, "barring an unmistakable and massive invasion of South Viet Nam from without we have no intention of employing combat U.S. forces in Viet Nam or using even naval or air-support which is but the first step in that direction." Johnson cryptically warned that if the Saigon regime proved unable to establish its legitimacy in the public's eyes and defend itself even with dollops of American aid, Washington "had better remember the experience of the French who wound up with several hundred thousand men in Vietnam and were still unable to do it . . . without engaging a single Chinese or Russian" as it considered taking on an active combat role. "Before we take any such plunge," Johnson argued, "we had better be sure we are prepared to become bogged down chasing irregulars and guerrillas over the rice fields and jungles of Southeast Asia while our principal enemies China and the Soviet Union stand outside the fray and husband their strength."[87]

In advance of his summit meeting with de Gaulle, Kennedy had been both made aware of the potential consequences of deepening American involvement in Vietnam by his vice president and advised to consult more closely with France on Third World matters by one of his principal national security advisors. Kennedy had asked de Gaulle for a frank dialogue on the Congo and was somewhat disappointed with the results, but when he committed to finding a diplomatic solution in Laos he found his French counterpart to be a constructive partner. Still, as de Gaulle learned to his great frustration later in 1961, Kennedy compartmentalized allied offers of assistance, accepting it in some areas without granting status as a full partner on all matters of joint concern. In early 1961 Kennedy was willing to accept diplomatic help from France only where he was weak (Laos), or relatively unworried (Africa and South America), but not in key regions where he felt that the United States had the resources to achieve its goals alone. As important as de Gaulle's actions had been in Algeria, they were not sufficient to lead Kennedy to reevaluate his core perceptions of France's role in Vietnam, which remained wholly negative.

5

Drinking Sour Wine

The Kennedy-de Gaulle disagreement over Vietnam began innocently enough during the Paris summit in the spring of 1961, but it was exacerbated in subsequent months by fundamental disagreements over the nature of the Atlantic alliance and tolerance for neutral regimes outside the bloc system. On May 31 the two presidents sat down for a calm, dispassionate discussion of their respective views on how best to proceed in Southeast Asia as they moved down a checklist of roughly half a dozen major topics of conversation. Kennedy had well-established reservations about French policy in Vietnam, but he was willing to listen to de Gaulle out of curiosity and respect for his role in bringing a resolution to the Algerian War. Kennedy made a strong case that there were legitimate strategic concerns that focused his attention on South Vietnam, while a Western defeat there would do untold damage to America's global prestige. De Gaulle emphasized the region's unsuitability for a military confrontation with the communists and its peripheral importance to the Cold War. What separated the two presidents at this point was de Gaulle's preference for a low-risk diplomatic course of action that acknowledged the possibility, which he believed to be small, of strategic defeat, while Kennedy was willing to gamble on an idealistic, maximum effort campaign to forestall a communist victory.

The dispute began at the summit as a clash of perception, but quickly evolved into one where the Kennedy administration fell back on clichéd views of de Gaulle to dismiss the French position rather than undertake the awkward, difficult task of questioning the assumptions that turned Vietnam into an American problem. Frank Costigliola argues that while the coded, feminized descriptions of France disappeared from official American documents after de Gaulle returned to power in 1958, the penchant for overly simplistic stereotyped explanations of French behavior remained. He writes, "Washington officials found overbearing de Gaulle's insistence on an equal voice for France in managing NATO and his push for a more autonomous French policy. They often coded de Gaulle's stubbornly nationalist policy as pathological self-aggrandizement and the crotchets of a too-old leader, as the product of the general's overblown sense of France's natural place and his underdeveloped appreciation for the 'reality' of America's power and wisdom."[1]

While Kennedy and de Gaulle were able to exchange their views on Vietnam respectfully despite their sharp disagreement, two of Kennedy's aides, Schlesinger and Bundy, fed him Francophobic and anti-de Gaulle pre-summit reports that focused attention on de Gaulle's supposed character defects rather than the actual substance of the proposals he was expected to make. They wanted the president to believe that while de Gaulle's France was no longer outwardly effeminate, it was still a troublesome, uncooperative partner ruled by a deeply flawed leader with suspect mental capabilities. Cumulatively, these reports conveniently reinforced preexisting prejudices—that de Gaulle was a doddering, old, uncooperative anti-American, that the French had nothing to teach the administration about its former colony, and that France had delusions of grandeur that manifested themselves in an attempt to play an overly ambitious role in the world—making it easier for Kennedy to dismiss de Gaulle's opposition to American policy in Vietnam. The more time that passed after the summit, the easier it became for Kennedy to retreat into comfortable stereotypes about French foreign policy and to look past the more trenchant points de Gaulle had made in face to face conversation.

If judged by the enthusiastic response Kennedy met with from the adoring throngs in Paris, his three-day summit with de Gaulle was a smashing public relations success. Even the normally reserved de Gaulle allowed himself to be swept away by the charms of Kennedy's "French wife," born Jackie Bouvier with genealogy tracing back to New France, a secret weapon who melted hearts across Europe while her husband was engaged in tough summit diplomacy. In its 1962 Man of the Year cover story on Kennedy, *Time* wrote of Jackie Kennedy:

> Few diplomats have scored more triumphs than Jacqueline Kennedy in her year as the nation's First Lady. She has charmed Britain's Macmillan, France's De Gaulle, Germany's Adenauer and, for that matter, Khrushchev himself (said Khrushchev of Jackie's gown: "It's beautiful!") "Jackie wants to be as great a First Lady in her own right

> as Jack wants to be a great President," says a friend. Toward that end, Jackie has worked hard and effectively. She has done over the White House with unexceptionable taste. She has introduced into the White House, for the first time in years, good food, great music, Shakespeare, warmth and informality—all along with a deep respect for American tradition. In so doing, she has managed to stay very much herself.[2]

De Gaulle truly delighted in conversation with Mrs. Kennedy, who spoke good French and was well-versed in French history. She presented de Gaulle with a letter from George Washington to Vicomte de Noailles which had been bought for $90,000, an incredibly generous and thoughtful gift that further enamored her to the French president.[3] The outward warmth of summit participants was a natural honeymoon period extension as the new players in the post-Eisenhower era sought to become better acquainted with one another. Kennedy had only been in office for five months and it was a great honor to France to host his first official trip to Europe as president. When the summit was announced in early April, the German press viewed it as a significant gesture to de Gaulle, while the British expressed surprise that Kennedy was not planning to come to London first.[4] De Gaulle had been in office for three years, but he was still shoring up his position domestically. The contentious issues that later forced a near breach between Paris and Washington were still off on the horizon. This was the high point in Franco-American relations in the 1960s, and the 1961 summit was of great importance for both presidents, given that it was scheduled just days ahead of what was expected to be a blistering round of talks between Kennedy and Khrushchev in Vienna. De Gaulle spared no detail in making the Kennedys feel welcome. The pomp and ceremony of the lavish banquets and the last-minute paint job for the car they were going to be riding in were among the measures designed to ensure that de Gaulle's honored American guests enjoyed a pleasant stay.

Summit diplomacy, which grew exponentially during the Roosevelt presidency partly out of wartime exigency, had become a permanent fixture of American foreign policy by the 1960s that was embraced by both Kennedy and Johnson.[5] While bringing heads of state together for direct negotiations opens the possibility of relatively quick settlements on major issues, summit diplomacy also contains the risk of setting overly enthusiastic domestic audiences up for disappointment when it stalls.[6] De Gaulle's tour of the United

States in 1960 had been a veritable public relations smash and his approval rating there was never higher, but he failed to secure any concessions on the *directoire* or nuclear matters from Eisenhower.[7] Even if no one in the White House expected Kennedy to iron out a handful of substantive policy disagreements after only three days in Paris, there was some hope that he could at least take an important first step toward restoring some of the cordiality in Franco-American relations that had been lost during the later years of the Eisenhower administration. This relatively modest expectation was shared by de Gaulle, who had been preparing for the summit with the palpable anticipation of a man who saw an opportunity to break an impasse that had dragged on from the earliest days of his presidency.

During the Cold War, presidential visits took on symbolic and emotional importance for both American audiences and the people of the host country.[8] Kennedy's carefully crafted "Ich bin ein Berliner" speech in June 1963, a masterstroke of political theater and possibly the most memorable presidential moment in the history of the Cold War, emphasized to half a million rapt German spectators that the United States would not abandon them for détente with the communist bloc.[9] Reassuring as this was to the cheering masses, it was a forceful political display of solidarity at a time of growing tensions between Washington and Bonn over America's commitment to its continental European allies. Many Americans feared that Washington was losing its grip over West Germany after de Gaulle and Adenauer signed the symbolic Franco-German Treaty of Cooperation (also known as the Élysée Treaty) in January.[10] While the treaty had little long-term impact beyond the two countries, it appeared to many observers as though de Gaulle, having been rebuffed in his attempts to secure a consultative apparatus with Britain and the United States, had found another dissatisfied NATO partner to collaborate with when his first attempts at reform had failed.[11] Kennedy's unambiguous reiteration of his support for the rights of Berliners to choose their own political destiny five months later, however, gave birth in West Germany to "a new degree of political loyalty and legitimacy on behalf of the transatlantic alliance."[12]

Kennedy's 1961 trip to Paris was more symbolic for what it omitted. Unlike in his memorable "Ich bin ein Berliner" speech in Berlin two years later, he failed to offer any words of substance to a French audience beyond the usual platitudes. France was drifting further from the American orbit than West Germany, but Kennedy had no stirring public declaration of shared political values and hopes for the future to reel it back, nor did he show any empathy for the national soul-searching that came out of the Algerian War. Berlin fit better in Kennedy's view of the Cold War as a black-white divide between the democratic and communist camps. At the same time, he found it easier to relate to Germans living on the front line of the Cold War than with Frenchmen who clung to an imperial past because they were uncertain about their future. This instinctive sympathy toward Germans and cautiousness toward the French had been apparent in numerous public speeches from the House of Representatives and the Senate before he became president. If Kennedy's 1963 Berlin trip was a carefully orchestrated piece of political theater, Paris in 1961 was simply an early dress rehearsal. This visit was in some respects nothing more than an obligatory courtesy call while Kennedy was on his way to see Khrushchev for more pressing business in Vienna.

Kennedy had been prepared in his pre-summit briefs for an awkward meeting with de Gaulle, and the American press cautioned the public to limit their expectations, but the president found himself greeted with an overwhelming display of affection from large crowds in Paris.[13] The *Washington Post* reported that as Kennedy disembarked from his plane at Orly Airport, "de Gaulle put his arm around the American President's shoulder and firmly guided him to the place of honor for the playing of the French and American national anthems."[14] In the city itself, an estimated 200,000 people, more than either Eisenhower or Khrushchev had drawn for their visits to the French capital, lined streets along the Kennedys' motorcade route into the city in the hopes of getting a glimpse of the handsome, young presidential couple.

Red, white, and blue bunting lined the avenues, handmade signs welcoming the Kennedys were displayed in café windows, and bohemian students in the Left Bank even held up a crude Harvard banner as a salute to Kennedy's alma mater.[15] Kennedy rode through the city in de Gaulle's open-top Citroën limousine escorted by saber-toting mounted Republican Guardsmen in red-plumed helmets and full breastplates, while the first ladies traveled separately in a closed car. As the cheers grew louder and gave no sign of abating, de Gaulle encouraged Kennedy to stand in the back seat to give the crowd a better look at him. Confetti showered down upon them from second- and third-story windows along the Rue de Rivoli as they moved through the city's posh commercial district. Later, a thunderstorm rolled through as the convoy approached the Champs-Elysées en route to the Arc de Triomphe, but the crowds remained undeterred by the foul weather that drenched both presidents riding in de Gaulle's convertible.[16] Paris greeted Kennedy like a conquering hero.

No creature comfort was spared during the Kennedys' stay in Paris. Kennedy's "favorite brands of cigars and beer and American cream" were shipped off from Washington to the president's quarters in advance of the summit. After learning that Jackie Kennedy had expressed hopes that she would have the occasion to visit at least one Parisian museum, de Gaulle himself issued orders that a selection of famous paintings by Renoir, Nicolas Lancret, and Jean-Baptiste-Siméon Chardin be sent over from the Louvre to decorate the couple's guest apartment at the Quai d'Orsay.[17] After an obligatory stop at the Arc de Triomphe to pay tribute to French veterans, Kennedy spent his first evening in Paris at a white tie state dinner in his honor where he spoke of the usual litany of historical ties that had bonded France and America together from their revolutionary days.

Kennedy adopted an ineffective strategy of trying to charm de Gaulle with effusive flattery that sounded embarrassingly deferential coming from the leader of the free world.[18] He laid the rhetoric on especially thick at his first opportunity to depart from his prepared statement before supper, saying of de Gaulle that "already he lives in history—history he has both made and written. Any yet he never dwells in the past. His mind is firmly fixed on the future. His face is radiant with the sunrise he intently watches."[19] Kennedy later toasted de Gaulle's "wise and courageous leadership," promising that the United States would not abandon France in its time of need as President Franklin Roosevelt had in 1940. On this awkward point he offered no real specifics, but it was meant to comfort those who doubted his word. De Gaulle, forced to respond to the purple praise of his guest, offered back that Kennedy was "the true statesman who selects his course and holds to it without letting himself be stopped nor deviated because of incidents."[20] This statement does not necessarily read as a compliment in retrospect.

Kennedy's charm offensive did nothing to bridge the generational and temperamental gaps between the two presidents, nor did it contribute to the resolution of any outstanding bilateral differences.[21] They did part company in strong agreement that France and the United States would not abrogate Western rights in Berlin in the face of Soviet pressure, but they failed to reach an understanding on the independent French nuclear program, which had much greater significance in their bilateral relationship. Paris's pursuit of its own *force de frappe* was motivated by a desire to restore France's global prestige and reflected a lack of confidence in the American security guarantee, but Kennedy said nothing in public or private to assuage de Gaulle's worries, nor did he think doing so was necessary.[22] All of the banquet glad-handling had been for the benefit of the cameras, while the legitimacy of these fundamental French concerns was not easily understood or accepted by Kennedy. Deeper rapprochement ultimately proved elusive, but, as Schlesinger noted, "in 1961 each man was primarily concerned with exploring the mind of the other . . . [and] the talks turned up no insuperable obstacles to cooperation."[23]

Unsurprisingly, Kennedy and de Gaulle's relatively brief discussion of Vietnam was subsumed in a broader communications breakdown that occurred after the summit. Kennedy left Paris with the mistaken impression that de Gaulle would not oppose American plans in South Vietnam even though he did not agree with them, similar to the noninterference pledge de Gaulle had made during their exchange on the Congo months before. The brevity of de Gaulle's comments on Vietnam might suggest that he felt the logic against deeper American involvement was self-evident to the point that it hardly warranted more detailed discussion.

De Gaulle's pitch on Vietnam would have been more persuasive to Kennedy had the French president laid bare his own mistaken assumptions and regrettable decisions leading to the First Indochina War before criticizing his American counterpart in the run-up to the Second. Perhaps de Gaulle's pride was too great to share his personal reflections, or perhaps the summit agenda was too full with other matters for this sort of conversation to unfold naturally. Either way, he could have distanced himself from embarrassment by delegating to his subordinates a more detailed explanation of the evolution of his thinking on the war in subsequent meetings with their American counterparts, but it appears that he did not choose this course either. Hindsight certainly proved de Gaulle right, but the arguments he presented would have been more effective if they had been prefaced with a more forthright admission of wrongdoing. This would have gone a long way to insulate de Gaulle from charges of knee-jerk anti-Americanism by an administration that was particularly sensitive to European critiques of its management of the Western alliance.

Pierre Journoud's *De Gaulle et le Vietnam* provides the definitive examination of the factors leading up to de Gaulle's summit comments to Kennedy, a remarkable and incremental fifteen-year process that saw him shake off his regressive early positions in order to put France in the role of an honest broker. De Gaulle returned to France in 1944 with stock views of the empire as a benevolent enterprise that had brought civilization and protection to a host of backward peoples across the globe. As was typical of French officials of his generation, he had little interest in the Vietnamese themselves, their history, or their own ambitions as a nation; they instead served as tools to validate French national self-esteem. He saw the reincorporation of Vietnam after Ho's independence declaration as a critical step toward showing the world that France was not in decline, and he showed no remorse for the war he had set in motion until it was almost over. Ho, he assumed, was nothing more than a Soviet puppet. During his many years on the political sidelines, however, de Gaulle began to reevaluate France's relationship with Vietnam and the meaning of its tenacious resistance to colonial rule, gaining for his "former Vietnamese adversary . . . increasing and reciprocal understanding and respect, [even] hues of admiration."[24]

There were earlier indications that de Gaulle was no conservative hard-liner on Vietnam and saw the merit in dealing with moderate nationalist leaders, but it was the death of Stalin in 1953 that finally removed his fears that negotiations with Ho would produce an "Asian Munich." De Gaulle's party, the *Rassemblement pour le peuple français,* had already endorsed the concept of reorganizing the empire into a looser French Union with some measure of local autonomy, but by the early 1950s many influential party members began to advocate full Vietnamese independence. Recognizing that the war was all but lost and that if France prolonged it much longer it would lose all of its remaining influence in Vietnam, de Gaulle accepted the premise of negotiating with Ho and bringing in Moscow and Beijing as coguarantors in a regional peace deal. De Gaulle expected that the elections prescribed by the Geneva settlement would unite Vietnam, but at the same time leave it politically divided between a communist-oriented North and Western-oriented South, giving France an opportunity to intervene diplomatically as a mediator and reestablish itself as a major outside power in the region.[25]

De Gaulle, however, was in no position to further this aim at this juncture. The prime minister of the day, Pierre Mendès France, was loathe to alienate the United States even further after the EDC debacle and the Eisenhower administration's disapproval of the Geneva settlement, so he chose to deal exclusively with the government of South Vietnam rather than pursue reconciliation with the North. As American advisers flooded in to take over from the vacating French, de Gaulle realized that the prospects for putting

Vietnam back together through a negotiated settlement were growing increasingly remote. The American presence, he understood, would harden and make permanent the division along the 17th parallel. Serious regrets began to creep in as Diem used American support to overcome his unsustainably narrow base in order to consolidate power. During the period of French withdrawal during the mid-1950s, "de Gaulle implicitly recognized that he was wrong not to fully support the [earlier] negotiation efforts with Ho Chi Minh."[26] When he did return to the presidency in 1958, de Gaulle cultivated ties in both North and South Vietnam, making pains not to show preference to one or the other, in order to leave open the possibility of returning France to the original mediator role he had envisioned years earlier.

Kennedy desperately needed to hear how all of this came to pass and how these conclusions were drawn, preferably from de Gaulle himself, if there was to be any hope of taking creative, multilateral steps to contain the war he had inherited. Kennedy's election presented de Gaulle with an opportunity for a fresh start, while everything in its recent history pushed France in the direction of opposing American escalation in Vietnam. The French foreign policy establishment, including many of de Gaulle's most trusted advisers, had mostly coalesced around a position of neutralization, negotiation, and the withdrawal of foreign military forces as part of a bid to calm Southeast Asia as a whole. It is difficult to imagine any French leader supporting the American program in 1961, given France's own military experience there, the difficulties it had faced during the war in Algeria, the reckless adventurism of the Eisenhower administration over the Taiwan Strait, and Kennedy's disastrous foray at the Bay of Pigs.[27]

French diplomatic records from the Paris summit show that the Foreign Ministry was of the impression that de Gaulle had clearly expressed the view that the problem in Vietnam was political in nature, and outside attempts to tip the balance through military intervention would end in failure.[28] This message, the first direct salvo on Vietnam during the de Gaulle-Kennedy years, was interpreted by the Kennedy administration as a mildly expressed reservation about the tough slog ahead for Americans as their involvement deepened. The blame for this and the subsequent misunderstanding it created must be apportioned equally. Americans missed linguistic nuance, while the French failed to express with sufficient conviction their fears that the American endeavor in Vietnam was shaping up for a massive failure. This initial miscommunication ensured that Vietnam would be added to the growing list of difficulties in Franco-American relations. In later years, American charges that the French, motivated by selfishness and anti-American jealousy, were undermining Washington's efforts in Vietnam grew increasingly frequent, as did French frustration with American inability to comprehend the political nature of the conflict.

Kennedy's Pre-Summit Briefings

Kennedy already had long-standing set ideas about France and the French national character as he embarked for Paris, but he had never met de Gaulle and depended on secondary accounts to prepare himself for his first encounter with *le général.* The White House solicited two long reports on de Gaulle in May to brief Kennedy in advance of his first meeting with his French counterpart.[29] The two de Gaulle experts consulted were Cy Sulzberger, a globe-trotting playboy journalist with wide access to world leaders who penned an influential thrice-weekly "Foreign Affairs" column in the *New York Times,* and Nicholas Wahl, a Harvard professor of government and a leading American specialist in French politics.

In broad terms there were elements of the Gaullist legend that appealed greatly to Kennedy. De Gaulle emerged as one of the great European heroes of World War II by demonstrating his "will to resist" while lesser countrymen collaborated with Nazi rule, he brought an end to the interminable squabbling of the effete, bourgeois politicians of the Fourth Republic, he rewrote the constitution to shore up the power of the president, and he had most recently engineered a solution to the Algerian crisis that looked like it would prevent North Africa from becoming a new Cold War battlefield. Though Wahl was on relatively good terms with de Gaulle and wrote with less cynicism than Sulzberger, both men offered views that counterbalanced the aforementioned positive qualities Kennedy saw in the French president.

Not only did the Sulzberger-Wahl papers set a pessimistic tone for the summit, but they reflected the administration's attempt to psychoanalyze de Gaulle and fit his words and actions into French national character flaws rather than simply review them based on their merits. These background reports went beyond the intellectual curiosity of an administration with a strong social science orientation and were an early example of a long-running search for the faults in de Gaulle that fit with Kennedy's stereotypes of French national character defects of jealousy, selfishness, and irrationality.

Schlesinger cultivated Sulzberger's fantasy of being a player in the Great Game disguised as a foreign correspondent at the *New York Times,* referring to him as someone "who probably has seen more of De Gaulle than any living American."[30] Sulzberger, a Harvard graduate like Kennedy, was the nephew of Arthur Hays Sulzberger, the publisher of the *New York Times* from 1935 to 1961. His familiarity with de Gaulle did not result in nuance-filled analysis; much of what Sulzberger wrote for Kennedy was insightful, but the disdainful tone running through his report illustrated a complete unwillingness to consider the legitimacy of de Gaulle's foreign policy goals. His assessment of de Gaulle betrayed an unspoken expectation that France should passively accept second-tier status and submit to American management of the Western alliance.

Sulzberger began his report with a specious tribute to de Gaulle as "a powerful personality and as a major and fascinating historical figure," but then immediately cut him down to size by adding that "many of his conceptions are, I believe, either false, outdated, or premature; at least not applicable to May 31, 1961."[31] While Sulzberger chose to appropriate André Malraux's characterization of de Gaulle as a "man of the day before yesterday and the day after tomorrow,"[32] he clearly viewed the former as the more apt half of this characterization. According to Sulzberger, de Gaulle was at heart an anti-American harboring old grudges left over from World War II. Sulzberger saw "resentment at the fact that the United States is now the great power of the West—in Europe and elsewhere—while France has fallen to a tertiary role" and "a kind of invisible Anglo-American conspiracy designed to keep France from recovering the prestige it held, above all, on the continent, during and after World War I."[33]

Sulzberger suggested that Kennedy had best remember that "the General doesn't really like us and he suspects our motives, even when they are above suspicion. . . . De Gaulle is an astute poker player—but with the European 'stripped deck.' We must remember this and not deceive ourselves."[34] This assessment, coupled with blanket statements like "de Gaulle has blazing areas of ignorance" and "it is blatantly apparent that de Gaulle has little use for our conceptions of either NATO or U.N.," perpetuated the stereotype that French foreign policy was motivated by feminine traits such as resentment, jealousy, and irrationality rather than the reasonable pursuit of a national interest that differed from that of the United States.[35]

When actual talks began, Sulzberger cautioned Kennedy that he would be facing a dour, humorless old man who deliberately chose "austere surroundings" unbefitting of his title. While de Gaulle was "very much the old-fashioned gentleman with impeccable manners, deliberate courtesy and an almost subconscious desire to speak and hear well-phrased sentences . . . [b] eneath his superior air and frequently disdainful manner, [he] is a rather shy and timid man." Sulzberger tentatively expressed hope that the president and his wife would find de Gaulle "favorably inclined towards [their] youth" and open to "a bit of quiet gaiety and laughter . . . in moments of relaxation between the major conversations."[36]

Sulzberger was apparently responsible for coming up with Kennedy's counterproductive summit strategy of trying to win de Gaulle over through superficial flattery. He suggested Kennedy consider "'buttering up' de Gaulle . . . [by] point[ing] out how pleased we are that the heritage of French culture . . . in former French colonies in Africa has helped bring many of these to the support of Western causes in the U.N. Assembly."[37] Similarly, he recommended paying lip service to de Gaulle's "conception of consultation" by "ask[ing] the General's advice on Cuba/Latin America to stoke his ego."[38] He noted that this would be a hollow nod to French vanity, as "we are no more bound to follow his advice than he is bound to follow ours."[39] Sulzberger's recommendations for Kennedy's approach to the summit—beginning talks with an assumption of bad faith from the Élysée, feigning interest in de Gaulle's monologues without ever considering the substance of his arguments, and avoiding areas of policy disagreement—did nothing to further mutual understanding.[40]

Wahl, the son of Hungarian Jewish immigrants to the United States, had the good fortune of securing a meeting with de Gaulle, then out of power, in the early 1950s as a Harvard graduate student doing thesis research on the politics of the French Resistance. The retired general took a shine to the intelligent young American, granting him numerous audiences through the decade as the Fourth Republic began to crumble. This gave Wahl an unprecedented insider's view to the redrafting of the French constitution that enabled him to write his first book, the well-received *The Fifth Republic: France's New Political System.*[41] In spite of his personal admiration for de Gaulle and the tremendous career boost their friendship had afforded him, Wahl's report to Kennedy painted a picture of the French president as a stubborn old windbag rather than a man of thoughtful conviction and strategic foresight. By focusing on the rigors of de Gaulle's formalism, his oratorical habits, tics, and so on, Wahl inadvertently threw a blinding spotlight on the cultural-generational gap between the young Cold Warrior from Brookline and the statesman from Lille whose formative years took place while European empires reigned supreme.

Whereas Sulzberger tended to take a mocking approach to everything from de Gaulle's conception of how the Atlantic alliance should operate to his mannerisms, Wahl placed his emphasis on the unpleasantness of the physical act of conversation with the French president. Though Wahl knew better than anyone the obstacles de Gaulle had overcome on his road to the Élysée, he skipped past the more relevant component of his makeup to focus on the idiosyncrasies of an elderly European. Wahl's memo helped further shift Kennedy's pre-summit focus from de Gaulle's message—that France was a willing partner, but had reservations about elements of American policy that led it to seek reassurance and more meaningful dialogue—to the medium: an old man who was widely assumed to be reflexively anti-American. In doing so Wahl unwittingly contributed to the delegitimization of a raft of French concerns about American leadership in the Western community that were poorly understood in Washington and thus went unaddressed during the Kennedy years.

Wahl forewarned Kennedy that conversation with de Gaulle was a "carefully managed" listening exercise that usually lacked a real, free-flowing exchange of ideas.[42] Without assigning any anti-American motive to the French president, Wahl further advised Kennedy that "nothing can oblige de Gaulle to 'give and take' when he has decided not to—and this is usually the case."[43] When de Gaulle did allow an opening to his interlocutor on a subject of disagreement, "he might give the impression that he [was] listening closely to your reformulation and will appear to agree with your view by nodding his head and grunting 'oui' occasionally."[44] After allowing the speaker to continue until he was "finally winded on the subject," de Gaulle would suggest returning to the matter in future discussions, at which time "he might give [one] satisfaction" only if the speaker had insisted and de Gaulle had found some advantage to conceding the point.[45]

By pressing one's insistence on matters where de Gaulle did not agree, the most likely outcome was that he would concur "that your point is very interesting and then . . . launch off into a long lecture on a parallel subject only somewhat relevant."[46] Outside of the staid confines of the Élysée, "his talk at meals or in automobiles is often of a critical and free swinging variety that allows him to escape the formal courtesies of his official discussions and to indulge his talent for epigram, cryptic rhetorical questions, and bitter, if not coarse, comment."[47] Disappointingly, however, "even in this sort of informal talk, de Gaulle pays little attention to the flow of conversations, but tosses off his opinion as they occur to him without any care for their immediate relevance."

The impression Kennedy would have taken from these two reports just as he was about to meet with de Gaulle was that he should brace himself for a tedious and ultimately pointless exercise. While the perspectives of Sulzberger and Wahl were certainly informative to Kennedy, both men seemed to operate under the assumption that de Gaulle received all men as equals and would treat an American president no differently than a foreign journalist or scholar. Although Kennedy had prepared himself for lengthy monologues, de Gaulle proved far more eager to engage in meaningful discussion with the American president than Sulzberger or Wahl would have had Kennedy believe.

The pre-summit briefing book prepared for Kennedy by Christian Chapman, then officer in charge of Laos affairs at the State Department, took a half-century's worth of American caricatures of France and applied them to French policy aims in Southeast Asia. Kennedy had been well-acquainted with the politics of the region during its anticolonial struggle, but this dossier sought to reacquaint him with post-Geneva elements of the Franco-American dynamic in Vietnam. Foreshadowing much of the State Department and embassy chatter as American involvement in South Vietnam deepened in 1962, Chapman delegitimized French policy aims in the region and assigned sinister motives to them by using the familiar tactic of assigning feminine characteristics to France.

Borrowing heavily from the feminizing language commonly used by Americans to describe France in the 1950s, Chapman painted France as a spurned ex-lover when it came to its views of American involvement in Vietnam. He argued that "the French are . . . attached to Indo-China by ties of emotion and interest. But with their power diminished, they have jealously sought to preserve a special position at whatever cost."[48] He expressed the view that France's hollow claim to world power centered on its control of a few small Pacific islands and the retention of some influence in its former Indochinese colonies.[49] As the United States replaced France as the chief foreign power in the region following the 1954 peace deal, "inevitably strong emotional frictions developed between French and Americans, the French feeling that we sought to supplant them and we considering that French policies were opening the area to Communist conquest." Paris refused to passively allow Washington to usurp its former role in Southeast Asia and "the French have interpreted the inclination of the native peoples toward the US as a perfidious American scheme to wean their loyalties away from France."[50] At no point did Chapman consider that France had long preferred negotiation to the use of force, the latter approach having already failed, and that this was the real source of worry when de Gaulle considered the Kennedy administration's policy direction in Vietnam.

The briefing book outlined a broad philosophical disagreement in the region that supposedly had its roots in French "selfishness," which manifested itself in indifference toward communism, the preservation of noncommunist regimes in the former Indochina, and the defense of Western interests in Asia in general. Chapman wrote, "The French, who no longer have the power to affect the situation, have taken a very narrow and selfish view and simply sought to preserve what they could of their own interests at whatever cost, even at the risk of losing the area to the Communists."[51] Chapman argued that France's similarly "soft" stance during the Laos Crisis, caused in large part by the inability of the French military mission in Laos to train an effective national army, stoked further discord. "The policy of complete laissez-faire" from the French, who backed centrist prime minister Souvanna Phouma, led France to mistakenly characterize American support for the rightist Colonel Phoumi Nosavan as an attempt "to make Laos into a militant anti-Communist bastion" rather than a last-ditch effort to prevent "the gradual take-over of the country by the Pathet Lao, supported and directed from the outside." As a result, "the recent crisis in Laos has produced renewed bitterness [as the] French consider that we have pursued what they call a 'hard' policy which, in their eyes, has caused an inevitable Communist reaction."[52]

The Pre-Summit Talking Points Paper issued to Kennedy on May 27 predicted a further bilateral schism to come in Southeast Asia before the two presidents had even had a chance to discuss their views of the region. De Gaulle, by failing to provide any specifics on the summit agenda or any indication of the order in which he planned to discuss major issues, certainly did little to aid American preparations for discussion on Vietnam. Nevertheless, the unnamed author of the document expected general agreement on "'East-West Issues,' Berlin, the future of the EEC, German integration, Africa, and the French role there."[53] The paper recognized that there was no prospect of winning de Gaulle's support for the UN, but felt Kennedy should explain to him once again why the United States felt the UN was important to Western policy.[54] Kennedy was encouraged to express a desire to see a greater French role in Latin America and Cuba, but the paper demonstrated uncertainty about de Gaulle's position on Southeast Asia and advocated a defensive posture on an area that was anticipated as a source of awkwardness.

The paper suggested discussing the region "under the general problem of Communist aggression and penetration," with the understanding that Thailand, Vietnam, and Laos would be addressed together. The paper's contradictory recommendation that "stress could be laid on obtaining French cooperation in creating a genuinely neutral government and not one dominated by the leftist elements" pointed toward radically different conceptions of what constituted neutralism. Whereas de Gaulle's neutrality implied emphasis on nonalignment in the Cold War, the American position seemingly denied that socialist regimes could even be neutral despite evidence to the contrary in Yugoslavia and India. The assertion that "we should combat de Gaulle's view that Laos is a peripheral area which can be abandoned with impunity, and continue our efforts to improve the performance of the Royal Army" further demonstrates a total incomprehension of Gaullist notions of neutrality.[55]

Kennedy was never boxed in by the binary choices presented in reports such as this and ultimately did develop a more progressive form of engagement with the Third World. As Robert Rakove argues, this process entailed Kennedy personally courting nonaligned leaders, tolerance for their socialist experimenting, offering generous no strings aid packages, and often giving them far more support in disputes with their former colonial rulers than any would have reasonably expected from President Eisenhower. Kennedy's approach bore fruit in parts of Africa and Asia that had been outside the American orbit in 1960, but had to be exercised with caution because it at times ran the risk of alienating domestic public opinion by making him appear too sympathetic to unsavory dictators. Rakove laments Johnson's abandonment of this approach and the subsequent hostility the Vietnam War engendered toward the United States from the nonaligned world. Nevertheless, Kennedy's efforts to woo parts of the Third World away from the Soviet bloc into a truer sort of neutralism in no way indicated a willingness to allow countries that were perceived to be Western-aligned to back out into the neutral camp.[56]

De Gaulle, by contrast, was well served by his ambassador, Alphand, who provided a very thoughtful pre-summit analysis of Kennedy's first hundred days as president. Alphand noted that despite "a run of bad luck, crises, and disenchantment" in Cuba, the Congo, Laos, and South Vietnam, Kennedy retained "his calm, his self-confidence, and his ambition to overcome obstacles and realize his goals." Still, he saw "a brilliant Harvard student" who typically acted "without great reflection" on his actions, most damagingly in Cuba. Alphand felt that Kennedy often assembled great minds to work together on assessing global challenges, and then typically failed to consult with them before making a decision. He wrote that part of this could be attributed to growing pains and a bureaucracy that needed to adapt to a new president, holding out hope that Kennedy could draw the right lessons from his earliest foreign policy setbacks. There were, reassuringly, early indications that Kennedy was exercising much greater caution in the wake of the Bay of Pigs disaster. When it came to France specifically, Alphand wrote that Kennedy's initial conversations with Prime Minister Harold Macmillan and Chancellor Konrad Adenauer had "only grazed certain subjects," but he hoped that Kennedy would delve deeper with de Gaulle. He saw reason for optimism in Kennedy's remarks to Alphand that "harmonious relations with France set the tone for those throughout the West" and in his willingness to consider French "positions . . . on major problems such as NATO organization, the future of Africa, and relations with the communist bloc." At the very least, his expectation was that Kennedy genuinely hoped to engage de Gaulle in serious discussion in the hopes of diffusing major differences that could not be settled entirely.[57]

While the French did assume that there was reason to believe that Kennedy would give de Gaulle a fair hearing, there was a sense of urgency when it came to pressing their antiwar message after a Vietnamese asset reported to the French embassy in Saigon on an alarming development during Vice President Johnson's summit with Diem in early to mid-May. The source indicated that Johnson had laid out two very stark extremes for Diem: either he could take American military and economic aid and then put American generals in charge of the ARVN, or he could go it alone, declare South Vietnam's neutrality, and hold national a reunification election in conjunction with Hanoi. Johnson wanted to force Diem into a corner, knowing that the latter option would almost certainly result in his ouster at the ballot box.[58] Roger Lalouette, the French ambassador in Saigon who typically wrote with great candor, informed de Gaulle just days before his summit with Kennedy that Diem's brother and adviser, Ngo Dinh Nhu, had in confidence vented his displeasure with what he described as out of touch, second-rate American officials in Vietnam and their "prefabricated assistance plans that come from Washington offices." More troublingly, Nhu told Lalouette that despite what Diem had told Johnson in person his government had no intention of ceding this degree of sovereignty to the United States. Lalouette believed that the Kennedy administration was very close to deploying combat troops to South Vietnam, which would be a complete disaster if the host government planned to resist Americanization of the war effort.[59]

Kennedy and de Gaulle finally got their first opportunity to measure each other up in face-to-face talks just after lunch on May 31, 1961, during the first afternoon of the summit. Between the niceties of banquet etiquette, de Gaulle sought real, tangible concessions from Kennedy. Most notably, he wanted greater cooperation between Paris, Washington, and London on external "Western policy," confirmation that Kennedy would not yield Western rights in Berlin under pressure from Khrushchev, and reassurance that the United States would come to Western Europe's defense in the event of a Soviet invasion, even if doing so meant running the risk of a nuclear attack on the American mainland. When they finally sat down to talk politics, de Gaulle invited Kennedy to speak on issues that interested him the most and Kennedy ranked Southeast Asia second, after Berlin, but before Latin America and Africa.

Discussion of Vietnam concluded without any definitive agreement, but a clear picture emerges where both men at least presented their cases, though neither conceded any ground. De Gaulle expressed his position broadly—or "vaguely" as Americans would later charge—but firmly: no to military intervention, no to big aid programs, no to the logic that American prestige in the region forced it to act against the long-term interests of the West, that it would be wise to enlist the help of regional powers like India and Japan, and that the West should play for time as the communist bloc began to fragment.[60] This stance, expressed solely through diplomatic channels until de Gaulle's press release in August 1963, remained essentially unchanged up to Kennedy's tragic assassination.

Kennedy's position denied the presence of strong ideological and emotional impulses to intervene as he dispassionately outlined what appeared to be sound strategic reasons for American involvement in Vietnam. The president rejected de Gaulle's view that American intervention had turned South Vietnam into a Cold War battlefield, while countering that an American withdrawal would ensure the collapse of the Saigon regime, that American military intervention must be kept on the table as a bargaining chip with the Soviets, and that a failure to act vigorously in the face of communist pressure would have a catastrophic effect on the perception of American security guarantees in allied states running all the way from the Philippines to Greece.

It is likely that Kennedy's subsequent misunderstanding of de Gaulle's position on Vietnam arose from the latter's assurance that he would not publicly oppose American military intervention in Laos should Kennedy deem it necessary even though he firmly disagreed with this course of action.[61] Kennedy's disagreement with de Gaulle's views probably led him to misunderstand their seriousness. The final American summary notes of the summit mentioned Southeast Asia right after a recap of discussions on Africa, specifically the deteriorating situation in Portuguese Angola.[62] De Gaulle did not support a UN role there—he had earlier in 1961 made a similar argument that the Western powers should have imposed their will on the Belgians and Congolese outside of the UN to prevent Soviet meddling—but once again said that he understood the American position and would not oppose it. It appears that de Gaulle had inadvertently set a precedent where the White House made the reasonable assumption that his concerns over the shape of "Western Policy" in the Third World were serious, but of far less importance than European matters, and certainly not worth risking a diplomatic breach with Washington. By issuing another noninterference pledge on Laos, de Gaulle seemingly resolved the matter to the White House's satisfaction and fed the impression that Vietnam was not one of his core concerns.

Laos and South Vietnam were inextricably linked in American thinking on Southeast Asia. Historian Geoffrey Warner argues that the Kennedy administration had talked tough about Laos as a regional lynchpin whose defense was essential to the maintenance of American prestige, but Kennedy had dithered on military intervention during the spring crisis to the point that the rainy season forced a cease-fire that temporarily shelved the problem.[63] South Vietnam then became the administration's consolation prize when the McNamara and Gilpatric reports of April and early May reinforced perceptions that a communist victory there was a plausible short-term scenario that could only be prevented by a major overhaul of the American effort in the region.

Kennedy accepted Rostow's argument that the deployment of American troops would have broader political-diplomatic consequences, but he set out to prevent another Cuba- or Laos-style embarrassment by maxing out the American effort just short of a firm troop commitment. In practical terms, this meant shoring up the Diem regime and increasing the size of the US Military Assistance and Advisory Group beyond the limits authorized by the International Control Commission (ICC) in place since the Geneva Accords in 1954.[64] Warner writes that "after what we have learned about the President's behaviour over Laos, we should be wary of concluding that he had made a firm decision [about the nature of the American commitment to Saigon. . . . Nevertheless,] having in effect abandoned Laos, the administration had taken a decision to stand firm in South Vietnam."[65]

If de Gaulle did leave ambiguity as to how he would respond to an American policy in Southeast Asia that he did not support, there was none in his assessment of Western prospects in the region. He forcefully shared the opinion that "the situation in Laos is badly compromised. . . . It's a poor country, without unity, without will, freedom, almost lacking in everything."[66] The problem, in his mind, was that "because the United States is engaged, the Russians were engaged in their turn and they have the advantage mostly because of their propaganda, of the determination of their agents and on site supporters."[67] De Gaulle's preferred course of action was to encourage Laotians to keep free from communist control, while at the same time recognizing that the Pathet Lao would have to be given a share of power in order to keep the peace.

De Gaulle felt that Souvanna Phouma, a French-backed neutralist, was the least bad candidate to lead a coalition government, in part because he had demonstrated an ability to work with the communists without being used by them. France planned to continue using the small military base at Seno permitted under the Geneva Accords as a forward listening post. Kennedy, who had abandoned Eisenhower's attempts to establish a Western-oriented rightist regime in Laos, tepidly concurred that Souvanna was an acceptable candidate to lead the country, but he wondered how the moderate would hold up if the tenuous balance of power tipped in the Pathet Lao's favor. De Gaulle responded by admitting that Souvanna might not prove able to hold off the communists, but warned, "One must not lose sight . . . that in general South East Asia (Laos, South Vietnam, Cambodia and even Siam) is not a good combat ground for the West. For the rest of the region, the best course is to let it develop its own neutrality that will not force the Soviets to penetrate the area, as they seem to have no desire to do so."[68] Kennedy, de Gaulle felt, was losing sight of Western limitations.

Kennedy responded that American prestige was tied to a favorable outcome in Laos, which had a SEATO guarantee that he had reaffirmed in the hopes of securing a cease-fire. If the communists were to triumph there, Kennedy argued, "the effect could be disastrous" for America's Asian allies from Turkey to the Philippines.[69] De Gaulle, no doubt sensing that his line of reasoning was not gaining any traction, let Kennedy know that he was aware of the dangers to the United States and parried from another angle. He stressed that France was able to retain some influence in its former Indochinese colonies precisely because it had abandoned the notion of playing a military role in the region.[70] De Gaulle then attempted to reaffirm that this view in no way implied that he advocated passively allowing Asia fall into communist hands; rather, he preferred taking a stand where conditions were favorable to the West. He cited India and Japan as more advanced Asian powers—as he termed them, "real countries"—in terms of national unity, civilization, government, and independence that were both defensible and worthy of serious aid.[71] This position reflected a realist worldview that opposed idealistic crusades to impose Western-style values and expectations where they had no foundation. In a more strongly worded reiteration of his earlier rejection of military intervention in Southeast Asia, he stated that limited economic and technical aid along with cultural diplomacy was the only appropriate course of action.[72] Kennedy was not prepared to concede the point, however, even though this was very much his preferred course with nonaligned Third World nations.

Reformulating his own argument, Kennedy hoped to touch on a matter dearer to de Gaulle by drawing parallels between the American role in Southeast Asia and the defense of Western interests in Berlin. He returned to the SEATO security guarantees to Thailand and South Vietnam, claiming that there was a real possibility the Saigon regime could collapse even with American aid and that it certainly would not survive an American withdrawal from the country. Kennedy questioned, "Would the effect produced on Asia not be of the same nature as that of an allied retreat from Berlin on the West?"[73] De Gaulle tried to steer the conversation back to common ground, replying that he did not disagree with the Berlin analogy and that unfortunate policy decisions made during the Eisenhower years, principally the effort to replace France as the region's primary economic and cultural link, had consequences that were not of Kennedy's doing. In future discussions with Kennedy officials, de Gaulle added the salient point that the fundamental difference between Berlin and Vietnam was that the Soviet Red Army already had a physical presence in the former.

In the meantime, however, de Gaulle stated fatalistically, "the wine has been opened, now we must drink it."[74] De Gaulle made clear that France had no intention of intervening militarily in Southeast Asia again and advised Kennedy that he should abide by the same policy. Kennedy expressed a deep reluctance to risk seeing American forces get bogged down in Laos, but resisted taking military options off the table by citing the need to keep pressure on the Soviets during upcoming negotiations and close the communist infiltration route to South Vietnam and Thailand.[75] This forced de Gaulle to repeat that the poor terrain in Laos meant military intervention should not be considered under any circumstances, adding that nonintervention from the West would lessen Soviet desire to interfere and allow real neutrality to take shape.[76]

The discussion began to draw to a close without broad agreement, but de Gaulle launched a final salvo nevertheless. He reminded Kennedy that French efforts to hold back the spread of communism in Indochina by military means had led to the rapid deterioration of the situation on the ground and an ultimate communist triumph. The United States would meet with the same fate if it repeated this mistake, but "if the US estimates that its security or honor—because of its engagements—forces it to intervene, France would not oppose."[77]

Building on the point, de Gaulle wondered whether the West would have greater ease of action in the region once the Chinese began to visibly show their hegemonic ambitions in Southeast Asia. He foresaw a point in the future where the West would have more allies in place—claiming that even Ho feared the Chinese—and a breach in Sino-Soviet relations would lead to more favorable circumstances. De Gaulle added that Western influence in Vietnam, even the communist North, was strong and that relations with France were considerably better than they had been a decade earlier. Still skeptical, Kennedy questioned whether the West had the luxury of waiting for a Sino-Soviet split or if this was a development that would not come until the West had been expelled from the region.[78] De Gaulle wrapped up the topic by expressing understanding that the situation there could turn out unfavorably for Washington while noting that there could be no worse result than an American military defeat.[79]

This exchange of views on Vietnam took place during the sole face-to-face encounter between Kennedy and de Gaulle. The pre-summit briefing files that had been prepared for Kennedy by Christian Chapman emphasized irrational, feminized stereotypes as an explanation for French behavior in Vietnam, and background reports on de Gaulle from Wahl and Sulzberger painted the French president as an old bore who should be flattered and politely ignored. Kennedy unfortunately decided to heed Sulzberger's advice and very little came out of summit. The only saving grace was that bilateral relations were not compromised even further because Kennedy offered to reconsider tripartism, an issue dear to de Gaulle. Both men had expressed their opinions frankly, though at this point it was unclear to Kennedy just how far de Gaulle would take his opposition to American policy, while de Gaulle was unsure of the extent to which Kennedy would fix his personal prestige on a noncommunist outcome in Vietnam. Kennedy was free to disagree with de Gaulle and even ignore his warnings, just as de Gaulle opposed elements of American policy in Europe. The stakes were high enough, however, to warrant a dispassionate discussion of de Gaulle's suggestion that the administration pursue diplomatic options rather than escalate the conflict.

De Gaulle later reflected on their only meeting that Kennedy was "a man whose ability, whose age and whose justifiable ambition inspired immense hopes. He seemed to me to be on the point of taking off into the heights, like some great bird that beats its wings as it approaches the mountain tops."[80] When it came to Vietnam, however, he wrote, "Kennedy had listened to me. But events were to prove that I had failed to convince him."[81]

6

Making the Best of It

The period from the end of the Franco-American summit in June 1961 to the Cuban Missile Crisis in October 1962 saw a considerable souring of bilateral relations between Paris and Washington under the weight of many lingering, unresolved disagreements ranging from the *force de frappe,* the Multilateral Force (MLF) nuclear weapons sharing deal, French opposition to British entry into the EEC, and the appropriateness of negotiating with the Soviets. At this juncture the policy dispute over Vietnam was neither the biggest stumbling block in the Franco-American relationship nor one that had come out into the open, but it certainly was a festering source of mutual dissatisfaction. The French response to the growing impasse was to cite the goodwill that had been built up during the Paris summit in the hopes of wrangling an invitation to the United States for de Gaulle, suggesting that a meeting should probably take place in Key West or New England, where the formal trappings of Washington could be avoided.

The White House, increasingly annoyed with French "obstructionism" and unable to see beyond a perception that de Gaulle harbored wartime grudges with the "Anglo-Saxons" and was reflexively anti-American, expected little from another presidential tete-à-tete and constantly rebuffed French efforts to restore some civility to the badly damaged relationship. At this point, voices in the bureaucracy sympathetic to French aims were either removed or marginalized and the American embassy in Saigon emerged as a particularly hostile voice against French policy in Vietnam. The hardening of American policy toward France grew to the point that Kennedy privately admitted in mid-1962 that he had completely given up on finding any common ground with de Gaulle.[1]

Distrustful of French motives and animated by a desire to break with past policy in the region, key members of the Kennedy-era bureaucracy were often guilty of mistakenly assuming that the Vietnamese shared their suspicions of Paris. They also dismissed evidence of growing French influence on both sides of the 17th parallel and signs that de Gaulle actually had the high-level connections necessary to engineer a diplomatic solution to the war. During the period in question, relations between Paris and Hanoi had improved considerably, while Ngo Dinh Nhu, the brother of and adviser to President Ngo Dinh Diem, had begun a subtle diplomatic campaign to reestablish France as a player in the country to counterbalance American influence and provide a discreet conduit for talks with representatives from the North.

There were, however, several important organs and actors that did have a better understanding of de Gaulle's aims and long-term vision, but they were either ignored or eased out of their positions. The CIA, for example, produced a detailed intelligence summary of de Gaulle's foreign policy aims for Kennedy in May of 1961 that outlined how his belief that ideologies were a transitory phenomenon led to his ability to scold the Soviet leadership for its current policy yet still see the possibility of détente. The agency also outlined the reasoning behind de Gaulle's conviction that a Sino-Soviet split was inevitable. Hindsight proved that de Gaulle had a better grasp than Kennedy of how the Cold War would really play out, but acknowledging his assessment would have required the administration to accept that France had a different, yet legitimate worldview. This proved impossible, however, as key administration officials were convinced that America's relationship with France had been and would continue to be an adversarial one.

CIA analysts did not feel that reflexive anti-Americanism or old wartime grievances with "les Anglo-Saxons"—so frequently cited by members of the administration, Kennedy included, as root causes of de Gaulle's opposition to American policy—were worthy of further examination because they distracted attention from de Gaulle's true aims.[2] In Paris, James "Jim" Gavin, a decorated World War II general and political maverick whose dispatches to Washington revealed a considerable amount of sympathy toward de Gaulle, was in 1962 replaced as American ambassador to France by Charles "Chip" Bohlen, whose hostility better reflected the administration's orientation toward Paris.[3] In the Washington political bureaucracy, the alarmist reports about policy drift in Vietnam from Chester Bowles, the president's special representative and adviser on African, Asian, and Latin American affairs, were ignored as retribution after he leaked his opposition to the Bay of Pigs invasion to the press. As the few nuanced American voices relatively close to the president capable of rationalizing how de Gaulle's worldview applied to Southeast Asia were silenced through 1962, the Kennedy administration retreated further into historical prejudices against France and de Gaulle.

De Gaulle's top diplomats, Foreign Minister Maurice Couve de Murville, Ambassador Hervé Alphand, and Minister of Cultural Affairs André Malraux, all doggedly stuck to de Gaulle's summit message that American military intervention in Vietnam would backfire. In numerous conversations with Kennedy, Rusk, McNamara, and other members of the bureaucracy, they repeated several explanations for the French position. They argued that the United States simply could not maintain a position of strength in Asia from Iran to Japan when it no longer enjoyed a nuclear monopoly, that Indochina had an unsuitable terrain for fighting, that increased American material and economic aid for the Diem regime was drawing the Soviets into an area of peripheral interest where they had no previous presence, and that a Sino-Soviet split was coming in the near future, pointing to more favorable playing conditions for the West in Southeast Asia.

French officials did, however, make sure that their Vietnamese policy dispute with Washington stayed out of the press to avoid the appearance of disunity in the Western camp. Nor did their apparent inability to reach a common position on Vietnam shake the French appetite for further dialogue on the region or de Gaulle's personal amity for Kennedy. French diplomats in Hanoi continually furnished the Americans with pertinent intelligence they were unable to obtain otherwise on a variety of military and economic matters in the North without being solicited by Washington. British officials and Canadian members of the ICC operating in the North rarely stayed in dour Hanoi any longer than they had to, preferring the chaotic bustle and cowboy capitalism of Saigon. While both groups shared information with the Americans, neither enjoyed anything remotely close to the degree of access to communist officials as the French.

French concerns were, for the most part, noted with growing but passive annoyance until a remarkably frank May 1962 exchange between Kennedy, Bundy, Alphand, and Malraux in which an angry Kennedy castigated France and Germany for their criticism of American leadership of NATO, threatening to bring American troops home unless Western Europeans started to show more appreciation for the sacrifices Washington was making for them.[4]

Kennedy had publicly expressed concern since he was a presidential candidate over how the United States' healthy trade surpluses of the early

1950s had evaporated as a byproduct of a deliberate American Cold War strategy to defend and feed economic recovery in Western Europe and Japan.[5] American generosity had its costs, however, in the form of domestic inflation and higher unemployment, neither of which would help Kennedy sell the American people on his party during the upcoming mid-term elections or would serve the interests of his own reelection campaign in 1964. Kennedy did not plan any sort of dramatic policy reversal to preserve American economic supremacy at his allies' expense, but he did hold an understandable expectation that the wave of dollars flowing out of his country should have bought a good degree of cooperation from its beneficiaries, such as France. Kennedy's wounded, defensive assertion that United States would gladly put an end to the massive expense of its commitment in Europe signaled that France's dissension on Vietnam was viewed as an unwelcome component of a wider and inappropriate attack on American leadership. Consequently, it was little surprise then that he chose to stop listening to the French rather than reevaluate his perceptions of them.

South Vietnam: Chaos and Competing Agendas

Key members of the Kennedy administration who traveled with the president to Paris acknowledged that while the French and American positions on Laos appeared to be coming closer, major disagreement remained on South Vietnam. During an early June 1961 ministerial meeting on Laos between Charles Bohlen, then special assistant to the secretary of state, Bundy, Gavin, Couve de Murville, and Alphand, Bundy expressed skepticism for de Gaulle's reliance on cultural diplomacy and outlined his preference for injecting military might.[6] Playing "bad cop," Bohlen implied that France was not living up to the military responsibilities assigned to it in the 1954 Geneva Accords and chided Couve de Murville for associating neutralism with demilitarization. Bundy tried to steer the discussion back to matters on which both sides agreed, arguing that "perhaps there was no difference on Laos, or the existent difference relates to [a] different estimate of what is needed or what can be saved." There was mutual acknowledgment, however, on Bundy's point that "there were real differences, and that these extended to South Vietnam." Couve de Murville responded by arguing that South Vietnam should be viewed as a "separate matter" and that disagreement on Laos should be keep private to prevent compromising ongoing negotiations to neutralize the country, with the outcome of diplomatic efforts still uncertain. Neither party left satisfied, but they did make a tacit agreement to publicly stress areas of agreement on Laos and avoid complicating matters by making linkages to issues related to Vietnam.[7]

Temporarily shelving substantive policy disagreement on Vietnam did not make it disappear, as both French and American actors were painfully aware. By early July relatively localized issues pertaining to Laos and South Vietnam had spiraled into a philosophical debate over the nature of Washington's role in the Cold War that entrenched the Kennedy administration's view that de Gaulle could not see reason. From mid-1961 to late 1962 the patient efforts of top French diplomats to continue dialogue on Vietnam and clearly explain the historical factors that motivated their position contrasted starkly with the hurt, defensive tone of key Kennedy administration members who viewed expressions of policy disagreement as a personal attack on American leadership of the Western alliance.

When the dispute over Vietnam resurfaced in late autumn following the release of the Taylor-Rostow Report in early November 1961, American officials tended to downplay the extent of French opposition to deepening American involvement in South Vietnam, or consciously misinterpreted ambiguity in French statements to make it appear that there was more consensus with American positions than actually existed.[8] The French had already concluded that the "American presence is . . . imposing and weighs too heavily on a newly emancipated country" before Kennedy took office, thus it was entirely predictable that they would express their disapproval at the suggestion that American assistance to Saigon should be ramped up even further.[9] When it became clear by late spring 1962 that de Gaulle would not mute his opposition to American policy in Vietnam, internal American discussion once again shifted from the substance of de Gaulle's views back to an examination of the historical factors that supposedly made him such a difficult ally.

Following inconclusive discussions in Paris a month earlier, Couve de Murville felt compelled to write Dean Rusk in early July 1961 to clarify outstanding matters on Laos, principally assertions from Bundy and Bohlen that France was indifferent toward the fate of the beleaguered country.[10] Alphand had reported back to Paris earlier in the year that the American secretary of state had been "open, attentive, and very keen on educating himself" during their first encounter, which likely gave the French the impression that he was the Kennedy official most likely to give them a fair hearing.[11] In previous high-level Franco-American discussions on Southeast Asia, French officials spoke of their strategic view of the West's role in the region in broad terms, perhaps assuming that their American colleagues would not prove resistant to a realist assessment. This approach failed to yield the results France desired, prompting Couve de Murville to outline the French strategic view in greater detail. He wrote to Rusk: "Laos, the Congo and Cuba . . . are problems that arise on the periphery of the Communist world or even outside it where Russia's vital interests are not directly involved. They differ from that country's basic national problems. In that periphery the Soviet Union seeks to exploit to the maximum the crises that arise, and thereby to extend its advantages. But it is not disposed to take major risks, that is to say risks of war, for its very existence is in no way at stake."[12]

He recognized that Washington had "vital interests" in the Far East and Southeast Asia and was directing regional defense against the Soviet Union and China, but attacked the notion of French indifference by noting that France too "attaches very great importance" to Indochina because of its "cultural and economic legacy" as a former colonial power.

Still, Couve de Murville countered that the Kennedy administration had ambitions that vastly outstripped even Washington's considerable resources. He wrote that it was "unrealistic" that the United States could continue with its early Cold War policy of propping up and supplying a ring of anticommunist states running all the way from Iran to Japan when it no longer enjoyed an atomic monopoly. He made clear that he was not arguing for pacifism, conceding that "military intervention by the West would be necessary immediately and would be justified" if China sent its forces into Southeast Asia.[13] He then sought to convince Rusk that the same principles that the West applied to the defense of Berlin or key East Asia allies need not be applied to Southeast Asia and that acceptable neutral regimes could be established in Indochina at very little cost or risk to Western prestige.

Couve de Murville argued that standing firm on Berlin, the focal point of the Cold War, was a special case because of the divided city's unquestionable importance to the West and proximity to other NATO allies.[14] So far as Asia was concerned, he also hoped to create a distinction between Japan and the Philippines, where the United States was firmly entrenched in a position of military strength, and the contested nations of Southeast and Southern Asia. This essentially outlined a conservative regional strategy whereby the Western powers would not intervene militarily in theaters of relative weakness until

China or the Soviet Union had given them a clear pretext by firing the first shot. In the meantime, Couve de Murville argued that "apart from such an eventuality, it seems to us normal to limit ourselves to political, economic and cultural means, with the least possible intervention in the internal policy of these countries."[15] This approach would dictate an active but discrete French policy "in Laos, Cambodia, and South Vietnam [where] we think that we are capable of exerting in the long run a not inconsiderable influence."[16]

The foreign minister asserted that France would accept neutralization of disputed countries, especially a "very special case" like South Vietnam, as an acceptable alternative to the unpredictable consequences of unprovoked military intervention. Moving on to Laos, Couve de Murville acknowledged that the opposition there was looking to communize the country, not neutralize it, and that it would not accept partition. Even if the outlook there was not optimistic, he argued, military intervention was the only alternative and one that was unacceptable for reasons stated earlier. He concluded his remarks on Southeast Asia pessimistically, telling Rusk "let us make the best of it, then, and try not to come out too badly in the end."[17]

Couve de Murville's attempt to repackage the French position on Southeast Asia by explaining it in greater detail than de Gaulle had in summit conversations with Kennedy failed to provoke any deeper discussion on regional strategy in the administration. Within a week Rostow and Rusk were discussing how "[Washington] must be ready to go" in South Vietnam, weighing a series of military options designed to buttress the Diem regime's counterinsurgency campaign.[18] Rostow suggested increasing the number of American military personnel in the South to support ARVN training and logistics, a Viet Cong-style "counter-guerrilla operation" in the North with American air and naval support, and a limited military operation against the Hanoi regime, such as the seizure of the North's second city and main seaport, Haiphong. Rostow felt that the United States had to put more military pressure on North Vietnam because "a posture aimed more directly against North Viet-Nam is more likely to be diplomatically persuasive" and "we are unlikely to be able to negotiate anything like a satisfactory Laos settlement unless the other side believes that we are prepared, as an alternative to a satisfactory settlement, to fight."[19] On a broader strategic level, Rostow envisioned a response that was diametrically opposed to the one expressed by Couve de Murville to Rusk, making an express linkage between American action in Laos and Vietnam to wider policy in the rest of Asia and Berlin.

The administration not only ignored French pleas to consider Southeast Asia in isolation from other Cold War theaters, it also unfairly interpreted the differing French conception of the Cold War as the byproduct of parochial self-interest. Even Dean Acheson, Harry Truman's secretary of state and an elder statesmen of the Democratic Party who served as an unofficial foreign policy advisor to Kennedy, gave in to this lazy thinking. His address to State Department employees in late July 1961 typified the administration's feminized characterization of continental Europeans as narrow-minded complainers incapable of seeing the full scope of the global challenges that faced American decision-makers.[20] The theme of Acheson's address was the importance of returning the State Department to its rightful, proper role as the central organ of foreign policy formation and the necessity of putting an end to bureaucratic infighting with other agencies, but he also emphasized greater American unilateralism in the face of a cacophony of critical European voices.

Acheson had worked hard to modernize the Democratic Party's positions on defense and nuclear weapons in the late 1950s, adding his support to Kennedy's new flexible response program, much of which was rooted in General Maxwell Taylor's policy prescriptions in *The Uncertain Trumpet,* his 1960 book that argued against President Eisenhower's overreliance on nuclear weapons at the expense of conventional forces.[21] At Kennedy's request, Acheson outlined a new, more active strategy in March 1961 to update the American approach to Western alliance management.[22] Acheson advised "consulting frankly [with European allies] about policies which are still in a formative stage, and being willing to alter policies, if warranted, in the light of discussion," but he recognized that the former colonial areas would continue to be "a fertile source of disagreement between the U.S. and its NATO allies."[23] However, as Acheson and Kennedy framed it, consultation was to be a one-way affair in which Washington convinced hesitant Europeans to toss away their anachronistic colonial-era worldviews and submit to the American program.

There were serious reservations about American leadership across Western Europe in 1961 and 1962, but France emerged during this period as the one NATO member willing to voice its concerns about the consequences of nonconsultation with the United States. The MLF nuclear sharing scheme was typical of the Kennedy administration's efforts to offer a token concession that created the veneer of equality within the Western alliance. The MLF was designed by the Eisenhower administration to discourage other continental NATO allies, West Germany especially, from following the British and French, partners that had developed or were in the process of developing their own national programs, by giving international NATO crews shared control of American seaborne nuclear-armed Polaris missiles. The Kennedy administration first balked at equipping the MLF with modern nuclear submarines, then made it clear that Washington was to retain veto power over the actual use of MLF missiles.[24] The MLF was meant to give Europeans the comfort of knowing they had their finger on the button and could defend themselves in the event of nuclear attack, but it did not give them the right to actually push it. This was unacceptable to de Gaulle for all of the same reasons that prompted the Mendès France government to allow the EDC program to die almost a decade earlier.

Politically, the Kennedy administration's program for Western Europe called for the creation of an integrated political community that shed narrow-minded national interests in favor of a large-tent anticommunist grouping. Washington lobbied hard to include Britain in the EEC, mostly because London's presence would help ensure a firm Atlanticist orientation for Western Europe and undermine any drift toward neutralism. De Gaulle saw American intentions for what they were, an attempt to plant an American Trojan horse in a dynamic new political project and to chip away at European national sovereignty politically just as NATO did militarily, and emerged as the unelected spokesman for a contrarian European position. Through 1962 de Gaulle and Adenauer, authors of the January 1963 bilateral Treaty of Friendship, were already closing ranks on key Cold War issues, such as making overtures to China that would force the Soviets to reevaluate their position in Europe, superpower arms control, and building on de Gaulle's vision of "a single European community extending from Paris to the Urals."[25] De Gaulle had no intention of surrendering to the Soviet Union, nor did he accept that Washington had the right to decide the continent's fate.

Acheson was not speaking in an official capacity in his July 25 speech, but he was addressing State Department employees with a message that the secretary of state and various other members of the administration would have privately agreed with: that continental Europeans—he had no critical words for Britain—were generally predisposed toward insular national thinking, that they refused to acknowledge their own shortcomings, and that America's NATO allies were often obstacles that jeopardized wider American and Western interests.

Referencing an April trip to Europe that took him to five NATO capitals, Acheson noted that "in each of these countries people nursed a sense of grievance against the United States, though in no two cases was the grievance the same one. They had troubles which largely were the result of their own stupidity, or foolishness, or lack of foresight, but in order to blame somebody other than themselves, they blamed us."[26]

Kennedy had frequently employed these irrational, female descriptors for France in his own addresses from the 1950s. Acheson added that there were great early expectations of the Kennedy administration in Europe, but that the response there to the Bay of Pigs invasion was incredulity. Europeans likened Kennedy to "a gifted amateur practicing with a boomerang and suddenly knocking himself cold. They were amazed that so inexperienced a person should play with so lethal a weapon."[27] Still, Acheson did not believe that the young administration's blunder in Cuba added any legitimacy to a handful of unrelated European grievances he was subjected to during his voyage.

After dropping several joking remarks about how unpleasant it was to find himself in the company of European "intellectuals," the Yale and Harvard Law graduate said, "I began to have a reluctant feeling that we perhaps are the only nation in the world which is capable of having a broad outlook on the world, an outlook which perhaps can at times comprise some of the interests or many of the interests of the whole free world." His prescription for American policy-makers was to listen less to Europeans and "always act ahead of the discussion . . . doing things which we urge others to follow, rather than making proposals and talking about them forever."[28]

With Franco-American policy discussions on Southeast Asia at an impasse, the dispute over Vietnam remained dormant until the release of the Taylor-Rostow Report in early November 1961. In this prelude to the intense negotiations in November–December and a deeper reassessment of Franco-American relations in Washington in the spring of 1962, there was an early indication that the administration was more focused on trying to figure out what "motivated" de Gaulle and his top officials, who had always been forthright on why France opposed American policy in Vietnam, than on debating his ideas. More nuanced assessments emerged, but they were overlooked in favor of reports that played up traditional charges of French anti-Americanism.

Nicholas Wahl, the Harvard-based expert on French politics, reported to Rusk in early August 1961 on separate conversations he held with de Gaulle and French prime minister Michel Debré in late July, noting the resignation in de Gaulle's thinking since his return to power and his pursuit of much more limited national goals than those usually ascribed to him.[29] Wahl contrasted de Gaulle's aggressive confidence that he could restore French prestige in 1958 with the reality of 1961 that "three years in power have considerably affected his general view of France's future and his estimation of his own role in influencing the course of her history."[30] Under the weight of the confused ambitions of the people he led, coup plotting in the army, and the chaos in Algeria, de Gaulle's grandiose visions had given way to new priorities of maintaining national unity and reforming the French state while France husbanded its economic, scientific, and spiritual strength for a return to great power status at some distant point in the future.[31]

Wahl noted that despite de Gaulle's short-term pessimism, he was still "guardedly optimistic about France's ultimate future" even if a "fatalistic attitude . . . had come to dominate all his thinking."[32] Wahl's portrait of de Gaulle was that of a man consumed by internal developments beyond his control, his own political legacy as he neared the end of his public life, and the future of his divided, confused country, rather than the mischief-making anti-American he had been characterized as by many in Washington.

The release of the Taylor-Rostow Report, which advocated the deployment of American military personnel to South Vietnam and a potential combat role for them, sparked a renewed flurry of activity from French officials frustrated that Washington was preparing itself for entry into the war. General Maxwell Taylor had been the commander of the famed 101st Airborne Division during World War II, led UN forces in the final months of the Korean War, and was the author of *The Uncertain Trumpet,* a critique of the Eisenhower administration that had brought him to Kennedy's attention.[33] A rising star in the administration, he became the president's most valued military advisor as Kennedy's distrust of the Joint Chiefs of Staff grew out of his belief that they had withheld crucial information during the Bay of Pigs invasion.

Fresh off heading a task force charged with writing the postmortem of the Cuban fiasco, Taylor left for South Vietnam on October 15, 1961, with the hawkish Rostow and Brigadier General Edward Lansdale, an assistant to the secretary of defense who had coordinated American counterinsurgency support for the Philippines and the Diem government, among others.[34] Taylor concluded that the United States must show resolve in South Vietnam because its regional prestige was at risk, that the ARVN was characterized by "bad tactics and bad administrative arrangements" that rendered it incapable of defeating a guerrilla force one tenth its size, and that the defensive-mindedness the ARVN inherited from the French "permit[ted] a relatively small Viet-Cong force . . . to create conditions of frustration and terror certain to lead to a political crisis, if a positive turning point is not soon achieved."[35]

When he arrived in South Vietnam, Taylor discovered that the ARVN was handicapped by a series of major weaknesses. Its intelligence arm was especially inadequate and rarely provided forewarning of surprise attacks, forcing Saigon to tie up roughly 80 percent of its troops with static guard duty.[36] The ARVN also was incapable of deploying its reserves quickly enough to protect villages from communist raids, creating a vicious circle where the peasants withheld badly needed intelligence from a government that was unable to guarantee their security. The situation was still far from hopeless, though, Taylor argued. Like many Americans, he viewed Diem as a deeply flawed leader, but one who was still the best candidate to rule the country. He hoped that a new generation of young postcolonial officials and army officers would inject a new sense of professionalism into the ARVN's counterinsurgency campaign. Rostow added wishfully that the vast majority of the peasants were apolitical and could be won over if the right reform programs were implemented correctly.[37]

Taylor's prescription for the ills facing the Diem regime was to put the ARVN on a mobile offensive footing that involved a more hands-on role for the six thousand to eight thousand new American military personnel he wanted to see deployed in South Vietnam. He recommended that the US military support the ARVN by performing specialized roles ranging from "air reconnaissance and photography, airlift (beyond the present capacity of SVN forces), special intelligence, and air-ground support techniques" to coastal defense.[38] Had these recommendations for "working collaboration" been accepted, they would have transformed the United States from a patron to an active combatant bound to the defense of the Diem regime.[39] Kennedy made his opposition to the introduction of American troops clear in advance of follow-up discussions on the report between Taylor, Rostow, McNamara, Bundy, and Undersecretary of State George Ball on November 6, but he remained interested enough to have key members of the administration debate the plan and outline how it might be implemented.[40]

The language of the Taylor Report was Rostowian, referring to "communist strategy" as though the Soviet Union, China, and North Vietnam were engaged in a unified campaign of subversion in South Vietnam. It made no mention of the strategic implications of the recent Sino-Soviet split and how the United States could exploit them.[41] The report also revealed that Washington knew relatively little about the forces the ARVN was fighting. Despite conflicting evidence in an early October National Intelligence Estimate that 80 to 90 percent of the roughly seventeen thousand Viet Cong were South Vietnamese armed with homemade or captured weapons rather than infiltrators from the North, Rostow was fixated on the idea that the North was leading an international communist conspiracy to conquer the South. A Rand Corporation study from 1961 similarly concluded that the communist insurgency was overwhelming home-grown and that even limitless foreign economic-military aid would do little to halt it unless the Diem government took serious measures to address the grievances of the masses.[42] That many of the Taylor-Rostow Report's central tenets escaped challenge testifies to the administration's tunnel vision on Vietnam and its inability to weigh countering points of view.

Rusk informed the president the following day that he, McNamara, and the Joint Chiefs were in agreement that "the chances are against, probably sharply against, preventing the fall of South Viet-Nam by any measures short of the introduction of U.S. forces on a substantial scale" and that "the fall of South Viet-Nam to Communism would lead to the fairly rapid extension of Communist control, or complete accommodation to Communism, in the rest of mainland Southeast Asia and in Indonesia."[43] They acknowledged that direct American military intervention could easily spark highly unwelcome consequences—such as formal Chinese and North Vietnamese entry into the war along the lines of Korea a decade earlier or a renewed Pathet Lao offensive in Laos, serious considerations that motivated de Gaulle's preference for diplomacy—and would potentially require as many as six divisions, totaling 205,000 men, to be effective.[44]

Short of the injection of American troops, Rusk, McNamara, and the Joint Chiefs offered a token nod to the view that the ARVN might be capable of stabilizing the country provided that it underwent a massive doctrinal and organizational overhaul, American troops "sharply increased" their role in logistics, transport, intelligence, and command, and the communist bloc was induced to lessen its support for the Viet Cong. In the end, Rusk stated that they should "now take the decision to commit ourselves to the objective of preventing the fall of South Viet-Nam to Communism and [show] willingness to commit whatever United States combat forces may be necessary to achieve this objective."[45] McNamara reaffirmed that he and the Joint Chiefs would prefer to "commit the U.S. to the clear objective of preventing the fall of South Vietnam to Communism and that we support this commitment by the necessary military actions."[46]

This discussion on the Taylor-Rostow Report was typical of internal debate over American policy in Vietnam, focusing on what shape the intervention should take rather than the broader question of whether the US military belonged in the country in the first place. Kennedy did not meet with his cabinet for a discussion of the report until November 11, and the partial records that remain show that he did not share the hawks' enthusiasm for an immediate deployment of American forces. While de Gaulle had made clear during the Paris summit that no Western country should intervene military without a clear pretext, namely a Chinese or North Vietnamese invasion of the South, Kennedy did not rule out a future combat role for the United States and proceeded to gradually increase troop levels over the next two years. For the moment, however he stressed that he would not make a snap decision, "troops [were] a last resort," that he would not risk war with China, and that his preference was to deploy a multilateral SEATO contingent if military intervention proved necessary.[47]

Kennedy's decision to put the brakes on his more hawkish lieutenants did not prevent, however, an adverse French reaction to news of the report's contents. French observers noted that the ARVN had shown some ability to modify its strategy and that the increase in American aid following the Johnson visit in the spring had boosted its morale. The biggest military obstacle they saw was widespread distrust with the Diem regime, which showed little inclination for meaningful reforms. So long as the government denied the noncommunist opposition the right to demonstrate and refused to decentralize power, ever greater numbers of disgruntled Vietnamese would be driven into the arms of the National Liberation Front (NLF). These French observers felt that it was unrealistic to expect any improvement in the military situation without addressing the toxic political environment Diem had created.[48]

Rusk met with Ambassador Alphand on November 13 to outline American intentions in Vietnam in light of discussions on the Taylor-Rostow Report. He began by restating the administration's mantra that it would "take the necessary measures which will make it possible for Viet-Nam to win its own war," an end that would require a greater military support and training role from the United States.[49] Rusk added, "We do not, however, visualize sending U.S. forces of the battle-group type, although this may become necessary later."[50]

Alphand's response built on the same logic that motivated de Gaulle's advice to Kennedy in late May and Couve de Murville's longer elaboration on French thinking to Rusk in July. He questioned whether sending American military engineers to the Mekong Delta for flood relief operations was actually a pretext for a larger deployment of combat troops. Rusk admitted that no deployment of engineers was imminent, but it had been considered, prompting the ambassador to again offer a general summary of his government's opposition to any form of military intervention by Washington. Alphand argued against a deployment on the additional grounds that it would complicate ongoing negotiations over Laos with the Soviets in Geneva and that it would give Moscow a pretext to broaden its own limited intervention in Vietnam.

Rusk said he agreed with Alphand's concerns over Laos, but he dismissed the second component of the ambassador's argument on the grounds that Soviet involvement had already grown to the point that there were enough company-sized Viet Minh groupings equipped with modern Soviet weaponry to fill out three regiments. Alphand repeated de Gaulle's view that Indochina, Vietnam specifically, was a poor place to fight, as the French knew from firsthand experience. The loss of Vietnam would be "disastrous . . . but France does not want to see the involvement of forces escalated by the introduction of American troops," he argued.[51]

Rusk responded that Washington could not let South Vietnam go down the same path as Laos because the "bad precedent" it set would be devastating to public opinion in the United States and in allied countries. He stated that West Europeans no longer had global concerns to worry over and did not see the importance of the region to Washington's international prestige. The secretary of state was bracing for new Geneva talks to lead not to "a genuine coalition and true neutrality but rather to disguised surrender" in Laos. He figured that the Soviets would "see no need to compromise [in Vietnam] if they can pick up Southeast Asia without it."[52] Alphand pressed Rusk to confirm that the United States had not rejected the option of deploying troops, to which Rusk replied, "We realize that sending troops would represent a risk. It might be a greater risk not to send them." He concluded, "We hope that we can work together, but if the issue comes to be one of the possible loss of Southeast Asia and our European friends do not agree with our policies to prevent this, then our paths may have to diverge."[53]

High-level Franco-American discussions on Vietnam did resume the following month, though they failed to lead to any sort of breakthrough. Ambassador Gavin had forewarned Rusk that the French government was concerned that the administration seemed "likely to overstress military aspects of solution at expense of political and social reform . . . [and that the] Quai [d'Orsay] also appears to fear that we may be presented with 'reform measures' satisfactory on paper but lacking necessary motivating spirit."[54] Gavin added that the French had reluctantly ceded the initiative in Southeast Asia to the United States and had little bargaining leverage left because of their total rejection of military options. Still, they were greatly concerned "that hasty US action in Vietnam might preclude chances for [a] neutrality experiment in Laos on which [the] French bank for continuation [of the] French presence in Southeast Asia and [the] precarious non-alignment of Cambodia."[55] The French position was that major action in Vietnam should be postponed until negotiations on Laos had played out in the hopes that a Laotian solution would have a positive spillover effect in Vietnam.

Vietnam's role in the communist bloc dominated the tripartite talks on Vietnam in Washington involving Rusk, Alphand, British ambassador David Ormsby-Gore, and Lord Hood in early December 1961.[56] Alphand questioned "whether [the American] decision to increase support for Vietnam would not create the danger of an escalation in the area and lead to increased Chinese-Communist assistance." Rusk responded that the stakes were high enough to warrant running the risk of escalation, especially given that communist forces had ramped up their guerrilla campaign substantially. Alphand later asked whether the American government had taken "Sino-Soviet differences" into consideration. Rusk replied that the American "decision was not influenced by these considerations but simply by the need that the time had come to stand firm, if Southeast Asia was to be defended." Rusk noted that the Chinese were more inclined toward escalation in Vietnam than the Soviets, but countered "that [the US government] could not base [its] policy on the assumption of a Chinese-Soviet rift." The British delegation remained neutral, making minor suggestions and asking questions rather than outlining a firm position.

When Rusk and Gavin met with de Gaulle and Couve de Murville in Paris on December 13, 1961, they addressed Southeast Asia only briefly after inconclusive talks on negotiations with the Soviets, which de Gaulle opposed on principle so long as Moscow took an aggressive posture on Berlin, to the exasperation of the Kennedy administration.[57] De Gaulle disarmed his American guests with an unfamiliar degree of cordiality, but he recognized that the prospect of dissuading Rusk was remote and chose not to press the issue. For the better part of a year, both sides had been circling around the same positions on Vietnam without making any significant impact on each other's thinking. After Rusk brought de Gaulle up to speed on American plans for South Vietnam, assuring him that no combat troops would be deployed in the short term, de Gaulle chose to add little beyond some cryptic remarks about the failure of the French campaign in Indochina and his hope that the United States "would succeed in what it was endeavoring to do."[58] At this point de Gaulle alluded to the advice he had offered Kennedy during the spring summit, leaving his key aides to conduct more substantive discussions on the topic.

Vietnam was set aside for the time being as the French became consumed by the final stages of peace negotiations with Algerian rebels that would produce the Évian Accords in March of 1962. Although the Algerian War was drawing to a close, there were still major residual issues that demanded de Gaulle's full attention until late spring 1962, such as counterterrorism operations against General Raoul Salan's *Organisation armée secrète,* a hard right faction of the French military that rejected the peace and continued the fight against the FLN, and the repatriation of roughly 1 million European *pieds noirs* settlers to metropolitan France.[59] France's Algerian distraction conveniently provided a welcome reprieve for Rusk, who had little interest in further bilateral discussions on Vietnam with de Gaulle's representatives.

In May 1962 it became evident that the Kennedy White House had grown tired of the long parade of fruitless discussions and had begun to take insult from de Gaulle's continued pressure for a diplomatic solution. This was a period of great internal American reflection on the administration's relationship with France that concluded with a return to the familiar anti-American caricature of de Gaulle and a feminized view of France as an inherently irrational actor with whom discussion or agreement were unrealistic goals. Charles Bohlen, appointed ambassador to France later in the year, recounted that Kennedy "had a curious fascination for" de Gaulle and "was always trying to find out what made the man tick, why he acted the way he did, and what particular motivation he was working on."[60] Bohlen speculated that Kennedy "finally came to the conclusion that de Gaulle needed some form of friction with the United States for his own personal policies, domestic and otherwise, but Kennedy was equally determined that he was not going to oblige him on this."[61] Kennedy's argument, which overlooked de Gaulle's earlier attempts to shore up policy coordination with his administration via the *directoire* plan, was a means of shifting responsibility for difficulties in Franco-American relations from Washington to Paris. Ignoring strains in the alliance did not make them disappear and ultimately aggravated bilateral relations even further.

Bohlen, who was still serving as the ambassador to France when he gave his interview to Arthur Schlesinger as part of the John F. Kennedy Oral History Project that began after the president was assassinated, is probably guilty of understating the extent to which Kennedy personalized Gaullist opposition to his policies. In contrast, de Gaulle had always held Kennedy in high esteem and was able to separate personal from political differences. As Ambassador Alphand noted after Kennedy's death, "We had differences of opinion on many subjects, but there was no difference of principle between us and this we saw especially in the time of great crises."[62]

A remarkably frank exchange between Kennedy, Alphand, and Malraux in Washington on May 11, 1962, illustrated just how badly the administration's view of France had deteriorated within a year of the Paris summit, long before de Gaulle had taken any provocative steps regarding the American campaign in Vietnam.[63] The conversation began as Malraux tried to clarify elements of the French position on British entry into the Common Market—supported by the United States and opposed by France unless Britain chose to fully orient its trade toward Europe rather than the Commonwealth—that he believed were misunderstood in Washington. Kennedy quickly steered the discussion to what he believed was the real issue: that France wanted to kick the "Anglo-Saxons" out of Western Europe while still saddling them with the responsibility for its defense.

Kennedy was so fixated on the idea that de Gaulle harbored an anti-American grudge from President Roosevelt's efforts to sideline him during World War II that he repeated the charge several times despite Malraux's attempt to convince him that de Gaulle had shown himself to be very pragmatic in his postwar dealings with Germany, France's longtime enemy, evidence that he could leave the past behind.[64] Malraux could have added that de Gaulle's rejected *directoire* plan refuted the anti-American obstructionist charges by offering further evidence that the French president had in fact been seeking greater meaningful consultation with Washington when Kennedy took office, not opposition.

Malraux tried to explain the French obsession with national self-defense that manifested itself in the independent *force de frappe* and a desire to gain real decision-making power within NATO by arguing "the French army of today had faced twenty years of fighting all over the world without defending France, and that is why it has gone mad."[65] Rather than acknowledge the point, Kennedy raised the ante by stating that the United States would gladly withdraw its forces from Europe because of the massive expense of the American commitment there. No one in the French government had publicly suggested an American military withdrawal from Europe.

Kennedy argued that he would be content to let the so-called Franco-German axis handle the Berlin crisis on its own, but he knew that it did not have the military resources to credibly deter the Soviet bloc. Had the United States not been "carrying the load . . . , [he] could understand a policy of every man for himself," but France had refused to do "the military work" to defend Berlin, it had opposed negotiations with the Soviets, and now its obstructionist views had supposedly contaminated West German thinking.[66]

The president alluded to his feminized notion of the French national character when he stated: "The United States was carrying a very large load and in particular he found it very difficult to understand this latent, almost female, hostility which appeared in Germany and France, and an apparent sentiment that we might not be reliable in keeping our engagements."[67]

To Kennedy, the United States was a masculine power with a global responsibility to offer protection to its weaker feminine charges who lacked the conviction, "realism," and "will to resist" to defend themselves. For their part, NATO allies still had an obligation to play a supporting role, assisting the United States as best they could through burden-sharing. It was bad enough that irrational France was throwing up roadblocks at American leadership of the Western alliance, but the administration felt that spreading the anti-American contagion to loyal West Germany was intolerable. In his mind, Kennedy associated the different goals of French policy with larger faults of America's European allies rather than accepting them as the legitimate expression of a differing politico-historical outlook.

Kennedy had lost his patience, "[did] not understand the posture of France," and was not planning to alter his thinking.[68] In an attempt to lighten the tone, Kennedy claimed that "he thought that General de Gaulle was right 80 percent of the time, but he did wish that de Gaulle might say that we were right 20 percent of the time."[69] Malraux appreciated the effort at humor, but the exchange left him deeply shaken and marked a turning point in Franco-American relations during the Kennedy-de Gaulle era.

Kennedy was still livid weeks after the meeting despite Malraux's best efforts to patiently explain the roots of French thinking. In a May 30 conversation with *Newsweek* political reporter Benjamin Bradlee, Kennedy allegedly complained that "that bastard de Gaulle" would not deploy any French troops to support American efforts in Southeast Asia even though France was a member of SEATO.[70]

As the administration's anger with de Gaulle's France grew, Ambassador Gavin found himself increasingly marginalized and was ultimately replaced by the more confrontational Charles Bohlen in late 1962. Gavin was one of the few figures with access to Kennedy who made a genuine effort to understand de Gaulle's thinking and explain it to an American audience, but the president had concluded that he was inadequately communicating American policy aims in Paris and had perhaps shown too much sympathy to French positions that opposed those coming out of Washington. Gavin had warned the administration in March 1961 that Franco-American relations would deteriorate badly unless Kennedy offered de Gaulle the serious tripartite consultation he had been seeking for three years, but his dire prediction did nothing to alter the administration's approach to France.[71] His numerous uncritical reports on French thinking on Vietnam and Southeast Asia beginning in late May 1961 hinted that he agreed with the French position that Vietnam was facing political problems first and foremost, putting him at odds with Rusk and most of Kennedy's advisors.[72] It was only a matter of time before his position became untenable.

On May 10, 1962, the day before Kennedy's fateful exchange with Alphand and Malraux, Gavin cabled Rusk twice from Paris to express his sympathy with French frustration over the American policy of expressing dissatisfaction with France to third parties and to argue that the Paris embassy really could not do anything further to spin American policy in a positive light without real change in the White House's approach.[73] Kennedy deflected, cabling Gavin on May 18, 1962, to reiterate to de Gaulle the message he had sent back with Alphand and Malraux: the United States could not be excluded from internal West European affairs and still be expected to provide a defense guarantee.[74]

Gavin responded to the president's mild rebuke by attempting once again to outline his understanding of French foreign policy aims and motivations. In the first of two cables to Rusk on May 28, 1962, Gavin reported that in his last conversation with de Gaulle he found the French president "unfriendly," "tense," and fearful that NATO would collapse if the United States treated Western European countries as protectorates rather than allies.[75] Gavin argued that the official American stance that France should not have nuclear weapons for its own defense fed that view. More importantly, however, he informed Rusk that the message Malraux had taken back from Kennedy was received very unfavorably in Paris, contributing to a growing bilateral gap that created a "need for an agonizing reappraisal of our relations vis-à-vis Europe."[76]

In his second memo of the day he attempted to explain the French cabinet's concerns over the American stance on the *force de frappe* and Washington's growing hawkishness in Vietnam. He stated that France feared that the United States "as sole proprietor of [an] atomic force . . . might regard some conflicts in Europe as limited and thus would not participate. On the other hand, [the] US might become involved in [a] war in which France would have no interest." France felt that possession of a token nuclear force would give it "some freedom of action . . . [and] responsibility for its own future."[77] Gavin understood that the American policy of nonconsultation on strategic matters fed French fears that Washington and Moscow would make a deal over Europe's head and created uncertainty bordering on mistrust regarding American intentions. He attempted to counter Rusk's perception of de Gaulle's reflexive anti-Americanism on July 6, 1962, by arguing, "Some people have made the mistake of interpreting many of [the] general's actions as being in some sense primarily directed against the US. . . . Fundamentally his concern is French national interest, which, on basic issues, he regards as largely [the] same as the United States."[78] Still, no matter how many times he restated his views, Gavin was unable to swing his political masters to this more fair-minded appraisal of French thinking.

None of the major historical works have found any evidence to support Kennedy's theory that France's Vietnam policy was motivated by anti-Americanism. Marianna P. Sullivan refuted charges of anti-Americanism in the first major study of Vietnam in Franco-American relations, *France's Vietnam Policy: A Study in French-American Relations,* arguing that de Gaulle's peace initiatives were "a dynamic response to changing Vietnamese circumstances and evolving French-American relations."[79] More recently, Yuko Torikata, after an exhaustive search of recently released French archival material, has shown that de Gaulle's Vietnam policy slowly evolved from suggestions for a negotiated peace to criticizing the war in the press only once it became clear that Washington would not heed his advice to avoid military escalation. Initially, de Gaulle hoped that using his good offices to help Washington find a way out of Vietnam would in fact "avoid troubles in the Atlantic Alliance" rather than exacerbate them. However, "with American military escalation, this consideration gradually diminished to be replaced by his aspiration for greater support from the Third World and the Eastern bloc."[80]

Eugenie Blang concurs in her study of French, British, and German responses to the war, *Allies at Odds: America, Europe, and Vietnam, 1961–1968*. She writes, "Regardless of his own ambitions, [de Gaulle] genuinely tried to save the Americans from undertaking a doomed Vietnam policy. Despite a decade of tensions with Washington, de Gaulle provided good judgement on Vietnam."[81] Taking a longer view, Pierre Journoud sees Gaullist Vietnam policy as a "process of exorcizing a century of common history with Vietnam, finished in blood at Dien Bien Phu, defeat, and humiliation, by a painful separation of the body."[82] Douglas Snyder has concluded that the Johnson administration similarly misjudged de Gaulle's intentions in Vietnam in 1966–67, echoing the same anti-American dismissal that Kennedy had employed earlier in the decade.[83] In short, France's pursuit of peace in Vietnam during the Kennedy years was driven most of all by a desire to atone for past sins and provide experience-based advice, not some vain manifestation of schadenfreude that came from showing up misguided Americans.

In early 1962, however, Kennedy rejected Gavin's argument that de Gaulle was simply pursuing French national interests when charges of anti-Americanism were such a convenient excuse to avoid a discussion on legitimate policy aims. Kennedy assumed de Gaulle's proposals on Vietnam were little more than another minor irritant in a grander scheme to oppose American leadership in the Western alliance. McGeorge Bundy weighed in on Franco-American relations in late May with a short note arguing that Kennedy had left Paris in 1961 with de Gaulle's confidence, adding that some rapprochement was definitely still possible.[84] Still, Bundy remained fixated on the idea that de Gaulle was animated by reflexive anti-Americanism and sought documentary evidence from his subordinates to counter Gavin's anecdotal reports to the contrary.

Bundy's folio included a pair of memos Kennedy had requested from William Averell Harriman, Roosevelt's special envoy to Europe in the early 1940s and wartime ambassador to the Soviet Union, "to indicate to the President that Presidential difficulties with de Gaulle did not start in 1961."[85] Harriman was an elder statesman in the Democratic Party and served Kennedy in a variety of capacities, first as a roving ambassador, then as assistant secretary of state for Far Eastern affairs, before finally settling in as undersecretary of state for political affairs. Harriman's first memo addressed de Gaulle's difficulties with Churchill and Roosevelt, bringing up American-backed General Henri Giraud's rivalry with de Gaulle for leadership of French forces in North Africa in late 1942 to underline his view that de Gaulle was stubborn, irrational, and obsessed with honor. Harriman buttressed feminized stereotypes of France by recounting that "it was at Casablanca that Churchill christened DeGaulle [*sic*] 'Joan of Arc' because of his emotional attitude towards his role in reestablishing the honor of France."[86] Harriman also cited a 1943 conversation where de Gaulle allegedly dismissed Giraud's idea of going to war with the Soviet Union after the Germans had worn them out by arguing that Russia and France had always been partners and should control Europe together, excluding the insular British and distant Americans. None of the observations from this fishing expedition were particularly germane to Vietnam in the early 1960s.

After internal discussions in May on how to proceed with de Gaulle's France, the Kennedy administration opted for confrontation rather than rapprochement. In mid-June 1962 talks between Alphand and a combative McNamara in Washington, the secretary of defense was dismissive of French concerns over NATO, which he argued did not exist in other allied capitals.[87] McNamara went on to flippantly reject the concept of a neutral European "Third Force" independent of the superpowers—a project that, as Alphand noted, de Gaulle had never endorsed—as fanciful considering that Europe was the main source of friction between the United States and the Soviet Union. He went on to skewer the logic behind de Gaulle's notions of tripartism, arguing that it was highly doubtful that other NATO members would accept being reduced to second- or third-tier status.[88] This remark indicated that McNamara had failed to consider de Gaulle's main grievance against American leadership: NATO as it was then organized confined *all* of its European members to second-rate status, even those with useful experience and resources in contested regions of the Third World.

Rusk adopted a more conciliatory tone in a series of high-level *tour d'horizon* meetings with de Gaulle and his cabinet from June 19–21 in Paris, but Kennedy had already given up on rebuilding his relationship with de Gaulle.[89] Robert Kleiman at the State Department's French Affairs Desk met with Kennedy in late May to try to convince him to keep an open dialogue with de Gaulle, who gave nothing away in negotiations and would often make sudden grand reversals months later, but his entreaties made little headway. Kleiman noted that "the only response he got from [Kennedy] was that the differences were too great between the United States and de Gaulle . . . , thus [his] unwillingness to get involved in any further discussions with the General."[90]

From the Paris summit in the spring of 1961 to late spring 1962, American suspicion of French motives in Vietnam continued to grow as it became clear that de Gaulle would never endorse Washington's military program there. De Gaulle and several other high-ranking French officials, engrossed as they were by events in Algeria, repeatedly made clear their fundamental opposition to the introduction of American troops into Vietnam throughout this period. They consistently expressed a preference for a low-risk diplomatic strategy over a military confrontation that threatened to draw China and the Soviet Union into yet another civil war, offering to help the United States by employing France's substantial resources in Southeast Asia to the pursuit of a negotiated peace.

The Kennedy administration, which had uncritically accepted most of the Taylor Report's recommendations on accelerating the American counterinsurgency program, had no interest whatsoever in heeding French advice. That the French position was constantly rebuffed was less significant than the manner in which administration officials shaped their response. At no point did they acknowledge (much less debate) a rival, but reasonable interpretation of the conflict. Rather, they chose to seek an explanation for de Gaulle's position in the French president's supposed character flaws or historically rooted anti-Americanism, a counterproductive exercise that merely shifted the focus of attention away from the substance of his viewpoint. The disunited and feeble voices in the American bureaucracy that opposed the administration's policy in Vietnam were similarly marginalized during this period as well, creating conditions for fantasies of a grand French conspiracy to grow to truly absurd proportions in 1963.

7

Ignoring Nosey Charlie

Subtle transformations in the international system from the summer of 1962 to Kennedy's assassination in November 1963 created new opportunities for de Gaulle, who saw a window to modify the global Cold War status quo in a manner more fitting with French national interests. In turn, a series of developments emboldened de Gaulle and ultimately led him to make his first public appeal for peace and nonintervention in Vietnam in August 1963. The erection of the Berlin Wall brought an uneasy truce to that divided Cold War flashpoint, the Évian Accords of March 1962 wrapped up France's last remaining colonial war and eliminated a major complication in French relations with the Third World, while the negotiated settlement to the Cuban Missile Crisis in October seemed to indicate to de Gaulle that the superpowers would not go beyond the nuclear brink and that the Cold War was effectively over.[1] In Vietnam, the Diem regime's bloody repression of Buddhists and students protesting against the government's autocratic nature from spring to autumn 1963 sparked American revulsion and widespread distaste for the Kennedy administration's wayward client state.

De Gaulle increasingly turned toward strengthening relations with France's European partners, West Germany especially, in response to American unwillingness to reform NATO and put his *directoire* proposal in place.[2] The end of the Algerian War in early 1962 allowed him to focus French efforts more firmly on reorganizing and unifying Western Europe in a manner that would better position it to bargain with both of the superpowers. In pursuing a program designed to enhance French independence and prestige, de Gaulle adopted more assertive European policies that had the unfortunate consequence of being interpreted in Washington as an ungrateful attempt to exclude the United States from West European political considerations while leaving it saddled with the burden of mutual defense.

De Gaulle first rebuffed the American-sponsored MLF as a poor substitute for a *force de frappe* under exclusive French command. His subsequent refusal to join the United States, the Soviet Union, and Britain as signatories to the Partial Test Ban Treaty in August 1963—France lagged behind in its nuclear program and was loathe to sign an agreement that would limit Paris's ability to develop a credible deterrent—was viewed as another example of French insolence.[3] His veto of the British entry into the EEC and the signing of the Franco-German Treaty of Friendship with West Germany in January 1963 pointed toward a narrower, Anglo-Saxon-free vision of Western Europe's future that infuriated the Kennedy administration. These actions were designed above all to strengthen France, and by extension Western Europe, but seemingly conformed to the stereotype of de Gaulle as an anti-American actor obsessed with French prestige and aloof toward the greater good of the Atlantic alliance, shaping negative perceptions of his motives on all other concerns.

The Kennedy administration viewed French actions in Vietnam through the same lens that colored perceptions of de Gaulle's aims in Europe. After James Gavin had been replaced as ambassador to France in 1962, the two remaining voices in the president's coterie willing to share their reservations about administration policy in Vietnam in a manner that unintentionally reflected elements of the Gaullist critique were quietly eased out of their respective positions the following year. J. K. Galbraith, who had been serving as ambassador to India since the spring of 1961, stepped aside in July 1963 to return to academia. His infrequent attempts to sway the president against military intervention with simple logic and humor rather than economic tables and detailed reports bore no fruit. Chester Bowles was a former undersecretary of state who had been quietly demoted to the elaborately titled position of the president's special representative and adviser on African, Asian, and Latin American affairs and ambassador at large. He spent most of 1962 futilely drafting unread memos to Kennedy on the dangers of policy drift and groupthink in Vietnam before being put out of his misery with an exile posting to India in mid-1963 as Galbraith's replacement.

As the situation in South Vietnam grew increasingly tumultuous during the summer of 1963, American embassy telegrams out of Saigon revealed a profound distrust of French motives despite French willingness to share intelligence gleaned from sources in Hanoi and continued openness on Paris's long-term hopes for the country. The administration fixated on the notion that Roger Lalouette, the French ambassador in Saigon, was plotting with Ngo Dinh Nhu, President Diem's younger brother and main political advisor, to arrange a cease-fire with the Viet Cong and potentially secure a reunification deal with the North in exchange for the removal of American forces. As Schlesinger later remembered, the administration thought that "de Gaulle's interest was plain enough—to show up the blundering Americans, to rescue the west from a hopeless predicament, [and] restore French influence in Indochina."[4] Lalouette was indeed in contact with Nhu and high-level members of the Hanoi regime, but his aim was to hammer out a deal that would give the Kennedy administration a "peace with honor" and an opportunity to exit the country before the situation spiraled out of control.

By the middle of 1962, the French had clearly identified the obstacles that would prevent the Kennedy administration from succeeding in Vietnam. On the campaign trail, Kennedy had sensibly indicated that his support for Diem would be conditional on reforms and good government in South Vietnam, a position he appeared to have abandoned after taking office.[5] On the ground the Diem regime talked progressive-sounding reforms with the American ambassador, Frederick Nolting, but it made no real move toward actually implementing them because tackling graft and implementing land reform would have hurt the mostly Catholic, French-educated elites upon whose support Diem depended. Saigon played up its successes on the battlefield, but the ARVN was losing an eye-watering three hundred men per month to desertion alone. At the same time, British and Australian advisors, hardened by their successful counterinsurgency in Malaya, were becoming increasingly pessimistic about the government's war effort due to Saigon's disregard for their advice. Where American officials saw progress, they saw strategic hamlets thrown up in haste, before the ARVN and militias were capable of defending them, without any consideration of the psychological effects that relocation had on the rural population.

As Lalouette argued, the United States had entered a war that was nothing like the last one it had fought in Korea, and it simply was not prepared.[6] Compounding matters, "scorched earth" tactics that involved the heavy use of chemical defoliants were a massive propaganda gift to Viet Cong recruiters.[7] By July, Ambassador Alphand predicted that if the situation continued to deteriorate, the Kennedy administration would be caught between the unpleasant options of replacing Diem with a military junta or sending in American combat units as a last-ditch effort to save the regime.[8] The time for a solution to these weighty problems was running short; France's decision to become a more active diplomatic player going forward was a response to the gravity of the situation and de Gaulle's personal interest in securing a peaceful outcome.

American analysts heavily studied reports on the farewell conversation between Jean-François Doudinot de la Boissière, the outgoing the French *délégué général* in Hanoi, and North Vietnamese premier Pham Van Dong in June 1963 for signs of a potential North Vietnamese overture toward Diem, while the movements of Nhu and Lalouette were subject to considerable diplomatic chatter. The French, who had made their preference for a negotiated settlement abundantly clear to the Kennedy administration from early 1961, had never denied that Nhu was in frequent contact with representatives from the North and did not share American perceptions of him as a toxic element in South Vietnamese politics. Nhu, well-known to the French since his student days in France in the 1930s, was cunning enough to recognize the value of speaking directly to his political rivals and confided to Lalouette about the difficulties his brother's regime faced, caught as it was between the domestic insurgency and the demands of its American patrons.[9] The French recognized that Nhu's pragmatism was a potential key for the entire Vietnamese deadlock. Mieczysław Maneli, a Polish member of the ICC in Vietnam who later defected to the United States, discusses Nhu's thinking in the summer of 1963 at length in *War of the Vanquished,* concluding that he genuinely was interested in making peace with the NLF.[10]

All of the major players in Vietnam understood that Nhu was the indisputable lynchpin for any possible settlement in 1963. Diem's younger brother held no official government title, but he wielded incredible power behind the scenes. The political and personal relationship between Diem and Nhu was perhaps even closer than that of John F. Kennedy and his brother Bobby, the attorney general. Seth Jacobs writes, "The bond between the two men grew stronger over the course of Diem's reign, until by 1963 Nhu was virtually the only person to whom the South Vietnamese leader would listen."[11] Where the United States disagreed with France and a host of other third-party countries with a diplomatic presence in Saigon was whether Nhu was a malevolent influence on Diem or if he was cagey enough to become the architect of an understanding that would bring the war to an early end.

Nhu was born in 1910, the fourth of six boys in a family that had once served the imperial court before French colonization. By all accounts he was in his youth much more reserved than his brothers, a bookish intellectual who appeared to have no interest in entering political life. Frederick Nolting, Kennedy's first ambassador to South Vietnam, was sympathetic toward Nhu in his memoirs, arguing that he was fairly easy to talk to, relatively candid, and would have been perfectly content pursuing his interests in academia had circumstances not thrown him into the spotlight.[12] Nhu had spent most of the 1930s studying in France, first obtaining a literature degree and then pursuing his interests in paleography and librarianship at École des Chartes in Paris. He returned to Vietnam in the late 1930s, married Tran Le Xuan in the middle of the war, and had become the senior archivist at the National Library in Hanoi by 1945. When the French sacked him as punishment for Diem's anticolonial agitation, he relocated to Dalat, where he occupied himself by editing a newspaper and growing orchids.

There is some disagreement as to when Nhu became politically engaged. Edward Miller signals that the August Revolution of 1945 was his turning point, while Jessica Chapman argues that he did not get actively involved in politics until 1953, almost at the end of the colonial era.[13] Either way, his new path was most likely heavily influenced by the murder of his eldest brother, Ngo Dinh Khoi, in 1945 by Viet Minh agents who suspected him of collaborating with the Japanese and then the self-imposed exile of Diem in 1950, a move that was in large part motivated by a desire to avoid meeting a similar fate. Once committed, Nhu proved remarkably adept at clandestine organizing and in 1954 founded the Revolutionary Personalist Workers Party (Can lao Nhan vi Cach Mang Dang or Dang Can lao Nhan vi, usually shortened to Can Lao), an outgrowth of the informal networks and secret societies he developed during the French War to serve as the basis of Ngo family power. The party had no firm ideological grounding, but Nhu convinced an array of Catholics, intellectuals, civil servants, professionals, labor leaders, and younger army officers across different sections of the country that his family was the best bet to safeguard their interests during a period of revolutionary upheaval.[14] Edward Miller writes, "In the factionalized and fragmented world of Indochinese politics during the 1950s, Nhu's ability to wield power through both mass organizations and clandestine networks was a potent tool. Diem understood this, and he counted heavily on Nhu to lay the political groundwork for his return."[15] Nhu essentially formed the right alliances and wrote the playbook that elevated Diem to power.

Seth Jacobs writes, "An intelligent and courageous man, Nhu was also devious, cruel, arrogant, and, by many accounts, an opium addict."[16] He was personally responsible for a number of disastrous actions that undercut his brother's ability to establish a viable state and prosecute an effective counterinsurgency campaign. Nhu was behind a botched 1959 assassination attempt of Norodom Sihanouk, the premier and former king of Cambodia, that was motivated by Sihanouk's perceived coziness with communist bloc leaders. The Diem regime's hostility ultimately drove Sihanouk into a secret alliance with Vietnamese communists in early 1964 that opened the port of Sihanoukville to shipments of war materiel and supplies bound for the rebels in South Vietnam.[17] Nhu also controlled the Special Forces and was widely believed to have ordered the violent crackdown on Buddhists across the country in late August 1963 that left dozens of pagodas in ruins and sent hundreds of protesters to jail for demanding religious liberties that were taken for granted in the West.[18] Nhu's heavy-handedness drove student protestors into the streets, unnecessarily opening up a second urban front when the government should have been focused on its counterinsurgency campaign in the field. Nhu's image was certainly not helped by his wife, who had a knack for saying the wrong thing at the worst time to American reporters. Still, France was willing to work with Nhu despite all of his flaws because his willingness to at least engage the NLF and the DRV offered the best hope of averting a catastrophic American military intervention.

The Kennedy administration refused to accept that surreptitious French efforts to use Nhu as a vehicle to foster North-South dialogue was the logical byproduct of a long-standing regional peace policy first articulated in the spring of 1961, interpreting Lalouette's actions instead as part of a sinister Gaullist conspiracy to drive Americans out of Southeast Asia that mirrored his alleged anti-American program in Europe. Washington's obstruction of de Gaulle's efforts put the United States in a position to fail in Vietnam on its own terms when it could have succeeded by taking French assistance.

South Vietnam plunged even further into chaos in June of 1963 as Diem, a member of the country's dominant Catholic minority, launched a campaign to brutally suppress the civil liberties of restless Buddhists and their university student sympathizers that badly damaged already strained relations with the United States.[19] Photographs in American newspapers of the self-immolation of Buddhist monk Thich Quang Duc in heavy Saigon traffic coupled with facetious comments from Tran Le Xuan, known to Americans as Madame Nhu, bachelor Diem's sister-in-law and the unofficial first lady, calling the suicides "barbecues" shocked American audiences. Diem and his inner coterie came off as completely tone-deaf to the concerns of their primary foreign benefactor, forcing the Kennedy administration to begin internal discussions on a potential coup.

De Gaulle's August Statement

De Gaulle responded to the deepening crisis on August 29, 1963, the same day Kennedy authorized a coup against Diem intended to bolster South Vietnam's capacity to carry on the war effort, by taking the unusual step of having a statement he had made to his cabinet expressing French interest in Vietnam, his sympathy for hardships of the Vietnamese people, and his hopes for progress, independence, and cooperation cited verbatim to the press via Minister of Information Alain Peyrefitte.[20] De Gaulle's statement was classically ambiguous and designed for a broad global audience, making no direct reference to the United States, but there was no mistaking that his underlying message was that Paris backed Vietnamese reunification rather than status quo American efforts to prop up the independent anticommunist regime in Saigon.[21]

Indirect and diplomatically cautious as it was, the de Gaulle statement marked the first time that the French president had made public his opposition to the Kennedy administration's program in Vietnam. The American response—a mix of incomprehension, curiosity, and suspicion—was truly odd; Kennedy's top officials reacted as though de Gaulle had dropped a massive bombshell on them when in fact he had said little publicly beyond the oft-repeated stance on Vietnam that he, Couve de Murville, Alphand, and Malraux had been advancing in numerous private conversations with their American counterparts over the previous two and a half years. With little to no internal opposition to the thinking behind the administration's policy in Vietnam beyond the private reservations of George Ball and unpopular suggestions from Chester Bowles, the de Gaulle statement did not provoke meaningful reflection in the Kennedy White House on American policy in a country that was rapidly careening out of control.

McGeorge Bundy summed up the cabinet's view of the statement in a September 1, 1963, memo to Kennedy in which he cautioned that "we find only our own personal irritation as an argument against [the] well-established conclusion that we do best when we ignore Nosey Charlie."[22] When Kennedy appeared on CBS News the following day for an interview with Walter Cronkite at Hyannis Port, he hinted at "impatience" with America's "candid friend" and dismissed the de Gaulle statement as an inconsequential generalization from a leader who was doing nothing to "carry the burden" of defending South Vietnam from communism.[23] In a White House cabinet meeting on September 3, Kennedy "commented that the French were doing practically nothing and their [economic and military programs in Vietnam] had been minimal in the last ten years." When the discussion turned to the expected French response to his televised comments on the de Gaulle statement, "the President said he doubted Ambassador Alphand had the guts to protest."[24]

Confronting an Unpleasant Dilemma in Vietnam: The Domestic Opposition to Intervention Suffers Defeat

It is difficult to quantify the extent to which de Gaulle's history and policies in other areas preconditioned the Kennedy administration against serious consideration of his Vietnam program, given that it also ignored internal voices making similar arguments. George Ball openly shared his reservations about Vietnam policy with Kennedy just once before quickly retreating upon meeting opposition.[25] Senator Mike Mansfield, the majority leader, was a longtime friend of Kennedy and an early supporter of the Diem regime who had reversed course in late 1962 after a disappointing fact-finding visit to the country. He later became a vocal public opponent of the war during the Johnson administration, one of a small number of Democrats active on Vietnam that came out of the era with their reputations enhanced. His pessimistic December report to Kennedy on the consequences of deepening American involvement in Vietnam contained the sort of detailed analysis lacking from the broader philosophical opposition from de Gaulle and his top lieutenants, but it still failed to convince the president that the benefits of a withdrawal outweighed the risks.[26]

Despite his expertise on Southeast Asia and long-standing relationship with the president, Mansfield never possessed the influence necessary to convince Kennedy to reevaluate his strategy of discretely expanding the support role of American military personnel while playing for time before making a final commitment to Saigon. Bowles was predictably ignored as punishment for earlier disloyalty to the administration, and Ball chose self-censorship over sustained opposition. It is possible, however, that Mansfield's entreaties for a policy reversal were handicapped because Kennedy associated his position with the critique that had been presented ad nauseum by the unpopular de Gaulle and his aides.

Bowles first raised his concerns regarding American policy in Southeast Asia in an April 1962 memo to Kennedy and repeated his fears of a dangerous policy drift through four more unanswered letters before the year was out. He returned to the subject with renewed vigor in another mid-June 1962 memo to Kennedy, again urging that the government "clearly define and publicly state 'a coherent over-all political objective' for our involvement in Southeast Asia."[27] He cited the recent settlement in Laos and Mansfield's stated desire to have Congress focus more attention on the administration's grand regional strategy as "an excellent opportunity for a positive clarification of our overall political objectives."[28]

Bowles did not object to any decision taken by the administration on Vietnam; rather, his main concern was that a series of crises had regrettably forced it to shape policy on the fly rather than follow a strategic blueprint. He saw additional cause for alarm in the lack of coordinated military and political planning, noting that the administration had already formulated an advanced counterinsurgency program without stating its political aims beyond a repetition of Eisenhower's domino theory. Until the administration set out a regional "grand design . . . the initiative will continue to rest with our adversaries and with our allies and camp followers," leaving the administration vulnerable to unpredictable future events.[29] Citing examples from the world wars and Korea, his fear was that if the administration delayed in the formulation of a clear regional policy it could ultimately be left in a position where it had missed the "honorable avenue of retreat" and had no alternative save war.[30]

Bowles continued to warn that fighting a war in Vietnam with "no clear definition" could very well lead to losses similar to those suffered by France—ninety thousand men and a bill that exceeded all of the aid money that it received under the Marshall Plan—a point that de Gaulle and his lieutenants had been attempting to impress upon the administration without success. In playing for time, Kennedy was confusing America's Vietnamese allies, the enemy, and millions of Southeast Asians who had witnessed major overt and covert American intervention in a variety of hot spots with mostly unfavorable results. Bowles recommended that "we present ourselves in a fresh and affirmative role . . . [by outlining that here], as elsewhere in the world, what we want for the people of the region is almost precisely what the people want for themselves: guaranteed national independence, more rapid economic development, and maximum choice within their own cultures and religions."[31]

Bowles argued that such a public statement of American objectives in Southeast Asia would appeal to nationalist and neutralist opinion in the region, position the United States firmly in the peace and development camp in contrast with militaristic communists, isolate the Chinese by appealing to Soviet elements that preferred deescalation in the region, shore up bipartisan support at home for the administration's program, and "provide a compelling rationale for whatever future action—military, political or economic—we may be required to take in the region."[32]

The underlying assumptions behind Bowles's call for a reevaluation of American policy were driven by many beliefs that de Gaulle and his team had already expressed to Kennedy: that most Southeast Asians would embrace a policy of peace after almost two decades of uninterrupted warfare, that American military intervention in the former Indochina would be too costly in terms of manpower and dollars, that military intervention could potentially lead to an even worse result than the status quo, and that the United States simply lacked the resources to maintain a position of military strength all along the Asian perimeter. Bowles did not view neutralism as a stalking horse for communism because he felt the United States, not the Soviet Union, had the commercial resources and experience fostering regional integration to spark the rapid economic development desired by Southeast Asians.

As reasoned as Bowles's argument sounds in hindsight, his plea for a policy reexamination fell on deaf ears. His letter received no reply from the White House and no record exists to indicate that it was even read by anyone in the cabinet, preoccupied as those engaged in Vietnam planning were with hashing out details for the strategic hamlet program and various aid streams. The following month, Bowles, sensing that his proposed forthcoming trip to the region would amount to little more than "a series of vague discussions with Southeast Asian leaders," pressed Rusk in a letter for a presidential statement of policy aims in Southeast Asia, though the evidence appears to indicate that he was ignored once again.[33]

W. Averell Harriman, at this point serving as the assistant secretary of state for Far Eastern affairs, wrote a short note to Rusk on July 30, 1962, referring to the Bowles plan as "impractical" on the grounds that it would require another Geneva-style international conference when the United States had no reason to believe that the Soviets or Chinese would show good faith and would probably end up lacking reasonable enforcement mechanisms.[34] It was a moot point in any event, since Harriman and the rest of Kennedy's foreign policy team were of a mind that "suggested economic objectives can be achieved only after there is peace." Rostow concurred with this assessment of the Bowles proposal.[35] When word reached an unhappy Bowles that the Far East Bureau of the State Department rejected his idea for a presidential statement on political aims in Southeast Asia, he penned an emotional missive to Kennedy on August 18, 1962, accurately predicting, among other things, that a situation was brewing in the coming year that would force Washington to commit more troops and money to a deteriorating situation or abandon South Vietnam with its tail between its legs.[36]

Bowles argued that his opponents appeared to have learned little from the French experience or the mistakes of the Eisenhower administration. He repeated Mansfield's assertion, one that paralleled earlier claims from de Gaulle that American intervention in the region had drawn in the Soviets when no previous interest existed and that the countries with the smallest American presence, Cambodia and Burma, were in fact the freest of communist influence. Bowles railed against his colleagues' notion that the United States could not accept "paper guarantees" from the Soviet Union when the Austrian precedent of 1955 had clearly demonstrated that Moscow was capable of cosponsoring neutralism with Washington when it perceived such a policy to be in its best interests. He went on to argue further that the administration ought to "improve our almost non-existent intelligence capability in regard to Ho Chi Minh's attitudes and objectives" as part of a broader reassessment of accepted wisdom that would see greater tolerance for anticommunist neutralism at the expense of the "military bastion" approach.[37]

As with all of Bowles's other unsolicited memos on the Third World written during 1962, there is no documentary evidence that his ideas provoked any follow-up discussions between Kennedy and other members of the administration. On December 1, 1962, Bowles finally admitted defeat, writing Kennedy to express continued support for his presidency mixed with dismay that he had been unable to navigate the bureaucracy and affect real change for the better.[38] Thereafter, Bowles, one of the more thoughtful and earliest Cassandras on Vietnam in Kennedy's coterie, quietly stepped down from what he finally understood to be a ceremonial position with no real duties or influence.

Unconstrained by the opposition from Kennedy's advisors, Senator Mansfield used his commencement address at Michigan State University on June 10, 1962, to call for greater public discussion of Vietnam as American involvement deepened. Through the 1950s Mansfield had been one of Diem's firmest American backers, but he had begun to grow increasingly disillusioned with the South Vietnamese president's autocratic tendencies. Though he did not mention de Gaulle by name, he did echo the French president's conviction that the United States could not spend its way to a desired result. Mansfield expressed concern that "from a minimum of contact and cost scarcely a dozen years ago [America's role in Southeast Asia has] moved, today, to a point of saturated involvement and immense expense."[39]

Mansfield argued that as the United States entered the region in earnest to contain Communist China, it sent in American personnel to build up local military capabilities at great cost and funded ambitious economic aid programs that made no tangible improvements to the lives of millions of ordinary Vietnamese and Laotians who Washington was supposedly protecting from communism. A vast portion of the $3 billion in American aid allocated to Southeast Asia over the previous decade had in fact ended up lining the pockets of Saigon's military and political elite.[40] Mansfield did not oppose American efforts on the grounds of cost alone, but rather because they were so costly without "yield[ing] a durable peace and safeguard[ing] an opportunity for the growth of stable free nations in the region."[41] South Vietnam, he claimed, was even more unstable than it had been five years earlier, before the massive American aid flow had begun, and nearby countries with limited contact with the United States, principally Burma and Cambodia, had enjoyed far more success in maintaining their independence and resisting communist pressure. Above all, Mansfield urged Americans to consider whether this expensive, ineffective aid effort in a faraway region where the United States had few commercial or cultural ties was worth continuing in its present form, suggesting that "traditional diplomacy" was quite likely the best avenue.[42]

Mansfield's speech had the most impact on Bowles, who embarked on the aforementioned futile, but noble, campaign to promote the Senator's new thinking to other members of the administration. After several months of reflection, Mansfield penned a letter to Kennedy warning him of the findings of the upcoming Senate Foreign Relations Committee report due in February.[43] Mansfield wrote candidly, repeating many of the points that Couve de Murville had made to Rusk in 1961 about the limits of American resources in Asia without mentioning France or parallel Gaullist arguments. Mansfield charged that the Diem regime had lost any momentum for positive change five years earlier and was now totally dependent on American largesse in the form of billions of aid dollars and development programs that yielded few tangible results. He noted local optimism toward the Strategic Hamlet Program, Special Forces cooperation with the Montagnards to cut off communist supply lines, and other new initiatives, but added that General Henri Navarre had tried a similar list of ideas when he took command of French forces in Indochina in the spring of 1953.[44] Mansfield believed that the Viet Cong were adaptable enough to counter the Strategic Hamlet Program, dictating that expectations for the initiative should remain limited.

With no short-term prospects for victory, the only hope of saving South Vietnam was "enlightened" government in post-Diem Saigon coupled with massive dollops of American aid. The only remaining alternative means of propping up Saigon was the unpalatable option of official American entry into the war and putting South Vietnam under neo-colonial management. Mansfield vehemently opposed choosing this path, arguing, "Our role is and must remain secondary in present circumstances. It is their country, their future which is most at stake, not ours."[45] While there was theoretical merit to Kennedy's attempts to play for time in an attempt to keep as many options open as possible, Mansfield and others had correctly recognized that this delay made it much more difficult to opt for a policy of disengagement.

Mansfield went on to warn Kennedy that American planning did not take into account the real possibility that the political situation in Saigon could get worse rather than better. He urged a broad strategic reevaluation of Vietnam's importance from a realist perspective, suggesting that the United States needed to decide just how far it would ultimately go to defend its regional interests.[46] Mansfield left no ambiguity; he had independently arrived at the same conclusions as de Gaulle regarding Washington's role in the conflict, closing with the suggestion that a combination of gradual disengagement and "vigorous diplomacy" would serve American interests by lightening its burdens while simultaneously bringing stability to the region. "We may well discover," he wrote, "that it is in our interests to do less rather than more than we are now doing."[47]

De Gaulle Accelerates the French Peace Program

Two major events in 1962 emboldened de Gaulle to transform his critique of American policy on Vietnam to active, if discreet, support for Vietnamese actors willing to talk over terms for a comprehensive settlement. The Évian Accords brought a formal cease-fire with the FLN and finally brought peace to Algeria after a bloody eight-year guerrilla war that had cost at least 350,000 lives and pushed France to the brink of civil war.[48] The point at which de Gaulle finally reconciled himself to the loss of Algeria is a matter for historical debate, but the resolution of the conflict certainly did remove the biggest obstacle to a genuine policy of peace and goodwill toward another former colony that had similarly fought hard for its independence.[49]

The denouement of the Cuban Missile Crisis in October 1962 also had tremendous consequences for de Gaulle's thinking on France's role within the Atlantic alliance. He took two principal lessons from the standoff: first, that the superpowers had both backed down when faced with the prospect of nuclear war, which had profound implications on the Cold War; and, second, that the Kennedy administration would dictate to America's allies during major crises rather than consult with them, definitively shattering any residual French hopes for tripartism. The Cuban Missile Crisis was a seminal event for de Gaulle, who viewed the superpowers' recoil from the use of nuclear weapons as an indication that nuclear war was far less likely in the future. De Gaulle took this as a signal that the bipolar superpower era was effectively over and America's Western allies no longer had to support the United States unequivocally.[50] In combination with the new freedom of action gained by wrapping up the Algerian War, this reinforced de Gaulle's conviction that it was in the interests of both France and Western Europe to secure greater independence.

De Gaulle's foreign policy up to 1962 had focused on French relations with the United States and Europe, but after the events in Cuba he shifted his attention to Third World countries that would now play a more significant role in superpower confrontations. This reorientation was followed by overtures to countries on both sides of the Cold War divide and the promotion of a policy of détente, which would allow France "to deemphasize total solidarity with its major ally and to concentrate less on Europe, the focus of Soviet-American conflict."[51] De Gaulle had long aspired to Franco-Soviet rapprochement, but this was impossible until Moscow relented over Berlin and began granting greater autonomy to its European satellites. France's postcolonial reposturing did, however, create the prospect of a diplomatic opening to mainland China, which de Gaulle identified as a major player that could help shape a Vietnamese peace settlement.[52] Like many elements of Gaullist foreign policy, his ambitions greatly surpassed the resources necessary to fulfill them, but the development of a clearer French policy of moral support for the peoples of the Third World caught in the middle of the US-Soviet rivalry, respect for national independence, and opposition to the bipolarity of the Cold War status quo did help contrast France's new global role against American "imperialism" as the conflict in Vietnam intensified in 1963.

As important as developments in Algeria were, de Gaulle would not have felt as confident as he did, openly recasting France as a global player with interests and a strategic vision different from those of the United States, if not for the Kennedy administration's nonconsultation of America's European allies during the Cuban Missile Crisis. Costigliola argues that the decision of Kennedy's Executive Committee (ExComm) to reject any consultation with Western European leaders during a crisis that put them in as much danger of nuclear annihilation as the United States emerged from thinking that viewed Western Europeans as irrational partners incapable of solving major crises.[53] Whereas the Kennedy administration felt that including Europeans or Canadians in the decision-making process during the crisis would make negotiations and military planning more difficult while increasing the risk of a security breach, Western Europeans saw American unilateralism as bitter evidence of their own helplessness.[54]

Widely read contemporary French political commentator Raymond Aron, usually known for his pro-American sympathies, told Walter Lippmann of the *Washington Post* that American conduct during the crisis had effectively reduced America's European allies to "the status of protectorate nations."[55] When Kennedy sent Dean Acheson to inform de Gaulle of the coming Cuba blockade mere hours before announcing it in a speech, de Gaulle began the conversation with typical bluntness, asking, "In order to get our roles clear . . . have [you] come . . . to inform me of some decision taken by your President—or have you come to consult me about a decision which he should take[?]"[56] Unsurprised by Acheson's response that the former was indeed the case, de Gaulle, like most other leaders of NATO countries, was intensely troubled by the Kennedy administration's reluctance to include American allies in a discussion of such a grave matter of mutual concern. It was at this point the

French president felt free to begin a more assertive, independence-oriented foreign policy program.

De Gaulle struck first in Europe. The Kennedy administration had strongly backed Britain's candidacy for the EEC in the hopes that London would steer the six original members in a more pro-American direction, a transparent motive that de Gaulle naturally opposed as a challenge to French leadership on the continent. Kennedy and Bundy lacked the enthusiasm of the Grand Design enthusiasts like Ball, Rostow, and others who saw Western European integration as a catch-all solution to contain West Germany, build a viable export market for the United States, and prevent the rise of neutralism. Still, they had been slowly shifting to the view that the EEC could be used as a vehicle to solve an interrelated series of political and economic challenges.[57] Impressive growth rates in Common Market countries outstripped those of the United States, which was suffering chronic balance of payments deficits with Europe, developments that had potentially negative implications for Washington as it pertained to the Atlantic alliance. Europeanist promoters of the Grand Design viewed British entry in the EEC as a means of injecting a pro-American, liberal trading regime that would oppose any possible future moves toward raising tariffs or closing the Western European trading bloc to American commerce. More importantly, "Great Britain's desire to preserve its 'special relationship' with the United States meant that London would serve as Washington's ear and spokesperson within the Common Market."[58]

On January 14, 1963, de Gaulle dropped a major bombshell that killed American plans for the EEC by issuing a statement that vetoed the British application for membership. The matter had become tied to the seemingly unrelated issue of the French *force de frappe,* which, unlike Britain's independent nuclear deterrent, was being developed without the aid of American technology. British prime minister Harold Macmillan, having been strongly warned in advance by the Kennedy administration against an "unholy alliance" with de Gaulle's France, had rejected de Gaulle's suggestion in a December 14, 1962, meeting that their two countries develop a joint nuclear missile program to replace the soon-to-be-cancelled Skybolt system.[59] Macmillan badly wanted de Gaulle's support for British entry into the EEC, but he was unwilling to jeopardize London's relationship with Washington and could not offer de Gaulle the nuclear quid pro quo he was seeking.

De Gaulle was unimpressed by Macmillan's "[hints] at the long-term nuclear opportunities, albeit with the unspoken if quite obvious condition that Britain must first be admitted to the EEC."[60] Several days later at Nassau, Bahamas, Macmillan secured a deal from Kennedy that would see the American sale of submarine-based Polaris missiles to replace the V-bomber-based Skybolt force, closing the door on any prospect of Franco-British nuclear cooperation. The following month de Gaulle justified his EEC veto on the grounds that British trade deals with the Commonwealth threatened to undermine the institution of the Common Agricultural Policy, an elaborate subsidy program dear to French farmers, by flooding Western Europe with cheap agricultural products.[61] Still, there was little doubt in Washington that de Gaulle's veto "was linked to the Nassau Agreement, and . . . [was part of] a strong attack on the American vision of an Atlantic Community as a subterfuge for hegemony."[62]

In the first National Security Council meeting after de Gaulle's veto speech, Kennedy expressed his belief that the move was part of a broader French conspiracy to leave the United States responsible for the burden of guaranteeing European security while undermining its influence on NATO allies. Kennedy felt that "if France keeps Britain out, this will be a setback for us but a more severe setback for the U.K."[63] He was more concerned with de Gaulle's opposition to the MLF, which was designed to "increase our influence in Europe . . . provide a way to guide NATO . . . [and] weaken de Gaulle's control of the [Common Market] Six." Kennedy established France as an opponent by explaining, "It is through the multilateral concept that we increase the dependence of the European nations on the United States and tie these nations closer to us. Thus, we thwart de Gaulle who wants to cause a split between Europe and the United States." He correctly argued that de Gaulle had turned to Germany after being rebuffed by Britain and the United States on his *directoire* proposal, a development that threatened to undermine NATO, but at least prevented Bonn from considering a deal with the Soviets. As annoying as these events were, he argued, "We should not be overly distressed because the problems caused by de Gaulle are not crucial in the sense that our problems in Latin America are."[64]

De Gaulle followed up his British EEC veto on January 22, 1963, with the equally provocative signing of the Franco-German Treaty of Friendship with Chancellor Adenauer, with whom the French president had been consulting regularly on East-West issues over the previous year. The pact, controversial in both countries, emerged out of mutual dissatisfaction with Kennedy and lingering doubts over the extent of Washington's commitment to Europe in the event of nuclear war. The two senior statesmen had spent many hours discussing how they could present a united European front on peace and development across the Iron Curtain, dwelling specifically on issues such as how to diplomatically exploit the Sino-Soviet split and bring stability to Central Europe via an arms limitation pact between the superpowers, and pledged to coordinate foreign policy in the future.[65] Their intention to provide an alternative vision to the American-led Cold War status quo was predictably interpreted as a minor rebellion in the White House, which expected such behavior from de Gaulle, but was disappointed to see cooperation from a West German leader so heavily dependent on American troops to deter Soviet aggression.

An emotional Adenauer, who sought to draw West Germany closer to France without repudiating its close ties to United States, told Undersecretary of State Gilpatric on February 14, 1963, that he was "flabbergasted" by American opposition to the treaty when growing Franco-German solidarity was largely motivated by perceptions in Germany that Kennedy was reneging on his promise not to discuss German matters with the Soviets without prior consultation with Bonn.[66] Gilpatric had told Adenauer earlier in the conversation that Kennedy blamed "recent signs of greater Soviet intransigence [on] de Gaulle's January 14 press conference, citing as examples both nuclear test negotiations and Soviet attitude on removal of troops from Cuba," indirectly expressing American concern that its hitherto compliant ally was being sold Gaullist snake oil.[67]

There was some justification for Adenauer's anger toward the United States in early 1963. When Kennedy chose to temporarily back down on bilateral talks with the Soviets on Berlin, he did so not because he thought it was wrong to break a promise to Bonn, but rather out of concern that disgruntled Europeans could sabotage unilateral American initiatives. In a high-level meeting with Bundy, Rusk, William Tyler, and his ambassadors to London and Berlin on February 15, 1963, Kennedy rejected Rusk's suggestion that the administration continue talks despite Franco-German objections on the grounds that "unless they were fully locked in, the Germans would be in a position to take advantage of the accomplishments of the talks, but remain ever ready to criticize us if things went wrong."[68]

The following day Kennedy authorized instructions for the ambassador to Bonn, who was to inform Adenauer that the administration had not initiated this latest round of talks with the Soviets and noted the West German position that there was "no advantage in reacting swiftly to [the Foreign Minister Andrei] Gromyko overture."[69] The ambassador was to make clear that the administration hoped that Bonn would not object to future bilateral Soviet-American talks on the understanding that they would be kept exploratory in nature and that acceptance of the Western position in Berlin was nonnegotiable. Reasserting American concern over the nature of the new Franco-German relationship, Adenauer was to be told that "it seems to us that [the] position now taken by the German [government] toward talks is more negative than it was a year ago, and that there is now no difference between the German and French positions on this point."[70] This message was delivered on February 19 and apparently resolved the matter to Adenauer's satisfaction, but de Gaulle was not excused for his supposed role in stoking German-American discord.

The events of January and February 1963 illustrated how the Kennedy administration had come to view de Gaulle as a minor irritant, yet one capable of "seducing" less assertive continental European NATO members into opposing American designs. By framing opposition to American aims from de Gaulle and fellow travelers in Western Europe and Canada as the product of emotion over rationality, of narrow national interest over burden-sharing, of bitterness over magnanimousness, the Kennedy administration was able to delegitimize a raft of European concerns. Its incomplete reading of history coupled with deeply ingrained national stereotypes fostered a mythology of de Gaulle as an intractable foe that precluded any serious reappraisal of American policy toward France.

In a long letter to Kennedy on January 29, 1963, Arthur Schlesinger Jr., special assistant to the president and a key speechwriter, lamented how badly the administration had damaged its relationship with France.[71] He argued that "our delinquency lies less in failing to change [de Gaulle's] course than in failing to recognize what his course was—and doing so in spite of the singularly frank and lucid declaration he made to the world of his policies and purposes."[72] Citing direct quotes from published memoirs that he doubted had been widely read within the administration, Schlesinger found numerous declarations from de Gaulle that he would resist Anglo-American attempts to relegate France to second-class status, that he sought to reestablish French primacy in Western Europe, that he would not accept dependence on any ally, and that he would cooperate with members of the communist bloc who sought peace and stability. "This misjudgement of de

Gaulle's intentions," he wrote, "in face of the evidence he so obligingly provided as to what he planned to do, is so massive that it deserves appraisal so that the error will not be repeated."[73]

The administration's stance toward de Gaulle was reversible at any time, while the more diligent evaluation of his aims and motivations that Schlesinger was calling for would have left Washington better prepared to deal with France in the future. By the spring of 1963, Kennedy appeared to have come around to this view and made a tentative effort to mend fences. Kennedy, Couve de Murville, and Alphand had not all spoken together in person since the president's outburst a year earlier, but in a late May discussion Kennedy tried to calm worries over a deteriorating bilateral relationship by making a series of conciliatory statements. This sudden and welcome change in tone sent off all the wrong signals to French officials, whose subsequent actions indicate that they concluded that they had been given Kennedy's blessing to begin a more active peace policy in Vietnam.

Kennedy first claimed that he found the French conception of European unity entirely reasonable.[74] He added that he had come around to de Gaulle's view that the risk of war in Europe had lessened considerably as a result of the breakdown in Sino-Soviet relations. When Couve de Murville expressed his view that China's goal in Southeast Asia was a defensive one designed at producing a buffer zone to separate it from the United States rather than overt takeover, Kennedy seemed receptive to his suggestion that, this assumption proving true, a political solution for Vietnam would be optimal.[75] It appeared that Kennedy had finally come around to the French position on Vietnam, an extremely encouraging development. Shortly after Couve de Murville's return to Paris, de Gaulle's ambassadors to North and South Vietnam began a discreet campaign to foster a French-supported dialogue with the ultimate aim of laying the groundwork for a future cease-fire and reunification negotiations.

The Last Chance for Peace Slips Away

In South Vietnam late in the summer of 1963, Diem and Nhu were showing growing resentment toward American infringements on South Vietnamese sovereignty, while the economically strained North made subtle indications that Ho was willing to make major concessions in exchange for a comprehensive reunification deal. Ambassador Lalouette's reports to Couve de Murville emphasized the ARVN's incompetent leadership and poor performance on the battlefield, growing Viet Cong assertiveness, Diem's continued unwillingness to implement reforms, and the cancerous spread of disillusion among American advisers in country.[76] In French eyes, America was like a man that had stepped into quicksand, with each effort to break free sucking him down ever deeper. In these circumstances de Gaulle felt the need to pursue a deal that would satisfy the absolute minimum demands of all parties, draw a draining war to a close for the Vietnamese, allow the United States to withdraw with honor intact, and permit the North's communist patrons to similarly disengage from a peripheral conflict. This was the logical extension of the May 25 conversation between Kennedy, Alphand, and Couve de Murville.

Supporters of the incipient withdrawal theory, those who believe Kennedy was on the cusp of disengagement in Vietnam near the end of his life, will typically cite his June 10 commencement address at American University in the capital as evidence that his entire thinking on the Cold War was in flux and that a thaw was afoot. In the address, Kennedy called for a global "peace for all time" and decried "the expenditure of billions of dollars every year on weapons acquired for the purpose of making sure we never need to use them." He then went on to express optimism that Soviet leaders could be induced to make a grand bargain and, more remarkably, encouraged his countrymen to reevaluate their own assumptions about the evil nature of America's primary adversary so the peoples of the world could "live together in mutual tolerance." He commended the Soviet Union's scientific achievements and suggested that his countrymen empathize with its wartime devastation, calling the brutal Nazi push deep into Soviet territory the equivalent of the destruction of virtually all of the United States east of Chicago.[77] Kennedy used the address to send a crystal clear signal to Moscow, where his speech met with pleasant approval, as evidenced by Khrushchev's willingness to allow the country's biggest circulation daily newspapers, *Izvestia* and *Pravda,* to publish a full transcript.[78]

Within two months, Rusk had put his signature alongside those of his British and Soviet counterparts, Lord Home and Andrei Gromyko, to the Limited Nuclear Test Ban Treaty, which established a moratorium on nuclear testing in space, underwater, and in the atmosphere. This pact set new limits on the nuclear arms race and created optimism that there was further room for the sort of disarmament projects in the conventional military sphere that Washington had championed since the 1920s.

While Kennedy talked up the mutual benefits of the pursuit of superpower détente by the summer of 1963, his core assumptions on the Cold War in the Third World were left unchanged by recent events. The president's ill-advised decision to authorize the Bay of Pigs invasion had prompted Havana and Moscow to take measures that precipitated the Cuban Missile Crisis, yet orders to pursue highly aggressive anti-Castro measures continued to pour out of the White House despite what should have been a very cautionary tale on the dangers of meddling in this particular neighbor's affairs. The very month of Kennedy's American University Speech the National Security Council signed off on an escalation of the sabotage campaign against Cuba, while the CIA plotted Castro's assassination and a military coup with disaffected revolutionary Rolando Cubela.[79] It was only after Kennedy's assassination that Lyndon Johnson opted to scale these efforts back as Cuba came to be seen as secondary challenge after the war in Vietnam began to ramp up.

If the administration had really been in the midst of a major Cold War reevaluation in the summer of 1963, it would not have been so badly caught off guard by the process Kennedy had set in motion during his May conversation on Vietnam with Couve de Murville and Alphand. The paranoia in Washington that surrounded French initiatives there through the summer of 1963 illustrated that the administration still rejected the French assessment of the conflict even though Kennedy had just signaled that he was starting to understand it better. Here as elsewhere, Kennedy and his advisers viewed their European allies as unfocused, narrow-minded wards who lacked Washington's global vision. As such, they were to be gently cajoled into accepting the American position rather than given shared responsibility, or credit, for policy formation. The sheer distrust of de Gaulle's peace initiatives in Vietnam was the natural outgrowth of American perceptions that sabotage was his principal aim in Europe.

The seeds for a new French effort had been planted at the end of March 1963, when Lalouette identified more favorable signs for North-South reconciliation than at any point since independence. Nhu understood that the heavy American presence in South Vietnam fed into Viet Cong propaganda that Saigon was an illegitimate puppet regime. To counter this, he wanted to progressively reduce the American role over the next three years and balance Washington's predominance by building new foreign friendships. France, he explained, could play a supporting role on the latter point.

At the same time, Lalouette's sources in the North indicated that the communist regime had similarly concluded that greater French involvement might end up breaking the impasse to the benefit of all parties. Premier Pham Van Dong, a moderate who was one of Ho's longest-serving and closest allies, told Lalouette's source that the DRV could accept a political solution for Vietnam based on a series of conditions that would have sounded quite reasonable to France. These included an end to American military intervention, a democratically elected government in Saigon, neutralization for the South, and eventual reunification. Meanwhile in the South, Diem was having difficulty containing his displeasure with the demands of his American advisers and began a more active search for a new course that would allow him to regain sovereignty without compromising the aid flow. He and de Gaulle had to this point been extremely hostile toward one another, but Diem felt that circumstances dictated reopening the door to French involvement in Vietnamese affairs even though he disliked the concept of Gaullist-supported neutralism.[80] Major questions remained: Did Diem agree with Nhu that the South could wean itself off of American aid? Could the DRV work with Diem if he won a free and fair election? Could Saigon be reconciled to neutralization, an option Diem steadfastly opposed, but perhaps only as a bargaining chip? But Lalouette did see enough room for concessions on both sides to at least warrant the start of preliminary talks. He proceeded on the understanding that both parties were rational and understood that pouring ever more scarce resources into the conflict had thus far failed to turn the tide in their favor.[81]

France may have viewed Nhu as an essential player in any grand bargain, but he had by the spring of 1963 become a toxic element in the eyes of most American officials. Nolting cabled back to Washington in late March that Nhu was becoming much more tentative and was reluctant to commit to discussions on funding for counterinsurgency programs, a product of his uncertainty over American policy.[82] A little over a month later, Nhu spoke with Warren Unna of the *Washington Post,* a reporter many saw as hostile to the Diem regime, expressing his view that it would be desirable to reduce the number of American advisers in half. Unna spun the corresponding article that ran on May 12 to make it seem as though Nhu had suggested he wanted American money to fight the war without committing to any conditions or oversight. American readers would have been left wondering why American lives were being put at risk conducting military missions, financed by the

American taxpayer, at the behest of a regime that was trying to push the United States out and resisted American-sponsored reforms. Diem responded by attacking Unna's credibility, prompting Unna to further inflame South Vietnamese-American relations by suggesting that Nhu had said Americans were not advisers, but "unnecessary observers."[83]

French efforts to facilitate North-South talks in Vietnam began in earnest after *Délégué Général* Jean-François Doudinot de la Boissière's farewell conversation with Premier Pham Van Dong in Hanoi on June 29, 1963. De la Boissière had spoken freely with American officials in Saigon on North Vietnamese economic plans and reunification strategy, passing along much useful information that was not otherwise available to Washington. In June 1963 he had informed American officials that Hanoi was taking a patient, political approach with the South while it waited for the inevitable collapse of the Diem regime and its replacement by a new government reconciled to reopening Geneva talks on reunification.[84] He also warned that the United States was in danger of being backed into a position where it was seen as an opponent of reunification, the dearest desire of the majority of the Vietnamese people.[85] While the consular and State Department officials who noted his views expressed appreciation for his unique access in the North, they typically dismissed him as a "colonialist French official" with "defeatist" views on the future of South Vietnam who "greatly exaggerated" Hanoi's willingness to negotiate peace with the South in good faith.[86]

De la Boissière spoke with two American embassy officers in Saigon on July 3, 1963, to inform them of the substance of his farewell conversation with Premier Pham a week earlier.[87] He said that Pham admitted that the South was making economic progress, but "professed to believe that the Diem regime would be dragged down by the weight of the American presence and was therefore doomed." Pham warned of a trap facing the United States: the more men it sent, the harder it would be for it to win. Pham argued: "The Americans will be unable to reduce their commitment as the struggle drags on, for the more they pour in the more the 'people' (Viet Cong) will struggle against them. In this situation the population will begin to chafe under the miseries caused by the American presence and will turn to a neutral solution as the only way of ridding South Viet Nam of the Americans."[88]

De la Boissière added that Hanoi was taking deliberate steps to leave room open for negotiations with Saigon. It had adopted a policy of strict neutrality in the Sino-Soviet dispute to maintain further room for diplomatic manoeuver, it was "anxious to keep operations in the South well below the threshold of open warfare," and it was preparing a direct overture for a comprehensive settlement to a post-Diem government.[89]

De la Boissière not only acknowledged that France was aware that discrete negotiations between the North and South were taking place, but also, provocatively to American ears, described official communications between the foes as "excellent."[90] In a subsequent report on the conversation, de la Boissière stated that he had told Pham that South Vietnam's Foreign Minister Vu Van Mau hoped for "peaceful competition with Hanoi instead of Viet Cong destruction."[91] Pham felt this overture might be genuine, but added that South Vietnam was still controlled by the United States, which was building up its military presence in the country, and that "inevitably [a] diplomatic settlement would establish [a] neutralist [South Vietnam]."[92] The last thing Pham reportedly said to de la Boissière was "see you in Geneva," indicating his belief that France would play a part in securing a negotiated settlement to the war along Laotian lines.[93]

By sharing such sensitive information with American officials, de la Boissière explicitly revealed that France was working to position itself as a mediator between North and South Vietnam and felt no need to hide its actions from Washington. As explosive as news of the Pham-de la Boissière conversation should have been, it was simply catalogued with hundreds of other tidbits of information on the region and there is no documentary evidence to indicate that it provoked any sustained discussion in the State Department or White House.

While South Vietnam plunged further into crisis as Buddhists and their sympathizers launched a wave of protests against the government in July and August, American newspapers openly discussed the advantages for Washington of an anti-Diem coup after hardly making mention of Ho's public announcement on terms for a negotiated settlement at the end of May. All of the momentum seemed to be moving toward a decision that would make a messy situation much worse, so France opted to change course and try a new approach: a grand public appeal for peace.

De Gaulle responded personally to the crisis on August 29, 1963, by having his minister of information, Alain Peyrefitte, cite verbatim to the press a short cabinet statement that de Gaulle had made on Vietnam. Without naming the United States or the communist patrons of North Vietnam, de Gaulle reasserted French interest in its former colony, offering to help all Vietnamese people unify the country and secure "independence from foreign influences."[94] De Gaulle stated:

> The serious events taking place in Vietnam are being followed in Paris with attention and emotion.
>
> The work which France accomplished in the past in Cochin-China, Annam and Tonkin, the ties which she has in its development lead her to understand particularly well, and share sincerely, the hardships of the Vietnamese people.
>
> On the other hand, the knowledge which France has of this people's valor makes her appreciate the role this people would be capable of playing in the present situation of Asia, for its own progress and for the benefit of international understanding, once it is able to carry on its activity in independence from exterior influences, in internal peace and unity, and in concord with its neighbors.
>
> Today more than ever it is this that France wishes for all of Vietnam.
>
> Naturally it is up to this people and to them alone to choose the means to bring this about. But every national effort which might be undertaken in Vietnam toward this end would find France ready, to the extent of her own possibilities, to set up a cordial cooperation with this country.[95]

The "de Gaulle statement" was well-intentioned and sensitive enough to avoid blaming Washington for the sorry state of affairs in South Vietnam, which makes the reaction it elicited from the Kennedy administration all the more remarkable. De Gaulle's missive first caught American officials badly off-guard and then, after it had been fully digested, became the source of derision.[96]

The impact was felt the following day when Ambassador Alphand was summoned to a meeting with Rusk at the State Department. In the American summary of the conversation, Alphand said the statement "in essence . . . reiterated the points which General de Gaulle had made in his meeting with the President in the spring of 1961. The French did not feel that a military solution could work."[97] Rusk returned to the arguments he too had made many times in the past, replying that it was North Vietnam, not the United States, that was seeking a military solution to the conflict, that Washington never sought out Saigon as an ally and that the Kennedy administration "would be perfectly happy if it were truly nonaligned as many other countries are." In response, Alphand clarified that France had "no immediate solution to the problem" and described the statement "as a long term proposition, not as something that could be put into effect in the near future."[98]

Rusk did seem interested in tapping French knowledge of North Vietnamese thinking, posing a series of questions that led Alphand to tell him that Ho Chi Minh sincerely wanted peace, but Chairman Mao was pushing him to ramp up the war and that the Soviets truly had little influence in Southeast Asia beyond what Ho gave them to counterbalance the Chinese. Whereas Alphand saw many signs indicating support for neutralism, Rusk would not waver from the hard-line position that American actions were forced on them by communist aggression and that "a truly neutral Vietnam was [probably not] possible."[99] Nevertheless, Alphand promised that he would "emphasize to the press that it was absurd to think that France was looking for an arrangement with Diem or was trying to extend her influence at the expense of the U.S.," agreeing to Rusk's request that the de Gaulle statement be painted as a long-term plan.[100]

On the ground, Lalouette painted a picture that same day of a highly combustible situation. The Kennedy administration had recently dispatched Henry Cabot Lodge Jr., a Republican who had lost his Senate seat to Kennedy in 1952 and was the vice presidential candidate on Richard Nixon's losing ticket in 1960, to replace Ambassador Frederick Nolting in early August 1963. Kennedy hoped the appointment of a bitter rival to such a key position would help win bipartisan support for his Vietnam policy, but early indications were that Lodge was either unprepared for or overwhelmed by his new assignment. Lodge's political memoirs disappointingly skip past his time in Vietnam, merely refuting that he had played an active role in planning the coup that led to Diem's murder.[101] Soon after he had settled in, however, he began leaking sensitive information on Nhu's contacts with the North to his old friend Joe Alsop at the *Washington Post* in a deliberate campaign to smear Nhu, undercut tentative peace feelers in the South, and prepare the American public for a coup. Lodge insisted that Kennedy had given him a mandate for these sorts of activities, efforts that were in direct opposition to the ongoing French peace initiative.[102]

Lalouette reported that Ambassador Lodge had begun "deliberately confining himself to trivial matters . . . [as the] beginning of a policy of disassociation," refusing even to meet with officials of the South Vietnamese government. Based on his most recent conversation with Lodge, Lalouette concluded that a coup against Diem was imminent, perhaps coming within the next week. Lalouette reminded Lodge that as diplomats they had a responsibility to work to "peacefully resolve the serious problems that South Vietnam was currently facing," then he asked his American counterpart to request "patience and moderation" from the Kennedy administration. Lodge responded by soliciting Lalouette's opinion as to whether a coup would do much physical damage to Saigon and how it would be perceived in the suburbs, to which Lalouette bleakly replied that fighting would be severe, that the civilian population would be caught in the crossfire, and that Viet Cong elements in the capital could exploit the disorder.[103]

To de Gaulle's probable satisfaction, his August statement took on a life of its own, provoking a debate within the United States on alternatives to war in Vietnam. American public opinion was firmly focused on the drama in Saigon in September 1963, with most media outlets arguing against a unilateral American withdrawal, but supportive of efforts to find a diplomatic solution. *Newsweek, The New Republic,* and the respected Pulitzer Prize-winning political commentator Walter Lippmann all saw de Gaulle's willingness to facilitate a deal as a productive development.[104] Noted war correspondent and Vietnam expert Bernard Fall reported later in the month that Hanoi welcomed French efforts because it knew that a protracted war with the United States would leave North Vietnam overly dependent on Beijing. The Viet Cong insurgency even began to slacken by late summer–early autumn, which may have been a deliberate North Vietnamese attempt to bolster Diem's position in the hopes of bringing about an accommodation.[105]

Still, *New York Times* journalist Tad Szulc wrote on August 30, 1963, that the Kennedy administration's official view of the de Gaulle statement was that it "must be viewed as a hypothetical issue," revealing that the "administration deeply resented his intervention."[106] He added that the White House saw the statement as "another effort to undercut the United States' position in the Western alliance" and found its timing during a crisis in relations between Washington and Saigon "particularly irksome."[107] Other newspaper reports in the immediate aftermath of the statement echoed administration fears that France was looking to work around the United States, its NATO ally, by seeking Soviet support for its neutralization plan, or that it had given Nhu an opportunity to evade American pressure on the regime for major reforms by cutting a deal with the North.[108]

Kennedy was in the midst of agonizing internal discussions over whether to encourage an ARVN coup against Diem, and French efforts to promote a negotiated solution created massive problems for his administration.[109] McGeorge Bundy told Ambassador Alphand that "he didn't understand [France's] Vietnam policy," questioning whether de Gaulle's statement should be interpreted as a condemnation of the American military program there.[110] American embassy officials in Paris urged that it would be unwise to respond harshly to the de Gaulle statement, "toplofty and irritating though it may be," because "we do not find [it] inconsistent with this attitude of relative aloofness." The embassy suggested that "we would do well for [the] time being to pass it over in complete silence and treat it as [a] French definition of long term objectives for Viet-Nam unless we see signs that some kind of initiative is developing from it."[111]

Still, Lodge, the newly minted ambassador to South Vietnam, succeeded in convincing the administration that de Gaulle's "idiotic" statement was an affront to the American effort in Vietnam.[112] He surmised that Nhu, with the help of Ambassador Lalouette, was trying to play Paris off against Washington to secure a deal with the North to eject the United States from the South in exchange for peace.[113] This would indicate that Lodge had merely been feigning interest in Lalouette's views and had no real interest in pursuing actual diplomacy. Ambassador Bohlen in Paris cabled Rusk on September 2, 1963, to inform him that the French had been taken aback by the hostile American reaction to the statement, which de Gaulle hoped would be "helpful to [Washington] if it in any way shook up Diem and made him tractable."[114]

Undeterred by American bitterness for de Gaulle's statement and suspicion of his potential role as a conduit between the North and South, Lalouette called on Lodge again on September 4. In the French account of the meeting, Lodge at first told Lalouette that Diem was finished as president. He described the South Vietnamese government as the biggest obstacle to winning the war, while the acid-tongued Madame Nhu had to be removed in order to restore some normalcy to bilateral US-Vietnamese relations. Lodge conceded that Nhu was highly intelligent, of "an international class" in terms of his political sense, but was a total disaster when it came to his dealings with the press and the public. The tone of the conversation shifted when Lodge told Lalouette that Nhu had informed him of his contacts with the NLF, which Lalouette spun as a positive development. If Nhu was speaking with the rebels, Lalouette suggested, it should be taken as a sign that he and Diem were ready to begin a peace initiative.

When Lalouette argued that the United States should support these efforts, Lodge seemed to indicate that he would share this perspective with the Kennedy administration. Lodge elaborated on his dismay over the general apathy he saw from the general population, adding that American military advisors could not see "the light at the end of the tunnel" and assumed the war could continue for years. Lodge also explained that he understood that American actions could provoke a more active role from Hanoi and in turn Beijing and Moscow, dictating great caution. Lalouette interpreted this as a deeper, more realistic assessment than he was used to from Lodge, taking relief in Lodge's suggestion that the United States give Diem some breathing room and even invite Nhu stateside for an extended discussion on his long-term plans. Lodge promised to support a program from Nhu that allowed for a return to the pre-1960 situation and left the door open for political, economic, and social reform, provided that it did not damage American prestige.[115]

An optimist would have seen cause for hope in Lalouette's cable, but Lodge's account indicates that the American ambassador was engaged in an act of deception designed to take the wind out of French initiatives. Lodge wrote that Lalouette had come to remind him that "Nhu believed he could work out an arrangement with the [Viet Cong] whereby the guerrilla war would be ended . . . [in exchange for] the withdrawal of some US troops."[116] Lodge believed that it was Lalouette's view that if the United States eventually tired of the conflict, France would like to help it lay the groundwork for a future withdrawal.[117] Lalouette's attempts to assuage Lodge's fears had quite the opposite effect; the French ambassador's every movement thereafter was subjected to incredible scrutiny as Lodge attempted to pin down Lalouette's role in Nhu's supposed anti-American plot.

The de Gaulle statement had provoked far too much chatter in the press for Kennedy to remain silent, forcing the president to clarify his reaction to it on national television during a September 2 CBS interview with Walter Cronkite from Hyannis, Massachusetts. In a draft statement for the president in preparation for the interview, Bundy wrote a stinging riposte asserting that de Gaulle had never offered to inject the military resources necessary to defend South Vietnam and that he appeared willing to hand the country over to the communists, but Bundy suggested that Kennedy not use this rebuttal on air.[118] Bundy argued that it would be detrimental to American interests in Southeast Asia for Kennedy to reference the French role in Laos, which he and Harriman now considered "most unhelpful" and one that "raises [the] spectre of neutralist solution" for Vietnam.[119] More importantly, however, Bundy advised that "we find only our own personal irritation as an argument against [the] well-established conclusion that we do best when we ignore Nosey Charlie."[120]

On air with Cronkite, Kennedy was guarded when the discussion turned to Vietnam, stressing that it was up to the South Vietnamese themselves to win the war, with the United States reluctantly playing a secondary support role with equipment and advisors.[121] He repeated the importance of the domino theory, arguing: "These people who say that we ought to withdraw from Viet-Nam are wholly wrong because if we withdraw from Viet-Nam, the Communists would control Viet-Nam. Pretty soon Thailand, Cambodia, Laos, Malaya would go, and all of Southeast Asia would be under the control of the Communists and under the domination of the Chinese, and then India and Burma would be the next target. So I think we should stay."[122]

When asked if he had an opinion of de Gaulle's statement specifically, Kennedy largely heeded Bundy's advice, cautiously dismissing it as much ado about nothing: "I guess it was an expression of his general view, but he doesn't have any forces there or any program of economic assistance, so that while these expressions are welcome, the burden is carried, as it usually is, by the United States and the people there. But I think anything General de Gaulle says should be listened to, and we listened."

When Cronkite asked Kennedy if the statement warranted a personal meeting "to call off President de Gaulle from this kind of sniping at us," Kennedy replied:

> I mean President de Gaulle follows a policy of advancing the interest of France and he is a man of great stature. We are trying to advance the interests of the U.S. and we think the interests of the U.S. are tied up with maintaining the balance of freedom in the world. What, of course, makes Americans somewhat impatient is that after carrying this load for 18 years, we are glad to get counsel, but we would like a little more assistance, but we are going to meet our responsibility anyway. It doesn't do us any good to say, 'Well, why don't we all just go home and leave the world to those who are our

enemies.' General de Gaulle is not our enemy. He is our friend and candid friend—and, there, sometimes difficult—but he is not the object of our hostility.[123]

After having viewed the broadcast, Lalouette reported to the Foreign Ministry that "JFK had taken a friendly tone when speaking of General de Gaulle, which sheds new light on his take on the French position," but this was wishful thinking.[124] Kennedy followed up his Cronkite interview with an elaboration on NBC's *Huntley-Brinkley Report* a week later, again calling for patience and reiterating his belief in the domino theory.[125] With these two interviews Kennedy was signaling to Paris that de Gaulle's peace initiatives were unwelcome, that his administration had decided to stay the course, playing for time in the hopes that the coup leaders could produce a more responsive and popular government than Diem had.

With French interest in brokering a comprehensive Vietnamese peace settlement and the existence of clandestine North-South contacts already established by early September, American attention shifted to Nhu's prospects for success as he used the potential withdrawal of American advisors in the South as a diplomatic bargaining chip with his communist adversaries. On September 11, Lodge cabled Rusk that de Gaulle's statement had been welcomed by the press in South Vietnam, but the government and most Vietnamese had little appetite for a more active French role in the country. Lodge felt that the "only possibly interested party seems to be Nhu[,] who from recent reports [is] conceivably cooking up some sort of deal with [the] French in anticipation [of a] possible showdown with [the] U.S."[126] He concurred with the view that de Gaulle, who had long been on bad terms with Diem, had been persuaded by Lalouette that protecting the president and his brother were essential to any potential peace deal with the North. Lodge assumed that France's real motivation was to "open up all of what was formerly Indo-China to French business activity and political influence."[127]

Though specifics on any particular deal were lacking, Lodge identified Lalouette and Nhu as the greatest threats to American influence in South Vietnam. He concluded that if the French would not curtail their initiatives of their own accord, then ridding the country of Nhu was the next best means of scuppering them. The State Department and CIA both issued less sensationalistic reports around the same time, arguing that Nhu viewed the de Gaulle statement as a means of evading American pressure for governmental reform, that Moscow and Beijing respectively might welcome a deal that got the United States out of country, and that France was more than likely involved in secret negotiations, but both organizations concluded that no major moves were imminent.[128]

Many elements of these assessments were accurate, particularly when it came to how far along a Nhu-led peace push had gone. The French were aware that they had only arrived at the earliest stages of setting the groundwork for talks. Diem had described the de Gaulle statement as little more than an expression of his long-term aim of seeing the country reunited, while Pham Van Dong had yet to comment officially by mid-September. What existed at this point was merely the hope of exploring the possibility of negotiations, not a guarantee that they would succeed.

It was, however, a positive sign that neither the North nor the South had disavowed de Gaulle's offer to help facilitate dialogue, as was word that a North Vietnamese diplomat in Algiers had told his French counterpart that his government looked favorably on de Gaulle's statement.[129] A Polish interlocutor, Mieczysław Maneli, who served as his country's head delegate on the ICC, had informed Nhu in early September that Hanoi appeared willing to make a major concession: the reopening of commerce across the 17th parallel.[130] Nhu's response, knowing Maneli had direct access to Hanoi, was to instruct him to tell the North that discussions for a cease-fire could possibly begin within a few months.[131] This was the second channel for North-South dialogue that emerged late in the summer of 1963. At the same time, Ramchundur Goburdhun, a French-educated Indian ICC representative who enjoyed good relations with leaders on both sides of the DMZ, had offered to bring Nhu in contact with senior DRV officials to discuss a temporary peace. This overture apparently went so far as to include a private meeting at Goburdhun's Saigon home between Nhu and an unknown DRV agent, followed by an invitation for a more formal round of secret talks in New Delhi.[132]

Whether or not this could have resulted in a real settlement if the process had been given room to breathe is a matter for historical debate. Fredrik Logevall and Ellen Hammer find signs indicating that North and South Vietnam were moving toward the opening phase of a potential bargain that could have given them both more independence from their respective superpower patrons, stanched the bleeding in the field, and yielded some economic benefits.[133] Diem was fully aware that Ambassador Lodge had been plotting his ouster from the moment he arrived in Vietnam in August, leading Seth

Jacobs to conclude that this pressure forced him "to entertain the possibility of reducing his dependence on Washington by making a deal with Hanoi that would neutralize both North and South Vietnam and lead to a reconciliation between the two countries."[134] This position would have been anathema at the start of the year, but circumstances had changed dramatically over the summer. Francis X. Winters and Gareth Porter go somewhat further in suggesting that Diem and Nhu had grown so weary of American pressure that neutralism had finally begun to gain a certain appeal.[135] Edward Miller and Philip Catton are skeptical of these views, however, arguing that Diem and Nhu were confident in their prospects for victory and viewed talks with the NLF and Hanoi primarily as a means of learning more about the communist negotiating position, not as the prelude to a grand bargain.[136] Meanwhile on the communist side, Pierre Asselin counters that Hanoi had no intention of making any meaningful concessions at this juncture unless Diem was ready to hand over his country, while Margaret Gnoinska sees the North's overtures through Maneli as a limited effort to open trade and cultural ties rather than the beginnings of summit diplomacy.[137]

Elements of all of these arguments are convincing, and there is currently no definitive piece of evidence that advances one interpretation over the other. In any event, it would have taken a perfect storm of an endorsement from the Kennedy administration, a hitherto unseen willingness to compromise from both North and South Vietnam, and diplomatic support from France for neutralization to succeed. Only the latter had been secured. Nevertheless, the remote possibility of peace was greater than at any point since partition, even if all of the hard work was still left to be done.

Lodge would not relent in his crusade to uncover evidence of a French-supported plot engineered by Nhu, who was described in the same sort of feminizing language that was typically found in early Cold War American descriptions of the French. He reported to Rusk that Nhu, who he alleged was in the midst of an opium bender, was "manic," held "delusions of grandeur," was "somewhat irrational, highly emotional, wound up and very self centered," and "had seduced" Lalouette, who was being manipulated rather than pulling strings.[138] Diem was "cut off from reality and very slow in his reactions," no longer capable of sustaining the vigor he had brought to his office only few years earlier.[139]

By the end of the month, however, it had become clear that American preparations for a coup had outpaced Nhu's efforts to reach some sort of understanding with the North. On September 30, Melvin Manful, counsellor for political affairs at the Saigon embassy, cabled on this "cagey game" between Nhu, Hanoi, and the French, "who have all along chafed over their loss of influence, would be more than happy to have the opportunity to play the role of the chief Western influence upon the departure of the U.S." Nhu saw a showdown with Washington approaching within three months and hoped to parlay the success of the Strategic Hamlet Program into a better deal with the North while the United States was still in the country in force.[140] While Nhu welcomed the long-term vision expressed in the de Gaulle statement, he still viewed the Strategic Hamlet Program as the best means of creating favorable grounds for eventual negotiations, perhaps in December or early 1964, with Ho's representatives, who would probably have to delay any response as they waited on instructions from Moscow and Beijing.[141]

In the end, however, Nhu overestimated the length of this brief window of opportunity to save his own position and, more importantly, to finally bring peace to his country. Administration discussion continued almost to the end of October, and Kennedy's indirect position was that while the United States did not necessarily want a coup, it would not oppose one. Washington was forewarned of the coup at least a week before it was launched, with Kennedy and McNamara willing to take a hands-off approach. Ambassador Lodge, who was micromanaging an amateurish operation that was barely concealed from the regime, was, however, far more enthusiastic for taking active measures to get rid of Diem.

South Vietnam had been rife with talk of a coup for over two months, but on November 1 it finally came to pass. Lalouette's earlier prediction to Lodge that a coup would result in heavy fighting across Saigon was unfounded; it proved to be a relatively bloodless affair for all but the president and his brother. A group of ARVN generals led by General Duong Van Minh stormed the presidential palace in Saigon after Diem and Nhu refused an offer of safe passage out of the country and attempted to flee, but they were captured and summarily executed the following day. Everyone, Lodge included, was shocked by Diem's murder, and Kennedy in particular was dismayed by the moral implications of American actions.[142]

Diem had alienated most of his countrymen and driven many to armed revolt, but his ouster at this particular juncture quashed tentative, cautiously executed, French-supported initiatives to create the conditions for talks on a neutral, reunited Vietnam. Nhu was cunning, clever, and the only major player in South Vietnamese politics with the will and contacts to bring about an accommodation with the North. What might have come to pass had he and his brother been given only a few more months in power is one of the great unknowns of the Vietnam wars.

As flawed as Diem had been, his post-coup successors increased South Vietnam's dependency on the United States and fed North Vietnamese propaganda that portrayed the leadership in Saigon as little more than a cabal of American stooges. None were capable of playing Nhu's double game of simultaneously negotiating with enemy and ally alike. The collapse of the Diem regime also had profound implications on decision-making north of the DMZ. As Pierre Asselin outlines in *Hanoi's Road to the Vietnam War,* Le Duan, one of the most ardent hawks in the North Vietnamese leadership, seized a dominant role within the Communist Party on the strength of his argument that diplomacy and political efforts had failed to yield any tangible movement toward national reunification.[143] By year's end he had outmaneuvered his more moderate rivals, including those who had opened their ears to French peace overtures. He then charted a course toward open war with South Vietnam, pushing "Resolution 9" at the Ninth Plenum of the party's Central Committee in December 1963, a plan that hoped to rapidly defeat the ARVN before the United States could introduce its own forces. Asselin writes, "With [the] adoption [of Resolution 9] by the Central Committee, the earlier effort to separate the revolutionary processes in the North and South was abandoned. Henceforth, the DRVN would invest itself comprehensively in the liberation of the South by military struggle."[144] With this more aggressive orientation heading into 1964, Hanoi mobilized all of its resources for war, ramped up its aid to the Viet Cong, prepared the PAVN for conventional operations on South Vietnamese territory, and girded itself for a fight with American troops. Under these conditions, there was no hope for a resumption of peace efforts until a tragic amount of blood had been spilled.

Kennedy too was killed, taking an assassin's bullet as his presidential motorcade traveled through Dallas on November 22, 1963. With his death, the French campaign for a peaceful solution to the conflict before the United States committed to a direct military intervention effectively drew to a close. De Gaulle soon discovered that Kennedy's successor, Lyndon Johnson, had no desire to even listen to French proposals, and the two men never spoke directly at any point between Kennedy's funeral and the Gulf of Tonkin Incident. In five years as president, Johnson met de Gaulle only twice, the second occasion being Konrad Adenauer's funeral in 1967, and justified his near total avoidance of the French president with colorful baseball metaphors that portrayed Johnson as a slugger facing a fearsome curveball artist.[145] De Gaulle had failed to sway either president to his correct assessment of America's prospects for success if it entered the conflict, and Johnson's tragic decision to formally bring America into the war with the Tonkin Gulf Resolution in August 1964 was the logical outcome of his predecessor's dangerous policy of sidelining French advice.

The events of 1963 mark a tragic final chapter in the Kennedy administration's rejection of the Gaullist program for Vietnam. Diem's resistance to American guidance was an insurmountable obstacle for the ambitious counterinsurgency and nation-building programs the Kennedy administration had laid out. His government's brutal repression of Buddhists and other disaffected sections of South Vietnamese society caused a massive propaganda embarrassment for the United States, the American public was turning against the conflict, and, most importantly, leaders in both halves of Vietnam were willing to explore the possibility of a cease-fire deal. The arguments for pursuing a peace policy seemingly grew stronger by the day, but the Kennedy administration never even considered exploring the French alternative to military escalation. In the process, it authored the opening chapter of America's single greatest defeat of the Cold War era.

Conclusion

The French consul in Da Nang, Jacques Boizet, took a trip to the DMZ late in the winter of 1962. An experienced Asia hand who had grown as cynical of the Kennedy administration's war effort as most of his French colleagues by this point, Boizet often shared with Roger Lalouette blindingly simple observations, usually delivered with literary panache, in a format that no American Foreign Service officer would have dared submit to his superior. Boizet's journey north to the frontier took him to an old colonial-era bridge on the Ben Hai River that served as a border crossing between the Vietnams. Different flags flew on opposite sides of the river, surrounded by obligatory signs denouncing the regime that controlled the other half of the country. Officials had gone so far as to mark every last centimeter of their territory by painting their zone of control on the bridge in the proper national color, red for the communist northern section and green for the southern noncommunist span, just as one would expect on the front line of a Cold War divide.

The comic tension of this border scene was broken when guards on both sides ultimately chose not to observe strict orders to avoid fraternization with their mortal enemies. The bridge saw very little traffic, so when the northern police saw the French group approach the southern side of the bridge, curiosity got the better of them. Naturally, they crossed over the bridge on foot to ask their southern counterparts who these pale foreigners were and what was the nature of their visit. Once the strictest of rules had been broken, the northerners decided that they might as well take the mail over and sit down for tea with their neighbors. Boizet commented, "A world finishes and yet the rice paddies continue in a landscape typical of Central Vietnam, laying at the bottom of the Annamite Range. A cold wind blows and everything seems to protest against the absurdity of this invisible barrier." Boizet's words could have come from any number of members of the French foreign policy establishment, unable as it was to comprehend why the United States would continue fighting to perpetuate the artificial border mistakenly erected right through the heart of a coherent, ancient nation eight years earlier.[1]

The Vietnam War fell roughly in the middle of the "American Century" that was bookended by costly, divisive military interventions in the Philippines in 1898 and Iraq in 2003.[2] That the Kennedy administration, so confident in its understanding of American exceptionalism, committed a tremendous amount of lives, money, and effort in remaking a far corner of the world in America's image is hardly remarkable; many of his predecessors and successors have done the same elsewhere in one form or another, with increasingly poor results over the course of the past half century. It is also true that Kennedy had inherited momentum toward a robust intervention in Southeast Asia from Dwight Eisenhower, who had steadily positioned the United States as the major foreign power in Vietnam after the French withdrawal in 1954. Kennedy was tragically assassinated while in office, leaving the ultimate decision on whether to formally join the fighting to Johnson, an accidental president who would have much preferred to focus on his ambitious, noble-minded domestic reform agenda. Was Vietnam really Kennedy's war?

At its essence, Kennedy's real fault in Vietnam was that he did not apply the brakes in time and reevaluate the consequences of this slow-motion march to war. Playing for time, as he had in Laos in 1962, was no longer a viable option for Vietnam in the summer of 1963 once monks started self-immolating in central Saigon to protest repressive government policies and the countryside had largely fallen to communist guerrillas. The administration's tacit authorization of the coup that led to Diem's and Nhu's murders effectively marked a major, unpleasant evolution of the client-patron relationship that all but tied South Vietnam's fate to Washington. For that, Kennedy bears responsibility.

Despite Camelot myth-making, Kennedy was flawed and human, which is entirely forgivable. What is less so is the New Frontiersmen's boastfulness of their "objective vision," their cherished ability to manage crises under extreme pressure, and the sound social science grounding of the modernization theory that shaped their approach to the Third World. The men of the Kennedy administration were, for the most part, rank conformists who never saw the contradiction in fighting for the supposed interests of the free world while remaining completely intolerant of dissent, either internally from men like Ball, Galbraith, Bowles, Gavin, and Mansfield, or externally from de

Gaulle and occasionally, to a more muted extent, Adenauer. They were so wrapped up in managing day-to-day crises across the globe that they were never able to comprehend the interests of other players, much less imagine a way out of the Cold War. Their casual dismissal of experienced statesmen from allied countries, such as de Gaulle, Adenauer, and Macmillan, was terribly misguided in hindsight.

Kennedy's natural overconfidence was combined with long-standing suspicions of French national character and France's colonial legacy. He had bought into popular negative views of France and French foreign policy circulating in interwar America by the time he was an undergraduate at Harvard. These prejudices were revealed in the diary from his 1937 trip to Europe. From the House of Representatives and the Senate, Kennedy's writing and speeches on France employed subtle cultural stereotypes and gendered language that reflected his mistrust of the country. When de Gaulle shattered the feminized stereotypes of Fourth Republic France by bringing strength to the French presidency and securing an honorable withdrawal from Algeria, Kennedy shifted to the mistaken notion that Franco-American policy disagreements were explained by de Gaulle's supposed character flaws and the French president's historically rooted anti-Americanism. When de Gaulle disagreed with Kennedy on Vietnam at the Paris summit and afterward, familiar stereotypes of France flooded back, providing the administration with a convenient justification to dismiss his position without debating it on its merits. Kennedy too often assumed that malevolent intent was the driving force behind French foreign policy, and as a result he made too little effort to understand the French national interest as de Gaulle understood it. America suffered greatly in Vietnam over the course of the following decade due to Kennedy's closed-mindedness when it came to America's oldest foreign ally.

Charles de Gaulle was portrayed as many things over the course of his long and storied career—messianic advocate of tank warfare in the interwar years, rallying figure for a painfully divided nation in the 1940s, and the president who finally brought an end to *le bourbier algérien* in 1962—but he is best remembered both at home and abroad as one who seemed to take his greatest pleasure in sabotaging the American superpower's designs. It is often argued that any French president of the era undoubtedly would have pursued the same ends as de Gaulle, but *le général* brought the means, high drama, public moralizing, and conflict escalation that entrenched his hero status for so many of his countrymen. De Gaulle's diplomacy naturally rankled across the Atlantic, yet he had the ability to see Cold War issues with a degree of clarity that was absent in American corridors of power. De Gaulle, having just extricated France from its own bloody war in Algeria, knew that American intervention in Vietnam would only complicate a very delicate local dispute and was sure to end in failure. He expressed his views privately at first and then went to the press only after he found himself completely ignored by the Kennedy and Johnson administrations.

Several key historiographical questions arise when examining de Gaulle's Vietnam policy: Had de Gaulle set himself on an irreversible path toward confrontation with the Anglo-Saxons all along, or did Washington "lose" him somewhere along the way? Was he simply using Vietnam as a means of humiliating the United States in front of the entire world?

In effect, the Americans did lose de Gaulle, a "rebel by inclination" to Jean Lacouture, but one who most likely could have functioned within the constraints of an American-dominated alliance that acknowledged French national interests and accepted the need for real consultation on matters of joint concern. The Kennedy administration, like its predecessor, proved unwilling to offer the symbolic concession of an informal *directoire* in exchange for more tractability from Paris; doing so would have required an admission that there were serious flaws to the manner in which Washington led NATO, something Kennedy could not fathom. De Gaulle's critique of growing American involvement in Vietnam, which began politely and privately in discussions with Kennedy administration officials, was shaped by a belief that the ideological differences between East and West that so absorbed Washington were really of little import. Vietnam was a peripheral theater; Europe was where the Cold War would ultimately be won or lost. His critique was not the product of a genuine expression of solidarity with Third World peoples and their national liberation movements, but neither was it the product of reflexive anti-Americanism as many have argued. There is huge significance to the fact that de Gaulle made public his Vietnam position only after the Kennedy administration had closed the door on greater consultation.

De Gaulle spent two and a half years patiently trying to sway the Kennedy administration to his—correct—view of the conflict. He knew that Kennedy needed to hear his critique because other American allies who shared his view, principally Britain, West Germany, and Canada, were too reticent to step forward and offer their own challenge. Only after Johnson had formally made the decision to go to war did de Gaulle become an increasingly vocal and public critic of the American Vietnam policy, culminating in a dramatic speech from Phnom Penh on September 1, 1966, in which he reiterated his long-standing call for the neutralization of Indochina. De Gaulle knew no one in the White House was listening by this point, but this mattered little to him. He was privately infuriated by Johnson's decision to tune him out, though he accepted that his words alone would not alter American policy. Only when the United States reordered the way it viewed its alliances would it be able to wind down its commitment in Vietnam. His audience was world public opinion, and this time his critique of the Vietnam War *was* part of a calculated bid to embarrass the reckless hegemon that ignored its allies one time too many.

From the Cambodian capital, de Gaulle publicly summarized his assessment of the Vietnam conflict. Unlike in his August 1963 statement, this time he did mention the United States by name and his criticism was clearly directed at Washington. He stated:

> [France] is [calling for withdrawal and negotiation] because of the exceptional and two-century-old friendship that . . . she has for America, because of the idea she has up to now had of her—like the one America has of herself—that is, the idea of a country championing the concept that we must allow people to determine their own destiny in their own way. She is saying this in consideration of the warnings which Paris long repeated to Washington when nothing irreparable had yet been done.
>
> She is saying this, lastly, with the conviction that, in view of the power, wealth and influence at present attained by the United States, the act of renouncing, in its turn, a distant expedition once it appears unprofitable and unjustifiable and of substituting for it an international arrangement organizing the peace and development of an important region of the world, will not, in the final analysis, involve anything that could injure its pride, interfere with its ideals and jeopardize its interests.
>
> On the contrary, in taking a path so true to the Western genius, what an audience would the United States recapture from one end of the world to the other, and what an opportunity would peace find on the scene and everywhere else. In any event, lacking this outcome, no mediation will offer a prospect of success, and that is why France, for her part, has never thought and does not think of proposing one.[3]

These words very succinctly recapitulated not only the French critique of America's involvement in the Vietnam War, but a position that a growing number of Americans were beginning to share.

In the early 1960s de Gaulle was not battling Kennedy on Vietnam alone; there were significant, but disunited, ineffective, and often timid antiwar voices within the American bureaucracy, such as George Ball, John Galbraith, Chester Bowles, and others. That the Kennedy administration also boxed out the few critical voices on Vietnam at home in its march to war would have provided little solace to de Gaulle. One is still left to wonder how events would have played out had men such as these been as bold and steadfast with Kennedy regarding their opposition as de Gaulle had been.

The reality is that Johnson fully committed to the war and a terrible bloodletting ensued. Vietnam broke his presidency, overshadowing tremendous progress on Civil Rights, education, and a whole raft of domestic concerns. It continued through Richard Nixon's first term, but the French came back in the end, providing diplomatic support for the Paris Peace Accords that finally let the United States disengage from Vietnam in 1973. As it turned out, Kennedy's decision to sideline de Gaulle ultimately set off a chain of events leading to a humiliating defeat that claimed over fifty-eight thousand American military personnel, shattered the lives of hundreds of thousands of veterans, killed well over a million people in Southeast Asia, and left three countries—Vietnam, Cambodia, and Laos—cratered from years of aerial bombardment and ravaged by highly toxic chemical defoliants. This was the staggering cost of Kennedy's mistrust, the result of pursuing the worst course of action that had been open to him in 1963.

Notes

Introduction

1. Frank Costigliola, "Kennedy, the European Allies, and the Failure to Consult," *Political Science Quarterly* 100, no. 1 (1995): 113.

2. Frequent participants included Secretary of State Dean Rusk, Secretary of Defense Robert McNamara, National Security Adviser McGeorge Bundy, Ambassador to France Charles "Chip" Bohlen, Ambassador to the Soviet Union Llewellyn Thompson, and Kennedy's most trusted military adviser, General Maxwell Taylor.

3. Alphand to Couve, January 25, 1963, Ministère des Affaires étrangères, AM 1952–1963, USA, 376, "politique extérieur," 9-5-0, La Courneuve.

4. Ibid.

5. Yuko Torikata argues in "Reexamining de Gaulle's Peace Initiative on the Vietnam War," *Diplomatic History* 31, no. 5 (2007), that American scholars have tended "to see in de Gaulle's criticism another attempt to defy American hegemony in the Western Alliance" (910), while their French counterparts "maintain that de Gaulle's initiatives can be best explained by France's colonial experience in Indochina and learned from the Algerian War" (910–11). Regarding the period examined in this work, she argues, "de Gaulle hoped France's mediation would contribute to a peace settlement; he took every opportunity to intervene in person, putting forward his neutralization plan. Although it is certain that he intended to enhance French prestige by interceding between the two blocs, his main objective was to avoid any serious trouble in the Atlantic Alliance. In particular, he feared that if the United States was dragged into a morass of war in Vietnam, American military forces would probably be reduced in Western Europe; this would definitely threaten France's own security" (912).

6. Marianna P. Sullivan, *France's Vietnam Policy: A Study in French-American Relations* (Westport, Conn.: Greenwood, 1978), 20.

7. There is little to no mention of Vietnam before the late summer of 1963 in the context of Kennedy-de Gaulle conversations/correspondence in all of the major overviews of Franco-American relations during the Cold War, such as: Charles G. Cogan, *Oldest Allies, Guarded Friends: The United States and France since 1940*

(Westport, Conn.: Praeger, 1994), and Charles G. Cogan, *Forced to Choose: France, the Atlantic Alliance, and NATO—Then and Now* (Westport, Conn.: Praeger, 1997); Frank Costigliola, *France and the United States: The Cold Alliance since World War II, 1940–1990* (New York: Twayne, 1992); Jean-Baptiste Duroselle, *France and the United States from the Beginnings to the Present,* trans. Derek Coltman (Chicago: Univ. of Chicago Press, 1978); Michael M. Harrison, *The Reluctant Ally: France and Atlantic Security* (Baltimore, Md.: Johns Hopkins Univ. Press, 1981); Erin R. Mahan, *Kennedy, de Gaulle, and Western Europe* (New York: Palgrave Macmillan, 2002); and Marvin R. Zahniser, *Uncertain Friendship: American-French Diplomatic Relations through the Cold War* (New York: Wiley, 1975).

8. Robert S. McNamara, with Brian VanDeMark, *In Retrospect: The Tragedy and Lessons of Vietnam* (New York: Times Books, 1995). This was followed by another collaborative effort, Robert S. McNamara, James G. Blight, and Robert K. Brigham's *Argument without End: In Search of Answers to the Vietnam Tragedy* (New York: Public Affairs, 1999). The most notable works to address Kennedy's role from this post-1995 tidal wave of Vietnam War scholarship include Robert Buzzanco, *Masters of War: Military Dissent and Politics in the Vietnam Era* (New York: Cambridge Univ. Press, 1996); Robert Buzzanco and Marilyn Young, eds., *A Companion to the Vietnam War* (Malden, Mass.: Blackwell Publishing, 2002); Lawrence Freedman, *Kennedy's Wars: Berlin, Cuba, Laos, and Vietnam* (New York: Oxford Univ. Press, 2000); Lloyd C. Gardner and Ted Gittinger, eds., *Vietnam: The Early Decisions* (Austin: Univ. of Texas Press, 1997); Lloyd C. Gardner, *Pay Any Price: Lyndon Johnson and the Wars for Vietnam* (Chicago: Dee, 1995); George C. Herring, *LBJ and Vietnam: A Different Kind of War* (Austin: Univ. of Texas Press, 1994); Michael H. Hunt, *Lyndon Johnson's War: America's Cold War Crusade in Vietnam, 1945–1968* (New York: Hill and Wang, 1996); David Kaiser, *American Tragedy: Kennedy, Johnson, and the Origins of the Vietnam War* (Cambridge, Mass.: Belknap Press of Harvard Univ. Press, 2000); Fredrik Logevall, *Choosing War: The Lost Chance for Peace and the Escalation of War in Vietnam* (Berkeley: Univ. of California Press, 1999); Peter Lowe, ed., *The Vietnam War* (London: Macmillan, 1998); Robert J. McMahon, *The Limits of Empire: The United States and Southeast Asia since World War II* (New York: Columbia Univ. Press, 1999); H. R. McMaster, *Dereliction of Duty: Lyndon Johnson, Robert McNamara, the Joint Chiefs of Staff, and the Lies That Led to Vietnam* (New York: HarperCollins, 1997); Edwin E. Moïse, *Tonkin Gulf and the Escalation of the Vietnam War* (Chapel Hill: Univ. of North Carolina Press, 1996); Mark Moyar, *Triumph Forsaken: The Vietnam War, 1954–1965* (New York: Cambridge Univ. Press, 2006); Gareth Porter, *Perils of Dominance: Imbalance of Power and the Road to War in Vietnam* (Berkeley: Univ. of California Press, 2004); Jeffrey Record, *The Wrong War: Why We Lost in Vietnam* (Annapolis, Md.: Naval Institute Press, 1998); Robert D. Schulzinger, *A Time for War: The United States and Vietnam, 1941–1975* (New York: Oxford Univ. Press, 1997); Orrin Schwab, *Defending the Free World: John F. Kennedy, Lyndon Johnson, and the Vietnam War, 1961–1965* (Westport, Conn.: Praeger, 1998); Blema S. Steinberg, *Shame and Humiliation: Presidential Decision Making on*

Vietnam (Montreal, Quebec: McGill-Queen's Univ. Press, 1996); Frank E. Vandiver, *Shadows of Vietnam: Lyndon Johnson's Wars* (College Station: Texas A&M Univ. Press, 1997); and Francis X. Winters, *The Year of the Hare: America in Vietnam, January 25, 1963–February 15, 1964* (Athens: Univ. of Georgia Press, 1997).

9. There is a numerically small revisionist school that seeks to justify the war. Leading historians here include the aforementioned Mark Moyar (*Triumph Forsaken*) and Michael Lind, who wrote *Vietnam: The Necessary War: A Reinterpretation of America's Most Disastrous Military Conflict* (New York: Free Press, 1999).

10. The text of his address can be found in George C. Herring, "'Peoples Quite Apart': Americans, South Vietnamese, and the War in Vietnam," *Diplomatic History* 14, no. 1 (1990): 1–23.

11. See numerous articles from Pierre Asselin and his most recent book, *Hanoi's Road to the Vietnam War, 1954–1965* (Berkeley: Univ. of California Press, 2013); Philip E. Catton, *Diem's Final Failure: Prelude to America's War in Vietnam* (Lawrence: Univ. Press of Kansas, 2002); Jessica M. Chapman, "Staging Democracy: South Vietnam's 1955 Referendum to Depose Bao Dai," *Diplomatic History* 30, no. 4 (2006): 671–703; and Jessica M. Chapman, *Cauldron of Resistance: Ngo Dinh Diem, the United States, and 1950s Southern Vietnam* (Ithaca, N.Y.: Cornell Univ. Press, 2013); James T. Fisher, "The Second Catholic President: Ngo Dinh Diem, John F. Kennedy, and the Vietnam Lobby, 1954–1963," *U.S. Catholic Historian* 15, no. 3 (1997): 119–37; Seth Jacobs, "'Our System Demands the Supreme Being': The U.S. Religious Revival and the 'Diem Experiment,' 1954–55," *Diplomatic History* 25, no. 4 (2001): 589–624; Seth Jacobs, *America's Miracle Man in Vietnam: Ngo Dinh Diem, Religion, Race, and U.S. Intervention in Southeast Asia, 1950–1957* (Durham, N.C.: Duke Univ. Press, 2004); Seth Jacobs, *Cold War Mandarin: Ngo Dinh Diem and the Origins of America's War in Vietnam, 1950–1963* (Lanham, Md.: Rowman and Littlefield, 2006); Howard Jones, *Death of a Generation: How the Assassinations of Diem and JFK Prolonged the Vietnam War* (New York: Oxford Univ. Press, 2003); Matthew Masur, "Exhibiting Signs of Resistance: South Vietnam's Struggle for Legitimacy, 1954–1960," *Diplomatic History* 33, no. 2 (2009): 293–313; Lien-Hang T. Nguyen, *Hanoi's War: An International History of the War for Peace in Vietnam* (Chapel Hill: Univ. of North Carolina Press, 2012); and, Geoffrey C. Stewart, "Hearts, Minds and Cong Dan Vu: The Special Commissariat for Civic Action and Nation-Building in Diem's Vietnam, 1955–1957," *Journal of Vietnamese Studies* 6, no. 3 (2011): 44–100.

12. James Hershberg provides a fascinating look at a valiant but failed Polish-Italian peace initiative in 1966 in *Marigold: The Lost Chance for Peace in Vietnam* (Stanford, Calif.: Stanford Univ. Press, 2012). For Hungary's diplomatic efforts in Vietnam, see Zoltán Szőke, "Delusion or Reality?: Secret Hungarian Diplomacy during the Vietnam War," *Journal of Cold War Studies* 12, no. 4 (fall 2010): 119–80. For Romania's role, see Mircea Munteanu, "Over the Hills and Far Away: Romania's Attempts to Mediate the Start of U.S.-North Vietnamese Negotiations, 1967–1968," *Journal of Cold War Studies* 14, no. 3 (summer 2012): 64–96.

13. Kathryn C. Statler makes note of the gap in studies of Franco-American disagreement over Vietnam from the Geneva Conference to the Tonkin Gulf Resolution in her excellent study *Replacing France: The Origins of American Intervention in Vietnam* (Lexington: Univ. Press of Kentucky, 2007), 7. Nevertheless, *Replacing France* focuses on American intervention in Vietnam from 1950 to 1961, prior to Kennedy's arrival in the White House.

14. Logevall's *Choosing War,* one of the most influential works on the origins of the Vietnam War, does open with de Gaulle's first public critique of Kennedy's Vietnam policy in August 1963 and argues that Kennedy should have followed de Gaulle's advice, which was the least bad alternative he had at the time. Still, Logevall leaves the two-year buildup to de Gaulle's August 1963 statement untouched before launching into the Johnson-era developments. An earlier Logevall article ("De Gaulle, Neutralization and American Involvement in Vietnam, 1963–64," *Pacific Historical Review* 61, no. 1 (February 1992): 69–102), written while he was a Ph.D. candidate at Yale, follows a similar time line. Charles G. Cogan, a leading Harvard-based American historian of twentieth-century Franco-American relations, addressed the topic in *Oldest Allies, Guarded Friends,* but he paints Vietnam in the Kennedy-de Gaulle relationship in broad strokes before devoting the bulk of his efforts to the Johnson-de Gaulle period. The earliest and most detailed work on the subject, Marianna P. Sullivan's 1978 *France's Vietnam Policy,* similarly chooses to focus on the Johnson-de Gaulle dynamic without exploring the crucial Kennedy-era prelude to it.

15. The best of the first generation of French scholarship on Vietnam came from former officials and journalists who had an intimate, firsthand acquaintance with the conflict and focused on the collapse of the colonial regime. Jean Sainteny, a resistance hero who served as the Fourth Republic's commissaire for Tonkin and North Annam from October 1945 to December 1947, detailed how his early attempts to negotiate a comprehensive settlement with Ho Chi Minh were compromised by a series of unstable governments in Paris in *Histoire d'une paix manquée, Indochine 1945–1947* (Paris: A. Fayard, 1967) and *Face à Ho Chi Minh* (Paris: Seghers, 1970). Paul Mus, author of *Viet-Nam: sociologie d'une guerre* (Paris: Éditions du Seuil, 1952), added his voice as another highly competent colonial official in de Gaulle's first postwar government who, after having negotiated with Ho, was equally convinced that Vietnamese nationalism could not be defeated by force. Étienne Manac'h's three-volume *Mémoires d'extrême Asie* (Paris: Fayard, 1977–1982) devotes a considerable amount of space to Vietnamese developments from 1960 to 1969, when he served as the Foreign Ministry's directeur du Département de L'Asie-Océanie before taking over as France's ambassador to mainland China. Journalists would make a significant contribution as well. Phillipe Devillers, the Indochina correspondent for the notable daily newspaper *Le Monde,* wrote the classic *Histoire du Viêt-Nam de 1940 à 1952* (Paris: Éditions du Seuil 1952) and collaborated with Jean LaCouture on *End of a War; Indochina, 1954,* trans. Alexander Lieven and Adam Roberts (New York: Praeger, 1969) and *Viet-Nam: de la guerre française à la guerre américaine* (Paris: Éditions du Seuil, 1969). Bernard Fall, an Austrian Jew and

resistance fighter who later joined the French army, became a history professor at Howard University and war correspondent during the French and American counterinsurgency campaigns. A prolific writer best known for *Street without Joy: Indochina at War, 1946–63* (London: Pall Mall, 1963), Fall's fascinating life came to a premature end when he was killed by a landmine in Vietnam in 1967 at age forty. Fall's work was characterized by lucid writing, penetrating analysis, and a consistently pessimistic outlook for American forces that was shaped by his front row seat to the collapse of French rule. Georges Chaffard of the news magazine *L'Express* penned an early historical account of transition from French rule to American hegemony, *Les deux guerres du Vietnam: de Valluy à Westmoreland* (Paris: La Table Ronde, 1969), but like *Viet-Nam: de la guerre française à la guerre américaine* from Devillers and Lacouture, it was published with the outcome of the war still very much in doubt. Weightier second-generation works continued to place more emphasis on the colonial period than the American-led war of the 1960s. The war did not provoke the same emotional response for these writers as it had for American academics who had lived through that turbulent decade. See, for example, Jacques Dalloz's *La guerre d'Indochine: 1945–1954* (Paris: Seuil, 1987); Pierre Brocheux's *The Mekong Delta: Ecology, Economy, and Revolution, 1860–1960* (Madison: Center for Southeast Asian Studies, University of Wisconsin-Madison, 1995); and Pierre Brocheux and Daniel Hémery's *Indochine: la colonisation ambiguë, 1858–1954* (Paris: Découverte, 1995). Also of importance are *La Bureaucratie au Viet Nam* (Paris: L'Harmattan: 1983) and *Cent fleurs écloses dans la nuit du Viet Nam* (Paris: Bertoin, 1991) from the controversial Georges Boudarel, a Marxist who lived in Vietnam until 1964 and was a respected lecturer of Indochinese history at a branch of the University of Paris until it was revealed in 1991 that he had brutalized French prisoners of war as the deputy chief of the notorious Camp 113 in the 1950s. In typical *longue durée* fashion, the most notable recent French works have tended to take a broader focus on Vietnam in relations between France and the United States from the founding of the Fifth Republic in 1958 to the North's triumph in 1975. Laurent Cesari's *L'Indochine en guerres, 1945–1993* (Paris: Belin, 1995); Christopher Goscha and Maurice Vaïsse, eds., *La guerre du Vietnam et l'Europe, 1963–1973* (Brussels: Bruylant, 2003); and Pierre Brocheux and Charles Robert Ageron's *Du conflit d'Indochine aux conflits Indochinois* (Brussels: Complexe, 2000) are among the best works from this wave of scholarship. Two promising younger French scholars, Thierry Dahan and Pierre Journoud, have recently made substantial contributions to the historiography of Vietnam in Franco-American relations during the Fifth Republic. Dahan argues in his Ph.D. dissertation, "La Vème République et le Vietnam, 1959–1976" (Ph.D. thesis, L'Université de Nice, 1998), that Fourth Republic governments grew disinterested with Vietnam after the Geneva Accords were signed, leaving the Americans as the primary foreign sponsor of newly independent South Vietnam. He examines how de Gaulle focused French interest in the country after returning to power as part of his policy of restoring grandeur, how the efforts of a team of French officials in the 1960s toward a peace deal resulted in Paris being chosen as the site of the negotiated settlement that ended American participation in the war in 1973, and the futile efforts of President Giscard d'Estaing to ensure that Vietnamese signatories respect the terms of the Paris Accords from 1973 to the North's ultimate victory in 1975. Journoud's 2007 Ph.D. dissertation, "Les relations franco-américaines à l'épreuve du Vietnam entre 1954 et 1975: de la défiance dans la guerre à la coopération pour la paix" (Ph.D. thesis, Université de Paris I-Sorbonne, 2007) argues that the United States actually defended French economic and cultural interests in South Vietnam after the Geneva Accords despite sharply divergent views of the region's future. He shows that Franco-American discord over Vietnam has perhaps been overstated, given that rapprochement came about easily in the late 1960s once Washington committed to the peace deal that the French government was willing to broker. There will be more commentary to come on his monograph *De Gaulle et le Vietnam, 1945–1969* (Paris: Tallandier, 2011).

16. Robert D. Dean, *Imperial Brotherhood: Gender and the Making of Cold War Foreign Policy* (Amherst: Univ. of Massachusetts Press, 2001).

17. There is some temptation to search for more traditional answers behind Kennedy's decision-making on Vietnam in the peer-influence "groupthink" theory of Irving L. Janis, who provides case studies of major American foreign policy decisions in the mid-twentieth century in two significant works on the subject. See Irving L. Janis, *Groupthink: Psychological Studies of Policy Decisions and Fiascoes* (Boston: Houghton Mifflin, 1982), an elaborated version of his earlier work, *Victims of Groupthink: A Psychological Study of Foreign-policy Decisions and Fiascoes* (Boston: Houghton, Mifflin, 1972). Janis defines groupthink as "a mode of thinking that people engage in when they are deeply involved in a cohesive in-group, when the members' strivings for unanimity override their motivation to realistically appraise alternative courses of action" (*Victims of Groupthink,* 3). To prevent groupthink, leaders should consider various alternatives, allow subordinates to voice dissenting views, have separate groups work independently on the same problem, and consult with trusted observers outside the group. The greatest obstacle to accusing the Kennedy administration of groupthink on Vietnam comes out of a contradiction that Janis himself identifies: the Bay of Pigs fiasco in the spring of 1961 provides a textbook example of the disastrous consequences of groupthink, while Kennedy's handling of the Cuban Missile Crisis the following autumn demonstrates exemplary nongroupthink decision-making. Janis argues that the Bay of Pigs prompted Kennedy to take active measures to combat groupthink that bore fruit during the Cuban Missile Crisis (*Victims of Groupthink,* 148–49). Surveying recent literature on the early Vietnam decisions of President Johnson, who left Kennedy's foreign policy team intact, John Garofano argues in "Tragedy or Choice in Vietnam? Learning to Think Outside the Archival Box," *International Security* 26, no. 4 (2002), that "arguments about groupthink or bureaucratic or organizational roadblocks do not stand up to the archival evidence" (157).

18. Vincent Bugliosi, *Reclaiming History: The Assassination of John F. Kennedy* (New York: Norton, 2007).

19. See, for example, James K. Galbraith, “JFK’s Vietnam Withdrawal Plan Is a Fact, Not Speculation,” *The Nation,* November 22, 2013, https://www.thenation.com/article/jfks-vietnam-withdrawal-plan-fact-not-speculation/.

20. Frank Costigliola and Thomas Paterson, “Defining and Doing the History of American Foreign Relations: A Primer,” in *Explaining the History of American Foreign Relations,* ed. Michael J. Hogan and Thomas G. Paterson (Cambridge, UK: Cambridge Univ. Press, 2004), 285.

21. Ibid., 284.

22. The French held firm in their belief that a maximum effort had been made on the battlefield and that political negotiations were the sole means forward, whereas the Americans were loath to negotiate with communists under any circumstances and refused to contemplate entering into talks until military advantage had been secured.

23. Frank Costigliola concludes in his excellent examination of American decision-making during the Cuban Missile Crisis, “Kennedy, the European Allies, and the Failure to Consult,” that Kennedy’s ExComm (the leading voices in his National Security Council) “summarily dismissed any idea of sharing with the allies decisions that could have led to the nuclear destruction of Western Europe as well as North America.” Costigliola argues that the language used by American decision-makers indicated a perception of Western Europeans “as the shaky, often impractical and emotional ‘others’ of the NATO family, unequal and inexperienced partners who were too ready to compromise with the Soviets (or, conversely, prone to resist the compromises decided upon by Americans) and who, therefore, had to be manipulated rather than consulted by the hard-headed, responsible officials of Washington” (107).

24. Kennedy earned the nickname “the Senator from Algeria” in the late 1950s for his support for Algerian independence. See Frank Kelley, “Kennedy Talk on Algeria Stirs Protests in France,” *Washington Post,* July 4, 1957, B10. The issues surrounding the American difficulties with the *force de frappe* are inevitably surveyed in most works on Franco-American relations in the early 1960s. For articles that focus specifically on French nuclear policy before and during the Kennedy years, see Wilfrid Kohl, *French Nuclear Diplomacy* (Princeton, N.J.: Princeton Univ. Press, 1971); Hans-Peter Schwarz, “Adenauer, le nucleaire, et la France,” *Revue d’histoire diplomatique* 106, no.4 (1992): 297–311; Georges Henri-Soutou, “Les problems de sécurité dans les rapports franco-allemand de 1956 à 1963,” *Relations Internationales,* no. 58 (1989): 227–51; David Tal, “From the Open Skies Proposal of 1955 to the Norstad Plan of 1960: A Plan Too Far,” *Journal of Cold War Studies* 10, no. 4 (2008): 66–93; and Mervyn O’Driscoll, “Explosive Challenge: Diplomatic Triangles, the United Nations, and the Problem of French Nuclear Testing, 1959–1960,” *Journal of Cold War Studies* 11, no. 1 (2009): 28–56.

25. This was Kennedy’s charge against French ambassador Herve Alphand on September 3, 1963. US Department of State, *Foreign Relations of the United States, 1961–1963,* vol. 4, *Vietnam, August–December 1963* (Washington, D.C.: GPO, 1991), 54, https://history.state.gov/historicaldocuments/frus1961-63v04/pg_100.

26. Ibid., 43, http://www.state.gov/r/pa/ho/frus/kennedyjf/iv/12645.htm.

1. *Cultural Imaging of the French "Other"*

1. William L. Chew III, "Literature, History and the Social Sciences?" in William L. Chew III, ed., *National Stereotypes in Perspective: Americans in France, Frenchmen in America* (Atlanta: Rodopi, 2001), 4. For a thorough examination of popular stereotypes of the French around the time of the American Revolution, see Eugen Weber, "Of Stereotypes and of the French," *Journal of Contemporary History* 25, nos. 2/3 (1990): 169–203.

2. Chew, "Literature, History, and the Social Sciences," 4, 11. He defines this as the study of "national stereotypes so current in our collective memory [that] color, to a large extent, not only our self-perception (our 'auto-image') via the image of the other (our 'hetero-image'), but determine for better and, regrettably, more often, for worse our behavior toward the other."

3. John G. Gazley, *American Opinion of German Unification, 1848–1871* (New York: Columbia University, 1926), 232.

4. Ibid., 239–41.

5. Ibid., 252.

6. Ibid., 300.

7. Ibid., 321.

8. Stuart Anderson, *Race and Rapprochement: Anglo-Saxonism and Anglo-American Relations, 1895–1904* (London: Associated Univ. Presses, 1981), 65.

9. Duroselle, *France and the United States,* 46.

10. Ibid., 48.

11. Kristen Hoganson, *Consumers' Imperium: The Global Production of American Domesticity, 1865–1920* (Chapel Hill: Univ. of North Carolina Press, 2007), 66–69.

12. Michael H. Hunt, *Ideology and US Foreign Policy* (New Haven, Conn.: Yale Univ. Press, 1987), preface, xi. Hunt defines "ideology" as "an interrelated set of convictions or assumptions that reduces complexities of a particular slice of reality to easily comprehensible terms and suggests appropriate ways of dealing with that reality." The two earliest general works on American Anglo-Saxonism in the nineteenth century still stand out as the best examinations of the subject: Anderson, *Race and Rapprochement,* and Reginald Horsman, *Race and Manifest Destiny: The Origins of American Racial Anglo-Saxonism* (Cambridge, Mass.: Harvard Univ. Press, 1981). Other relevant works include Paul McCartney, "Anglo-Saxonism and U.S. Foreign Policy during the Spanish-American War," in *Ethnic Identity Groups and U.S. Foreign Policy,* ed. Thomas Ambrosio (Westport, Conn.: Praeger, 2002), 21–46; Stuart Anderson, "Racial Anglo-Saxonism and the American Response to the Boer War," *Diplomatic History* 2, no. 3 (1978): 219–36; Paul A. Kramer, "Empires, Exceptions, and Anglo-Saxons: Race and Rule between the British and United States Empires," *Journal of American History* 88, no. 4 (2002): 1315–53; Eric T. L. Love, *Race over Empire: Racism and U.S. Imperialism, 1865–1900* (Chapel Hill: Univ. of North Carolina Press, 2004); Cynthia J. Davis, "Nation's Nature: 'Billy Budd, Sailor,' Anglo-Saxonism, and the Canon," and Maria DeGuzman, "Consolidating Anglo-American

Imperial Identity Around the Spanish-American War (1898)," both in *Race and the Production of Modern American Nationalism,* ed. Reynolds J. Scott-Childress (New York: Garland, 1999), 43–66, 97–126; and Audrey Smedley, *Race in North America: Origin and Evolution of a Worldview,* 3rd ed. (Boulder, Colo.: Westview Press, 2007).

13. In *Race and Rapprochement,* Anderson explains "Anglo-Saxonism" as "the belief—part of the prevailing orthodoxy in Great Britain and the United States in the late nineteenth and early twentieth centuries—that the civilization of the English-speaking nations was superior to that of any other group of people on the planet; and that the primacy of English and American civilization was largely due to the innate racial superiority of the people who were descended from the ancient Anglo-Saxon invaders of Britain" (12).

14. Ibid., 19.

15. Ibid., 24.

16. Ibid., 46. The Kennedy family was Irish Catholic, but as integrated, wealthy elites their sensibilities were similar to those of East Coast White Anglo-Saxon Protestants.

17. Hunt, *Ideology and US Foreign Policy,* 78–79.

18. Ibid.

19. Horsman, *Race and Manifest Destiny,* 26.

20. Alexis de Tocqueville, *Democracy in America,* trans. Henry Reeve (London: Longman, 1875), 370. There is a long discussion of slavery in the chapter "Present and Future Conditions of Negroes," 360–88. On the sectional divide, see the chapter "Chances of Duration of the Union," 389–425.

21. He writes, "I know of no country, indeed, where the love of money has taken stronger hold on the affections of men" (48). For other comments, see pages 51, 267, and 311.

22. Jacques Portes, *Fascination and Misgivings: The United States in French Opinion, 1870–1914,* trans. by Elborg Forster (New York: Cambridge Univ. Press, 2000), 2–3.

23. Ibid., 22.

24. Philippe Roger, *L'Ennemi américain: Généalogie de l'antiaméricanisme français* (Paris: Seuil, 2002), 56.

25. Irwin Wall, *The United States and the Making of Postwar France, 1945–1954* (New York: Cambridge Univ. Press, 1991), 11–12.

26. Cogan, *Oldest Allies, Guarded Friends,* 9–11.

27. For recent works on Anglo-American rapprochement in the late nineteenth and early twentieth centuries, see Kathleen Burk, *Old World, New World: The Story of Britain and America* (London: Little, Brown, 2007); Duncan Andrew Campbell, *Unlikely Allies: Britain, America and the Victorian Origins of the Special Relationship* (New York: Hambledon Continuum, 2007); Alan P. Dobson, ed., *Anglo-American Relations in the Twentieth Century: Of Friendship, Conflict and the Rise and Decline of Superpowers* (New York: Routledge, 1995); B.J.C. McKercher, ed., *Anglo-American Relations in the 1920s: The Struggle for Supremacy* (Basingstoke: Macmillan, 1991);

Anne Orde, *The Eclipse of Great Britain: The United States and British Imperial Decline, 1895–1956* (New York: St. Martin's Press, 1996); David Reynolds, *The Creation of the Anglo-American Alliance, 1937–1941: A Study in Competitive Co-Operation* (London: Europa, 1981); David Reynolds and David Dimbleby, *An Ocean Apart: The Relationship between Britain and America in the Twentieth Century* (New York: Random House, 1988); and Priscilla Roberts, "The Anglo-American Theme: American Visions of an Atlantic Alliance, 1914–1933," *Diplomatic History* 21, no. 3 (1997): 333–64.

28. This is the general theme of Michael J. Hogan's *Informal Entente: The Private Structure of Cooperation in Anglo-American Economic Diplomacy, 1918–1928* (Columbia: Univ. of Missouri Press, 1977).

29. Reynolds, *The Creation of the Anglo-American Alliance,* 3.

30. Robert J. Young, *Marketing Marianne: French Propaganda in America, 1900–1940* (New Brunswick, N.J.: Rutgers Univ. Press, 2004), 65.

31. Ibid., 68.

32. William R. Keylor, "How They Advertised France: The French Propaganda Campaign in the United States during the Breakup of the Franco-American Entente, 1918–1923," *Diplomatic History* 17, no. 3 (1993): 355.

33. Margaret MacMillan's *Paris 1919: Six Months That Changed the World* (New York: Random House, 2002) is the most significant recent account of deliberations in Paris. The most thorough international collection of essays on the Treaty of Versailles remains Manfred F. Boemeke, Gerald D. Feldman, and Elisabeth Glaser, eds., *The Treaty of Versailles: A Reassessment after 75 Years* (New York: Cambridge Univ. Press, 1998). For French security aims at Versailles and after, see especially Anthony Adamthwaite, *Grandeur and Misery: France's Bid for Power in Europe, 1914–1940* (New York: St. Martin's Press, 1995); Robert Boyce, ed., *French Foreign and Defence Policy, 1918–1940: The Decline and Fall of a Great Power* (New York: LSE/Routledge, 1998); Wm. Laird Kleine-Ahlbrandt, *The Burden of Victory: France, Britain, and the Enforcement of the Versailles Peace, 1919–1925* (Lanham, Md.: Univ. Press of America, 1995); and David Stevenson, *French War Aims Against Germany, 1914–1919* (Oxford: Clarendon Press, 1982). The myth of French "vindictiveness" toward Germany at Versailles has proven especially enduring in the United States. Even Costigliola, whose work often highlights the clumsiness of American cultural diplomacy and insensitivity to European concerns, portrays France as vindictive and determined to use reparations as a means of keeping Germany down in *Awkward Dominion: American Political, Economic, and Cultural Relations with Europe, 1919–1933* (Ithaca, N.Y.: Cornell Univ. Press, 1984), in spite of serious attacks against this view in the late 1970s from fellow American historians such as Sally Marks, *The Illusion of Peace: International Relations in Europe, 1918–1933* (London: Macmillan, 1976); Marc Trachtenberg, *Reparation in World Politics: France and European Economic Diplomacy, 1916–1923* (New York: Columbia Univ. Press, 1980); Stephen Schuker, *The End of French Predominance in Europe: The Financial Crisis of 1924 and the Adoption of the Dawes Plan* (Chapel Hill: Univ. of North Carolina Press, 1976); Charles S. Maier, *Recasting Bourgeois Europe: Stabilization in France, Germany, and*

Italy in the Decade after World War I (Princeton, N.J.: Princeton Univ. Press, 1975); and Melvyn Leffler, *The Elusive Quest: America's Pursuit of European Stability and French Security, 1919–1933* (Chapel Hill: Univ. of North Carolina Press, 1979).

34. Duroselle argues that American soldiers in France in 1917–18 who came in frequent contact with prostitutes formed the unfair stereotype that all French women in general were of loose morals (*France and the United States,* 117). Also see, for example, Byron Farwell, *Over There: The United States in the Great War, 1917–1918* (New York: Norton, 1999), especially chapter 14, "Venereal Disease." For examinations of Francophilia among African American troops and artists during and after World War I, see Arthur E. Barbeau and Florette Henri, *The Unknown Soldiers: African-American Troops in World War I* (New York: Da Capo, 1996); Michel Fabre, *From Harlem to Paris: Black American Writers in France,1840–1980* (Chicago: Univ. of Illinois Press, 1991); Tyler Stovall, *Paris Noir: African Americans in the City of Light* (Boston: Houghton, 1996), Tyler Stovall, "The Color Line behind the Lines: Racial Violence in France during the Great War," *American Historical Review* 103, no. 3 (1998): 737–69; and Mark Whalan, "'The Only Real White Democracy' and the Language of Liberation: The Great War, France, and African-American Culture in the 1920s," *MFS Modern Fiction Studies* 51, no. 4 (2005): 775–800.

35. John L. Balderson, "US Now Blamed for Ruhr Crisis," *Boston Daily Globe,* January 28, 1923, 15. See also Drew Pearson, "Ruhr Crisis Due to Politics, French Steel King Says," *Boston Daily Globe,* June 8, 1924, 66.

36. "A View of Germany," *Hartford Courant,* February 5, 1923, 8.

37. See, for example, Major General Henry T. Allen's *Boston Globe* column "My Rhineland Journal."

38. For a populist take, see Will Rogers, "How Rude of Us to Lend France Money!," *Hartford Courant,* August 15, 1926, C1. Similar arguments were advanced for a more erudite audience in Frank H. Simonds, "Europeans Are Drawing Together with America as Common Enemy," *Hartford Courant,* October 31, 1926, D2. Also see Edwin L. James, "The America that Europe Sees," *New York Times,* April 10, 1927, SM1.

39. Costigliola, *France and the United States,* 4.

40. For the best Kennedy biographies that avoid the "Camelot School's" deliberate lack of criticism, see Robert Dallek, *An Unfinished Life: John F. Kennedy, 1917–1963* (Boston: Little, Brown, 2003); Nigel Hamilton, *JFK: Reckless Youth* (New York: Random House, 1992); Seymour Hersh, *The Dark Side of Camelot* (Boston: Little, Brown, 1997); Doris Kearns Goodwin, *The Fitzgeralds and the Kennedys* (New York: St. Martin's Press, 1991); Barbara Leaming, *Jack Kennedy: The Education of a Statesman* (New York: Norton, 2006); Thomas Maier, *The Kennedys: America's Emerald Kings* (New York: Basic Books, 2003); Michael O'Brien, *John F. Kennedy: A Biography* (New York: Thomas Dunne Books/St. Martin's Press, 2005); Thomas C. Reeves, *A Question of Character: A Life of John F. Kennedy* (New York: Maxwell Macmillan International, 1991); and Gary Wills, *The Kennedy Imprisonment: A Meditation on Power* (Toronto: Little, Brown, 1982).

41. Joseph P. Kennedy, *I'm for Roosevelt* (New York: Reynal and Hitchcock, 1936).
42. Goodwin, *The Fitzgeralds and the Kennedys,* 512–17.
43. Maier, *The Kennedys,* 136.
44. Goodwin, *The Fitzgeralds and the Kennedys,* 516.
45. Wills, *The Kennedy Imprisonment,* 76–77.
46. Hersh, *The Dark Side of Camelot,* 61–63.
47. Leaming, *Jack Kennedy,* 21–24.
48. Dallek, *Unfinished Life,* 53–54.
49. Leaming, *Jack Kennedy,* 21–24.
50. John F. Kennedy, *Why England Slept* (New York: Funk, 1961).
51. Winston S. Churchill, *While England Slept: A Survey of World Affairs, 1932–1938* (New York: G. P. Putnam's Sons, 1938).
52. Reeves, *A Question of Character,* 49.
53. John F. Kennedy, *Why England Slept,* 50–51.
54. Ibid., 217.
55. Ibid., 218–24.
56. Wills, *The Kennedy Imprisonment,* 82.
57. See Allport's best known work, *The Nature of Prejudice* (Cambridge, Mass.: Addison-Wesley, 1954). Marilynn Brewer discusses contemporary views of his findings in "The Psychology of Prejudice: Ingroup Love and Outgroup Hate?," *Journal of Social Issues* 55, no. 3 (1999): 429–44.
58. Henri Tajfel's first major work on the subject was his influential article "Cognitive Aspects of Prejudice," *Journal of Biosocial Sciences* 25 (1969): 79–97.
59. Michael Billig, "Henri Tajfel's 'Cognitive Aspects of Prejudice' and the Psychology of Bigotry," *British Journal of Social Psychology* 41, no. 2 (2002): 175–76.
60. Stanley Allen Renshon, "The Role of Personality Development in Political Socialization," in *New Directions in Political Socialization,* ed. David C. Schwartz and Sandra Kenyon Schwartz (New York: Free Press, 1975), 37.
61. Christopher Endy, "Travel and World Power: Americans in Europe, 1890–1917," *Diplomatic History* 22, no. 4 (1998): 565–94.
62. Ibid., 571–72.
63. Ibid., 585.
64. Hamilton, *JFK,* 179.
65. Diary, European Trip, 1937, Personal Papers of John F. Kennedy (1917–1963), series 2, Early Years, 1928–1940, box 1, John F. Kennedy Presidential Library and Museum (hereafter JFKL), 4–5.
66. Ibid., 7.
67. Ibid., 8. American travelers to Italy and France frequently railed against poor standards of sanitary facilities there and the poor personal hygiene of the locals. Many viewed this as evidence that the "Latins" were not full members of the civilized community of nations, unlike Americans and Britons. See Endy, "Travel and World Power," 582–83.
68. Diary, European Trip, 1937, JFKL, 8.

69. Ibid., 11.

70. Ibid., 12.

71. Ibid., 14.

72. Ibid., 13. He wrote, "Went for a swim and then that night, after a cocktail party of Wilson's, played Boule—lost seventy francs. Was out with French girl. Their customs very strict requiring a chaperone until 21 or so."

73. Ibid., 15.

74. Hamilton, *JFK*, 194.

75. Ibid., 183.

76. Ibid., 199.

2. Building the Perfect Candidate

1. Valuable English-language additions to the French literature on the First Indochina War noted earlier include Lawrence S. Kaplan, Denise Artaud, and Mark R. Rubin, eds., *Dien Bien Phu and the Crisis of Franco-American Relations, 1954–1955* (Wilmington, Del.: SR Books, 1990); Mark Atwood Lawrence and Fredrik Logevall, eds., *The First Vietnam War: Colonial Conflict and Cold War Crisis* (Cambridge, Mass.: Harvard Univ. Press, 2007); Fredrik Logevall, *Embers of War: The Fall of an Empire and the Making of America's Vietnam* (New York: Random House, 2014); Martin Shipway, *The Road to War: France and Vietnam, 1944–1947* (Providence, R.I.: Berghahn, 1996); Statler, *Replacing France*; and Stein Tønnesson, *Vietnam 1946: How the War Began* (Berkeley: Univ. of California Press, 2009). For accounts of the French counterinsurgency in Algeria and the American view of the conflict, see Martin S. Alexander and John F. V. Keiger, *France and the Algerian War, 1954–62: Strategy, Operations and Diplomacy* (London: Cass, 2002); Jeffrey James Byrne, *Mecca of Revolution: Algeria, Decolonization, and the Third World Order* (New York: Oxford Univ. Press, 2016); Matthew Connelly, *A Diplomatic Revolution: Algeria's Fight for Independence and the Origins of the Post–Cold War Era* (New York: Oxford Univ. Press, 2002); Martin Evans, *Algeria: France's Undeclared War* (New York: Oxford Univ. Press, 2012); David Galula, *Pacification in Algeria, 1956–1958* (Santa Monica, Calif.: RAND Corporation, 2006); Constantine A. Pagedas, *Anglo-American Strategic Relations and the French Problem, 1960–1963: A Troubled Partnership* (Portland, Oreg.: Cass, 2000); Todd Shepard, *The Invention of Decolonization: The Algerian War and the Remaking of France* (Ithaca, N.Y.: Cornell Univ. Press, 2006); Benjamin Stora, *Imaginaires de guerre: Algérie, Viêt-Nam, en France et aux Etats-Unis* (Paris: Editions La Découverte, 1997); John Talbott, *The War without a Name: France in Algeria, 1954–1962* (New York: Knopf, 1980); Martin Thomas, *The French North African Crisis: Colonial Breakdown and Anglo-French Relations, 1945–62* (New York: St. Martin's Press, 2000); and Irwin Wall, *France, the United States, and the Algerian War* (Berkeley: Univ. of California Press, 2001).

2. For Vietnamese views of French rule, see the exhaustive Arthur J. Dommen, *The Indochinese Experience of the French and the Americans: Nationalism and Communism in*

Cambodia, Laos, and Vietnam (Bloomington: Indiana Univ. Press, 2001). Peter Zinoman's *The Colonial Bastille: A History of Imprisonment in Vietnam, 1862–1940* (Berkeley: Univ. of California Press, 2001) is a fascinating look at how draconian conditions in the colonial prison system stoked nationalist sentiment and unintentionally served as an institutional setting for revolutionary education. Relevant general studies include Nicola Cooper, *France in Indochina: Colonial Encounters* (Oxford, UK: Berg, 2001); J. P. Daughton, *An Empire Divided: Religion, Republicanism, and the Making of French Colonialism, 1880–1914* (New York: Oxford Univ. Press, 2006); Alec G. Hargreaves, ed., *Memory, Empire, and Postcolonialism: Legacies of French Colonialism* (Lanham: Lexington Books, 2005); John E. Dreifort, *Myopic Grandeur: The Ambivalence of French Foreign Policy toward the Far East, 1919–1945* (Kent, Ohio: Kent State Univ. Press, 1991), and Truong Buu Lam, *Colonialism Experienced: Vietnamese Writings on Colonialism, 1900–1931* (Ann Arbor: Univ. of Michigan Press, 2000). While the Fourth Republic has traditionally been viewed as weak and fractious—see, for example, Raymond Aron, *France: Steadfast and Changing: The Fourth to the Fifth Republic,* trans. J. Irwin and Luigi Einaudi (Cambridge, Mass.: Harvard Univ. Press, 1960)—newer interpretations are somewhat kinder. Works from Alan Milward and William Hitchcock have shattered illusions that weak and divided Fourth Republic governments meekly accepted American direction and by implication that de Gaulle later allowed his own wartime bitterness to dictate his foreign policy. Milward's *The Reconstruction of Western Europe, 1945–51* (London: Methuen, 1984) shows that Marshall Plan–era French governments proved surprisingly adept at thwarting American objectives and applied American aid in a fashion that better suited their own national economic agendas. Building on Milward's work, William I. Hitchcock argues in *France Restored: Cold War Diplomacy and the Quest for Leadership in Europe, 1944–1954* (Chapel Hill: Univ. of North Carolina Press, 1998) that the institutional weakness of the early Fourth Republic did allow for innovation and maneuver in policy-making, as political division inspired seemingly technocratic, apolitical solutions. He finds that there was a similar effect on French foreign policy, and that France was able to build consensus on regional stabilization that led to reconciliation with Germany on terms designed to suit France's economic needs. He believes that Fourth Republic governments crafted a more coherent and successful national recovery strategy than they were given credit for, reinforcing Milward's view that France was able to use Marshall Plan aid to pursue its own national interests. Generally concurring with this view are most notably Richard Vinen in *France, 1934–1970* (New York: St. Martin's Press, 1996); Tyler E. Stovall, *France since the Second World War* (New York: Longman, 2002); and Irwin Wall, *The United States and the Making of Postwar France, 1945–1954.*

3. For American relations with Tito's regime, see Henry W. Brands Jr., "Redefining the Cold War: American Policy toward Yugoslavia, 1948–60," *Diplomatic History* 11, no. 1 (1987): 41–54; Beatrice Heuser, *Western Containment Policies in the Cold War: The Yugoslav Case, 1948–53* (New York: Routledge, 1989); David L. Larson, *United States Foreign Policy toward Yugoslavia, 1943–1963* (Washington, D.C.:

Univ. Press of America, 1979); John R. Lampe, Russell O. Prickett, and Ljubiša S. Adamović, *Yugoslav-American Economic Relations since World War II* (Durham, N.C.: Duke Univ. Press, 1990).

4. John Fitzgerald Kennedy, *Prelude to Leadership: The Postwar Diary of John F. Kennedy,* ed. Hugh Sidey, and Deirdre Henderson (Washington, D.C.: Regnery, 1995), xiii.

5. Ibid., 58. There was no residual warmth for America's former wartime ally, the Soviet Union, in this diary. He wrote that "in many ways the 'SS' were as bad as the Russians" who had terrorized the civilian population with an orgy of stealing, raping, and looting.

6. Ibid., xl–xli.

7. Ibid., 11.

8. Ibid., 13.

9. For social conditions in France in 1944–45, see especially Anthony Beevor and Artemis Cooper, *Paris after the Liberation, 1944–1949* (New York: Penguin, 2004); Shannon L. Fogg, *The Politics of Everyday Life in Vichy France: Foreigners, Undesirables, and Strangers* (New York: Cambridge Univ. Press, 2009); Robert Gildea, *France since 1945* (New York: Oxford Univ. Press, 1996); and Rod Kedward, *La vie en bleu: France and the French since 1900* (London: Lane, 2005).

10. Kennedy, *Prelude to Leadership,* 41.

11. Ibid.

12. For French economic conditions at the end of World War II, see especially William James Adams, *Restructuring the French Economy: Government and the Rise of Market Competition since World War II* (Washington, D.C.: Brookings Institution, 1989); Frances M. B. Lynch, *France and the International Economy: From Vichy to the Treaty of Rome* (New York: Routledge, 1997); Alan S. Milward, *New Order and the French Economy* (London: Oxford Univ. Press, 1970); and Valérie-Anne Montassier, *Les années d'après-guerre, 1944–1949: La vie politique en France, l'économie les relations internationales, l'Union française* (Paris: Fayard, 1980).

13. Kennedy, *Prelude to Leadership,* 42.

14. John F. Kennedy, "Issues in the Defense of the West" address, February 6, 1951, Pre-Presidential Papers: House of Representatives (#2.1), series 2.2, Boston Office Speech Files, 1946–1952, box 95, JFKL, 1. Kennedy said, "The issue of whether and how Western Europe can be defended, with or without American aid, depends as everyone agrees . . . on the existence in these countries of a will to resist—a determination to build up within them singly and collectively forces that, together with such aid as we may supply them, have a reasonable chance of dealing with the threatened aggression from the East."

15. Ibid., 2.

16. Ibid., 4.

17. Ibid., 3.

18. Ibid., 4.

19. Ibid., 5.

20. Ibid., 4. Returning to long-standing American grievances about the nature of the French tax system, Kennedy stated, "The control of materials and the diversion of production into military channels has not really begun nor is it even being adequately planned. The tax structure, where only 15 percent of tax receipts come from direct taxation with the balance derived from hidden taxes, seems to slant away from bringing home to the public the burdens that a defense effort must entail."

21. Ibid.

22. Ibid.

23. Richard H. Immerman, "Introduction," in *Dien Bien Phu and the Crisis of Franco-American Relations, 1954–1955,* ed. Lawrence S. Kaplan, Denise Artaud, and Mark R. Rubin (Wilmington, Del.: SR Books, 1990), 1.

24. Ibid., 2. See, for example, Walter Lippmann, "Judgements and Prophecies: The Second U.S. Foreign Policy Failure of 1954," *Time,* September 13, 1954, http://www.time.com/time/magazine/article/0,9171,820155,00.html.

25. Schulzinger, *A Time for War,* 14. See also Walter LaFeber, "Roosevelt, Churchill, and Indochina: 1942–45," *American Historical Review* 80, no. 5 (1975): 1277–95.

26. Schulzinger, *A Time for War,* 13.

27. Ibid., 17.

28. Immerman, "Introduction," in Kaplan et al., eds., *Dien Bien Phu and the Crisis of Franco-American Relations, 1954–1955,* 3.

29. Mark Atwood Lawrence, *Assuming the Burden: Europe and the American Commitment to War in Vietnam* (Berkeley: Univ. of California Press, 2005), 286.

30. Immerman, "Introduction," in Kaplan et al., eds., *Dien Bien Phu and the Crisis of Franco-American Relations, 1954–1955,* 11–12.

31. Gary R. Hess, "Redefining the American Position in Southeast Asia: The United States and the Geneva and Manila Conferences," in Kaplan et al., eds., *Dien Bien Phu and the Crisis of Franco-American Relations, 1954–1955,* 125.

32. Ibid., 126.

33. Ibid., 140. Ilya V. Gaiduk argues in *Confronting Vietnam: Soviet Policy toward the Indochina Conflict, 1945–1963* (Washington, D.C.: Woodrow Wilson Center Press, 2003) that Stalin was wary of intervening in Vietnam during the Korean War era because past experience had shown that it was difficult for Moscow to control other Asian communist movements it had been involved with since the 1920s. After Stalin died, Nikita Khrushchev also tried to keep his distance from the region by deescalating the conflict with diplomacy. See Gaiduk's chapter 3 especially.

34. Statler, *Replacing France,* 1–2.

35. Ibid., 5.

36. Ibid., 4.

37. Ibid.

38. Ibid.

39. Ibid., 6.

40. Ibid., 5

41. In *American Tragedy,* Kaiser paints Kennedy as a moderate who courageously resisted the hawkish policy he inherited from Eisenhower and the national security establishment, arguing that the long-term roots of American intervention in Vietnam began with "Cold War policies adopted by the State and Defense Departments in 1954–1956 and approved secretly by President Eisenhower—policies that called for a military response to Communist aggression almost anywhere that it might occur, and specifically in Southeast Asia" (1). This does not accord with the position of Fred I. Greenstein and Richard H. Immerman, who argue in "What Did Eisenhower Tell Kennedy about Indochina? The Politics of Misperception," *Journal of American History* 79, no. 2 (September 1992): 568–87, that Eisenhower, while ambiguous, did not advise Kennedy to intervene militarily in Vietnam, but rather to make contingency plans for a unilateral intervention in Laos to prevent a communist takeover.

42. Logevall, *Choosing War,* 44.

43. Christopher E. Goscha, review of *The Road to War: France and Vietnam, 1944–1947,* by Martin Shipway, *Journal of Asian Studies* 57, no. 3 (1998): 922–23.

44. "Indo-China," undated, John F. Kennedy Pre-Presidential Papers: Senate Files (#2.3), series 6.8. General Files, 1953–1960, box 488, JFKL, 43.

45. Ibid., 1.

46. Ibid., 3. Kennedy copied this passage from Bao Dai's letter: "You have suffered too much in 4 mortal years, not to realize that the Vietnamese people, who have 20 centuries of history and a past frequently glorious, cannot and will not stand for any domination or any foreign intervention. You would understand this even better if you could see what is happening here, if you could feel the will for independence which smoulders in every heart, which no human force can repress."

47. Ibid., 5–6.

48. Ibid., 8.

49. Ibid., 17.

50. Ibid., 43. Emphasis in the original.

51. Ibid.

52. Ibid.

53. Ibid., 44.

54. Ibid., 62–63. Kennedy notes, "The [Vietnamese] left is communist because french [*sic*] policy has pushed the progressives into the communists [*sic*] arms. But the majority of Vietnamese are still the same peaceful moral people. Experience has proved that every time France or Viet Minh resorted to violence they have played the game their enemies wanted them to play. These people have grown up more in the past 10 years than they did in the preceding century. They want a new way of life—no foreign domination, no corrupt mandarinat [*sic*], no miserable living conditions."

55. Ibid., 63.

56. Ibid., 65.

57. "Indo-China: Mutual Security Act Amendment Speech," June 30, 1953, Pre-Presidential Papers: Senate Files, series 6.8 General Files, 1953–1960, box 481, JFKL, 4.

58. Ibid., 2.
59. Ibid., 2–3.
60. Ibid., 4.
61. Ibid., 5.
62. Ibid.
63. Ibid, 7.
64. Ibid, 10.
65. Ibid. Kennedy stated, "Unless the people of this area are assured that they are fighting for their own independence and not for the maintenance of French control when victory is won, all of our military assistance and all the French sacrifices of their youth and their treasure will go for naught."
66. Ibid., 10–13.
67. Ibid., 14.
68. Ibid., 14–15.
69. "Indochina Speech of 1954," April 6, 1954, Pre-Presidential Papers: Senate Files, series 12.1 Speech Files, 1953–1960, box 894, JFKL, 5.
70. Ibid., 3–4.
71. Ibid., 5.
72. Ibid., 6.
73. Ibid., 7–8.
74. "Remarks of Senator John F. Kennedy at Temple Emmanuel in New York City," November 19, 1957, JFKL, https://www.jfklibrary.org/Asset-Viewer/ZkLp-poxhHEySzBMYcAQM5A.aspx.
75. Stephen G. Rabe, *The Most Dangerous Area in the World: John F. Kennedy Confronts Communist Revolution in Latin America* (Chapel Hill: Univ. of North Carolina Press, 1999), 20–21.
76. Eugene Burdick and William Lederer, *The Ugly American* (Thorndike, Maine: Hall, 1994).
77. Dean, *Imperial Brotherhood,* 173. For example, Kennedy evoked *The Ugly American* during a campaign trail speech in West Virginia in which he decried the inadequacy of foreign language training in American schools. "Remarks of Senator John F. Kennedy at Athens, West Virginia," May 4, 1960, JFKL, www.jfklibrary.org/Asset-Viewer/UCNGR39I4EmDRUcWqql36w.aspx.
78. Freedman, *Kennedy's Wars,* 287–88.
79. Burdick and Lederer, *The Ugly American,* 105–8.
80. Ibid., 104.
81. Ibid., 99–100.
82. Ibid., 108.
83. Ibid., 107.
84. Ibid., 217–18.
85. Ibid., 177, 180.
86. Ibid., 216, 220.

3. *Masculinity and Modernization in Democratic Party Politics during the 1950s*

1. For good regional examinations of how gender politics shaped American foreign policy in other areas during this period, see Michelle Mart, "Tough Guys and American Cold War Policy: Images of Israel, 1948–1960," *Diplomatic History* 20, no. 3 (1996): 357–80; and Andrew J. Rotter, "Gender Relations, Foreign Relations: The United States and South Asia, 1947–1964," *Journal of American History* 81, no. 2 (1994): 518–42. More generally, see Carol Cohn, "Sex and Death in the Rational World of Defense Intellectuals," *Signs* 12, no. 4 (1987): 687–718; Frank Costigliola, "The Nuclear Family: Tropes of Gender and Pathology in the Western Alliance," *Diplomatic History* 21, no. 2 (1997): 163–83; Frank Costigliola, "Unceasing Pressure for Penetration: Gender, Pathology, and Emotion in George Kennan's Formation of the Cold War," *Journal of American History* 83, no. 4 (1997): 1309–39; K. A. Cuordileone, "'Politics in an Age of Anxiety': Cold War Political Culture and the Crisis in American Masculinity, 1949–1960," *Journal of American History* 87, no. 2. (2000): 515–45; Robert D. Dean, "Masculinity as Ideology: John F. Kennedy and the Domestic Politics of Foreign Policy," *Diplomatic History* 22, no. 1 (winter 1998): 29–62; Amy Kaplan, "Commentary: Domesticating Foreign Policy," *Diplomatic History* 18, no .1 (1994): 97–105; Emily S. Rosenberg, "Gender," *Journal of American History* 77, no. 1 (1990): 116–24; Emily S. Rosenberg, "'Foreign Affairs' after World War II: Connecting Sexual and International Politics," *Diplomatic History* 18, no. 1 (1994): 59–70.

2. Cuordileone, "Politics in an Age of Anxiety," 518.

3. For more on the EDC and its defeat, see Irwin Wall's aforementioned *The United States and the Making of Postwar France, 1945–1954*; Martin J. Dedman, *The Origins and Development of the European Union, 1945–95: A History of European Integration* (New York: Routledge, 1996); Edward Fursdon, *The European Defence Community, A History* (London: Macmillan, 1980); Daniel Lerner and Raymond Aron, eds., *France defeats EDC* (New York: Praeger, 1957); and Kevin Ruane, *The Rise and Fall of the European Defence Community: Anglo-American Relations and the Crisis of European Defence, 1950–55* (New York: St. Martin's Press, 2000).

4. Costigliola, *France and the United States,* 4.

5. Arthur Schlesinger Jr. later served as a special assistant to President Kennedy and earned a Pulitzer in 1965 for writing the most comprehensive early examination of the administration, *A Thousand Days: John F. Kennedy in the White House* (Boston, Mass.: Houghton Mifflin, 1965). For further elaboration on his worldview, see John Patrick Diggins, ed., *The Liberal Persuasion: Arthur Schlesinger, Jr., and the Challenge of the American Past* (Princeton, N.J.: Princeton Univ. Press, 1997).

6. Cuordileone, "Politics in an Age of Anxiety," 521. See Arthur M. Schlesigner Jr., *The Vital Center: The Politics of Freedom* (Boston, Mass.: Houghton Mifflin, 1949).

7. Cuordileone, "Politics in an Age of Anxiety," 523.

8. Dean, *Imperial Brotherhood,* 167.

9. Gareth Porter, *Perils of Dominance: Imbalance of Power and the Road to War in Vietnam* (Berkeley: Univ. of California Press, 2004), 2. For a thorough account of internal Democratic politics in the Kennedy era, see Sean J. Savage, *JFK, LBJ, and the Democratic Party* (Albany: State Univ. of New York Press, 2004).

10. As undersecretary of state and secretary of state under President Truman, Dean Acheson played a major role in developing the European Recovery Program, which anchored Western Europe to the United States, and the Truman Doctrine, which pledged hundreds of millions of dollars of economic and military aid to countries resisting communist pressure. Nevertheless, he was the frequent target of vicious attacks from Senator Joseph McCarthy for being "a pompous diplomat in striped pants" and "soft on communism." In retirement Acheson wrote several works reflecting on his role in shaping Cold War American foreign policy, the most notable of which is *Present at the Creation: My Years in the State Department* (New York: Norton, 1987). For biographies and examinations of his policies, see Robert L. Beisner, *Dean Acheson: A Life in the Cold War* (New York: Oxford Univ. Press, 2006); Douglas Brinkley, ed., *Dean Acheson and the Making of U.S. Foreign Policy* (New York: St. Martin's Press, 1993); Douglas Brinkley, *Dean Acheson: The Cold War Years, 1953–71* (New Haven, Conn.: Yale Univ. Press, 1992); David S. McLellan, *Dean Acheson: The State Department Years* (New York: Dodd, Mead, 1976); Ronald L. McGlothlen, *Controlling the Waves: Dean Acheson and U.S. Foreign Policy in Asia* (New York: Norton, 1993); and Gaddis Smith, *Dean Acheson* (New York: Cooper Square Publishers, 1972).

11. See Howard B. Schaffer, *Chester Bowles: New Dealer in the Cold War* (Cambridge, Mass.: Harvard Univ. Press, 1993); Chester Bowles, *The Conscience of a Liberal: Selected Writings and Speeches,* ed. Henry Steele Commager (Westport, Conn.: Greenwood, 1974).

12. Brinkley, *Dean Acheson: The Cold War Years, 1953–1971,* 57–58.

13. Gary W. Reichard, "Divisions and Dissent: Democrats and Foreign Policy, 1952–1956," *Political Science Quarterly* 93, no. 1 (1978): 51–72.

14. Ibid., 59–61.

15. John Kenneth Galbraith, *A Life in Our Times: Memoirs* (Boston, Mass.: Houghton Mifflin, 1981), 359.

16. Ibid.

17. Ibid., 106–7.

18. Brinkley, *Dean Acheson: The Cold War Years, 1953–1971,* 196. Acheson saw Kennedy as dangerously indecisive and Bundy, McNamara, Rostow, and Rusk as overrated, with George Ball and Paul Nitze being the only standouts.

19. Walter Isaacson and Evan Thomas, *The Wise Men: Six Friends and the World They Made* (New York: Simon and Schuster, 1986), 590–91.

20. Cuordileone, "Politics in an Age of Anxiety," 544.

21. Vinen, *France, 1934*–1970, 101.

22. John Newhouse, *De Gaulle and the Anglo-Saxons* (New York: Viking, 1970), 20–21.

23. Kenneth Moure and Martin S. Alexander, "Introduction," in *Crisis and Renewal in France, 1918–1962*, ed. Kenneth Moure and Martin S. Alexander (New York: Berghahn, 2002), 3.

24. Costigliola, *France and the United States,* 2.

25. Wall, *The United States and the Making of Postwar France,* 304.

26. "France: The Assassination," *Time,* September 13, 1954, http://www.time.com/time/magazine/article/0,9171,820157,00.html.

27. "Western Europe: The Death Struggle," *Time,* September 6, 1954, http://www.time.com/time/magazine/article/0,9171,820080,00.html.

28. Marquis Childs, "Stakes High, But Paris Is Apathetic," *Washington Post and Times Herald,* September 7, 1954, 16.

29. "The Death of EDC Has Left a Vacuum," *Hartford Courant,* September 9, 1954, 12.

30. William Henry Chamberlain, "Pall Over Europe," *Wall Street Journal,* August 30, 1954, 4.

31. "French Politics and the E.D.C.," *New York Times,* August 28, 1954, 14.

32. Wall, *France, the United States, and the Algerian War,* 57.

33. Thomas, *The French North African Crisis,* 211.

34. See Alan S. Rosenthal, "The Gender-Coded Stereotype: An American Perception of France and the French," *French Review* 72, no. 5 (1999): 897–908. This excellent short article connects historical and contemporary American gendered stereotyping of France.

35. Costigliola, "The Nuclear Family," 166.

36. Ibid., 169.

37. Ibid., 171.

38. Ibid., 173.

39. Ibid., 175.

40. Ibid., 176–77.

41. The most readable account of Kennedy's New Frontiersmen remains David Halberstam's *The Best and the Brightest* (New York: Random House, 1972), while Arthur M. Schlesinger's *A Thousand Days* stands out as the most notable work from an individual member of the administration. Theodore C. Sorenson, Kennedy's speechwriter, has recently added his memoirs, *Counselor: A Life at the Edge of History* (New York: Harper, 2008), though it sheds little light on Kennedy's dealings with Paris beyond adding that the president assumed the French had bugged his quarters during his spring 1961 summit with de Gaulle. For internal administration politics and evaluations of the New Frontier program, see Moya Ann Ball, *Vietnam-on-the-Potomac* (New York: Praeger, 1992); Irving Bernstein, *Promises Kept: John F. Kennedy's New Frontier* (New York: Oxford Univ. Press, 1991); James N. Giglio, *The Presidency of John F. Kennedy* (Lawrence: Univ. Press of Kansas, 2006); and Mark J. White, ed., *Kennedy: The New Frontier Revisited* (Basingstoke, Hampshire, UK:

Macmillan Press, 1998). For Kennedy's relationship with his brother and fellow New Frontiersman, Attorney General Robert Kennedy, see David Talbot, *Brothers: The Hidden History of the Kennedy Years* (New York: Free Press, 2007).

42. Dean, *Imperial Brotherhood,* 170.

43. Ibid.

44. Ibid., 179.

45. "Inaugural Address of President John F. Kennedy," January 20, 1961, Washington, D.C., JFKL, https://www.jfklibrary.org/Research/Research-Aids/Ready-Reference/JFK-Quotations/Inaugural-Address.aspx. Kennedy's 1961 inaugural address was one of the most memorable of the twentieth century, mixing conviction, idealism, and confidence.

46. John F. Kennedy, "Indochina Speech of 1954," JFKL.

47. Remarks of Senator John F. Kennedy, "The New Dimensions of American Foreign Policy," November 1, 1957, JFKL, https://www.jfklibrary.org/Asset-Viewer/6AEjsFjkJU6DYmIEvL0YTg.aspx.

48. Rusk's own account of his service under Kennedy and Johnson is *As I Saw It: Dean Rusk as Told to Richard Rusk,* ed. Daniel S. Papp (New York: Norton, 1990), while the best biography is Warren I. Cohen's *Dean Rusk* (Totowa, N.J.: Cooper Square Publishers, 1980). Also relevant are Thomas J. Schoenbaum, *Waging Peace and War: Dean Rusk in the Truman, Kennedy, and Johnson Years* (Toronto: Simon and Schuster, 1988); and Lawrence W. Serewicz, *America at the Brink of Empire: Rusk, Kissinger, and the Vietnam War* (Baton Rouge: Louisiana State Univ. Press, 2007).

49. These included chief of the U.S. State Department's International Security Affairs Division, special assistant to the secretary of war, director of the U.S. State Department's Office of U.N. Affairs, deputy undersecretary of state, and assistant secretary of state for Far Eastern affairs.

50. Cohen, *Dean Rusk,* 109.

51. Bruce Kuklick, *Blind Oracles: Intellectuals and War from Kennan to Kissinger* (Princeton, N.J.: Princeton Univ. Press, 2006), 133.

52. Galbraith, *A Life in Our Times,* 404.

53. Dean Rusk, "The President," *Foreign Affairs* 38, no. 3 (1960): 355–56.

54. John B. Henry II and William Espinosa, "The Tragedy of Dean Rusk," *Foreign Policy,* no. 8 (autumn 1972): 166.

55. Rusk, "The President," 366–68.

56. Dean Rusk, "The Bases of United States Foreign Policy," *Proceedings of the Academy of Political Science* 27, no. 2 (1962), 99.

57. Logevall, *Choosing War,* 35–36.

58. Rusk, *As I Saw It,* 240.

59. Before joining the Kennedy administration, McGeorge Bundy collaborated with Henry L. Stimson, Roosevelt's secretary of war, to write *On Active Service in Peace and War* (London: Hutchinson, 1949), and later produced *The Pattern of Responsibility: Edited by McGeorge Bundy from the Record of Secretary of State Dean Acheson* (Boston, Mass.: Houghton, Mifflin, 1952). After retiring from politics, he

gave lectures and wrote several books on general strategic and geopolitical issues, but did not directly address his role in the Kennedy and Johnson administrations. Notable biographies and examinations of his role as a policy-maker include: Kai Bird, *The Color of Truth: McGeorge Bundy and William Bundy: Brothers in Arms: A Biography* (New York: Simon and Schuster, 1998); Gordon M. Goldstein, *Lessons in Disaster: McGeorge Bundy and the Path to War in Vietnam* (New York: Times Books/Holt, 2008); and Andrew Preston, *The War Council: McGeorge Bundy, the NSC, and Vietnam* (Cambridge, Mass.: Harvard Univ. Press, 2006).

60. Kuklick, *Blind Oracles,* 133.

61. Dean, *Imperial Brotherhood,* 162.

62. Schlesinger, *A Thousand Days,* 208–9. For examples of McGeorge Bundy's early academic writing, see "The Test of Yalta," *Foreign Affairs* 27, no. 4 (1949): 618–29, and "November 1952: Imperatives of Foreign Policy," *Foreign Affairs* 31, no. 1 (1952): 1–14.

63. Kuklick, *Blind Oracles,* 135–36.

64. Schlesinger, *A Thousand Days,* 350–51.

65. Dean, *Imperial Brotherhood,* 198.

66. For biographies and individual examinations of his role as a policy-maker, see Paul Hendrickson, *The Living and the Dead: Robert McNamara and Five Lives of a Lost War* (New York: Knopf, 1996); McMaster, *Dereliction of Duty*; and Deborah Shapley, *Promise and Power: The Life and Times of Robert McNamara* (Toronto: Little, Brown, 1993).

67. McNamara applied his background in statistical analysis to measure the efficiency and effectiveness of American bombers, an experience he recounted in Errol Morris' Oscar-winning 2003 documentary *The Fog of War: Eleven Lessons from the Life of Robert S. McNamara,* DVD, directed by Errol Morris (New York: Sony Pictures Classics, 2003).

68. "Six for the Kennedy Cabinet," *Time,* December 26, 1960, http://content.time.com/time/magazine/article/0,9171,895133,00.html.

69. David K. Shipler, "Robert McNamara and the Ghosts of Vietnam," *New York Times,* August 10, 1997, SM30. In June 1997, McNamara took an unprecedented step for a former secretary of defense by traveling to Hanoi with a pair of retired American generals, a half dozen historians, and others to discuss the war with a delegation of former North Vietnamese officials, generals, and academics led by ex-Foreign Minister Nguyen Co Thach, who had unsuccessfully campaigned to normalize Vietnamese-American relations during the Reagan years. McNamara had publicly admitted that "we were wrong, terribly wrong" in his Vietnam memoir *In Retrospect: The Tragedy and Lessons of Vietnam* two years earlier. The conference was dominated by his acceptance that "each of us could have achieved our geopolitical objectives without that terrible loss of life" and that both sides had failed to capitalize on several opportunities to negotiate peace while McNamara was in office.

70. A prolific writer at all stages of his adult life, Rostow penned dozens of works on development economics and various other pet projects after he left politics. For

the best examinations of his role in the Kennedy administration, see Kimber Charles Pearce, *Rostow, Kennedy, and the Rhetoric of Foreign Aid* (East Lansing: Michigan State Univ. Press, 2001), and David Milne's *America's Rasputin: Walt Rostow and the Vietnam War* (New York: Hill and Wang, 2008).

71. Walt W. Rostow, *The Stages of Economic Growth: A Non-Communist Manifesto* (Cambridge, UK: Cambridge Univ. Press, 1971).

72. Halberstam, *The Best and the Brightest,* 44.

73. Freedman, *Kennedy's Wars,* 337.

74. Neil Sheehan et al., *The Pentagon Papers: As Published by the New York Times* (New York: Bantam, 1971). For Mansfield's transformation from Diem cheerleader in the 1950s to outspoken critic of Johnson's decision to go to war, see Gregory Allen Olson, *Mansfield and Vietnam: A Study in Rhetorical Adaptation* (East Lansing: Michigan State Univ. Press, 1995). For biographies and general accounts of his political career, see Louis Baldwin, *Hon. Politician: Mike Mansfield of Montana* (Missoula, Mont.: Mountain Press, 1979); and Francis R. Valeo, *Mike Mansfield, Majority Leader: A Different Kind of Senate, 1961–1976* (Armonk, N.Y.: Sharpe, 1999).

75. George Ball recounted his reservations over Vietnam in *The Past Has Another Pattern: Memoirs* (New York: Norton, 1982). The best secondary account is David L. DiLeo's *George Ball, Vietnam, and the Rethinking of Containment* (Chapel Hill: Univ. of North Carolina Press, 1991).

76. Schulzinger, *A Time for War,* 163.

77. Ball became very close to Jean Monnet during his time in Europe as a lawyer crafting trade legislation with the French government after the war, but he loathed de Gaulle for his challenge to deeper European integration. For all their disagreement over European issues, Ball at least recognized that de Gaulle had outlined his worldview in his memoirs and that his actions in office were largely consistent with his published writings. When it came to Vietnam, Ball and de Gaulle broadly agreed on major philosophical issues: that the country was of peripheral interest to the West, that American military intervention would not succeed where France had failed, and that large dollops of aid money were unlikely to be well spent by the Diem regime. However, subsequent elements of de Gaulle's European policy—such as rejection of the Multilateral Force (MLF) nuclear weapons sharing deal, the veto of British entry into the EEC, the withdrawal of French forces from NATO's integrated command—left Ball totally disinclined to risk his career by promoting the French president's position on Vietnam to the rest of the Kennedy administration.

78. Schulzinger, *A Time for War,* 176–77.

79. Freedman, *Kennedy's Wars,* 28.

80. Mark Peceny, *Democracy at the Point of Bayonets* (University Park: Pennsylvania State Univ. Press, 1999), 89.

81. Gerald S. Strober, *The Kennedy Presidency* (Lanham, Md.: Univ. Press of America, 1985), 413.

82. DiLeo, *George Ball, Vietnam, and the Rethinking of Containment,* 53.

83. Freedman, *Kennedy's Wars,* 32.

84. In recent years there has been fierce debate over the viability of Diem's regime. Revisionist scholar Mark Moyar argues in *Triumph Forsaken* that the overthrow of Diem was "by far the worst American mistake of the Vietnam War" (xvii). In his view, Diem knew Vietnam's political culture better than any American and governed appropriately under the circumstances. The real mistake was that Americans naively measured Diem against Western ideals that were totally incompatible with Vietnamese realities. Most contentiously, Moyar argues that the South could have bested the North on its own had Americans not interfered so deeply during the Diem years. Geoffrey Shaw makes similar arguments in *The Lost Mandate of Heaven: The American Betrayal of Ngo Dinh Diem, President of Vietnam* (San Francisco: Ignatius, 2015). James Carter totally rejects this line of thinking in *Inventing Vietnam: The United States and State Building, 1954–1968* (New York: Cambridge Univ. Press, 2008). It is his view that, "in reality, 'South Vietnam,' to the extent that it came into being at all, was a failed American invention" (13). He sees the failure of American state-building efforts despite substantial material and moral backing from Washington as the biggest problem related to the conflict in Vietnam. When this project failed to produce a viable state capable of conducting the war on its own, the United States felt compelled to intervene militarily on its behalf. A number of other historians working more closely with Vietnamese sources have taken a critical, but more sympathetic look at how Diem's ambitions for a nationalist social revolution fell short when confronted by postcolonial challenges such as industrial backwardness and overreliance on the United States. See, for example, Philip Catton's *Diem's Final Failure,* Jessica Chapman's *Cauldron of Resistance*, Edward Miller's *Misalliance: Ngo Dinh Diem, the United States and the Fate of South Vietnam* (Cambridge, Mass.: Harvard Univ. Press, 2013), and Geoff Stewart's *Vietnam's Lost Revolution: Ngo Dinh Diem's Failure to Build an Independent Nation, 1955–1963* (New York: Cambridge Univ. Press, 2016).

85. Christina Klein, *Cold War Orientalism: Asia in the Middlebrow Imagination, 1945–1961* (Berkeley: Univ. of California Press, 2003), 189.

86. For examinations of Kennedy-era modernization thinking on Vietnam, see Mark T. Berger, "Decolonisation, Modernisation and Nation-Building: Political Development Theory and the Appeal of Communism in Southeast Asia, 1945–1975," *Journal of Southeast Asian Studies* 34, no. 3 (2003): 421–48; Samuel Hale Butterfield, *U.S. Development Aid—An Historic First: Achievements and Failures in the Twentieth Century* (Westport Conn.: Praeger, 2004); Marc Frey, "Tools of Empire: Persuasion and the United States's Modernizing Mission in Southeast Asia," *Diplomatic History* 27, no. 4 (2003): 543–68; Nils Gilman, *Mandarins of the Future: Modernization Theory in Cold War America* (Baltimore, Md.: Johns Hopkins Univ. Press, 2003); Michael E. Latham, *Modernization as Ideology: American Social Science and "Nation Building" in the Kennedy Era* (Chapel Hill: Univ. of North Carolina Press, 2000); Michael E. Latham, "Ideology, Social Science, and Destiny: Modernization and the Kennedy-Era Alliance for Progress," *Diplomatic History* 22, no. 2 (1998): 199–229; and Jonathan Nashel, "The Road to Vietnam: Modernization Theory in

Fact and Fiction," in *Cold War Constructions: The Political Culture of United States Imperialism, 1945–1966,* ed. Christian G. Appy (Amherst: Univ. of Massachusetts Press, 2000).

87. Brian VanDeMark, "A Way of Thinking: The Kennedy Administration's Initial Assumptions about Vietnam and Their Consequences," in *Vietnam: The Early Decisions,* ed. Lloyd C. Gardner and Ted Gittinger (Austin: Univ. of Texas Press, 1997), 26–27.

88. Lawrence J. Bassett and Stephen E. Pelz, "The Failed Search for Victory: Vietnam and the Politics of War," in *Kennedy's Quest for Victory: American Foreign Policy, 1961–1963,* ed. Thomas G. Paterson (Toronto: Oxford Univ. Press, 1989), 224.

89. Schwab, *Defending the Free World,* 1–2.

90. Latham, *Modernization as Ideology,* 3–4.

91. Michael H. Hunt, *The American Ascendancy: How the United States Gained and Wielded Global Dominance* (Chapel Hill: Univ. of North Carolina Press, 2007), 208.

92. Ibid., 29.

93. Schwab, *Defending the Free World,* 7.

94. Ibid., 17–18.

95. Preston, *The War Council,* 76.

96. Freedman, *Kennedy's Wars,* 337–42.

97. Robert D. Schulzinger, "'It's Easy to Win on Paper': The United States and Vietnam, 1961–1968," in *The Diplomacy of the Crucial Decade: American Foreign Relations during the 1960s,* ed. Diane B. Kunz (New York: Columbia Univ. Press, 1994), 184–85.

98. Preston, *The War Council,* 77.

99. Ibid., 76–78.

100. Hunt, *The American Ascendancy,* 208.

101. Bassett and Pelz, "The Failed Search for Victory," 224.

4. Toward the First Encounter

1. The best general examinations of Kennedy's relationship with de Gaulle's France are Frank Costigliola's "The Failed Design: Kennedy, de Gaulle, and the Struggle for Europe," *Diplomatic History* 8, no. 3 (1984): 227–52; Mahan's *Kennedy, de Gaulle, and Western Europe*; and Pascaline Winand, *Eisenhower, Kennedy, and the United States of Europe* (New York: St. Martin's Press, 1996). Also see Douglas Brinkley and Richard T. Griffiths, eds., *John F. Kennedy and Europe* (Baton Rouge: Louisiana State Univ. Press, 1999); White's *Kennedy: The New Frontier Revisited*; Kunz's *Diplomacy of the Crucial Decade*; Paterson's *Kennedy's Quest for Victory*; and *Wilfried Loth, Europe, Cold War and Coexistence, 1953–1965* (London: Cass, 2004).

2. Respected British diplomat-historian Harold Nicholson in *The Evolution of Diplomacy* (New York: Collier, 1966) describes the "French method" that dominated

international relations from the era of Cardinal Richelieu in the seventeenth century to World War I as "courteous and dignified; it was continuous and gradual; it attached importance to knowledge and experience; it took account of the realities of existing power; and it defined good faith, lucidity and precision as the qualities essential to any sound negotiations" (99–100).

3. Stanley Hoffman, "The Foreign Policy of de Gaulle," in *The Diplomats, 1939–1979,* ed. Gordon A. Craig and Francis L. Loewenheim (Princeton, N.J.: Princeton Univ. Press, 1994), 231.

4. Josephine Brain, "Dealing with de Gaulle," in White, ed., *Kennedy: The New Frontier Revisited,* 160–61.

5. Phil Melling and Jon Roper, "Introduction," in *America, France and Vietnam: Cultural History and Ideas of Conflict,* ed. Phil Melling and Jon Roper (Brookfield, Vt.: Gower, 1991), 5–6.

6. Dean, *Imperial Brotherhood,* 179.

7. De Gaulle is undoubtedly one of the most fascinating political leaders of the twentieth century and, like Kennedy, has been the subject of dozens of biographies that range from highly critical to fawning. The best of this long list are Jean Lacouture, *De Gaulle,* 2 vols (New York: Norton, 1990–1992); Bernard Ledwidge, *De Gaulle* (New York: St. Martin's Press, 1982); Daniel J. Mahoney, *De Gaulle: Statesmanship, Grandeur, and Modern Democracy* (Westport, Conn.: Praeger, 1996); and Charles Williams, *The Last Great Frenchman: A Life of General de Gaulle* (London: Little, Brown, 1993). The author of several notable works on military strategy and geopolitics as an army officer in the interwar years, de Gaulle wrote *The Complete War Memoirs* (New York: Simon and Schuster, 1964), before returning to the presidency in 1958. He later added *Memoirs of Hope: Renewal and Endeavour,* trans. Terence Kilmartin (New York: Simon and Schuster, 1971), on the first four years of the Fifth Republic. Confidants and fellow travelers to leave their accounts of de Gaulle include: Pierre Maillard, *De Gaulle et le problème allemand: les leçons d'un grand dessein* (Paris: F.-X. Guibert, 2001); Jean Monnet, *Mémoires* (Paris: Fayard, 1976); Maurice Couve de Murville, *Une politique étrangère, 1958–1969* (Paris: Plon, 1971); and Alain Peyrefitte, *C'était de Gaulle,* 3 vols. (Paris: Fayard, 1994–2000). Edward A. Kolodziej's *French International Policy under De Gaulle and Pompidou: The Politics of Grandeur* (Ithaca, N.Y.: Cornell Univ. Press, 1974) stands out as the best work from the first generation of historians of de Gaulle's foreign policy, but W. W. Kulski's critical *De Gaulle and the World: The Foreign Policy of the Fifth French Republic* (Syracuse, N.Y.: Syracuse Univ. Press, 1966) is also notable even though it was published before the end of de Gaulle's presidency. Also relevant from this period are Edward L. Morse's *Foreign Policy and Interdependence in Gaullist France* (Princeton, N.J.: Princeton Univ. Press, 1973) and Simon Serfaty's *France, de Gaulle, and Europe: The Policy of the Fourth and Fifth Republics toward the Continent* (Baltimore: Johns Hopkins Press, 1968). The most significant of more recent works include Philip G. Cerny, *The Politics of Grandeur: Ideological Aspects of de Gaulle's Foreign Policy* (New York: Cambridge Univ. Press, 1980); Philip H. Gordon, *A Certain Idea of France: French*

Security Policy and the Gaullist Legacy (Princeton, N.J.: Princeton Univ. Press, 1993); Frédéric Bozo, *Two Strategies for Europe: De Gaulle, the United States, and the Atlantic Alliance,* trans. Susan Emanuel (Lanham, Md.: Rowman and Littlefield, 2001); and Maurice Vaïsse, *La Grandeur: politique étrangère du général de Gaulle, 1958–1969* (Paris: Fayard, 1998).

8. According to Gaullist mythology, de Gaulle neither wanted the Americans to accept his *directoire* proposal nor expected anything to come of it, but he needed a rejection to justify removing France from NATO's integrated command. French journalist Raymond Tournoux wrote in *La Tragédie du général* (Paris: Plon, 1967) that de Gaulle had confided to him, "I was looking for a means to get out of the Atlantic alliance and to resume a freedom of action which had been handed over by the Fourth Republic when it signed the NATO treaty. I therefore asked for the moon. I was certain they wouldn't give it to me. . . . But by not replying to my letter they enabled me to take measures to get out of the Atlantic alliance, which I couldn't have done if I hadn't first suffered this rebuff" (321–22). It is unlikely that the general was being completely honest with Tournoux on this point; if the *directoire* proposal was nothing more than a diplomatic ploy, he certainly would not have continued promoting it well into the second year of the Kennedy administration. Irwin Wall makes a compelling argument in *France, the United States, and the Algerian War* that de Gaulle believed France could retain Algeria if he secured Anglo-Saxon backing for a *directoire,* which was one of the main reasons why London and Washington rejected the proposal (169). In any event, the rejection of the *directoire* made clear to de Gaulle that he had little influence with Kennedy and should not expect even symbolic concessions from Washington.

9. Costigliola, *France and the United States,* 124–25.

10. Bozo, *Two Strategies for Europe,* 60.

11. See, for example, Newhouse, *De Gaulle and the Anglo-Saxons*; Brian Crozier, *De Gaulle* (New York: Scribner, 1973); F. Roy Willis, *De Gaulle: Anachronism, Realist, or Prophet?* (Huntington, N.Y.: Krieger, 1967).

12. Cerny, *The Politics of Grandeur,* 5.

13. Ibid.

14. Vaïsse, *La Grandeur,* 59.

15. Bozo, *Two Strategies for Europe,* xi.

16. Cerny, *The Politics of Grandeur,* 2.

17. Kaiser, *American Tragedy,* 89.

18. Jacobs, *America's Miracle Man in Vietnam,* 1.

19. Anne Sa'adah, "Idées Simples and Idées Fixes: De Gaulle, the United States, and Vietnam," in *De Gaulle and the United States: A Centennial Reappraisal,* ed. Robert O. Paxton and Nicholas Wahl (Providence, R.I.: Berg, 1994), 295–96.

20. Ibid., 307.

21. Logevall, *Choosing War,* 72.

22. The central argument of Peter Busch's *All the Way with JFK?: Britain, the US and the Vietnam War* (Oxford: Oxford Univ. Press, 2003) is that "Britain did

nothing to steer Washington away from the path that led to the Vietnam quagmire" (206) despite sharing much of de Gaulle's pessimistic outlook for the prospects of military intervention. Britain, by contrast, enjoyed privileged access to American corridors of power.

23. Lacouture, *De Gaulle,* 167.

24. Ministère des Affaires étrangères, *Documents diplomatiques français, 1961,* Tome I, *1er janvier–30 juin* (Paris: Impr. nationale, 1997), 581.

25. Ibid., 1:581–82. Alphand was not immune to the lure of lazy ethnic stereotypes, writing, "At one time, as a brilliant student of Harvard, he likes to study, surround himself with the most diverse and extensive advice, at another time, the reactions of an Irish politician reappeared so brusquely, without taking into account the multitude of opinions, sometimes contradictory that are presented to him generously, he acts without great reflection. During the Cuban affair that had been launched after extensive deliberation but on false intelligence, it seems to be that, in a few minutes, and under pressure from Mr. Stevenson that the president made the decision to forbid all support from American forces and to issue it officially . . . [via] a simple phone call from Mr. Stevenson without any consultation. These impulsive, confused moves contradict the necessity for serious studies of problems which should justify the proliferation of committees, study groups, expert missions created on all subjects."

26. In the early 1960s Adenauer was caught between rival attempts from Kennedy and de Gaulle to secure West Germany's backing for their respective vision of the Western alliance. Adenauer was torn, but ultimately chose Washington for the military protection it offered from the Soviet Union even though his instincts might have otherwise coincided with de Gaulle's. For relations between de Gaulle and Adenauer, see Oliver Bange, *The EEC Crisis of 1963: Kennedy, Macmillan, de Gaulle and Adenauer in Conflict* (New York: St. Martin's Press, 2000); Philip H. Gordon, *France, Germany, and the Western Alliance* (Boulder, Colo.: Westview Press, 1995); and Ronald J. Granieri, *The Ambivalent Alliance: Konrad Adenauer, The CDU/CSU and the West, 1949–1966* (New York: Berghahn, 2003).

27. Ministère des Affaires étrangères, *Documents diplomatiques français, 1961,* 1:612.

28. Ibid., 1:613.

29. Ibid.

30. Ibid., 1:614–15.

31. Ibid., 1:616.

32. John F. Kennedy, "letter to de Gaulle," February 2, 1961, President's Office Files (#3), series 9, Countries, box 116a—France Security 1961 (A), JFKL. It should be noted that this memo dates to within days of Kennedy's inauguration, indicating that it is reasonable to assume that he considered the commencement of an exchange of foreign policy ideas with de Gaulle a high priority.

33. On the UN's role in the Congo Crisis, see Trevor Findlay, *The Blue Helmets' First War?: Use of Force by the UN in the Congo, 1960–64* (Clementsport, Nova

Scotia: Canadian Peacekeeping Press, 1999); Eric Packham, *Freedom and Anarchy* (Commack, N.Y.: Nova Science Publishers, 1996); Eric Packham, *Success or Failure?: The UN Intervention in the Congo after Independence* (Commack, N.Y.: Nova Science Publishers, 1998).

34. John F. Kennedy, "letter to de Gaulle," February 2, 1961, JFKL, 1.

35. Ibid., 2.

36. Ibid., 3.

37. Ibid., 4.

38. Charles de Gaulle, "letter to John F. Kennedy," February 6, 1961, President's Office Files (#3), series 9, Countries, box 116a—France Security 1961 (A), JFKL, 1.

39. Ibid., 3.

40. Ibid., 2.

41. Ibid., 1.

42. Ibid., 2.

43. Ibid., 5.

44. Ibid., 4.

45. Ibid., 5.

46. Dean Rusk, "Suggested Reply to General de Gaulle," February 9, 1961, President's Office Files (#3), series 9, Countries, box 116a—France Security 1961 (A), JFKL.

47. Ibid.

48. McGeorge Bundy, "Memo for Mr. (Ralph) Dungan," February 10, 1961, President's Office Files (#3), series 9, Countries, box 116a—France Security 1961 (A), JFKL.

49. Alphand to ForMin, February 3, 1961, Ministère des Affaires étrangères, AM 1952–1963, USA, 356, "USA–France," 9-4-1, La Courneuve (hereafter COUR).

50. Alphand to ForMin, February 10, 1961, Ministère des Affaires étrangères, AM 1952–1963, USA, 356, "USA–France," 9-4-1, COUR.

51. Alphand to ForMin, February 23, 1961, Ministère des Affaires étrangères, AM 1952–1963, USA, 356, "USA–France," 9-4-1, COUR.

52. The best recent English-language survey of Laotian history is Martin Stuart-Fox, *A History of Laos* (New York: Cambridge Univ. Press, 1997). Somewhat dated but still useful examinations of Laos's relationship to the civil conflict in Vietnam are Arthur J. Dommen, *Conflict in Laos: The Politics of Neutralization* (New York: Praeger, 1971); and Norman B. Hannah, *The Key to Failure: Laos and the Vietnam War* (Lanham, Md.: Madison Books, 1987). For specific examinations of Washington's role in the country during the Kennedy era, see Jane Hamilton-Merritt, *Tragic Mountains: The Hmong, the Americans, and the Secret Wars for Laos, 1942–1992* (Bloomington: Indiana Univ. Press, 1993); William J. Rust, *So Much to Lose: John F. Kennedy and American policy in Laos* (Lexington: Univ. Press of Kentucky, 2014); Roger Warner, *Backfire: The CIA's Secret War in Laos and Its Link to the War in Vietnam* (New York: Simon and Schuster, 1995); and Edmund F. Wehrle, "'A Good,

Bad Deal': John F. Kennedy, W. Averell Harriman, and the Neutralization of Laos, 1961–1962," *Pacific Historical Review* 67, no. 3 (1998): 349–77.

53. L. D. Battle, "Memo for Mr. Ralph A. Dungan: Correspondence between the President and General de Gaulle," March 28, 1961, President's Office Files (#3), series 9, Countries, box 116a—France Security 1961 (A), JFKL.

54. The best accounts of Algeria's war for independence are Alistair Horne, *A Savage War of Peace: Algeria, 1954–1962* (London: Macmillan, 1977); and Talbott, *The War without a Name.*

55. Literally "black feet." The *pieds noirs* were French nationals living in Algeria, but they were a polyglot group drawn from all across the European half of the Mediterranean basin. They numbered just over 1 million in 1962, composing roughly 10 percent of the population of Algeria. Politically, they were dead set against independence and formed their own militias that perpetrated atrocities against the Algerian population, escalating the conflict. At the conclusion of the war almost all fled to metropolitan France—along with a smaller number of *harkis,* Algerian soldiers who had fought with the French against the rebels—where their political/economic impact has been likened to the arrival of millions of Germans from Central Europe to the Federal Republic of Germany in the late 1940s.

56. Dean Acheson, "letter to John F. Kennedy," March 19, 1961, President's Office Files (#3), series 2, Special Correspondence, box 27, JFKL.

57. Kennedy's friend and advisor John Kenneth Galbraith, then serving as the American ambassador in India, memorably observed that the Royal Laotian Army was "clearly inferior to a battalion of conscientious objectors from World War I." See John Kenneth Galbraith, *Letters to Kennedy,* ed. James Goodman (Cambridge, Mass.: Harvard Univ. Press, 1998), 70. Edmund Wehrle praises Kennedy for resisting pressure from his advisors to opt for a military solution, and instead using creative diplomacy to secure a cease-fire deal that brought relatively stability to the country for several years ("'A Good, Bad Deal,'" 350–51).

58. Charles de Gaulle, "letter to John F. Kennedy," March 26, 1961, President's Office Files (#3), series 9, Countries, box 116a—France Security 1961 (B), JFKL, 2.

59. Ibid.

60. Norman Hannah argues in *The Key to Failure* that the seeming compromise in Laos in 1962 was in fact a huge victory for Vietnamese communists that doomed the subsequent American war effort. The International Agreement on the Neutrality of Laos left communist forces in control of the border regions in southern Laos, an invaluable prize as the PAVN looked to expand its supply lines into South Vietnam. Gaining control over the government of Laos at this juncture was far less important to the communist cause than securing the Ho Chi Minh Trail and the ability to ratchet up operations south of the DMZ.

61. Walt Rostow, "Memo to the President of conversation with Habib Deloncle," March 26, 1961, President's Office Files (#3), series 9, Countries, box 116a—France Security 1961 (B), JFKL.

62. Ibid.

63. Ibid.

64. Walt Rostow, "Memo to McGeorge Bundy on meeting with de Gaulle, Part I," May 13, 1961, President's Office Files (#3), series 9, Countries, box 116a—France Security 1961 (C), JFKL, 1.

65. Ibid.

66. Ibid.

67. Ibid.

68. Ibid., 2.

69. Ibid.

70. In January 1961 discussions on Vietnam, Kennedy expressed skepticism that ramping up the military effort by having Washington pay for a twenty thousand-troop expansion to the South Vietnamese Army "would really permit a shift from the defense to the offense" in and of itself without a corresponding overhaul of the political landscape and a major public morale boost. See US Department of State, *Foreign Relations of the United States, 1961–1963,* vol. 1, *Vietnam, 1961* (Washington, D.C.: GPO, 1988), https://history.state.gov/historicaldocuments/frus1961-63v01/d4.

71. Ibid., 16, https://history.state.gov/historicaldocuments/frus1961-63v01/d16.

72. See James G. Blight and Peter Kornbluh, eds., *Politics of Illusion: The Bay of Pigs Invasion Reexamined* (Boulder, Colo.: Rienner, 1998); Trumbull Higgins, *The Perfect Failure: Kennedy, Eisenhower, and the C.I.A. at the Bay of Pigs* (New York: Norton, 1987); and Howard Jones, *The Bay of Pigs* (New York: Oxford Univ. Press, 2008).

73. US Department of State, *Foreign Relations of the United States, 1961–1963,* 1:31, https://history.state.gov/historicaldocuments/frus1961-63v01/d31.

74. Ibid., 1:37–39, https://history.state.gov/historicaldocuments/frus1961-63v01/d37, https://history.state.gov/historicaldocuments/frus1961-63v01/d38, https://history.state.gov/historicaldocuments/frus1961-63v01/d39.

75. Ibid., 1:42, https://history.state.gov/historicaldocuments/frus1961-63v01/d42.

76. Ibid.

77. Ibid.

78. Ibid., 1:13, https://history.state.gov/historicaldocuments/frus1961-63v01/d13.

79. Ibid., 1:42, https://history.state.gov/historicaldocuments/frus1961-63v01/d42.

80. Ibid., 1:43, https://history.state.gov/historicaldocuments/frus1961-63v01/d43.

81. It should be noted that American officers did seriously consider the efforts of France's Lieutenant Colonel David Galula, whose authoritarian methods had effectively pacified his sector of Kabylie during the Algerian War, after he moved to the United States in 1962 to take on a new role as a researcher at Harvard and began consulting for the Rand Corporation. Galula's most important works, however,

were published later in 1963 and 1964. See Galula, *Pacification in Algeria,* and David Galula, *Counterinsurgency Warfare: Theory and Practice* (Westport, Conn.: Praeger Security International, 1964). Brigadier General Paul Aussaresses, another veteran of World War II and Algeria, had the ears of a limited group of lower- and middle-ranking officers in the Kennedy-era military establishment after he took on a role as counterinsurgency instructor for the 10th Special Forces Group at Fort Bragg, North Carolina, beginning in 1961. As an intelligence officer in Algeria, Aussaresses oversaw a widespread, systemic, and deliberately brutal program of detention and torture of Muslim males that was completely incompatible with modern Western conceptions of human rights. Aussarresses felt that the United States could apply his model in Vietnam, but the American who translated his monograph on the Battle of Algiers acknowledges that his prescriptions were seen by his students at Fort Bragg as far too radical at this stage of the conflict. See Paul Aussaresses, *The Battle of the Casbah: Terrorism and Counter-Terrorism in Algeria, 1955–1957,* trans. by Robert L. Miller (New York: Enigma Books, 2002). Aussaresses died a publicly disgraced figure, stripped of his *Legion d'Honneur* and banned from wearing his military uniform, after giving shocking interviews late in his life with French and American media outlets in which he defended the use of torture during the Algerian War and advocated its use on al-Qaeda prisoners.

82. Walt Rostow, "Memo to McGeorge Bundy on meeting with de Gaulle, Part I," May 13, 1961, JFKL, 3.

83. Ibid.

84. Ibid.

85. US Department of State, *Foreign Relations of the United States, 1961–1963,* 1:60, https://history.state.gov/historicaldocuments/frus1961-63v01/d60.

86. Ibid. Johnson wrote, "In any event, if the present trend continues, there is the danger that the government will become a glittering facade. It will come to rest in the end, not on its people, but on a modern military establishment and an oriental bureaucracy both maintained for the indefinite future primarily by the United States Treasury. The power which is inherent in the ordinary Vietnamese people will be left to others to organize. In present circumstances, 'others' can only be the Communist Vietnamese since there is little promise that effective leadership will emerge from the noncommunist opposition to Ngo Dinh Diem at this time. If the point of no return in the present trend is reached—that is, if the preponderance of the people move from support of or at least acquiescence in the rule of the government to support of or acquiescence in the Viet Minh movement—a grave dilemma will be posed for our policies. Then, whatever aid we supply to the government to fight communism in the abstract will also be directed, in the specific, against the Vietnamese people. And if we use our own forces to help put down Communist rebellion in South Viet Nam we will also bear the onus of helping to put down the Vietnamese people."

87. Ibid.

5. *Drinking Sour Wine*

1. Costigliola, *France and the United States,* 121.

2. "John F. Kennedy," *Time,* January 5, 1962, http://content.time.com/time/magazine/article/0,9171,874369,00.html.

3. Sally Bedell Smith, *Grace and Power: The Private World of the Kennedy White House* (New York: Random House, 2004), 228–31.

4. On the German reaction, see Francois Seydoux to ForMin, April 4, 1961, Ministère des Affaires étrangères, AM 1952–1963, USA, 356, "USA–France," 9-4-1, COUR. For Britain's response, see Jean Chauvel (French Ambassador to Britain) to ForMin, April 4, 1961, Ministère des Affaires étrangères, AM 1952–1963, USA, 356, "USA–France," 9-4-1, COUR.

5. Elmer Plischke, *U.S. Department of State: A Reference History* (Westport, Conn.: Greenwood, 1999), 402.

6. Ibid., 409.

7. Bozo, *Two Strategies for Europe,* 47–48.

8. Andreas W. Daum argues in *Kennedy in Berlin* (Washington, D.C.: German Historical Institute, 2008) that "the use of symbolic politics was a decisive factor at critical moments in German-American relations in overcoming crises and maintaining the transatlantic bond between the United States and the Federal Republic" (9). President Ronald Reagan's famous June 12, 1987, speech at the base of the Brandenburg Gate, near the Berlin Wall, in which he implored, "Mr. Gorbachev, tear down this wall!" stands out to a slightly lesser extent than Kennedy's speech.

9. The Cuban Missile Crisis of 1962 had very nearly resulted in nuclear holocaust, prompting decision-makers in both Washington and Moscow to tone down their combative policies. In his June 10 commencement address at the American University in Washington, D.C., Kennedy reversed course and spoke in favor of détente with the Soviet Union, causing alarm in West Germany. The text of the speech can be found at John F. Kennedy, "Commencement Address at American University, June 10, 1963," Washington, D.C., June 10, 1963, JFKL, https://www.jfklibrary.org/learn/about-jfk/historic-speeches/american-university-commencement-address.

10. The treaty was designed as a sweeping gesture of Franco-German reconciliation. Politically, it established a framework for Franco-German consultation on issues of joint concern during biannual summits. The treaty also called for various cultural exchange initiatives to promote mutual understanding between the two countries.

11. The text of the treaty can be found in Christopher Hill and Karen Elizabeth Smith, *European Foreign Policy: Key Documents* (New York: Routledge, 2000), 62–65.

12. Daum, *Kennedy in Berlin,* 174.

13. Typical views from major dailies include Robert C. Doty, "The Man, the Monument Called de Gaulle," *New York Times,* May 28, 1961, SM10; Murrey Marder, "Kennedy Is Facing an Intransigent de Gaulle," *Washington Post,* May 28, 1961, E1.

14. “200,000 in Paris Give Kennedys Big Welcome,” *Washington Post,* June 1, 1961, A17.

15. Bill Henry, “Kennedy Turns on the Charm,” *Los Angeles Times,* June 1, 1961, B1.

16. “200,000 in Paris Give Kennedys Big Welcome,” *Washington Post,* June 1, 1961.

17. “Kennedy Flies to Paris,” *Chicago Tribune,* May 31, 1961, 1.

18. Mahan, *Kennedy, de Gaulle, and Western Europe,* 45.

19. Chalmers M. Roberts, “Kennedy Heaps Praise on Charles de Gaulle,” *Washington Post,* June 1, 1961, A1.

20. Ibid.

21. Mahan, *Kennedy, de Gaulle and Western Europe,* 7.

22. De Gaulle bluntly queried Kennedy, “Would you be willing to trade New York for Paris?” He and his countrymen painfully remembered that the United States had sat out two world wars until the latter stages, allowing France to be overrun before intervening in the most recent European conflict. Kennedy felt insulted by the insinuation that America’s response to a Soviet invasion of Western Europe would be less than total. Schlesinger, *A Thousand Days,* 350, 354.

23. Ibid., 357.

24. Journoud, *De Gaulle et le Vietnam,* 19.

25. Ibid., 46–49.

26. Ibid., 51.

27. Ibid., 96–97.

28. Ministère des Affaires étrangères, *Documents diplomatiques français 1961,* 1:674. American records of the conversation at the John F. Kennedy Presidential Library and Museum are much more condensed than the French account in *Documents diplomatiques français,* which makes an attempt to follow the flow of the conversation and paraphrase speakers as close to their original words as possible. All *Documents diplomatiques français* passages quoted in this work have been translated by the author.

29. Memos attached to these reports show that Arthur Schlesinger asked for the commentary from Cy Sulzberger, while McGeorge Bundy did likewise from Nicholas Wahl.

30. Cy Sulzberger, “Memo on General de Gaulle (to Arthur Schlesinger),” May 8, 1961, President’s Office Files (#3), series 9, Countries, box 116a—France Security 1961 (A), de Gaulle meeting, Part I, JFKL, 1.

31. Cy Sulzberger, “Memo on General de Gaulle (to Arthur Schlesinger),” May 8, 1961, JFKL, 1.

32. Ibid., 2.

33. Ibid., 8–9.

34. Ibid., 8.

35. Ibid., 20, 15.

36. Ibid., 4–6.

37. Ibid., 17.
38. Ibid.
39. Ibid., 18.
40. Ibid., 25.
41. Nicholas Wahl, *The Fifth Republic: France's New Political System* (New York: Random House, 1959).
42. Nicholas Wahl, "Conversation with General de Gaulle and the prime minister (to McGeorge Bundy)," undated (spring 1961), John F. Kennedy, President's Office Files (#3), series 9, Countries, box 116—France General 1961, JFKL, 1–3.
43. Ibid., 2.
44. Ibid.
45. Ibid.
46. Ibid.
47. Ibid., 3.
48. Christian Chapman, "Section I: SE Asia of President's Visit to de Gaulle, Paris, May 31–June 2 1961 Briefing Book," President's Office Files (#3), series 9, Countries, box 116a, JFKL, 1.
49. Ibid., 1.
50. Ibid., 2.
51. Ibid.
52. Ibid.
53. "President's Visit to de Gaulle, Paris, May 31–June 2, 1961, Talking Points," May 27, 1961, President's Office Files (#3), series 9, Countries, box 116a, JFKL, 1.
54. Ibid., 2.
55. Ibid.
56. Robert B. Rakove, *Kennedy, Johnson, and the Nonaligned World* (New York: Cambridge Univ. Press, 2013).
57. Alphand to de Gaulle, May 11, 1961, Ministère des Affaires étrangères, AM 1952–1963, USA, 356, "USA–France," 9-4-1, COUR.
58. No author, "Résultats du Voyage du Vice-Président des U.S.A. à Saigon (Remaniement Gouvernemental et Mesures Envisagées)," May 15, 1961, CLV, Vietnam Sud, 32-23-5, 76, January 1961–December 1961, COUR.
59. Lalouette to de Gaulle, May 25, 1961, CLV, Vietnam Sud, 32-23-5, 76, January 1961–December 1961, COUR.
60. "Talking Points Reviewing Conversations between President Kennedy and President de Gaulle," May 31, 1961–June 2, 1961, President's Office Files (#3), series 9, Countries, box 116a—France Security 1961 (D) de Gaulle Mtg. Part II, JFKL, 5.
61. Charles Lucet, untitled summary of JFK-de Gaulle meeting to European and NATO country embassies, June 3, 1961, Ministère des Affaires étrangères, AM 1952–1963, USA, 356, "USA–France," 9-4-1, COUR.
62. Ibid.
63. Geoffrey Warner, "Review: President Kennedy and Indochina: The 1961 Decisions," *International Affairs* 70, no. 4. (1994): 694–95.

64. Ibid.

65. Ibid., 696.

66. Ministère des Affaires étrangères, *Documents diplomatiques français 1961,* 1:674.

67. Ibid.

68. Ibid.

69. Ibid., 1:675.

70. Ibid. "France had been present in Indochina for a long time. President Kennedy recalls how she [France] decided to retire from there. If she still has a serious influence in Vietnam, Cambodia and in Laos, it is precisely because this influence no longer possesses a military character. Wanting to maintain influence and at the same time arming these countries are two contradictory goals. The populations think, in effect, that if the West arms their countries, it is to dominate them and the situation deteriorates immediately."

71. Ibid.

72. Ibid., 1:675–76. De Gaulle stated, "But South Vietnam, Laos, even Thailand are not realities, they are nebulous, invertebrate organisms. One should not engage oneself there too deeply. Without a doubt it is not easy to change policy, but it is not very difficult either on the condition of having the agreement of Mr. Nehru and of Japan. The favorable realities for the West, in the Indian Ocean and in the Pacific, are still considerable, but not in Southeast Asia, where the only favorable possibility is neutrality. The influence to conserve must not be military, but cultural, economic and technical like that of France. And, as well, one must not give these countries too much money that directly corrupts the government as well as the civil servants and creates unpopularity for the system as is the case in Vietnam."

73. Ibid., 1:676.

74. Ibid.

75. Ibid., 1:677–78.

76. Ibid., 1:677.

77. Ibid., 1:678.

78. Ibid.

79. Ibid., 1:679.

80. Charles de Gaulle, *Memoirs of Hope: Renewal and Endeavor,* trans. by Terence Kilmartin (New York: Simon and Schuster, 1971), 258

81. Ibid., 256.

6. *Making the Best of It*

1. Robert Kleiman and J. Robert Schaetzel, "French Affairs," June 1, 1962, General Records of the Department of State, Bureau of European Affairs Office of Political and Economic Affairs, RG 59, Alpha-Numeric Files 1948–1963, B.5D Canada-US trade area to C.3 de Gaulle Proposal 1962, Box 4, C3 De Gaulle Proposals 1962, NACP, 2.

2. CIA Briefing Packet, "Current Intelligence Weekly Summary of 18 May 1961," National Security Files, series 1, Countries, box 70A, France-General, JFKL.

3. See T. Michael Booth and Duncan Spencer *Paratrooper: The Life of General James M. Gavin* (New York: Simon and Schuster, 1994); and Buzzanco, *Masters of War.* Bohlen (1904–1974) was a Harvard graduate and Eisenhower-era ambassador to the Soviet Union. Under Kennedy and Johnson he served as special assistant to the secretary of state for Soviet affairs from 1960 to 1962 and later as ambassador to France from 1962–1967. See Charles E. Bohlen, *Witness to History, 1929–1969* (New York: Norton, 1973); and T. Michael Ruddy, *The Cautious Diplomat: Charles E. Bohlen and the Soviet Union, 1929–1969* (Kent, Ohio: Kent State Univ. Press, 1986).

4. "Meeting in the Cabinet Room (of John F. Kennedy, Ambassador Alphand, Malraux, Lebel and Bundy)," May 11, 1962, National Security Files, series 1, Countries, box 71, France-General, May 10, 1962–May 11, 1962, JFKL.

5. Statement by Senator John F. Kennedy on Balance of Payments, Philadelphia, Pennsylvania, October 31, 1960, http://www.presidency.ucsb.edu/ws/index.php?pid=74301.

6. "Memorandum of Conversation (between Bohlen, Bundy, Gavin, Murville, and Alphand at the Quai d'Orsay)," June 1, 1961, President's Office Files (#3), series 9, Countries, box 116a—France Security 1961 (D) de Gaulle Mtg. Part II, JFKL.

7. Ibid., 6–7.

8. The full text of the Taylor Report can be found at US Department of State, *Foreign Relations of the United States, 1961–1963,* 1:210, https://history.state.gov/historicaldocuments/frus1961-63v01/d210.

9. Lalouette to Couve, "Cinq ans d'experience americaine au Vietnam," September 17, 1960, CLV, Vietnam Sud, 32-23-5, 75, January 1958–November 1960, COUR.

10. Couve de Murville, "letter to Dean Rusk," June 7, 1961, RG 59, General Records of the Department of State, Records of Ambassador Charles E. Bohlen, 1942–71, box 18, Paris Foreign Ministers Meeting August 4–9, 1961, NACP.

11. Alphand to ForMin, January 23, 1961, Ministère des Affaires étrangères, AM 1952–1963, USA, 376, "politique extérieur," 9-5-0, COUR.

12. Ibid., 2.

13. Ibid.

14. Ibid., 3. He wrote, "A position of strength is certainly necessary since it is, for us, just as it is for the Russians, a question of paramount political interest. But it is more than that, for the very survival of the Atlantic Alliance and, consequently, the security of us all depend [*sic*] on the developments of a crisis in connection with Berlin."

15. Ibid., 2.

16. Ibid.

17. Ibid., 3.

18. Walt Rostow, "Memoradum for the Secretary of State," July 13, 1961, Confidential U.S. State Department Central Files, Vietnam: Internal and Foreign Affairs, 1960–1963, 59, Microfilm Rm., box 69, US-Relations with France 1960–1963, C92:

reel 3, NACP. Rostow explained his logic: "As I see it, the purpose of raising the Viet-Nam issue as a case of aggression is either to induce effective international action or to free our hands and our consciences for whatever we have to do. The optimum goal is to create a more persuasive deterrent position with respect to the Laos conference and Viet-Nam. At the minimum we put ourselves in a political position to salvage South Laos and save Viet-Nam with a more rational military plan than we now have."

19. Ibid.

20. "Address by Dean Acheson," July 25, 1961, President's Office Files (#3), series 2, Special Correspondence, box 27, JFKL, 1.

21. In early 1961, Kennedy overhauled Eisenhower's policy of massive retaliation to create a new flexible response doctrine that would allow the president to deploy conventional forces against the Soviet Union and its proxies rather than relying on total nuclear war. Kennedy had not abandoned nuclear deterrence, but he recognized that it was inappropriate in limited wars on the periphery. Europeans fretted that this shift indicated that Kennedy would not automatically come to their defense with America's full military weight in the event of Soviet attack. See John L. Gaddis, *Strategies of Containment: A Critical Appraisal of American National Security Policy during the Cold War* (New York: Oxford Univ. Press, 2005); Meena Bose, *Shaping and Signaling Presidential Policy: The National Security Decision Making of Eisenhower and Kennedy* (College Station: Texas A&M Univ. Press, 1998); Shaun R. Gregory, *Nuclear Command and Control in NATO: Nuclear Weapons Operations and the Strategy of Flexible Response* (New York: St. Martin's Press, 1996); and Jane E. Stromseth, *The Origins of Flexible Response: NATO's Debate over Strategy in the 1960s* (New York: St. Martin's Press, 1988).

22. Dean Acheson, "A Review of North Atlantic Problems for the Future," The Committee on U.S. Political, Economic and Military Policy in Europe's Policy Guidance to the National Security Council, March 1961, DNSA no. NH01131, JFKL, https://www.jfklibrary.org/asset-viewer/archives/JFKNSF/439/JFKNSF-439-001.

23. Ibid., 5–6.

24. Frank Costigliola, "The Pursuit of the Atlantic Community: Arms, Dollars, and Berlin," in Paterson, ed., *Kennedy's Quest for Victory,* 51.

25. Jeremi Suri, *Power and Protest: Global Revolution and the Rise of Détente* (Cambridge, Mass.: Harvard Univ. Press, 2005), 27.

26. "Address by Dean Acheson," July 25, 1961, JFKL, 2.

27. Ibid.

28. Ibid., 4.

29. Nicholas Wahl, "Memorandum on conversations with de Gaulle and Prime Minister Debré (to Ambassador Gavin)," National Security Files, series 1, Countries, box 70A, France-General, August 21, 1961–August 31, 1961, JFKL, 1–2.

30. Ibid.

31. De Gaulle was deeply shaken when Generals Maurice Challe, Raoul Salan, and others responded to Debré's secret peace negotiations with the FLN by

attempting a military putsch in April 1961. The coup quickly fizzled, but, echoing 1940, de Gaulle felt the need to give a televised address to the nation in uniform to urge his countrymen to resist the coup "by all means." French public opinion supported a negotiated settlement, conscripted soldiers had no interest in turning against the government, and local commanders in Oran and Constantine refused to go along with the plan.

32. Nicholas Wahl, "Memorandum on conversations with de Gaulle and Prime Minister Debré (to Ambassador Gavin)," National Security Files, series 1, Countries, box 70A, France-General, August 21, 1961–August 31, 1961, JFKL, 2.

33. The most comprehensive biography is John M. Taylor's *General Maxwell Taylor: The Sword and the Pen* (Toronto: Doubleday, 1989). General Taylor features prominently in Buzzanco's *Masters of War.* Also see Maxwell Taylor, *The Uncertain Trumpet* (New York: Harper, 1960).

34. Lansdale recounts his experiences in Southeast Asia in *In the Midst of Wars: An American's Mission to Southeast Asia* (New York: Fordham Univ. Press, 1991). For biographies, see Cecil B. Currey, *Edward Lansdale: The Unquiet American* (Boston, Mass.: Houghton Mifflin, 1988); and Jonathan Nashel, *Edward Lansdale's Cold War* (Amherst: Univ. of Massachusetts Press, 2005).

35. Taylor-Rostow Report, https://history.state.gov/historicaldocuments/frus1961-63v01/d210.

36. Moyar, *Triumph Forsaken,* 136.

37. Taylor-Rostow Report, https://history.state.gov/historicaldocuments/frus1961-63v01/d210.

38. Ibid.

39. Ibid. Specifically, the report called for the US government to:

> (a) Provide a U.S. military presence capable of raising national morale and of showing to Southeast Asia the seriousness of the U.S. intent to resist a Communist take-over.
> (b) Conduct logistical operations in support of military and flood relief operations.
> (c) Conduct such combat operations as are necessary for self-defense and for the security of the area in which they are stationed.
> (d) Provide an emergency reserve to back up the Armed Forces of the GVN in the case of a heightened military crisis.
> (e) Act as an advance party of such additional forces as may be introduced if CINCPAC or SEATO contingency plans are invoked.

40. US Department of State, *Foreign Relations of the United States, 1961–1963,* 1:211, https://history.state.gov/historicaldocuments/frus1961-63v01/d211.

41. Freedman, *Kennedy's Wars,* 324.

42. Ibid., 324–25.

43. US Department of State, *Foreign Relations of the United States,* 1:222, https://history.state.gov/historicaldocuments/frus1961-63v01/d222.

44. Ibid.

45. Ibid.

46. Ibid., 227.

47. Ibid., 236, https://history.state.gov/historicaldocuments/frus1961-63v01/d236.

48. No author, "La Situation en Extreme-Orient," September 29, 1961, Ministère des Affaires étrangères, Vietcong, *Asie-Océanie,* Conflit Vietnam, 90, "Positions des Etats Réunions de l'Otan (y compris dossier de la participation française," 1960–1964, COUR.

49. "Memoradum of Conversation (between Rusk, Ambassador Alphand, Barthelemy, Dean Brown, and Chalmbers B. Wood)," November 13, 1961, Confidential U.S. State Department Central Files, Vietnam: Internal and Foreign Affairs, 1960–1963, 59, Microfilm Rm., box 69, US-Relations with France 1960–1963, C92: reel 6, NACP.

50. Ibid.

51. Ibid.

52. Ibid.

53. Ibid.

54. James Gavin, "Embassy telegram (to Rusk)," November 17, 1961, Confidential U.S. State Department Central Files, Vietnam: Internal and Foreign Affairs, 1960–1963, 59, Microfilm Rm., box 69, US-Relations with France 1960–1963, C92: reel 7, NACP.

55. Ibid.

56. "Memorandum of Conversation (between Alphand, Ambassador Ormsby-Gore, Rusk, et al.)," December 6, 1961, Confidential U.S. State Department Central Files, Vietnam: Internal and Foreign Affairs, 1960–1963, 59, Microfilm Rm., box 69, US-Relations with France 1960–1963, C92: reel 7, NACP.

57. "Memorandum of Conversation (between Rusk, Gavin, de Gaulle and de Murville)," December 13, 1961, Confidential U.S. State Department Central Files, Vietnam: Internal and Foreign Affairs, 1960–1963, 59, Microfilm Rm., box 69, US-Relations with France 1960–1963, C92: reel 1, NACP. De Gaulle consistently refused the notion of negotiating with the Soviets while they were applying pressure on Western interests in Berlin because he viewed it as a reward for bad behavior.

58. Ibid.

59. Alexander and Keiger, *France and the Algerian War,* 151.

60. "Charles E. Bohlen, Oral History Interview," May 21, 1964, JFKL, 16, https://www.jfklibrary.org/Asset-Viewer/Archives/JFKOH-CEB-01.aspx.

61. Ibid.

62. "Herve Alphand Oral History Interview," October 14, 1964, JFKL, 9, https://www.jfklibrary.org/asset-viewer/archives/JFKOH/Alphand%2C%20H.E.%20Herve/JFKOH-HEHA-01/JFKOH-HEHA-01.

63. "Memorandum of Conversation (between Kennedy, Alphand, Malraux, Lebel, and Bundy in the White House)," May 11, 1962, National Security Files, series 1, Countries, box 71, France-General, May 10, 1962–May 11, 1962, JFKL.

64. Ibid.

65. Ibid., 8.

66. Ibid., 13.

67. Ibid., 11.

68. Ibid., 12.

69. Ibid., 14.

70. Benjamin C. Bradlee, *Conversations with Kennedy* (New York: Norton, 1975), 104.

71. James Gavin, "Embassy Telegram (to Dean Rusk)," March 22, 1961, National Security Files, series 1, Countries, box 70A, France-General, January 20, 1961–March 15, 1961, JFKL.

72. James Gavin, "Embassy Telegram (to Dean Rusk)," May 31, 1961, Confidential U.S. State Department Central Files, Vietnam: Internal and Foreign Affairs, 1960–1963, 59, Microfilm Rm., box 69, US-Relations with France 1960–1963, C92: reel 4, NACP.

73. James Gavin, "Embassy Telegram (to Dean Rusk)," May 10, 1962 (8:45 P.M.), National Security Files, series 1, Countries, box 71, France-General, JFKL; James Gavin, "Embassy Telegram (to Dean Rusk)," May 10, 1962 (9:22 P.M.), National Security Files, series 1, Countries, box 71, France-General, JFKL.

74. John F. Kennedy, "Memo for James Gavin," May 18, 1962, National Security Files, series 1, Countries, box 71, France-General, JFKL.

75. James Gavin, "Embassy Telegram (to Dean Rusk)," May 28, 1962 (10:20 A.M.), National Security Files, series 1, Countries, box 71, France-General, JFKL.

76. Ibid.

77. James Gavin, "Embassy Telegram (to Dean Rusk)," May 28, 1962 (2:07 P.M.), National Security Files, series 1, Countries, box 71, France-General, JFKL.

78. James Gavin, "Embassy Telegram (to Dean Rusk)," September 6, 1962 (4:56 P.M.), National Security Files, series 1, Countries, box 71, France-General, JFKL, 1–2.

79. Sullivan, *France's Vietnam Policy,* introduction, xi.

80. Torikata, "Reexamining de Gaulle's Peace Initiative on the Vietnam War," 912.

81. Eugenie Blang, *Allies at Odds: America, Europe, and Vietnam, 1961–1968* (Lanham, Md.: Rowman and Littlefield, 2011), 4.

82. Journoud, *De Gaulle et le Vietnam,* 26.

83. Douglas J. Snyder, "'Fantastic and Absurd Utterances': The Vietnam War and Misperception of Anti-Americanism in US-French Relations, 1966–1967," *Journal of Transatlantic Studies,* no. 1 (March 2012): 84–103.

84. McGeorge Bundy, "Memo for the President," May 28, 1962, National Security Files, series 1, Countries, box 71, France-General, JFKL, 1.

85. Ibid.

86. Ibid., 4. Harriman's second memo, originally written in 1960, added to the myth of Gaullist intransigence by noting that in December 1944 an exceedingly stubborn de Gaulle forced Stalin, who had had considerably more bargaining lever-

age, to abandon his demands that France recognize the communist "Lublin Poles" as the official government of Poland. At this point the Red Army was already occupying the eastern suburbs of Warsaw and the future composition of the Polish government was largely beyond the control of any of the Western Allies. Harriman meant to imply that de Gaulle was so obstinate that he was willing to comprise his greater strategic desire for Franco-Russian domination of Europe for a pointless gesture of solidarity toward the Polish government-in-exile in London.

87. "US-French Exploratory Talks," May 28, 1962, National Security Files, series 1, Countries, box 71, France-General, JFKL, 2–3.

88. Ibid.

89. Ministère des Affaires étrangères, *Documents diplomatiques français 1962,* Tome I, *1er janvier–30 juin* (Paris: Impr. nationale, 1998), 605–46.

90. Robert Kleiman and J. Robert Schaetzel, "French Affairs," June 1, 1962, General Records of the Department of State, Bureau of European Affairs Office of Political and Economic Affairs, RG 59, Alpha-Numeric Files 1948–1963, B.5D Canada-US trade area to C.3 de Gaulle Proposal 1962, box 4, C3 De Gaulle Proposals 1962, NACP, 2.

7. Ignoring Nosey Charlie

1. See Logevall, "De Gaulle, Neutralization, and American Involvement in Vietnam, 1963–1964," 78, and Sullivan, *France's Vietnam Policy,* 20–22.

2. De Gaulle's European platform is laid out in great detail in all of the major works on his foreign policy and biographies. See especially Bozo's *Two Strategies for Europe,* Mahan's *Kennedy, de Gaulle and Western Europe,* and Vaïsse's *La Grandeur,* as well as Garret Martin's solo effort, *General de Gaulle's Cold War: Challenging American Hegemony, 1963–68* (New York: Berghahn, 2013), and his coedited volume with Christian Nuenlist and Anna Locher, *Globalizing de Gaulle: International Perspectives on French Foreign Policy, 1958–1969* (Lanham, Md.: Lexington Books, 2010).

3. On the Partial Test Ban Treaty, see Paul Boyer, *Fallout: A Historian Reflects on America's Half-Century Encounter with Nuclear Weapons* (Columbus: Ohio State Univ. Press, 1998); Benjamin P. Greene, *Eisenhower, Science Advice, and the Nuclear Test-Ban Debate, 1945–1963* (Palo Alto, Calif.: Stanford Univ. Press, 2007); Kendrick Oliver, *Kennedy, Macmillan and the Nuclear Test-Ban Debate, 1961–63* (New York: St. Martin's Press, 1997); Glenn T. Seaborg, *Kennedy, Khrushchev, and the Test Ban* (Berkeley: Univ. of California Press, 1981); David Tal, *The American Nuclear Disarmament Dilemma, 1945–1963* (Syracuse, N.Y.: Syracuse Univ. Press, 2008); and Andreas Wenger and Marcel Gerber, "John F. Kennedy and the Limited Test Ban Treaty: A Case Study of Presidential Leadership," *Presidential Studies Quarterly* 29, no. 2 (1999): 460–87.

4. Arthur M. Schlesinger, *Robert Kennedy and His Times* (New York: Ballantine, 1979), 718.

5. No author, "Politique americaine au Vietnam," February 10, 1962, CLV, Vietnam Sud, 32-23-5, 77, January 1962–December 1962, COUR.

6. Lalouette to ForMin, May 9, 1962, CLV, Vietnam Sud, 32-23-5, 77, January 1962–December 1962, COUR.

7. No author, "Situation au Sud Vietnam," February 14, 1962, CLV, Vietnam Sud, 32-23-5, 77, January 1962–December 1962, COUR.

8. Alphand to ForMin, July 25, 1962, CLV, Vietnam Sud, 32-23-5, 77, January 1962–December 1962, COUR.

9. Journoud, *De Gaulle et le Vietnam,* 56, 84–87.

10. Mieczysław Maneli, *War of the Vanquished,* trans. Maria de Görgey (New York: Harper and Row, 1971), 118–25.

11. Jacobs, *Cold War Mandarin,* 86.

12. Frederick Nolting, *From Trust to Tragedy: The Political Memoirs of Frederick Nolting, Kennedy's Ambassador to Diem's Vietnam* (New York: Praeger, 1988), 100–101.

13. See Miller, *Misalliance,* 43; Chapman, *Cauldron of Resistance,* 52.

14. Miller, *Misalliance,* 44.

15. Ibid., 48.

16. Jacobs, *Cold War Mandarin,* 86.

17. David P. Chandler, *The Tragedy of Cambodian History: Politics, War, and Revolution since 1945* (New Haven, Conn.: Yale Univ. Press, 1991), 140.

18. Ellen Hammer, *A Death in November: America in Vietnam, 1963* (New York: Oxford Univ. Press, 1987), 167–68.

19. On Buddhist resistance to the Diem regime, see Mark Moyar, "Political Monks: The Militant Buddhist Movement during the Vietnam War," *Modern Asian Studies* 38, no. 4 (2004): 749–84; Robert J. Topmiller, *The Lotus Unleashed: The Buddhist Peace Movement in South Vietnam, 1964–1966* (Lexington: Univ. Press of Kentucky, 2006); and Robert J. Topmiller, "Struggling for Peace: South Vietnamese Buddhist Women and Resistance to the Vietnam War," *Journal of Women's History* 17, no. 3 (2005): 133–57.

20. Many of the documents concerning the administration's response to de Gaulle's statement at the National Archives in College Park, Maryland, remain classified. In the summer of 2007, I filed a Freedom of Information Act request that was acknowledged in writing the following year, but I never received any further indication as to whether permission to view these documents would be granted. I made a follow-up request in 2017 that similarly died on the vine.

21. Logevall, *Choosing War,* 2–3. De Gaulle unfortunately makes no mention of his August statement on Vietnam in *Memoirs of Hope: Renewal and Endeavor.*

22. McGeorge Bundy, "Draft Statement on South Vietnam for Cronkite Interview (to Kennedy)," September 1, 1963, National Security Files, series 1, Countries, box 199, Vietnam-General, September 1, 1963–September 10, 1963, State Cables, Memos and Misc, JFKL.

23. "Transcript: interview between President Kennedy and Walter Cronkite (CBS)," September 2, 1963, National Security Files, series 1, Countries, box 199, Vietnam-General, September 1, 1963–September 10, 1963, State Cables, Memos and Misc, JFKL.

24. US Department of State, *Foreign Relations of the United States,* 4:54, https://history.state.gov/historicaldocuments/frus1961-63v04/d54.

25. Strober, *The Kennedy Presidency,* 413.

26. US Department of State, *Foreign Relations of the United States, 1961–1963,* vol. 2, *Vietnam, 1962* (Washington, D.C.: GPO, 1990), 330, https://history.state.gov/historicaldocuments/frus1961-63v02/d330.

27. Chester Bowles, "Memo to the president," June 13, 1962, President's Office Files (#3), series 2, Special Correspondence, box 28, JFKL.

28. Ibid.

29. Ibid.

30. Ibid.

31. Ibid.

32. Ibid.

33. US Department of State, *Foreign Relations of the United States, 1961–1963,* 2:241, https://history.state.gov/historicaldocuments/frus1961-63v02/d241. Chester Bowles, "Memo to Dean Rusk," July 18, 1962, President's Office Files (#3), series 2, Special Correspondence, box 28, JFKL.

34. US Department of State, *Foreign Relations of the United States, 1961–1963,* 2:253, https://history.state.gov/historicaldocuments/frus1961-63v02/d253.

35. Ibid.

36. US Department of State, *Foreign Relations of the United States, 1961–1963,* 2:267, https://history.state.gov/historicaldocuments/frus1961-63v02/d267.

37. Ibid.

38. Chester Bowles, "Memorandum to the President," December 1, 1962, President's Office Files (#3), series 2, Special Correspondence, box 28, JFKL.

39. Mike Mansfield, "Commencement address at Michigan State University," June 10, 1962, President's Office Files (#3), series 2, Special Correspondence, box 31, JFKL.

40. Ibid. This was exactly the scenario de Gaulle had warned Kennedy against during the Paris summit.

41. Ibid.

42. Ibid.

43. Mike Mansfield, "Report on South Vietnam (to Kennedy)," December 18, 1962, President's Office Files (#3), series 2, Special Correspondence, box 31, JFKL.

44. For planning and implementation of the program, see Philip E. Catton, "Counter-Insurgency and Nation Building: The Strategic Hamlet Programme in South Vietnam, 1961–1963," *International History Review* 21, no. 4 (1999): 918–40.

45. Mike Mansfield, "Report on South Vietnam (to Kennedy)," December 18, 1962, JFKL.

46. Ibid.

47. Ibid.

48. The official French number of casualties was 350,000, while the FLN figured it to be closer to 1 million. Alistair Horne settles on 700,000 in *A Savage War of Peace.*

49. In *France, the United States, and the Algerian War,* Irwin Wall challenges the dominant Gaullist account that de Gaulle nobly and skillfully brought the conflict to a close, arguing instead that he initially hoped to retain some form of French control over Algeria. This would establish Paris as a major Mediterranean/African power and present France on a more equal footing with Britain and the United States. The election of Kennedy, a longtime foe of French colonialism, forced de Gaulle to give up this ambition and reluctantly accept Algerian independence. In any event, the Algerian War had been a mostly internal conflict for France, separate from other elements of the Cold War. Even if the settlement had not been entirely satisfying to the political right, the vast majority of French opinion took great relief that the long, draining period of colonial wars that had begun in 1945 had finally drawn to a close. Free of the Algerian burden, de Gaulle was able to begin rebuilding the national confidence necessary for France to assume its desired role as a major global player. As the man who had finally brought peace where a generation of politicians of all stripes had failed, de Gaulle had accumulated a considerable amount of political capital at home and abroad, establishing himself as a voice of authority on Third World conflicts.

50. Sullivan, *France's Vietnam Policy,* 5.

51. Ibid., 20.

52. Ibid., 21–22. De Gaulle had long been eager to restore diplomatic relations with the People's Republic, but he held off until January 1964 out of respect for wartime colleague Chiang Kai-shek, then president of Taiwan. France was the first major Western country to establish ambassadorial relations with Mao's China, and de Gaulle is still widely respected in present-day China.

53. Costigliola, "Kennedy, the European Allies, and the Failure to Consult," 107.

54. Ibid, 112.

55. Walter Lippmann, "Today and Tomorrow . . . The Agitated Alliance," *Washington Post,* December 20, 1962, A25.

56. Costigliola, "Kennedy, the European Allies, and the Failure to Consult," 113.

57. David DiLeo, "George Ball and the Revisionists in the State Department," in Brinkley and Griffiths, eds., *John F. Kennedy and Europe,* 273–74.

58. Costigliola, *France and the United States,* 129.

59. Paterson, ed., *Kennedy's Quest for Victory,* 49.

60. Peter Mangold, *The Almost Impossible Ally: Harold Macmillan and Charles de Gaulle* (London: Tauris, 2006), 171.

61. Andrew Moravcsik took on a provocative revisionist stance in *The Choice for Europe: Social Purpose and State Power from Messina to Maastricht* (London: Routledge/UCL Press, 1998), arguing that de Gaulle's veto was the product of commercial—not political—factors, just as de Gaulle publicly stated. He expanded on this position in "De Gaulle between Grain and Grandeur: The Political Economy of French EC Policy, 1958–1970 (Part 1)," *Journal of Cold War Studies* 2, no. 2 (2000): 3–43, and "De Gaulle between Grain and Grandeur: The Political Economy of French EC Policy, 1958–1970 (Part 2)," *Journal of Cold War Studies* 2, no. 3 (2000): 4–68. Robert H. Lieshout, Mathieu L. L. Segers, and Anna M. van der Vleuten dissected his work in "De Gaulle, Moravcsik, and *The Choice for Europe*: Soft Sources, Weak Evidence," *Journal of Cold War Studies* 6, no. 4 (2004): 89–139, arguing that Moravcsik misread two key documents on which his entire argument depends and generally failed to produce sufficient direct evidence that agricultural matters were de Gaulle's foremost concern regarding potential British EEC membership.

62. Harrison, *The Reluctant Ally,* 80.

63. US Department of State, *Foreign Relations of the United States, 1961–1963,* vol. 8, *National Security Policy* (Washington, D.C.: GPO, 1996), 125, https://history.state.gov/historicaldocuments/frus1961-63v08.

64. Ibid.

65. Suri, *Power and Protest,* 27.

66. US Department of State, *Foreign Relations of the United States, 1961–1963,* vol. 15, *Berlin Crisis, 1962–1963* (Washington, D.C.: GPO, 1994), 174, https://history.state.gov/historicaldocuments/frus1961-63v15/d174.

67. Ibid.

68. US Department of State, *Foreign Relations of the United States, 1961–1963,* 15:175, https://history.state.gov/historicaldocuments/frus1961-63v15/d175.

69. Ibid., 176.

70. Ibid.

71. Arthur Schlesinger Jr., "Memorandum for the president re: de Gaulle," January 29, 1963, The Personal Papers of Arthur Schlesinger Jr., box WH-34—France General, September 1961–October 1963, JFKL.

72. Ibid.

73. Ibid.

74. "Review of French Policy (between Kennedy, de Murville, et al.)," May 25, 1963, National Security Files, series 1, Countries, box 72A, France-General, JFKL.

75. Ibid.

76. See Lalouette to Couve, "Situation Politique au Vietnam (mois de janvier 1963)," January 30, 1963, C.L.V. Sud-Vietnam, 32-29, 145, January–March 1963, COUR; Lalouette to Couve, "Situation Politique au Vietnam (mois de fevrier 1963)," February 28, 1963, C.L.V. Sud-Vietnam, 32-29, 145, January–March 1963, COUR; and Lalouette to Couve, "Situation Politique au Vietnam (mois d'avril 1963)," April 30, 1963, C.L.V. Sud-Vietnam, 32-29, 146, April–July 1963, COUR.

77. John F. Kennedy, "Commencement Address at American University, 10 June 1963," https://www.jfklibrary.org/Asset-Viewer/BWC7I4C9QUmLG9J6I8oy8w.aspx.

78. Seymour Topping, "Russians Stirred by Kennedy Talk about Cold War," *New York Times,* June 13, 1963, 1.

79. Thomas G. Paterson, *Contesting Castro: The United States and the Triumph of the Cuban Revolution* (New York: Oxford Univ. Press, 1995), 261.

80. Journoud, *De Gaulle et le Vietnam,* 107.

81. No author, "Perspectives actuelles de la guerre du Vietnam," March 26, 1963, CLV, Vietnam Sud, 32-3-7, 28, January 1963–November 1964, COUR.

82. Telegram from the embassy in Vietnam to the Department of State, March 28, 1963, US Department of State, *Foreign Relations of the United States, 1961–1963,* vol. 3, *Vietnam, January–August 1963,* https://history.state.gov/historicaldocuments/frus1961-63v03/d68.

83. See Alphand to Couve, "De la presence americaine au Vietnam-interview de M. Ngo Dinh Nhu," May 17, 1963, CLV, Vietnam Sud, 32-23-5, 78, January 1963–December 1963, COUR; Lalouette to Couve, "interview de M. Ngo Dinh Nhu par le correspondant du Washington Post," May 22, 1963, CLV, Vietnam Sud, 32-23-5, 78, January 1963–December 1963.

84. Green, "Embassy telegram (to Rusk)," June 20, 1963, Confidential U.S. State Department Central Files, Vietnam: Internal and Foreign Affairs, 1960–1963, 59, box 69, US-Relations with France 1960–1963, C92: reel 9, Microfilm Rm., NACP.

85. Ibid.

86. Robert E. Barbour, "Embassy telegram (to Rusk)," May 7, 1963, Confidential U.S. State Department Central Files, Vietnam: Internal and Foreign Affairs, 1960–1963, 59, box 69, US-Relations with France 1960–1963, C92: reel 9, Microfilm Rm., NACP.

87. Robert E. Barbour, "Embassy telegram (to Rusk)," August 7, 1963, Confidential U.S. State Department Central Files, Vietnam: Internal and Foreign Affairs, 1960–1963, 59, box 69, US-Relations with France 1960–1963, C96: reel 13, Microfilm Rm., NACP.

88. Ibid.

89. Ibid.

90. Ibid.

91. Charles Bohlen, "Embassy telegram (to Rusk)," November 7, 1963, Confidential U.S. State Department Central Files, Vietnam: Internal and Foreign Affairs, 1960–1963, 59, box 69, US-Relations with France 1960–1963, C96: reel 13, Microfilm Rm., NACP.

92. Ibid.

93. Robert H. Miller, "Embassy telegram (to Rusk)," August 7, 1963, Confidential U.S. State Department Central Files, Vietnam: Internal and Foreign Affairs, 1960–1963, 59, box 69, US-Relations with France 1960–1963, C96: reel 13, Microfilm Rm., NACP.

94. Peter Grose, "De Gaulle Offers to Help End Foreign Role," *New York Times,* August 30, 1963, 1.

95. Ibid.

96. Tad Szulc, "Paris Premature on Vietnam Unity, Washington Says; It finds de Gaulle's Call for Merger and Neutrality Completely Unrealistic," *New York Times,* August 31, 1963, 1.

97. "Memoradum of Conversation (between Alphand, Rusk, et al.)," August 30, 1963, Confidential U.S. State Department Central Files, Vietnam: Internal and Foreign Affairs, 1960–1963, 59, box 69, US-Relations with France 1960–1963, C96: reel 13, Microfilm Rm., NACP.

98. Ibid.

99. Ibid.

100. Ibid.

101. Henry Cabot Lodge Jr., *The Storm Has Many Eyes: A Personal Narrative* (New York: Norton, 1973), 210–11. Also see William J. Miller, *Henry Cabot Lodge: A Biography* (New York: Heineman, 1967).

102. Anne E. Blair, *Lodge in Vietnam: A Patriot Abroad* (New Haven, Conn.: Yale Univ. Press, 1995), 52.

103. Lalouette to ForMin, August 30, 1963, CLV, Vietnam Sud, 32-23-5, 78, January 1963–December 1963, COUR.

104. Logevall, *Choosing War,* 55.

105. Ibid, 58.

106. Szulc, "Paris Premature on Vietnam Unity," 1.

107. Ibid.

108. Waverly Root, "France May Get Soviet Support on Plan to Neutralize Viet-Nam," *Washington Post,* September 1, 1963, A9. Also see Robert Trumbull, "Diplomats Say Brother of Diem Sees Accord as Way to Oust U.S.," *New York Times,* September 2, 1963, 1.

109. Logevall, *Choosing War,* 61.

110. Alphand to ForMin, September 13, 1963, CLV, Vietnam Sud, 32-23-5, 78, January 1963–December 1963, COUR.

111. Lyon, "Embassy telegram (to Rusk)," August 30, 1963 (6:23 P.M.), National Security Files, series 1, Countries, box 198A, Vietnam-General, August 24, 1963–August 31, 1963, State Cables, JFKL.

112. Henry Cabot Lodge Jr., "Embassy telegram (to Rusk)," September 1, 1963, National Security Files, series 1, Countries, box 199, Vietnam-General, September 1, 1963–September 10, 1963, State Cables, Part I, JFKL.

113. Henry Cabot Lodge Jr., "Embassy telegram (to Rusk)," August 30, 1963, National Security Files, series 1, Countries, box 198A, Vietnam-General, August 24, 1963–August 31, 1963, State Cables, JFKL; Henry Cabot Lodge Jr., "Embassy telegram (to Rusk)," August 31, 1963, National Security Files, series 1, Countries, box 198A, Vietnam-General, August 24, 1963–August 31, 1963, State Cables, JFKL; and Henry Cabot Lodge Jr., "Embassy telegram (to Rusk)," September 4, 1963, National

Security Files, series 1, Countries, box 198A, Vietnam-General, September 1, 1963–September 8, 1963, State Cables, JFKL.

114. Lyon, "Embassy telegram (to Rusk)," September 2, 1963, National Security Files, series 1, Countries, box 199, Vietnam-General, September 1, 1963–September 10, 1963, State Cables, Part I, JFKL.

115. Lalouette to Couve, "Entretien avec M. Cabot Lodge," September 4, 1963, CLV, Vietnam Sud, 32-23-5, 78, January 1963–December 1963, COUR.

116. Henry Cabot Lodge Jr, "Embassy telegram (to Rusk)," September 4, 1963 (10:40 A.M.), National Security Files, series 1, Countries, box 199, Vietnam-General, September 1, 1963–September 10, 1963, State Cables, Part I, JFKL.

117. Ibid.

118. Bundy, "Draft Statement on South Vietnam for Cronkite Interview (to Kennedy)," September 1, 1963, JFKL.

119. Ibid.

120. Ibid.

121. "Transcript: interview between President Kennedy and Walter Cronkite (CBS)," September 2, 1963, JFKL, https://www.jfklibrary.org/Asset-Viewer/Archives/JFKPOF-046-025.aspx.

122. Ibid.

123. Ibid.

124. "Situation au Vietnam," September 4, 1963, CLV, Vietnam Sud, 32-1-1, 17, September–November 1963.

125. Logevall, *Choosing War,* 52.

126. Henry Cabot Lodge Jr., "Embassy telegram (to Rusk)," September 11, 1963 (11:08 P.M.), National Security Files, series 1, Countries, box 199, Vietnam-General, September 11, 1963–September 17, 1963, State Cables, JFKL.

127. Henry Cabot Lodge Jr., "Embassy telegram (to Rusk)," September 11, 1963 (12:45 P.M.), National Security Files, series 1, Countries, box 199, Vietnam-General, September 11, 1963–September 17, 1963, State Cables, JFKL.

128. The State Department assessment is available in Thomas L. Hughes, "Hanoi, Paris, Saigon and South Vietnam's Future," September 11, 1963, National Security Files, series 1, Countries, box 199A, Vietnam-General, September 11, 1963–September 17, 1963, Memos and Misc. Part I, JFKL. The CIA's position is revealed in "CIA Memorandum on the possibility of a GVN deal with North Vietnam," September 14, 1963, National Security Files, series 1, Countries, box 199A, Vietnam-General, September 11, 1963–September 17, 1963, Memos and Misc. Part I, JFKL.

129. "Reactions dans le monde a la declaration du General de Gaulle," September 18, 1963, Ministère des Affaires étrangères, *Asie-Océanie,* Conflit Vietnam, 162, "Positions des Etats sur le Conflit," France 1961–1965, COUR.

130. See Margaret K. Gnoinska, "Poland and Vietnam, 1963: New Evidence on Secret Communist Diplomacy and the 'Maneli Affair,'" The Cold War International History Project Working Paper Series, no. 45 (Washington D.C.: Woodrow Wilson Center, 2005), https://www.wilsoncenter.org/sites/default/files/CWIHP_WP_45b.pdf.

131. "Indications sur le Vietnam communiquees par l'Ambassade britannique," September 19, 1963, CLV, Vietnam Sud, 32-1-1, 17, September–November 1963, COUR.

132. Miller, *Misalliance,* 307.

133. See Logevall, *Choosing War,* 12; Hammer, *A Death in November,* 223–24.

134. Jacobs, *Cold War Mandarin,* 164.

135. See Winters, *The Year of the Hare,* 99; Porter, *Perils of Dominance,* 126–27

136. See Miller, *Misalliance,* 304–8; Catton, *Diem's Final Failure,* 194–97.

137. See Asselin, *Hanoi's Road to the Vietnam War,* 155–56; Gnoinska, "Poland and Vietnam, 1963," 1–6.

138. Henry Cabot Lodge Jr., "Embassy telegram (to Rusk)," September 16, 1963, National Security Files, series 1, Countries, box 199, Vietnam-General, September 11, 1963–September 17, 1963, State Cables, JFKL.

139. Ibid.

140. Melvin Manful, "Vietnamese Reactions to de Gaulle's Statement of August 29 and Some Related Developments," September 30, 1963, Confidential U.S. State Department Central Files, Vietnam: Internal and Foreign Affairs, 1960–1963, 59, box 69, US-Relations with France 1960–1963, C96: reel 13, Microfilm Rm., NACP.

141. Ibid.

142. Freedman, *Kennedy's Wars,* 390–95.

143. Asselin, *Hanoi's Road to the Vietnam War,* 164–73.

144. Ibid., 168.

145. Lyndon Johnson, *The Vantage Point: Perspectives of the Presidency, 1963–1969* (New York: Holt, Rinehart, and Winston, 1971), 212.

Conclusion

1. Jacques Boizet, Consul de Gérance a Tourane (Da Nang), to Lalouette, "Au dix-septieme parallele," August 3, 1962, CLV, Vietnam Sud, 32-3-7, 17, January–June 1962, COUR.

2. This term was originally coined by *Time-Life* publisher Henry Luce in 1941.

3. Charles de Gaulle, "Discours de Phnom-Penh," September 1, 1966, Fondation Charles de Gaulle, http://www.charles-de-gaulle.org/wp-content/uploads/2017/03/Discours-de-Phnom-Penh.pdf.

Bibliography

Archival Sources

Digital National Security Archive, George Washington University, Washington, D.C.

Diplomatic Archive Center, Ministry of Foreign and European Affairs, La Courneuve, Paris

Ministère des Affaires étrangères, Vietcong, Asie-Océanie. Conflit Vietnam, 90, 1960—1964.

Ministère des Affaires étrangères, Asie-Océanie. Conflit Vietnam, 162, "Positions des Etats sur le Conflit," France 1961—1965.

Ministère des Affaires étrangères. AM 1952–1963, USA, 356. "Mich.:-France," 9-4-1

Ministère des Affaires étrangères. AM 1952–1963, USA, 376. "Politique extérieur," 9-5-0.

Ministère des Affaires étrangères, C.L.V. Vietnam Sud, 32-1-1, 17, September–November 1963.

Ministère des Affaires étrangères, C.L.V. Vietnam Sud, 32-3-7, 28, January 1963–November 1964.

Ministère des Affaires étrangères, C.L.V. Vietnam Sud, 32-23-5, 75, January 1958–November 1960.

Ministère des Affaires étrangères, C.L.V. Vietnam Sud, 32-23-5, 76, January 1961–December 1961.

Ministère des Affaires étrangères, C.L.V. Vietnam Sud, 32-23-5, 77, January 1962–December 1962

Ministère des Affaires étrangères, C.L.V. Vietnam Sud, 32-23-5, 78, January 1963–December 1963, COUR.

Ministère des Affaires étrangères, C.L.V. Sud-Vietnam, 32-29, 145, January–March 1963.

Ministère des Affaires étrangères, C.L.V. Sud-Vietnam, 32-29, 146, January–March 1963.

John F. Kennedy Presidential Library, Boston, Massachusetts

The Personal Papers of John F. Kennedy (1917–1963) (#1). Series 2. Early Years, 1928–1940.

Pre-Presidential Papers: House of Representatives (#2.1). Series 2.2. Boston Office Speech Files, 1946–1952.

John F. Kennedy Pre-Presidential Papers: Senate Files (#2.3). Series 6.8. General Files, 1953–1960.

Pre-Presidential Papers: Senate Files (#2.3). Series 12.1. Speech Files, 1953–1960.

President's Office Files (#3). Series 2. Special Correspondence.

President's Office Files (#3). Series 9. Countries.

National Security Files (#4). Series 1. Countries.

The Personal Papers of Arthur Schlesinger Jr. (#206).

National Archives, College Park, Maryland

General Records of the Department of State. Records of Ambassador Charles E. Bohlen, 1942–71. RG 59.

Confidential U.S. State Department Central Files. Vietnam: Internal and Foreign Affairs, 1960–1963. RG 59.

General Records of the Department of State. Bureau of European Affairs Office of Political and Economic Affairs. RG 59.

Published Sources

Acheson, Dean. "A Review of North Atlantic Problems for the Future." The Committee on U.S. Political, Economic and Military Policy in Europe's Policy Guidance to the National Security Council, March 1961. DNSA No. NH01131, JFKL.

———. *Present at the Creation: My Years in the State Department.* New York: Norton, 1987.

Adams, William James. *Restructuring the French Economy: Government and the Rise of Market Competition since World War II.* Washington, D.C.: Brookings Institution, 1989.

Adamthwaite, Anthony. *Grandeur and Misery: France's Bid for Power in Europe, 1914–1940.* New York: St. Martin's Press, 1995.

Alexander, Martin S., and John F. V. Keiger. *France and the Algerian War, 1954–62: Strategy, Operations and Diplomacy.* London: Cass, 2002.

Allen, Major General Henry T. "Allen's Move for New Franco-German Negotiations Halted by Hughes." *Boston Daily Globe,* November 25, 1923, 31.

Allport, Gordon. *The Nature of Prejudice.* Cambridge, Mass.: Addison-Wesley, 1954.

Anderson, Stuart. *Race and Rapprochement: Anglo-Saxonism and Anglo-American Relations, 1895–1904.* London: Associated Univ. Presses, 1981.

———. "Racial Anglo-Saxonism and the American Response to the Boer War." *Diplomatic History* 2, no. 3 (1978): 219–36.

Appy, Christian G., ed. *Cold War Constructions: The Political Culture of United States Imperialism, 1945–1966.* Amherst: Univ. of Massachusetts Press, 2000.

Aron, Raymond. *France: Steadfast and Changing: The Fourth to the Fifth Republic.* Translated by J. Irwin and Luigi Einaudi. Cambridge, Mass.: Harvard Univ. Press, 1960.

Ashton, Nigel John. *Eisenhower, Macmillan, and the Problem of Nasser: Anglo-American Relations and Arab Nationalism, 1955–59.* New York: St. Martin's Press, 1996.

Asselin, Pierre. *Hanoi's Road to the Vietnam War, 1954–1965.* Berkeley: Univ. of California Press, 2013.

Aussaresses, Paul. *The Battle of the Casbah: Terrorism and Counter-Terrorism in Algeria, 1955–1957.* Translated by Robert L. Miller. New York: Enigma Books, 2002.

"A View of Germany." *Hartford Courant,* February 5, 1923, 8.

Balderson, John L. "US Now Blamed for Ruhr Crisis." *Boston Daily Globe,* January 28, 1923, 15.

Baldwin, Louis. *Hon. Politician: Mike Mansfield of Montana.* Missoula, Mont.: Mountain Press, 1979.

Ball, George W. *The Past Has Another Pattern: Memoirs.* New York: Norton, 1982.

Ball, Moya Ann. *Vietnam-on-the-Potomac.* New York: Praeger, 1992.

Bange, Oliver. *The EEC Crisis of 1963: Kennedy, Macmillan, de Gaulle and Adenauer in Conflict.* New York: St. Martin's Press, 2000.

Barbeau, Arthur E., and Florette Henri. *The Unknown Soldiers: African-American Troops in World War I.* New York: Da Capo, 1996.

Bassett, Lawrence J., and Stephen E. Pelz. "The Failed Search for Victory: Vietnam and the Politics of War." In *Kennedy's Quest for Victory: American Foreign Policy, 1961–1963,* edited by Thomas G. Paterson, 223–52. Toronto: Oxford Univ. Press, 1989.

Bayly, Christopher, and Tim Harper. *Forgotten Wars: The End of Britain's Asian Empire.* New York: Allen Lane, 2007.

Beevor, Anthony, and Artemis Cooper. *Paris after the Liberation, 1944–1949.* New York: Penguin, 2004.

Berger, Mark T. "Decolonisation, Modernisation and Nation-Building: Political Development Theory and the Appeal of Communism in Southeast Asia, 1945–1975." *Journal of Southeast Asian Studies* 34, no. 3 (2003): 421–48.

Beisner, Robert L. *Dean Acheson: A Life in the Cold War.* New York: Oxford Univ. Press, 2006.

Bernstein, Irving. *Promises Kept: John F. Kennedy's New Frontier.* New York: Oxford Univ. Press, 1991.

Bernstein, Richard B. *Thomas Jefferson.* New York: Oxford Univ. Press, 2003.

Billig, Michael. "Henri Tajfel's 'Cognitive Aspects of Prejudice' and the Psychology of Bigotry." *British Journal of Social Psychology* 41, no. 2 (2002): 171–88.

Bird, Kai. *The Color of Truth: McGeorge Bundy and William Bundy: Brothers in Arms: A Biography.* New York: Simon and Schuster, 1998.

Blair, Anne E. *Lodge in Vietnam: A Patriot Abroad.* New Haven, Conn.: Yale Univ. Press, 1995.

Blang, Eugenie. *Allies at Odds: America, Europe, and Vietnam, 1961–1968.* Lanham, Md.: Rowman and Littlefield, 2011.

Blight, James G., and Peter Kornbluh, eds. *Politics of Illusion: The Bay of Pigs Invasion Reexamined.* Boulder, Colo.: Rienner, 1998.

Boemeke, Manfred F., Gerald D. Feldman, and Elisabeth Glaser, eds. *The Treaty of Versailles: A Reassessment after 75 Years.* New York: Cambridge Univ. Press, 1998.

Bohlen, Charles E. *Witness to History, 1929–1969.* New York: Norton, 1973.

Booth, T. Michael, and Duncan Spencer. *Paratrooper: The Life of General James M. Gavin.* New York: Simon and Schuster, 1994.

Bose, Meena. *Shaping and Signaling Presidential Policy: The National Security Decision Making of Eisenhower and Kennedy.* College Station: Texas A&M Univ. Press, 1998.

Boudarel, Georges. *La Bureaucratie au Viet Nam.* Paris: L'Harmattan, 1983.

———. *Cent fleurs écloses dans la nuit du Viet Nam.* Paris: Bertoin, 1991.

Bowles, Chester. *The Conscience of a Liberal: Selected Writings and Speeches.* Edited by Henry Steele Commager. Westport, Conn.: Greenwood, 1974.

Boyce, D. George. *Decolonisation and the British Empire, 1775–1997.* New York: St. Martin's Press, 1999.

Boyce, Robert, ed. *French Foreign and Defence Policy, 1918–1940: The Decline and Fall of a Great Power.* New York: LSE/Routledge, 1998.

Boyer, Paul. *Fallout: A Historian Reflects on America's Half-Century Encounter with Nuclear Weapons.* Columbus: Ohio State Univ. Press, 1998.

Bozo, Frédéric. *Two Strategies for Europe: De Gaulle, the United States, and the Atlantic Alliance.* Translated by Susan Emanuel. Lanham, Md.: Rowman and Littlefield, 2001.

Bradlee, Benjamin C. *Conversations with Kennedy.* New York: Norton, 1975.

Bradley, Mark. *Imagining Vietnam and America: The Making of Postcolonial Vietnam, 1919–1950.* Chapel Hill: Univ. of North Carolina Press, 2000.

Brands, Henry W., Jr. "Redefining the Cold War: American Policy toward Yugoslavia, 1948–60." *Diplomatic History* 11, no. 1 (1987): 41–54.

Brendon, Piers. *The Decline and Fall of the British Empire, 1781–1997.* New York: Knopf, 2008.

Brewer, Marilynn. "The Psychology of Prejudice: Ingroup Love and Outgroup Hate?" *Journal of Social Issues* 55, no. 3 (1999): 429–44.

Brinkley, Douglas. *Dean Acheson: The Cold War Years, 1953–71.* New Haven, Conn.: Yale Univ. Press, 1992.

———, ed. *Dean Acheson and the Making of U.S. Foreign Policy.* New York: St. Martin's Press, 1993.

Brinkley, Douglas, and Richard T. Griffiths, eds. *John F. Kennedy and Europe.* Baton Rouge: Louisiana State Univ. Press, 1999.

Brocheux, Pierre. *The Mekong Delta: Ecology, Economy, and Revolution, 1860–1960.* Madison: Center for Southeast Asian Studies, University of Wisconsin-Madison, 1995.

Brocheux, Pierre, and Daniel Hémery. *Indochine: la colonisation ambiguë, 1858–1954.* Paris: Découverte, 1995.

Brocheux, Pierre, and Charles Robert Ageron. *Du conflit d'Indochine aux conflits Indochinois.* Brussels: Complexe, 2000.

Bruce, Robert. *A Fraternity of Arms: America and France in the Great War.* Lawrence: Univ. Press of Kansas, 2003.

Buckley, Roger. *The United States in the Asia-Pacific since 1945.* Cambridge, UK: Cambridge Univ. Press, 2002.

Bugliosi, Vincent. *Reclaiming History: The Assassination of John F. Kennedy.* New York: Norton, 2007.

Bundy, McGeorge. *The Pattern of Responsibility.* Boston, Mass.: Houghton, Mifflin, 1952.

———. "November 1952: Imperatives of Foreign Policy." *Foreign Affairs* 31, no. 1 (1952): 1–14.

———. "The Test of Yalta." *Foreign Affairs* 27, no. 4 (1949): 618–29.

Bundy, McGeorge, and Henry L. Stimson. *On Active Service in Peace and War.* London: Hutchinson, 1949.

Burdick, Eugene, and William Lederer. *The Ugly American.* Thorndike, Maine: Hall, 1994.

Burk, Kathleen. *Old World, New World: The Story of Britain and America.* London: Little, Brown, 2007.

Busch, Peter. *All the Way with JFK?: Britain, the US and the Vietnam War.* Oxford: Oxford Univ. Press, 2003.

Buszynski, Leszek. *SEATO, The Failure of an Alliance Strategy.* Singapore: Singapore Univ. Press, 1983.

Butterfield, Samuel Hale. *U.S. Development Aid—An Historic First: Achievements and Failures in the Twentieth Century.* Westport, Conn.: Praeger, 2004.

Buzzanco, Robert. *Masters of War: Military Dissent and Politics in the Vietnam Era.* New York: Cambridge Univ. Press, 1996.

Buzzanco, Robert, and Marilyn Young, eds. *A Companion to the Vietnam War.* Malden, Mass.: Blackwell Publishing, 2002.

Byrne, Jeffrey James. *Mecca of Revolution: Algeria, Decolonization, and the Third World Order.* New York: Oxford Univ. Press, 2016.

Campbell, Duncan Andrew. *Unlikely Allies: Britain, America and the Victorian Origins of the Special Relationship.* New York: Hambledon Continuum, 2007.

Carter, James. *Inventing Vietnam: The United States and State Building, 1954–1968.* New York: Cambridge Univ. Press, 2008.

Catton, Philip E. "Counter-Insurgency and Nation Building: The Strategic Hamlet Programme in South Vietnam, 1961–1963." *International History Review* 21, no. 4 (1999): 918–40.

———. *Diem's Final Failure: Prelude to America's War in Vietnam.* Lawrence: Univ. of Kansas Press, 2002.

Cerny, Philip G. *The Politics of Grandeur: Ideological Aspects of de Gaulle's Foreign Policy.* New York: Cambridge Univ. Press, 1980.

———. "The Process of Personal Leadership: The Case of de Gaulle." *International Political Science Review/Revue internationale de science politique* 9, no. 2 (April 1988): 131–42.

Cesari, Laurent. *L'Indochine en guerres, 1945–1993.* Paris: Belin, 1995.

Chaffard, Georges. *Les deux guerres du Vietnam: de Valluy à Westmoreland.* Paris: La Table Ronde, 1969.

Chamberlain, William Henry. "Pall Over Europe." *Wall Street Journal,* August 30, 1954, 4.

Chandler, David P. *The Tragedy of Cambodian History: Politics, War, and Revolution since 1945.* New Haven, Conn.: Yale Univ. Press, 1991.

Chapman, Jessica M. *Cauldron of Resistance: Ngo Dinh Diem, the United States, and 1950s Southern Vietnam.* Ithaca, N.Y.: Cornell Univ. Press, 2013.

———. "Staging Democracy: South Vietnam's 1955 Referendum to Depose Bao Dai." *Diplomatic History* 30, no. 4 (2006): 671–703.

Chew, William, III, ed. *National Stereotypes in Perspective: Americans in France, Frenchmen ïn America.* Atlanta: Rodopi Press, 2001.

Childs, Marquis. "Stakes High, But Paris Is Apathetic." *Washington Post and Times Herald,* September 7, 1954, 16.

Churchill, Winston S. *While England Slept: A Survey of World Affairs, 1932–1938.* New York: G. P. Putnam's Sons, 1938.

Cogan, Charles G. *Forced to Choose: France, the Atlantic Alliance, and NATO—Then and Now.* Westport, Conn.: Praeger, 1997.

———. *French Negotiating Behavior.* Washington, D.C.: United States Institute of Peace Press, 2003.

———. *Oldest Allies, Guarded Friends: The United States and France since 1940.* Westport, Conn.: Praeger, 1994.

Cohen, Warren I. *Dean Rusk.* Totowa, N.J.: Cooper Square Publishers, 1980.

Cohn, Carol. "Sex and Death in the Rational World of Defense Intellectuals." *Signs* 12, no. 4 (1987): 687–718.

Connelly, Matthew. *A Diplomatic Revolution: Algeria's Fight for Independence and the Origins of the Post–Cold War Era.* New York: Oxford Univ. Press, 2002.

Cooper, Nicola. *France in Indochina: Colonial Encounters.* Oxford, UK: Berg, 2001.

Costigliola, Frank. *Awkward Dominion: American Political, Economic, and Cultural Relations with Europe, 1919–1933.* Ithaca, N.Y.: Cornell Univ. Press, 1984.

———. "The Failed Design: Kennedy, de Gaulle, and the Struggle for Europe." *Diplomatic History* 8, no. 3 (1984): 227–52.

———. *France and the United States: The Cold Alliance since World War II, 1940–1990.* New York: Twayne, 1992.

———. "Kennedy, the European Allies, and the Failure to Consult." *Political Science Quarterly* 110, no. 1 (1995): 105–23.

———. "The Nuclear Family: Tropes of Gender and Pathology in the Western Alliance." *Diplomatic History* 21, no. 2 (1997): 163–83.

———. "Unceasing Pressure for Penetration: Gender, Pathology, and Emotion in George Kennan's Formation of the Cold War." *Journal of American History* 83, no. 4 (1997): 1309–39.

Costigliola, Frank, and Thomas Paterson. "Defining and Doing the History of American Foreign Relations: A Primer." In *Explaining the History of American Foreign Relations,* edited by Michael J. Hogan and Thomas G. Paterson, 10–34. Cambridge, UK: Cambridge Univ. Press, 2004.

Couve de Murville, Maurice. *Une politique étrangère, 1958–1969.* Paris: Plon, 1971.

Craig, Gordon A., and Francis L. Loewenheim, eds. *The Diplomats, 1939–1979.* Princeton, N.J.: Princeton Univ. Press, 1994.

Crozier, Brian. *De Gaulle.* New York: Scribner, 1973.

Cullather, Nick. *The Hungry World: America's Cold War Battle against Poverty in Asia.* Cambridge, Mass.: Harvard Univ. Press, 2010.

Cumming, Henry H. *Franco-British Rivalry in the Post-War Near East: The Decline of French Influence.* Westport, Conn.: Greenwood, 1986.

Cuordileone, K. A. "'Politics in an Age of Anxiety': Cold War Political Culture and the Crisis in American Masculinity, 1949–1960." *Journal of American History* 87, no. 2 (2000): 515–45.

Currey, Cecil B. *Edward Lansdale: The Unquiet American.* Boston, Mass.: Houghton Mifflin, 1988.

Dahan, Thierry. "La Vème République et le Vietnam, 1959–1976." Ph.D. thesis, L'Université de Nice, 1998.

Dallek, Robert. *An Unfinished Life: John F. Kennedy, 1917–1963.* Boston: Little, Brown, 2003.

Dalloz, Jacques. *La guerre d'Indochine: 1945–1954.* Paris: Seuil, 1987.

Daughton, J. P. *An Empire Divided: Religion, Republicanism, and the Making of French Colonialism, 1880–1914.* New York: Oxford Univ. Press, 2006.

Daum, Andreas W. *Kennedy in Berlin.* Washington, D.C.: German Historical Institute, 2008.

Davis, Cynthia J. "Nation's Nature: 'Billy Budd, Sailor,' Anglo-Saxonism, and the Canon." In *Race and the Production of Modern American Nationalism,* edited by Reynolds J. Scott-Childress, 43–66. New York: Garland, 1999.

Dean, Robert D. *Imperial Brotherhood: Gender and the Making of Cold War Foreign Policy.* Amherst: Univ. of Massachusetts Press, 2001.

———. "Masculinity as Ideology: John F. Kennedy and the Domestic Politics of Foreign Policy." *Diplomatic History* 22, no. 1 (winter 1998): 29–62.

"The Death of EDC Has Left a Vacuum." *Hartford Courant,* September 9, 1954, 12.

Dedman, Martin J. *The Origins and Development of the European Union, 1945–95: A History of European Integration.* New York: Routledge, 1996.

DeGuzman, Maria. "Consolidating Anglo-American Imperial Identity Around the Spanish-American War (1898)." In *Race and the Production of Modern American Nationalism,* edited by Reynolds J. Scott-Childress, 97–126. New York: Garland, 1999.

Devillers, Phillipe. *Histoire du Viêt-Nam de 1940 à 1952.* Paris: Éditions du Seuil, 1952.

Devillers, Phillipe, and Jean Lacouture. *End of a War: Indochina,* 1954. Paris: Éditions du Seuil, 1960.

———. *Viet-Nam: de la guerre française à la guerre américaine.* Paris: Éditions du Seuil, 1969.

Diggins, John Patrick, ed. *The Liberal Persuasion: Arthur Schlesinger, Jr., and the Challenge of the American Past.* Princeton, N.J.: Princeton Univ. Press, 1997.

DiLeo, David L. *George Ball, Vietnam, and the Rethinking of Containment.* Chapel Hill: Univ. of North Carolina Press, 1991.

Dior, Eric. *Un couple infernal: Deux cents ans de francophobie et d'antiaméricanisme.* Paris: Perrin/Editions de la Bastille, 2003.

Dobson, Alan P., ed. *Anglo-American Relations in the Twentieth Century: Of Friendship, Conflict and the Rise and Decline of Superpowers.* New York: Routledge, 1995.

Dommen, Arthur J. *Conflict in Laos: The Politics of Neutralization.* New York: Praeger, 1971.

———. *The Indochinese Experience of the French and the Americans: Nationalism and Communism in Cambodia, Laos, and Vietnam.* Bloomington: Indiana Univ. Press, 2001.

Doty, Robert C. "The Man, the Monument Called de Gaulle." *New York Times,* May 28, 1961, SM10.

Dreifort, John E. *Myopic Grandeur: The Ambivalence of French Foreign Policy toward the Far East, 1919–1945.* Kent, Ohio: Kent State Univ. Press, 1991.

Duroselle, Jean-Baptiste. *France and the United States from the Beginning to the Present.* Translated by Derek Coltman. Chicago: Univ. of Chicago Press, 1978.

Elkins, Caroline. *Britain's Gulag: The Brutal End of Empire in Kenya.* London: Cape, 2005.

Elliott, David. *The Vietnamese War: Revolution and Social Change in the Mekong Delta, 1930–1975,* 2 vols. Armonk: Sharpe, 2003.

Endy, Christopher. "Travel and World Power: Americans in Europe, 1890–1917." *Diplomatic History* 22, no. 4 (1998): 565–94.

Evans, Martin. *Algeria: France's Undeclared War.* New York: Oxford Univ. Press, 2012.

Ermarth, Michael, ed. *America and the Shaping of German Society, 1945–1955.* Providence, R.I.: Berg, 1993.

Fabre, Michel. *From Harlem to Paris: Black American Writers in France, 1840–1980.* Chicago: Univ. of Illinois Press, 1991.

Fall, Bernard. *Street without Joy: Indochina at War, 1946–63.* London: Pall Mall, 1963.

Farwell, Byron. *Over There: The United States in the Great War, 1917–1918.* New York: Norton, 1999.

Findlay, Trevor. *The Blue Helmets' First War?: Use of Force by the UN in the Congo, 1960–64.* Clementsport, Nova Scotia: Canadian Peacekeeping Press, 1999.

Fisher, James T. "The Second Catholic President: Ngo Dinh Diem, John F. Kennedy, and the Vietnam Lobby, 1954–1963." *U.S. Catholic Historian* 15, no. 3 (1997): 119–37.

Fitzgerald, Frances. *Fire in the Lake: The Vietnamese and the Americans in Vietnam.* Boston: Little, Brown, 1972.

Fogg, Shannon L. *The Politics of Everyday Life in Vichy France: Foreigners, Undesirables, and Strangers.* New York: Cambridge Univ. Press, 2009.

The Fog of War: Eleven Lessons from the Life of Robert S. McNamara. DVD. Directed by Errol Morris. New York: Sony Pictures Classics, 2003.

"France: The Assassination." *Time,* September 13, 1954.

Freedman, Lawrence. *Kennedy's Wars: Berlin, Cuba, Laos, and Vietnam.* New York: Oxford Univ. Press, 2002.

"French Politics and the E.D.C." *New York Times,* August 28, 1954, 14.

Frey, Marc. "Tools of Empire: Persuasion and the United States's Modernizing Mission in Southeast Asia." *Diplomatic History* 27, no. 4 (2003): 543–68.

Fursdon, Edward. *The European Defence Community, A History.* London: Macmillan, 1980.

Gaddis, John L. *Strategies of Containment: A Critical Appraisal of American National Security Policy during the Cold War.* New York: Oxford Univ. Press, 2005.

Gaiduk, Ilya V. *Confronting Vietnam: Soviet Policy toward the Indochina Conflict, 1945–1963.* Washington, D.C.: Woodrow Wilson Center Press, 2003.

Galbraith, James K. "JFK's Vietnam Withdrawal Plan Is a Fact, Not Speculation." *The Nation,* November 22, 1963. https://www.thenation.com/article/jfks-vietnam-withdrawal-plan-fact-not-speculation/.

Galbraith, John Kenneth. *Letters to Kennedy.* Edited by James Goodman. Cambridge, Mass.: Harvard Univ. Press, 1998.

———. *A Life in Our Times: Memoirs.* Boston, Mass.: Houghton Mifflin, 1981.

Galula, David. *Counterinsurgency Warfare: Theory and Practice.* Wesport, Conn.: Praeger Security International, 1964.

———. *Pacification in Algeria, 1956–1958.* Santa Monica, Calif.: RAND Corporation, 2006.

Gardner, Lloyd C. *Pay Any Price: Lyndon Johnson and the Wars for Vietnam.* Chicago: Dee, 1995.

Gardner, Lloyd C., and Ted Gittinger, eds. *The Search for Peace in Vietnam, 1964–1968.* College Station: Texas A&M Univ. Press, 2004.

———. *Vietnam: The Early Decisions.* Austin, Tex.: Univ. of Texas Press, 1997.

Garofano, John. "Tragedy or Choice in Vietnam? Learning to Think Outside the Archival Box." *International Security* 26, no. 4 (2002): 143–68.

De Gaulle, Charles. *The Complete War Memoirs.* New York: Simon and Schuster, 1964.

———. *Memoirs of Hope: Renewal and Endeavor.* Translated by Terence Kilmartin. New York: Simon and Schuster, 1971.

Gaunson, A. B. *The Anglo-French Clash in Lebanon and Syria, 1940–45.* London: Macmillan, 1987.

Gazley, John G. *American Opinion of German Unification, 1848–1871.* New York: Columbia University, 1926.

Georges, Alfred. *Charles de Gaulle et la guerre d'Indochine.* Paris: Nouvelles Éditions latines, 1974.

Gildea, Robert. *France since 1945.* New York: Oxford Univ. Press, 1996.

Giglio, James N. *The Presidency of John F. Kennedy.* Lawrence: Univ. Press of Kansas, 2006.

Gilman, Nils. *Mandarins of the Future: Modernization Theory in Cold War America.* Baltimore, Md.: Johns Hopkins Univ. Press, 2003.

Gnoinska, Margaret K. "Poland and Vietnam, 1963: New Evidence on Secret Communist Diplomacy and the 'Maneli Affair.'" The Cold War International History Project Working Paper Series, no. 45. Washington D.C.: Woodrow Wilson Center, 2005.

Goedde, Petra. *GIs and Germans: Culture, Gender and Foreign Relations, 1945–1949.* New Haven, Conn.: Yale Univ. Press, 2003.

Golan, Galia. *The Soviet Union and National Liberation Movements in the Third World.* Boston, Mass.: Unwin Hyman, 1988.

Goldstein, Gordon M. *Lessons in Disaster: McGeorge Bundy and the Path to War in Vietnam.* New York: Times Books/Holt, 2008.

Goodwin, Doris Kearns. *The Fitzgeralds and the Kennedys.* New York: St. Martin's Press, 1991.

Gordon, Philip H. *A Certain Idea of France: French Security Policy and the Gaullist Legacy.* Princeton, N.J.: Princeton Univ. Press, 1993.

———. *France, Germany, and the Western Alliance.* Boulder, Colo.: Westview Press, 1995.

Goscha, Christopher, and Maurice Vaïsse, eds. *La guerre du Vietnam et l'Europe, 1963–1973.* Brussels: Bruylant, 2003.

Granieri, Ronald J. *The Ambivalent Alliance: Konrad Adenauer, The CDU/CSU and the West, 1949–1966.* New York: Berghahn, 2003.

Greene, Benjamin P. *Eisenhower, Science Advice, and the Nuclear Test-Ban Debate, 1945–1963.* Palo Alto, Calif.: Stanford Univ. Press, 2007.

Greenstein, Fred I., and Richard H. Immerman. "What Did Eisenhower Tell Kennedy about Indochina? The Politics of Misperception." *Journal of American History* 79, no. 2 (September 1992): 568–87.

Gregory, Shaun R. *Nuclear Command and Control in NATO: Nuclear Weapons Operations and the Strategy of Flexible Response.* New York: St. Martin's Press, 1996.

Grose, Peter. "De Gaulle Offers to Help End Foreign Role." *New York Times,* August 30, 1963, 1.

Hack, Karl. *Defence and Decolonisation in South-East Asia: Britain, Malaya and Singapore, 1941–1968.* Richmond, Surrey: Curzon, 2000.

Halberstam, David. *The Best and the Brightest.* New York: Random House, 1972.

Hamilton, Nigel. *JFK: Reckless Youth.* New York: Random House, 1992.

Hamilton-Merritt, Jane. *Tragic Mountains: The Hmong, the Americans, and the Secret Wars for Laos, 1942–1992.* Bloomington: Indiana Univ. Press, 1993.

Hammer, Ellen. *A Death in November: America in Vietnam, 1963.* New York: Oxford Univ. Press, 1987.

Hannah, Norman B. *The Key to Failure: Laos and the Vietnam War.* Lanham, Md.: Madison Books, 1987.

Hargreaves, Alec G., ed., *Memory, Empire, and Postcolonialism: Legacies of French Colonialism.* Lanham, Md.: Lexington Books, 2005.

Harrison, Michael M. *The Reluctant Ally: France and Atlantic Security.* Baltimore, Md.: Johns Hopkins Univ. Press, 1981.

Hendrickson, Paul. *The Living and the Dead: Robert McNamara and Five Lives of a Lost War.* New York: Knopf, 1996.

Henri-Soutou, Georges. "Les problems de sécurité dans les rapports franco-allemand de 1956 à 1963." *Relations Internationales,* no. 58 (1989): 227–51.

Henry, Bill. "Kennedy Turns on the Charm." *Los Angeles Times,* June 1, 1961, B1.

Henry, John B., II, and William Espinosa. "The Tragedy of Dean Rusk." *Foreign Policy,* no. 8 (autumn 1972): 568–87.

Herring, George C. *LBJ and Vietnam: A Different Kind of War.* Austin: Univ. of Texas Press, 1994.

Herring, George C. "'Peoples Quite Apart': Americans, South Vietnamese, and the War in Vietnam." *Diplomatic History* 14, no. 1 (1990): 1–23.

Hersh, Seymour. *The Dark Side of Camelot.* Boston: Little, Brown, 1997.

Hershberg, James. *Marigold: The Lost Chance for Peace in Vietnam.* Stanford, Calif.: Stanford Univ. Press, 2012.

Hess, Gary R. "Redefining the American Position in Southeast Asia: The United States and the Geneva and Manila Conferences." In *Dien Bien Phu and the Crisis of Franco-American Relations, 1954–1955,* edited by Lawrence S. Kaplan, Denise Artaud, and Mark R. Rubin, 123–48. Wilmington, Del.: SR Books, 1990.

Heuser, Beatrice. *Western Containment Policies in the Cold War: The Yugoslav Case, 1948–53.* New York: Routledge, 1989.

Higgins, Trumbull. *The Perfect Failure: Kennedy, Eisenhower, and the C.I.A. at the Bay of Pigs.* New York: Norton, 1987.

Hill, Christopher, and Karen Elizabeth Smith. *European Foreign Policy: Key Documents.* New York: Routledge, 2000.

Hitchcock, William I. *France Restored: Cold War Diplomacy and the Quest for Leadership in Europe, 1944–1954.* Chapel Hill: Univ. of North Carolina Press, 1998.

Hogan, Michael J. *A Cross of Iron: Harry S. Truman and the Origins of the National Security State, 1945–1954.* New York: Cambridge Univ. Press, 1998.

———. *Informal Entente: The Private Structure of Cooperation in Anglo-American Economic Diplomacy, 1918–1929.* Columbia: Univ. of Missouri Press, 1977.

———. *The Marshall Plan: America, Britain, and the Reconstruction of Western Europe, 1947–1952.* New York: Cambridge Univ. Press, 1987.

Hogan, Michael J., and Thomas G. Paterson, eds. *Explaining the History of American Foreign Relations.* Cambridge, UK: Cambridge Univ. Press, 2004.

Hoganson, Kristen. *Consumers' Imperium: The Global Production of American Domesticity, 1865–1920.* Chapel Hill: Univ. of North Carolina Press, 2007.

Horne, Alistair. *A Savage War of Peace: Algeria, 1954–1962.* London: Macmillan, 1977.

Horsman, Reginald. *Race and Manifest Destiny: The Origins of American Racial Anglo-Saxonism.* Cambridge, Mass.: Harvard Univ. Press, 1981.

Hunt, David. *Vietnam's Southern Revolution: From Peasant Insurrection to Total War.* Amherst: Univ. of Massachusetts Press, 2008.

Hunt, Michael. *The American Ascendancy: How the United States Gained and Wielded Global Dominance.* Chapel Hill: Univ. of North Carolina Press, 2007.

———. *Ideology and US Foreign Policy.* New Haven, Conn.: Yale Univ. Press, 1987.

———. *Lyndon Johnson's War: America's Cold War Crusade in Vietnam, 1945–1968.* New York: Hill and Wang, 1996.

Isaacson, Walter, and Evan Thomas. *The Wise Men: Six Friends and the World They Made.* New York: Simon and Schuster, 1986.

Jacobs, Seth. *America's Miracle Man in Vietnam: Ngo Dinh Diem, Religion, Race, and U.S. Intervention in Southeast Asia, 1950–1957.* Durham, N.C.: Duke Univ. Press, 2004.

———. *Cold War Mandarin: Ngo Dinh Diem and the Origins of America's War in Vietnam, 1950–1963.* Lanham, Md.: Rowman and Littlefield, 2006.

———. "'Our System Demands the Supreme Being': The U.S. Religious Revival and the 'Diem Experiment,' 1954–55." *Diplomatic History* 25, no. 4 (2001): 589–624.

James, Edwin L. "The America that Europe Sees." *New York Times,* April 10, 1927, SM1.

Janis, Irving L. *Groupthink: Psychological Studies of Policy Decisions and Fiascoes.* Boston, Mass.: Houghton Mifflin, 1982.

———. *Victims of Groupthink: A Psychological Study of Foreign-Policy Decisions and Fiascos.* Boston, Mass.: Houghton, Mifflin, 1972.

Jeffords, Susan. *The Remasculinization of America: Gender and the Vietnam War.* Bloomington, Ind.: Indiana Univ. Press, 1989.

"John F. Kennedy." *Time,* January 5, 1962.

Johnson, Lyndon. *The Vantage Point: Perspectives of the Presidency, 1963–1969.* New York: Holt, Rinehart, and Winston, 1971.

Jones, Howard. *The Bay of Pigs.* New York: Oxford Univ. Press, 2008.

———. *Death of a Generation: How the Assassinations of Diem and JFK Prolonged the Vietnam War.* New York: Oxford Univ. Press, 2003.

Journoud, Pierre. *De Gaulle et le Vietnam, 1945–1969.* Paris: Tallandier, 2011.

———. "Les relations franco-américaines à l'épreuve du Vietnam entre 1954 et 1975: de la défiance dans la guerre à la coopération pour la paix." Ph.D. thesis, Université de Paris I-Sorbonne, 2007.

Kaiser, David. *American Tragedy: Kennedy, Johnson, and the Origins of the Vietnam War.* Cambridge, Mass.: Belknap Press of Harvard Univ. Press, 2000.

Kaplan, Amy. "Commentary: Domesticating Foreign Policy." *Diplomatic History* 18, no. 1. (1994): 97–105.

Kaplan, Lawrence S., Denise Artaud, and Mark R. Rubin, eds. *Dien Bien Phu and the Crisis of Franco-American Relations, 1954–1955.* Wilmington, Del.: SR Books, 1990.

Kedward, Rod. *La vie en bleu: France and the French since 1900.* London: Lane, 2005.

Kelley, Frank. "Kennedy Talk on Algeria Stirs Protests in France." *Washington Post,* July 4, 1957, B10.

Kennedy, John Fitzgerald. *Prelude to Leadership: The Postwar Diary of John F. Kennedy.* Edited by Hugh Sidey and Deirdre Henderson. Washington, D.C.: Regnery, 1995.

———. *Why England Slept.* New York: Funk, 1961.

Kennedy, Joseph P. *I'm for Roosevelt.* New York: Reynal and Hitchcock, 1936.

"Kennedy Flies to Paris." *Chicago Tribune,* May 31, 1961, 1.

Keylor, William R. "How They Advertised France: The French Propaganda Campaign in the United States during the Breakup of the Franco-American Entente, 1918–1923." *Diplomatic History* 17, no. 3 (1993): 351–73.

Kleine-Ahlbrandt, Wm. Laird. *The Burden of Victory: France, Britain, and the Enforcement of the Versailles Peace, 1919–1925.* Lanham, Md.: Univ. Press of America, 1995.

Klein, Christina. *Cold War Orientalism: Asia in the Middlebrow Imagination, 1945–1961.* Berkeley: Univ. of California Press, 2003.

Kohl, Wilfrid. *French Nuclear Diplomacy.* Princeton, N.J.: Princeton Univ. Press, 1971.

Kolko, Gabriel. *Anatomy of a War: Vietnam, the United States, and the Modern Historical Experience.* New York: Pantheon Books, 1985.

Kolodziej, Edward A. *French International Policy under De Gaulle and Pompidou: The Politics of Grandeur.* Ithaca, N.Y.: Cornell Univ. Press, 1974.

Korbonski, Andrzej, and Francis Fukuyama, eds. *The Soviet Union and the Third World: The Last Three Decades.* Ithaca, N.Y.: Cornell Univ. Press, 1987.

Kramer, Paul A. "Empires, Exceptions, and Anglo-Saxons: Race and Rule between the British and United States Empires." *Journal of American History* 88, no. 4 (2002): 1315–53.

Kuisel, Richard. *Seducing the French: The Dilemma of Americanization.* Berkeley: Univ. of California Press, 1993.

Kuklick, Bruce. *Blind Oracles: Intellectuals and War from Kennan to Kissinger.* Princeton, N.J.: Princeton Univ. Press, 2006.

Kulski, W. W. *De Gaulle and the World: The Foreign Policy of the Fifth French Republic.* Syracuse, N.Y.: Syracuse Univ. Press, 1966.

Kunz, Diane B., ed. *The Diplomacy of the Crucial Decade: American Foreign Relations during the 1960s.* New York: Columbia Univ. Press, 1994.

———. *The Economic Diplomacy of the Suez Crisis.* Chapel Hill: Univ. of North Carolina Press, 1991.

Lacouture, Jean. *De Gaulle.* 2 vols. New York: Norton, 1990–1992.

LaFeber, Walter. "Roosevelt, Churchill, and Indochina: 1942–45." *American Historical Review* 80, no. 5. (1975): 1277–95.

Lam, Truong Buu. *Colonialism Experienced: Vietnamese Writings on Colonialism, 1900–1931.* Ann Arbor: Univ. of Michigan Press, 2000.

Lampe, John R., Russell O. Prickett, and Ljubiša S. Adamović. *Yugoslav-American Economic Relations since World War II.* Durham, N.C.: Duke Univ. Press, 1990.

Landsdale, Edward Geary. *In the Midst of Wars: An American's Mission to Southeast Asia.* New York: Fordham Univ. Press, 1991.

Larson, David L. *United States Foreign Policy toward Yugoslavia, 1943–1963.* Washington, D.C.: Univ. Press of America, 1979.

Latham, Michael E. "Ideology, Social Science, and Destiny: Modernization and the Kennedy-Era Alliance for Progress." *Diplomatic History* 22, no. 2 (1998): 199–229.

———. *Modernization as Ideology: American Social Science and "Nation Building" in the Kennedy Era.* Chapel Hill: Univ. of North Carolina Press, 2000.

Lawrence, Mark Atwood. *Assuming the Burden: Europe and the American Commitment to War in Vietnam.* Berkeley: Univ. of California Press, 2005.

Lawrence, Mark Atwood, and Fredrik Logevall, eds. *The First Vietnam War: Colonial Conflict and Cold War Crisis.* Cambridge, Mass.: Harvard Univ. Press, 2007.

Leaming, Barbara. *Jack Kennedy: The Education of a Statesman.* New York: Norton, 2006.

Ledwidge, Bernard. *De Gaulle.* New York: St. Martin's Press, 1982.

———. *De Gaulle et les Américains: conversations avec Dulles, Eisenhower, Kennedy, Rusk, 1958–1964.* Paris: Flammarion, 1984.

Leffler, Melvyn. *The Elusive Quest: America's Pursuit of European Stability and French Security, 1919–1933.* Chapel Hill: Univ. of North Carolina Press, 1979.

Lerner, Daniel, and Raymond Aron, eds. *France Defeats EDC.* New York: Praeger, 1957.

Lieshout, Robert H., Mathieu L. L. Segers, and Anna M. van der Vleuten. "De Gaulle, Moravcsik, and *The Choice for Europe*: Soft Sources, Weak Evidence." *Journal of Cold War Studies* 6, no. 4 (2004): 89–139.

Lind, Michael. *Vietnam: The Necessary War: A Reinterpretation of America's Most Disastrous Military Conflict.* New York: Free Press, 1999.

Lippmann, Walter. "Judgements and Prophecies: The Second U.S. Foreign Policy Failure of 1954." *Time,* September 13, 1954.

———. "Today and Tomorrow . . . The Agitated Alliance." *Washington Post,* December 20, 1962, A25.

Lodge, Henry Cabot, Jr. *The Storm Has Many Eyes: A Personal Narrative.* New York: Norton, 1973.

Logevall, Fredrik. *Choosing War: The Lost Chance for Peace and the Escalation of War in Vietnam.* Berkeley: Univ. of California Press, 1999.

———. "De Gaulle, Neutralization and American Involvement in Vietnam, 1963–64." *Pacific Historical Review* 61, no. 1 (February 1992): 69–102.

Logevall, Fredrik. *Embers of War: The Fall of an Empire and the Making of America's Vietnam.* New York: Random House, 2014.

Longrigg, Stephen Hemsley. *Syria and Lebanon under French Mandate.* New York: Octagon Books, 1972.

Loth, Wilfried. *Europe, Cold War and Coexistence, 1953–1965.* London: Cass, 2004.

Louis, William Roger. *Ends of British Imperialism: The Scramble for Empire, Suez and Decolonization: Collected Essays.* New York: Palgrave Macmillan, 2006.

Love, Eric T. L. *Race over Empire: Racism and U.S. Imperialism, 1865–1900.* Chapel Hill: Univ. of North Carolina Press, 2004.

Lowe, Peter, ed. *The Vietnam War.* London: Macmillan, 1998.

Lucas, W. Scott. *Divided We Stand: Britain, the US and the Suez Crisis.* Toronto: John Curtis Book, Hodder and Stoughton, 1991.

Lundestad, Geir. *"Empire" by Integration: The United States and European Integration, 1945–1997.* New York: Oxford Univ. Press, 1998.

———. *The United States and Western Europe since 1945: from "Empire" by Invitation to Transatlantic Drift.* New York: Oxford Univ. Press, 2003.

Lynch, Frances M. B. *France and the International Economy: From Vichy to the Treaty of Rome.* New York: Routledge, 1997.

MacMillan, Margaret. *Paris 1919: Six Months That Changed the World.* New York: Random House, 2002.

Mahan, Erin R. *Kennedy, de Gaulle, and Western Europe.* New York: Palgrave Macmillan, 2002.

Mahoney, Daniel J. *De Gaulle: Statesmanship, Grandeur, and Modern Democracy.* Westport, Conn.: Praeger, 1996.

Maier, Charles S. *Recasting Bourgeois Europe: Stabilization in France, Germany, and Italy in the Decade after World War I.* Princeton, N.J.: Princeton Univ. Press, 1975.

Maier, Thomas. *The Kennedys: America's Emerald Kings.* New York: Basic Books, 2003.

Maillard, Pierre. *De Gaulle et le problème allemand: les leçons d'un grand dessein.* Paris: F.-X. Guibert, 2001.

Manac'h, Étienne. *Mémoires d'extrême Asie.* 3 vols. Paris: Fayard, 1977–1982.

Maneli, Mieczysław. *War of the Vanquished.* Translated by Maria de Görgey. New York: Harper and Row, 1971.

Mangold, Peter. *The Almost Impossible Ally: Harold Macmillan and Charles de Gaulle.* London: Tauris, 2006.

Marder, Murrey. "Kennedy Is Facing an Intransigent de Gaulle." *Washington Post,* May 28, 1961, E1.

Marks, Sally. *The Illusion of Peace: International Relations in Europe, 1918–1933.* London: Macmillan, 1976.

Marlowe, John. *Perfidious Albion: The Origins of Anglo-French Rivalry in the Levant.* London: Elek Books, 1971.

Mart, Michelle. "Tough Guys and American Cold War Policy: Images of Israel, 1948–1960." *Diplomatic History* 20, no. 3 (1996): 357–80.

Martin, Garret. *General de Gaulle's Cold War: Challenging American Hegemony, 1963–68.* New York: Berghahn, 2013.

Masur, Matthew. "Exhibiting Signs of Resistance: South Vietnam's Struggle for Legitimacy, 1954–1960." *Diplomatic History* 33, no. 2 (2009): 293–313.

McCartney, Paul. "Anglo-Saxonism and U.S. Foreign Policy during the Spanish-American War." In *Ethnic Identity Groups and U.S. Foreign Policy,* edited by Thomas Ambrosio, 21–46. Westport, Conn.: Praeger, 2002.

McGlothlen, Ronald L. *Controlling the Waves: Dean Acheson and U.S. Foreign Policy in Asia.* New York: Norton, 1993.

McIntyre, W. David. *Background to the Anzus Pact: Policy-Making, Strategy, and Diplomacy, 1945–55.* New York: St. Martin's Press, 1995.

McKercher, B.J.C., ed. *Anglo-American Relations in the 1920s: The Struggle for Supremacy.* Basingstoke: Macmillan, 1991.

McLellan, David S. *Dean Acheson: The State Department Years.* New York: Dodd, Mead, 1976.

McMahon, Robert J. *The Limits of Empire: The United States and Southeast Asia since World War II.* New York: Columbia Univ. Press, 1999.

McMaster, H. R. *Dereliction of Duty: Lyndon Johnson, Robert McNamara, the Joint Chiefs of Staff, and the Lies That Led to Vietnam.* New York: HarperCollins, 1997.

McNamara, Robert S., James G. Blight, and Robert K. Brigham. *Argument without End: In Search of Answers to the Vietnam Tragedy.* New York: Public Affairs, 1999.

McNamara, Robert S., with Brian VanDeMark. *In Retrospect: The Tragedy and Lessons of Vietnam.* New York: Times Books, 1995.

Melandri, Pierre, and Serge Richard. *Les relations franco-americains au XXe siècle.* Paris: L'Harmattan, 2003.

Melling, Phil, and Jon Roper, eds. *America, France and Vietnam: Cultural History and Ideas of Conflict.* Brookfield, Vt.: Gower, 1991.

Méouchy, Nadine, and Peter Sluglet, eds. *The British and French Mandates in Comparative Perspectives.* Boston, Mass.: Brill, 2004.

Merritt, Richard L. *Democracy Imposed: U.S. Occupation Policy and the German Public, 1945–1949.* New Haven, Conn.: Yale Univ. Press, 1995.

Miller, Edward. *Misalliance: Ngo Dinh Diem, the United States and the Fate of South Vietnam.* Cambridge, Mass.: Harvard Univ. Press, 2013.

Miller, William J. *Henry Cabot Lodge: A Biography.* New York: Heineman, 1967.

Milne, David. *America's Rasputin: Walt Rostow and the Vietnam War.* New York: Hill and Wang, 2008.

Milward, Alan S. *New Order and the French Economy.* London: Oxford Univ. Press, 1970.

———. *The Reconstruction of Western Europe, 1945–51.* London: Methuen, 1984.

Ministère des Affaires étrangères. *Documents diplomatiques français, 1961.* Tome I, *1er janvier–30 juin* (Paris: Impr. nationale, 1997).

———. *Documents diplomatiques français, 1962.* Tome I, *1er janvier–30 juin* (Paris: Impr. nationale, 1998).

Moïse, Edwin E. *Tonkin Gulf and the Escalation of the Vietnam War.* Chapel Hill: Univ. of North Carolina Press, 1996.

Montassier, Valérie-Anne. *Les années d'après-guerre, 1944–1949: La vie politique en France, l'économie les relations internationales, l'Union française.* Paris: Fayard, 1980.

Monnet, Jean. *Mémoires.* Paris: Fayard, 1976.

Moravcsik, Andrew. *The Choice for Europe: Social Purpose and State Power from Messina to Maastricht.* London: Routledge/UCL Press, 1998.

———. "De Gaulle between Grain and Grandeur: The Political Economy of French EC Policy, 1958–1970 (Part 1)." *Journal of Cold War Studies* 2, no. 2 (spring 2000): 3–43.

———. "De Gaulle between Grain and Grandeur: The Political Economy of French EC Policy, 1958–1970 (Part 2)." *Journal of Cold War Studies* 2, no. 3 (2000): 4–68.

Morse, Edward L. *Foreign Policy and Interdependence in Gaullist France.* Princeton, N.J.: Princeton Univ. Press, 1973.

Moure, Kenneth, and Martin S. Alexander, eds. *Crisis and Renewal in France, 1918–1962.* New York: Berghahn, 2002.

Moyar, Mark. "Political Monks: The Militant Buddhist Movement during the Vietnam War." *Modern Asian Studies* 38, no. 4 (2004): 749–84.

———. *Triumph Forsaken: The Vietnam War, 1954–1965.* New York: Cambridge Univ. Press, 2006.

Munteanu, Mircea. "Over the Hills and Far Away: Romania's Attempts to Mediate the Start of U.S.-North Vietnamese Negotiations, 1967–1968." *Journal of Cold War Studies* 14, no. 3 (summer 2012): 64–96.

Mus, Paul. *Viet-Nam: sociologie d'une guerre.* Paris: Éditions du Seuil, 1952.

Nash, Knowlton. *Kennedy and Diefenbaker: Fear and Loathing across the Undefended Border.* Toronto: McClelland and Stewart, 1990.

Nashel, Jonathan. *Edward Lansdale's Cold War.* Amherst: Univ. of Massachusetts Press, 2005.

Newhouse, John. *De Gaulle and the Anglo-Saxons.* New York: Viking, 1970.

Nicholson, Harold. *The Evolution of Diplomacy.* New York: Collier, 1966.

Nguyen, Lien-Hang T. *Hanoi's War: An International History of the War for Peace in Vietnam.* Chapel Hill: Univ. of North Carolina Press, 2012.

Nolting, Frederick. *From Trust to Tragedy: The Political Memoirs of Frederick Nolting, Kennedy's Ambassador to Diem's Vietnam.* New York: Praeger, 1988.

Nuenlist, Christian, Anna Locher, and Garret Martin, eds. *Globalizing de Gaulle: International Perspectives on French Foreign Policy, 1958–1969.* Lanham, Md.: Lexington Books, 2010.

O'Brien, Michael. *John F. Kennedy: A Biography.* New York: Thomas Dunne Books/St. Martin's Press, 2005.

O'Driscoll, Mervyn. "Explosive Challenge: Diplomatic Triangles, the United Nations, and the Problem of French Nuclear Testing, 1959–1960." *Journal of Cold War Studies* 11, no. 1 (2009): 28–56.

Oliver, Kendrick. *Kennedy, Macmillan and the Nuclear Test-Ban Debate, 1961–63.* New York: St. Martin's Press, 1997.

Olson, Gregory Allen. *Mansfield and Vietnam: A Study in Rhetorical Adaptation.* East Lansing: Michigan State Univ. Press, 1995.

Orde, Anne. *The Eclipse of Great Britain: The United States and British Imperial Decline, 1895–1956.* New York: St. Martin's Press, 1996.

Ovendale, Ritchie. *Britain, the United States, and the Transfer of Power in the Middle East, 1945–1962.* New York: Leicester Univ. Press, 1996.

Pace, Eric. "Dean Rusk, Secretary of State in Vietnam War, Is Dead at 85." *New York Times,* December 22, 1994, A1.

Packham, Eric. *Freedom and Anarchy.* Commack, N.Y.: Nova Science Publishers, 1996.

———. *Success or Failure?: The UN Intervention in the Congo after Independence.* Commack, N.Y.: Nova Science Publishers, 1998.

Pagedas, Constantine A. *Anglo-American Strategic Relations and the French Problem, 1960–1963: A Troubled Partnership.* Portland, Oreg.: Cass, 2000.

Paterson, Thomas G. *Contesting Castro: The United States and the Triumph of the Cuban Revolution.* New York: Oxford Univ. Press, 1995.

———, ed. *Kennedy's Quest for Victory: American Foreign Policy, 1961–1963.* Toronto: Oxford Univ. Press, 1989.

Paxton, Robert O., and Nicholas Wahl, eds. *De Gaulle and the United States: A Centennial Reappraisal.* Providence, R.I.: Berg, 1994.

Pearce, Kimber Charles. *Rostow, Kennedy, and the Rhetoric of Foreign Aid.* East Lansing: Michigan State Univ. Press, 2001.

Pearson, Drew. "Ruhr Crisis Due to Politics, French Steel King Says." *Boston Daily Globe,* June 8, 1924, 66.

Peceny, Mark. *Democracy at the Point of Bayonets.* University Park: Pennsylvania State Univ. Press, 1999.

Percox, David A. *Britain, Kenya and the Cold War: Imperial Defence, Colonial Security and Decolonisation.* London: Tauris Academic Studies, 2004.

Petersen, Tore T. *The Middle East between the Great Powers: Anglo-American Conflict and Cooperation, 1952–7.* New York: St. Martin's Press, 2000.

Peyrefitte, Alain. *C'était de Gaulle.* 3 vols. Paris: Fayard, 1994–2000.

Plischke, Elmer. *U.S. Department of State: A Reference History.* Westport, Conn.: Greenwood, 1999.

Porter, Gareth. *Perils of Dominance: Imbalance of Power and the Road to War in Vietnam.* Berkeley: Univ. of California Press, 2004.

Portes, Jacques. *Fascination and Misgivings: The United States in French Opinion, 1870–1914.* Translated by Elborg Forster. New York: Cambridge Univ. Press, 2000.

Preston, Andrew. *The War Council: McGeorge Bundy, the NSC, and Vietnam.* Cambridge, Mass.: Harvard Univ. Press, 2006.

Purdum, Todd S. "Walt Rostow, Adviser to Kennedy and Johnson, Dies at 86." *New York Times,* 15 February 2003, A23.

Rabe, Stephen G. *The Most Dangerous Area in the World: John F. Kennedy Confronts Communist Revolution in Latin America.* Chapel Hill: Univ. of North Carolina Press, 1999.

Rakove, Robert B. *Kennedy, Johnson, and the Nonaligned World.* New York: Cambridge Univ. Press, 2013.

Record, Jeffrey. *The Wrong War: Why We Lost in Vietnam.* Annapolis, Md.: Naval Institute Press, 1998.

Reeves, Thomas C. *A Question of Character: A Life of John F. Kennedy.* New York: Maxwell Macmillan International, 1991.

Reichard, Gary W. "Divisions and Dissent: Democrats and Foreign Policy, 1952–1956." *Political Science Quarterly* 93, no. 1 (1978): 51–72.

Renshon, Stanley Allen. "The Role of Personality Development in Political Socialization." In *New Directions in Political Socialization,* edited by David C. Schwartz and Sandra Kenyon Schwartz, 29–68. New York: Free Press, 1975.

Reynolds, David. *The Creation of the Anglo-American Alliance, 1937–1941: A Study in Competitive Co-Operation.* London: Europa, 1981.

Reynolds, David, and David Dimbleby. *An Ocean Apart: The Relationship between Britain and America in the Twentieth Century.* New York: Random House, 1988.

Ricard, Serge, and Helene Christol. *Anglo-Saxonism in U.S. Foreign Policy: The Diplomacy of Imperialism, 1899–1919.* Aix-en-Provence, France: Publications de l'Université de Provence, 1991.

Robb, Peter. *A History of India.* New York: Palgrave, 2002.

Roberts, Chalmers M. "Kennedy Heaps Praise on Charles de Gaulle." *Washington Post,* June 1, 1961, A1.

Roberts, Priscilla. "The Anglo-American Theme: American Visions of an Atlantic Alliance, 1914–1933." *Diplomatic History* 21, no. 3 (1997): 333–64.

Roger, Philippe. *L'Ennemi américain: Généalogie de l'antiaméricanisme français.* Paris: Seuil, 2002.

Rogers, Will. "How Rude of Us to Lend France Money!" *Hartford Courant,* August 15, 1926, C1.

Root, Waverly. "France May Get Soviet Support on Plan to Neutralize Viet-Nam." *Washington Post,* September 1, 1963, A9.

Rosenthal, Alan S. "The Gender-Coded Stereotype: An American Perception of France and the French." *French Review* 72, no. 5 (1999): 897–908.

Rosenberg, Emily S. "'Foreign Affairs' after World War II: Connecting Sexual and International Politics." *Diplomatic History* 18, no. 1 (1994): 59–70.

———. "Gender." *Journal of American History* 77, no. 1 (1990): 116–24.

Rostow, Walt Whitman. *The Stages of Economic Growth: A Non-Communist Manifesto.* Cambridge, UK: Cambridge Univ. Press, 1971.

Rotter, Andrew J. "Gender Relations, Foreign Relations: The United States and South Asia, 1947–1964." *Journal of American History* 81, no. 2 (1994): 518–42.

Ruane, Kevin. *The Rise and Fall of the European Defence Community: Anglo-American Relations and the Crisis of European Defence, 1950–55.* New York: St. Martin's Press, 2000.

Ruddy, T. Michael. *The Cautious Diplomat: Charles E. Bohlen and the Soviet Union, 1929–1969.* Kent, Ohio: Kent State Univ. Press, 1986.

Rusk, Dean. *As I Saw It: Dean Rusk as Told to Richard Rusk.* Edited by Daniel S. Papp. New York: Norton, 1990.

———. "The Bases of United States Foreign Policy." *Proceedings of the Academy of Political Science* 27, no. 2 (1962): 98–110.

———. "The President." *Foreign Affairs* 38, no. 3 (1960): 353–69.

Rust, William J. *So Much to Lose: John F. Kennedy and American Policy in Laos.* Lexington: Univ. Press of Kentucky, 2014.

Sainteny, Jean. *Face à Ho Chi* Minh. Paris: Seghers, 1970.

———. *Histoire d'une paix manquée, Indochine 1945–1947.* Paris: A. Fayard, 1967.

Savage, Sean J. *JFK, LBJ, and the Democratic Party.* Albany: State Univ. of New York Press, 2004.

Schaffer, Howard B. *Chester Bowles: New Dealer in the Cold War.* Cambridge, Mass.: Harvard Univ. Press, 1993.

Schlesinger, Arthur M. *Robert Kennedy and His Times.* New York: Ballantine, 1979.

———. *A Thousand Days: John F. Kennedy in the White House.* Boston, Mass.: Houghton Mifflin, 1965.

———. *The Vital Center: The Politics of Freedom.* Boston, Mass.: Houghton Mifflin, 1949.

Schoenbaum, Thomas J. *Waging Peace and War: Dean Rusk in the Truman, Kennedy, and Johnson Years.* Toronto: Simon and Schuster, 1988.

Schuker, Stephen. *The End of French Predominance in Europe: The Financial Crisis of 1924 and the Adoption of the Dawes Plan.* Chapel Hill: Univ. of North Carolina Press, 1976.

Schulzinger, Robert D. *A Time for War: The United States and Vietnam, 1941–1975.* New York: Oxford Univ. Press, 1997.

Schwab, Orrin. *Defending the Free World: John F. Kennedy, Lyndon Johnson and the Vietnam War, 1961–1965.* Westport, Conn.: Praeger, 1998.

Schwarz, Hans-Peter. "Adenauer, le nucleaire, et la France." *Revue d'histoire diplomatique* 106, no.4 (1992): 297–311.

Seaborg, Glenn T. *Kennedy, Khrushchev, and the Test Ban.* Berkeley: Univ. of California Press, 1981.

Serewicz, Lawrence W. *America at the Brink of Empire: Rusk, Kissinger, and the Vietnam War.* Baton Rouge: Louisiana State Univ. Press, 2007.

Serfaty, Simon. *France, de Gaulle, and Europe: The Policy of the Fourth and Fifth Republics toward the Continent.* Baltimore, Md.: Johns Hopkins Press, 1968.

———. *La France vue par les États-Unis: réflexions sur la francophobie à Washington.* Paris: Institut Francais des Relations Internationales, 2003.

Shapley, Deborah. *Promise and Power: The Life and Times of Robert McNamara.* Toronto: Little, Brown, 1993.

Shaw, Geoffrey. *The Lost Mandate of Heaven: The American Betrayal of Ngo Dinh Diem, President of Vietnam.* San Francisco: Ignatius, 2015.

Sheehan, Neil, et al. *The Pentagon Papers: As Published by the New York Times.* New York: Bantam, 1971.

Shepard, Todd. *The Invention of Decolonization: The Algerian War and the Remaking of France.* Ithaca, N.Y.: Cornell Univ. Press, 2006.

Shipler, David K. "Robert McNamara and the Ghosts of Vietnam." *New York Times,* 10 August 1997, SM30.

Shipway, Martin. *The Road to War: France and Vietnam, 1944–1947.* Providence, R.I.: Berghahn, 1996.

Simonds, Frank H. "Europeans Are Drawing Together with America as Common Enemy." *Hartford Courant,* October 31, 1926, D2.

"Six for the Kennedy Cabinet." *Time,* December 26, 1960.

Smedley, Audrey. *Race in North America: Origin and Evolution of a Worldview,* 3rd ed. Boulder, Colo.: Westview Press, 2007.

Smith, Gaddis. *Dean Acheson.* New York: Cooper Square Publishers, 1972.

Smith, Sally Bedell. *Grace and Power: The Private World of the Kennedy White House.* New York: Random House, 2004.

Snyder, Douglas J. "'Fantastic and Absurd Utterances': The Vietnam War and Misperception of Anti-Americanism in US-French Relations, 1966–1967." *Journal of Transatlantic Studies,* no. 1 (March 2012): 84–103.

Sorenson, Theodore C. *Counselor: A Life at the Edge of History.* New York: Harper, 2008.

Springhall, John. *Decolonization since 1945: The Collapse of European Overseas Empires.* Houndmills, Basingstoke, Hampshire, UK: Palgrave, 2001.

Statler, Kathryn C. *Replacing France: The Origins of American Intervention in Vietnam.* Lexington: Univ. Press of Kentucky, 2007.

Steinberg, Blema S. *Shame and Humiliation: Presidential Decision Making on Vietnam.* Montreal, Quebec: McGill-Queen's Univ. Press, 1996.

Stephan, Alexander, ed. *Americanization and Anti-Americanism: The German Encounter with American Culture after 1945.* New York: Berghahn, 2005.

Stephanson, Anders. *Manifest Destiny: American Expansion and the Empire of Right.* New York: Hill and Wang, 1995.

Stevenson, David. *French War Aims Against Germany, 1914–1919.* Oxford: Clarendon Press, 1982.

Stewart, Geoffrey C. "Hearts, Minds and Cong Dan Vu: The Special Commissariat for Civic Action and Nation-Building in Diem's Vietnam, 1955–1957." *Journal of Vietnamese Studies* 6, no. 3 (2011): 44–100.

———. *Vietnam's Lost Revolution: Ngo Dinh Diem's Failure to Build an Independent Nation, 1955–1963.* New York: Cambridge Univ. Press, 2016.

Stora, Benjamin. *Imaginaires de guerre: Algérie, Viêt-Nam, en France et aux Etats-Unis.* Paris: Editions La Découverte, 1997.

Stovall, Tyler. *Paris Noir: African Americans in the City of Light.* Boston: Houghton, 1996.

———. "The Color Line behind the Lines: Racial Violence in France during the Great War." *American Historical Review* 103, no. 3 (1998): 737–69.

———. *France since the Second World War.* New York: Longman, 2002.

Strober, Gerald S. *The Kennedy Presidency.* Lanham, Md.: Univ. Press of America, 1985.

Stromseth, Jane E. *The Origins of Flexible Response: NATO's Debate over Strategy in the 1960s.* New York: St. Martin's Press, 1988.

Stuart-Fox, Martin. *A History of Laos.* New York: Cambridge Univ. Press, 1997.

Sullivan, Marianna P. *France's Vietnam Policy: A Study in French-American Relations.* Westport, Conn.: Greenwood, 1978.

Suri, Jeremi. *Power and Protest: Global Revolution and the Rise of Détente.* Cambridge, Mass.: Harvard Univ. Press, 2005.

Szőke, Zoltán. "Delusion or Reality?: Secret Hungarian Diplomacy during the Vietnam War." *Journal of Cold War Studies* 12, no. 4 (fall 2010): 119–80.

Szulc, Tad. "Paris Premature on Vietnam Unity, Washington Says; It Finds de Gaulle's Call for Merger and Neutrality Completely Unrealistic." *New York Times,* August 31, 1963, 1.

Tajfel, Henri. "Cognitive Aspects of Prejudice." *Journal of Biosocial Sciences* 25 (1969): 79–97.

Takeyh, Ray. *The Origins of the Eisenhower Doctrine: The US, Britain, and Nasser's Egypt, 1953–57.* New York: St. Martin's Press, 2000.

Tal, David. *The American Nuclear Disarmament Dilemma, 1945–1963.* Syracuse, N.Y.: Syracuse Univ. Press, 2008.

———. "From the Open Skies Proposal of 1955 to the Norstad Plan of 1960: A Plan Too Far." *Journal of Cold War Studies* 10, no. 4 (2008): 66–93.

Talbot, David. *Brothers: The Hidden History of the Kennedy Years.* New York: Free Press, 2007.

Talbott, John. *The War without a Name: France in Algeria, 1954–1962.* New York: Knopf, 1980.

Taylor, John M. *General Maxwell Taylor: The Sword and the Pen.* Toronto: Doubleday, 1989.

Taylor, Maxwell. *The Uncertain Trumpet.* New York: Harper, 1960.

Thomas, Martin. *The French North African Crisis: Colonial Breakdown and Anglo-French Relations, 1945–62.* New York: St. Martin's Press, 2000.

———. *The French Empire at War, 1940–45.* New York: Manchester Univ. Press, 1998.

Tocqueville, Alexis de. *Democracy in America.* Translated by Henry Reeve. London: Longman, 1862.

Tønnesson, Stein. *Vietnam 1946: How the War Began.* Berkeley: Univ. of California Press, 2009.

Topmiller, Robert J. *The Lotus Unleashed: The Buddhist Peace Movement in South Vietnam, 1964–1966.* Lexington: Univ. Press of Kentucky, 2006.

———. "Struggling for Peace: South Vietnamese Buddhist Women and Resistance to the Vietnam War." *Journal of Women's History* 17, no. 3 (2005): 133–57.

Topping, Seymour. "Russians Stirred by Kennedy Talk about Cold War." *New York Times,* June 13, 1962, 1.

Torikata, Yuko. "Reexamining de Gaulle's Peace Initiative on the Vietnam War." *Diplomatic History* 31, no. 5 (2007): 909–38.

Tournoux, Jean Raymond. *La Tragédie du général.* Paris: Plon, 1967.

Trachtenberg, Marc. *A Constructed Peace: The Making of the European Settlement, 1945–1963.* Princeton, N.J.: Princeton Univ. Press, 1999.

———. *Reparation in World Politics: France and European Economic Diplomacy, 1916–1923.* New York: Columbia Univ. Press, 1980.

Trumbull, Robert. "Diplomats Say Brother of Diem Sees Accord as Way to Oust U.S." *New York Times,* September 2, 1963, 1.

"200,000 in Paris Give Kennedys Big Welcome." *Washington Post,* June 1, 1961, A17.

US Department of State. *Foreign Relations of the United States, 1961–1963.* Vol. 1, *Vietnam, 1961* (Washington, D.C.: GPO, 1988).

———. *Foreign Relations of the United States, 1961–1963.* Vol. 2, *Vietnam, 1962* (Washington, D.C.: GPO, 1990).

———. *Foreign Relations of the United States, 1961–1963.* Vol. 4, *Vietnam, August–December 1963* (Washington, D.C.: GPO, 1991).

———. *Foreign Relations of the United States, 1961–1963.* Vol. 8, *National Security Policy* (Washington, D.C.: GPO, 1996).

———. *Foreign Relations of the United States, 1961–1963.* Vol. 15, *Berlin Crisis, 1962–1963* (Washington, D.C.: GPO, 1994).

Vaïsse, Maurice. *La Grandeur: politique étrangère du général de Gaulle, 1958–1969.* Paris: Fayard, 1998.

Valeo, Francis R. *Mike Mansfield, Majority Leader: A Different Kind of Senate, 1961–1976.* Armonk, N.Y.: Sharpe, 1999.

Vandiver, Frank E. *Shadows of Vietnam: Lyndon Johnson's Wars.* College Station: Texas A&M Univ. Press, 1997.

Van Hook, James C. *Rebuilding Germany: The Creation of the Social Market Economy, 1945–1957.* Cambridge, UK: Cambridge Univ. Press, 2004.

Vinen, Richard. *France, 1934–1970.* New York: St. Martin's Press, 1996.

Wahl, Nicholas. *The Fifth Republic: France's New Political System.* New York: Random House, 1959.

Wainwright, A. Martin. *Inheritance of Empire: Britain, India, and the Balance of Power in Asia, 1938–55.* Westport, Conn.: Praeger, 1994.

Wall, Irwin. *France, the United States, and the Algerian War.* Berkeley: Univ. of California Press, 2001.

———. *The United States and the Making of Postwar France, 1945–1954.* New York: Cambridge Univ. Press, 1991.

Wandel, Joseph. *The German Dimension of American History.* Chicago: Nelson-Hall, 1979.

Warner, Geoffrey. "Review: President Kennedy and Indochina: The 1961 Decisions." *International Affairs* 70, no. 4 (1994): 685–700.

———. "Review: The United States and Vietnam: From Kennedy to Johnson." *International Affairs* 73, no. 2 (April 1997): 333–49.

Warner, Roger. *Backfire: The CIA's Secret War in Laos and Its Link to the War in Vietnam.* New York: Simon and Schuster, 1995.

Weber, Eugen. "Of Stereotypes and of the French." *Journal of Contemporary History* 25, nos. 2/3 (1990): 169–203.

Wehrle, Edmund F. "'A Good, Bad Deal': John F. Kennedy, W. Averell Harriman, and the Neutralization of Laos, 1961–1962." *Pacific Historical Review* 67, no. 3 (1998): 349–77.

Wenger, Andreas, and Marcel Gerber. "John F. Kennedy and the Limited Test Ban Treaty: A Case Study of Presidential Leadership." *Presidential Studies Quarterly* 29, no. 2 (1999): 460–87.

"Western Europe: The Death Struggle." *Time,* September 6, 1954.

Whalan, Mark. "'The Only Real White Democracy' and the Language of Liberation: The Great War, France, and African-American Culture in the 1920s." *MFS Modern Fiction Studies* 51, no. 4 (2005): 775–800.

Whelan, Joseph G., and Michael J. Dixon. *The Soviet Union in the Third World: Threat to World Peace?* Toronto: Pergamon-Brassey's International Defense Publishers, 1986.

White, Mark J. ed. *Kennedy: The New Frontier Revisited.* Basingstoke, Hampshire, UK: Macmillan Press, 1998.

Willis, F. Roy. *De Gaulle: Anachronism, Realist, or Prophet?* Huntington, N.Y.: Krieger, 1967.

Wills, Gary. *The Kennedy Imprisonment: A Meditation on Power.* Toronto: Little, Brown, 1982.

Williams, Charles. *The Last Great Frenchman: A Life of General de Gaulle.* London: Little, Brown, 1993.

Winand, Pascaline. *Eisenhower, Kennedy, and the United States of Europe.* New York: St. Martin's Press, 1996.

Winters, Francis X. *The Year of the Hare: America in Vietnam, January 25, 1963–February 15, 1964.* Athens: Univ. of Georgia Press, 1997.

Young, Marilyn. *The Vietnam Wars, 1945–1990.* New York: Harper Collins, 1991.

Young, Robert J. *Marketing Marianne: French Propaganda in America, 1900–1940.* New Brunswick, N.J.: Rutgers Univ. Press, 2004.

Zahniser, Marvin. *Uncertain Friendship: American-French Diplomatic Relations through the Cold War.* New York: Wiley, 1975.

Zinoman, Peter. *The Colonial Bastille: A History of Imprisonment in Vietnam, 1862–1940.* Berkeley: Univ. of California Press, 2001.

Index

Studies in Conflict, Diplomacy, and Peace

Series Editors: George C. Herring, Andrew L. Johns, and Kathryn C. Statler

This series focuses on key moments of conflict, diplomacy, and peace from the eighteenth century to the present to explore their wider significance in the development of US foreign relations. The series editors welcome new research in the form of original monographs, interpretive studies, biographies, and anthologies from historians, political scientists, journalists, and policymakers. A primary goal of the series is to examine the United States' engagement with the world, its evolving role in the international arena, and the ways in which the state, nonstate actors, individuals, and ideas have shaped and continue to influence history, both at home and abroad.

Advisory Board Members

Books in the Series

Truman, Congress, and Korea: The Politics of America's First Undeclared War
Larry Blomstedt

The Gulf: The Bush Presidencies and the Middle East
Michael F. Cairo

Reagan and the World: Leadership and National Security, 1981–1989
Edited by Bradley Lynn Coleman and Kyle Longley

The Legacy of J. William Fulbright: Policy, Power, and Ideology
Edited by Alessandro Brogi, Giles Scott-Smith, and Daniel J. Snyder

American Justice in Taiwan: The 1957 Riots and Cold War Foreign Policy
Stephen G. Craft

Diplomatic Games: Sport, Statecraft, and International Relations since 1945
Edited by Heather L. Dichter and Andrew L. Johns

Nothing Less Than War: A New History of America's Entry into World War I
Justus D. Doenecke

Aid under Fire: Nation Building and the Vietnam War
Jessica Elkind

Enemies to Allies: Cold War Germany and American Memory
Brian C. Etheridge

Grounded: The Case for Abolishing the United States Air Force
Robert M. Farley

Foreign Friends: Syngman Rhee, American Exceptionalism, and the Division of Korea
David P. Fields

The Myth of Triumphalism: Rethinking President Reagan's Cold War Legacy
Beth A. Fischer

The American South and the Vietnam War: Belligerence, Protest, and Agony in Dixie
Joseph A. Fry

Lincoln, Seward, and US Foreign Relations in the Civil War Era
Joseph A. Fry

Obama at War: Congress and the Imperial Presidency
Ryan C. Hendrickson

The Cold War at Home and Abroad: Domestic Politics and US Foreign Policy since 1945
Edited by Andrew L. Johns and Mitchell B. Lerner

US Presidential Elections and Foreign Policy: Candidates, Campaigns, and Global Politics from FDR to Bill Clinton
Edited by Andrew Johnstone and Andrew Priest

Paving the Way for Reagan: The Influence of Conservative Media on US Foreign Policy
Laurence R. Jurdem

The Conversion of Senator Arthur H. Vandenberg: From Isolation to International Engagement
Lawrence S. Kaplan

Harold Stassen: Eisenhower, the Cold War, and the Pursuit of Nuclear Disarmament
Lawrence S. Kaplan

JFK and de Gaulle: How America and France Failed in Vietnam, 1961–1963
Sean J. McLaughlin

Nixon's Back Channel to Moscow: Confidential Diplomacy and Détente
Richard A. Moss

Breaking Protocol: America's First Female Ambassadors, 1933–1964
Philip Nash

Peacemakers: American Leadership and the End of Genocide in the Balkans
James W. Pardew

The Currents of War: A New History of American-Japanese Relations, 1899–1941
Sidney Pash

Eisenhower and Cambodia: Diplomacy, Covert Action, and the Origins of the Second Indochina War
William J. Rust

So Much to Lose: John F. Kennedy and American Policy in Laos
William J. Rust

Foreign Policy at the Periphery: The Shifting Margins of US International Relations since World War II
Edited by Bevan Sewell and Maria Ryan

Lincoln Gordon: Architect of Cold War Foreign Policy
Bruce L. R. Smith

Thomas C. Mann: President Johnson, the Cold War, and the Restructuring of Latin American Foreign Policy
Thomas Tunstall Allcock